Selma to Saigon

SELMA
TO
SAIGON

The Civil Rights Movement
and the Vietnam War

DANIEL S. LUCKS

UNIVERSITY PRESS OF KENTUCKY

Scholarly publisher for the Commonwealth,
serving Bellarmine University, Berea College, Centre College of Kentucky, Eastern
Kentucky University, The Filson Historical Society, Georgetown College, Kentucky
Historical Society, Kentucky State University, Morehead State University, Murray
State University, Northern Kentucky University, Transylvania University, University
of Kentucky, University of Louisville, and Western Kentucky University.
All rights reserved.

Editorial and Sales Offices: The University Press of Kentucky
663 South Limestone Street, Lexington, Kentucky 40508-4008
www.kentuckypress.com

The Library of Congress has cataloged the hardcover edition as follows:

Lucks, Daniel S., 1962–
  Selma to Saigon : the civil rights movement and the Vietnam War / Daniel S.
Lucks.
    pages cm
  Includes bibliographical references and index.
  ISBN 978-0-8131-4507-5 (hardcover : acid-free paper) —
  ISBN 978-0-8131-4509-9 (pdf) — ISBN 978-0-8131-4508-2 (epub)
  1. African Americans—Civil rights—History—20th century. 2. Civil rights
movements—United States—History—20th century. 3. Vietnam War, 1961–1975—
Social aspects—United States. 4. King, Martin Luther, Jr., 1929–1968. 5. Cold
War—Social aspects—United States. 6. United States—Race relations—History—
20th century. 7. War and society—United States—History—20th century. I. Title.
  E185.615.L82 2014
  323.1196'0730904—dc23   2013050472
  ISBN 978-0-8131-6846-3 (pbk. : alk. paper)

This book is printed on acid-free paper meeting the requirements of the American
National Standard for Permanence in Paper for Printed Library Materials.

Manufactured in the United States of America.

Member of the Association of
American University Presses

To my mother, Sheila Lucks,
and to the beloved memory of my father, Herbert Lucks,
and my brother, David Lucks, MD

Contents

Illustrations follow page 212

gress. At home, the antiwar ferment led to riots, bloodshed, and political upheaval that created deep fissures in American life. The Vietnam War soon eclipsed all other issues, including civil rights.[1]

Powerful memories of the civil rights movement and the Vietnam War continue to reverberate today. Many of the iconic images—from the first sit-ins in Greensboro, North Carolina, in 1960 to the evacuation of the U.S. embassy in Saigon in 1975—are engraved in our collective national consciousness. The scores of films, novels, plays, and popular and scholarly works on the Vietnam War and the civil rights movement affirm their persistent sway on the public imagination. Whereas the civil rights movement is viewed as a triumph for extirpating segregation, the Vietnam War is regarded as a colossal blunder—a national tragedy. The interplay between these two great protest movements has not received the scholarly treatment it deserves. Indeed, there is a paucity of work on the relationship between the two.[2] Aside from a modicum of works on African American soldiers in the armed forces during the Vietnam conflict, historians' treatments of African Americans and the war have focused on Martin Luther King Jr.'s wrenching and ultimately inspirational migration toward the antiwar camp during the last months of his life.[3] In contrast, this book goes beyond King to unearth the war's profound influence on the civil rights movement.[4] In general, the Vietnam War had a corrosive impact on the civil rights movement and adversely affected African American citizens and soldiers. Like their white counterparts, African Americans had to choose sides, and this book examines the consequence of those choices for the civil rights movement.

For blacks, the Vietnam War had a tragic subtext. The war unleashed tremors that occurred at a most inauspicious time for the civil rights movement. In the early 1960s, civil rights was the most urgent item on the nation's domestic agenda. The civil rights movement captured the imagination of the American public and the international community alike. And for a brief moment, it spurred the possibility of a biracial coalition between the nascent New Left and the young African American Freedom Riders in the Student Nonviolent Coordinating Committee (SNCC) and the Congress of Racial Equality (CORE).[5] But ultimately, the Vietnam War sucked much of the oxygen from the civil rights movement. After the Johnson administration's fateful decision to invest the national treasure in an attempt to prevent the fall of South Vietnam, civil rights, though still a significant issue, receded in importance. The war dominated the public and political discourse. Perhaps most devastating of all, the contentious nature of the war exacerbated preexisting tensions in the civil rights coalition along generational and ideological lines. By the end of the 1960s, the cacophonous debates over the Vietnam War had diverted the fervor from the movement for racial justice at home.

On January 6, 1966, SNCC became the first civil rights organization to oppose the war after Sammy Younge Jr., a twenty-one-year-old African American college student, SNCC worker, and veteran of the U.S. Navy, was murdered for attempting to use a restroom for whites in Tuskegee, Alabama. Three days after Younge's murder, SNCC's Executive Committee issued a statement condemning the United States' involvement in Vietnam as "racist and imperialist" and added that "Sammy Younge's murder indicated [SNCC's] role was not to fight in Vietnam, but [to fight] here in this county for freedoms [that African Americans] are denied here at home." SNCC compounded the resulting fury by affirming its support for draft resisters: "We believe that work in the civil rights movement and with other human relations organizations is a valid alternative to the draft. We urge all Americans to seek this alternative, knowing full well that it may cost them their lives—as painfully as in Vietnam."[6]

SNCC's broadside against the Vietnam War would resonate more profoundly with African Americans in the coming years. In the mid-1960s, however, most Americans still supported the war and perceived attacks on U.S. Cold War policy to be disloyal or even treasonous. SNCC's many opponents had long accused it of being infested with communists. As a result, reaction to the statement was so intense that the Alabama selective service director announced that he was considering reviewing the draft status of SNCC executive director John Lewis.[7]

SNCC's indictment of the Vietnam War became the lead story across the nation, and African Americans generally disapproved of the organization's temerity in speaking out against the war. Most Americans, black and white, believed that matters of foreign policy were beyond the competence of civil rights leaders. The American public had long coalesced around the need to combat the communist contagion, and Cold War liberalism reigned supreme. Furthermore, African Americans were deeply indebted to President Johnson for his passage of civil rights legislation, and they were eager to prove themselves worthy of their newly acquired civil rights—even on the battlefield. Accordingly, the African American press castigated SNCC's diatribe against the war. For example, the *Atlanta Daily World* summed up African Americans' collective outrage when it editorialized that SNCC's statements "are most deplorable, misleading and incorrect" and went on to insist that "Negroes must continue to be loyal to America, particularly when they are on the threshold of receiving full equality before the law."[8] By the beginning of 1966, acrimonious debates over the Vietnam War aggravated schisms in the civil rights movement, which would intensify over the next few years.

As this book demonstrates, the Cold War complicated the civil rights movement's response to the Vietnam War. The Cold War and the lingering memory of the Red scare and McCarthyism informed Americans' decisions about whether to support or oppose the war. African Americans were especially sensitive to the national obsession with the purported communist menace. As a vulnerable minority, African American leftists and pacifists had been targeted and marginalized for their early opposition to the Cold War. The witch hunts of the late 1940s and early 1950s had severed the civil rights movement's long-standing engagement with pacifism and its affinity for anticolonial movements in Africa and Asia. When the Vietnam War burst into the American consciousness in the mid-1960s, it was only a little more than a decade since the height of the Red scare and McCarthyism. As a result of the strength of the Cold War zeitgeist, the pall of McCarthyism persisted well into the mid-1960s, and criticism of American foreign policy was still deemed suspect. The convergence of the Americanization of the Vietnam War and the toppling of de jure segregation made many civil rights leaders wary of opposing America's Cold War policy abroad. Although segregation constituted an embarrassment to the United States in its ongoing propaganda war with the Soviet Union, and this eventually facilitated the dismantling of Jim Crow, the civil rights movement had to tread delicately because the hegemonic Cold War culture limited the parameters of permissible dissent. Indeed, segregationists and other opponents of racial reform had long branded the civil rights movement a communist plot.[9] The harassment of civil rights leaders and the initiation of the FBI's clandestine counterintelligence program (dubbed COINTELPRO) are testament to the government-sponsored intimidation that reached its pinnacle during the 1960s and early 1970s. Martin Luther King Jr., now revered by conservatives, was Red-baited and wiretapped, and his communist sympathies were seemingly validated when he came out against the war in April 1967.[10] From 1945 until the implosion of the Soviet Union, America lived under the shadow of the Cold War. The story of African Americans and the Vietnam War unfolded against the backdrop of Cold War hegemony, and an analysis of the civil rights movement's reaction to the Vietnam War cannot be divorced from this Cold War context.[11]

More than any other political figure, Lyndon Johnson occupies a central space in this book. He made the fateful decision to take the country into a large-scale war in Vietnam while contemporaneously shepherding the landmark Voting Rights Act of 1965 through Congress. Virtually all African Americans lauded his commitment to civil rights. Although he was often prodded into action by events on the ground, Johnson did more for African Americans and for civil rights than any other president since Lincoln.[12] Roy Wilkins, head of the NAACP, spoke for millions of his fellow African Americans when he marveled that "it will take many, many Presidents to match what LBJ did for blacks."[13] Clarence Mitchell, a chief lobbyist for the NAACP, went so far as to give LBJ a higher historical rank than both Abraham Lincoln and Franklin D. Roosevelt.[14] Johnson's prodigious skill in getting civil rights legislation passed justified the plaudits. Furthermore, Johnson cultivated close ties with the moderate wing of the civil rights movement, which eschewed mass demonstrations. But by the summer of 1965, Johnson's obsession with Vietnam precluded the realization of his goal of further remedying the historical stain of racism. A thin-skinned man, Johnson was quick to retaliate against antiwar activists and others who crossed him, banishing them from the corridors of power. For African Americans, buoyant from their historic civil rights victories and with a strong ally in the White House, opposing the war would have meant ending their relationship with LBJ. Whitney Young Jr., head of the National Urban League (NUL) and a staunch supporter of the president, summed it up best: "If we are not with Lyndon Johnson on Vietnam, then he is not going to be with us on civil rights."[15] In navigating the treacherous shoals of the issue of Vietnam, African Americans had to deal with the towering presence of Lyndon Johnson. The president's ambivalent relationship with Martin Luther King Jr., and its deterioration in the face of King's break with the Johnson administration over the war, highlights this tension and is explored in great detail.

Of course, the war in Vietnam was not the first time American foreign policy affected African Americans. They had fought at home and abroad against every foe since the Revolutionary War.[16] W. E. B. Du Bois had urged African Americans to close ranks and support Woodrow Wilson's decision to enter World War I, illustrating the accommodationism that characterized blacks' views of American military adventures. Most African Americans had long viewed military service as furthering the cause of civil rights. In 1948 they were jubilant when President Harry S. Truman issued Executive Order 9981 that eventually integrated the armed forces. In the mid-1960s African Africans initially supported the Vietnam War because it was the first war being fought by the ostensibly integrated military, and they were eager to prove themselves in the battle against communism. African Americans like Hattie Dodson, a middle-aged home-maker from Harlem, supported the war because she believed "we were fighting to preserve our democracy."[17]As the most integrated institution in American society, the military occupied an esteemed place in the minds of black America. Stories of the heroism of black soldiers flooded the African American press, and mainstream publications such as *Ebony* touted the exploits of the new black soldier. Military service afforded African Americans unprecedented opportunities for professional advancement and the chance to leave their impoverished urban ghettos or provincial southern hamlets. Many soldiers thus viewed Vietnam as their Harvard. A few years later, this positive sentiment had vanished, and racial problems rent the armed forces. No other foreign policy issue in American history has caused as much internal dissension within the African American population as the Vietnam War.

More than 300,000 African American men served in Vietnam before the end of U.S. involvement in 1973. Young African American men were rarely eligible for college deferments, and they lacked the requisite personal and professional connections to acquire a National Guard assignment. As a result, especially in the early years of the war, a disproportionate number of African American men fought and died in Vietnam. For the most part, they were the "grunts" consigned to the most dangerous assignments.[18] The thousands of African Americans who died in Vietnam left behind shattered families, and those who were fortunate enough to survive the ravages of the war returned home to a hostile public. Facing an uncertain future, many never overcame their physical and emotional combat scars. For many veterans, the festering wounds never healed. The travails of the African American soldier emerged as a pressing concern for the civil rights movement as the casualties mounted and racial strife plagued the armed forces. Civil rights leaders winced in horror as thousands of young black soldiers became "cannon fodder." The suffering and loss of life among black soldiers were important factors in the civil rights movement's reckoning with the war. Outrage at the unremitting carnage prompted King to choose sides and break his silence on the war.

King's circuitous migration to the antiwar movement dramatized the war's high stakes and polarizing effects on the civil rights movement. On April 4, 1967, after months of vacillation and private anguish, King publicly broke with the Johnson administration and indicted the U.S. government as "the greatest purveyor of violence in the world today."[19] The harsh and uncompromising tone of King's speech sparked an angry and shocked reaction from the African American press and representatives of the civil rights movement. Most civil rights leaders and King's white liberal allies derided his naïveté in speaking out against the U.S. Cold War policy, and admonished him for speaking on matters outside his competence. Only a smattering of the more radical members of the civil rights movement applauded King's stand. But just a few months later, King's eloquence and moral stature helped turn the tide of African American public opinion against the war. In King's final months, he paid a heavy price for his courageous stand. The liberal establishment and many of his moderate colleagues assaulted him as he spoke out for peace and addressed the intractable issues of poverty and inequality in the northern ghettos. In examining King's break with the Johnson administration over the Vietnam War, we must ask why King, a recipient of the Nobel Peace Prize, did not speak out against the war earlier. This book addresses King's turmoil as he came to the grim realization that the Vietnam War was wreaking havoc on African Americans and as the Great Society forced him to confront the Cold War leviathan. King's saga illustrates the enormous consequences blacks faced as they chose sides on the Vietnam War.

Only weeks after King's speech, Muhammad Ali's refusal to be inducted into the U.S. Army similarly provoked a national sensation. The most famous African American athlete in the world, Ali had cultivated an international network of black supporters. The voluble boxer famously said, "I ain't got no quarrel with the Viet Cong" because "they are considered as Asiatic black people and I don't have no fight against black people."[20] Ali's contretemps with the draft board highlighted blacks' growing critique of the war and the connection between the black freedom struggle and larger currents of the 1960s.[21] A member of the Nation of Islam, Ali had spent months with Malcolm X, but his local draft board in Louisville, Kentucky, denied his request for an exemption on religious grounds.[22] After Ali failed to report for duty in April 1967, boxing officials wasted no time in stripping the twenty-five-year-old champion of his heavyweight title.[23] The punishment did not end there: an all-white jury in Houston, Texas, convicted him of draft evasion, and a federal district court judge gave him five years in prison—a sentence that hung over him until 1971.[24] Meanwhile, Ali became a lightning rod. Although many prominent African Americans, such as baseball legend Jackie Robinson, objected to

Ali's conduct and described it as "unpatriotic," thousands of young blacks across the nation identified with Ali. Lionized abroad, at home, Ali became an inspiration to African Americans and provided a boost to the antiwar movement. Like King, Ali's extraordinary defiance unfolded in a highly public setting and highlighted the scope of the black rebellion against the war. Millions of other blacks had to choose sides in a more private setting, but for them, the stakes were no less important and the consequences no less profound. Confronted with a stark choice on the issue of Vietnam, the leadership of the civil rights movement made decisions that shaped the movement's trajectory.

The civil rights movement of the 1960s was the culmination of a long struggle to rectify slavery. It achieved the objective of ending Jim Crow in an inspirational fashion that continues to fascinate historians and the general public alike. As such, it occupies sacred ground in our twenty-first-century civic religion. While these heady and idealistic days defined the first half of the 1960s, the years following the U.S. military buildup in Vietnam were imbued with despair, confusion, and spasms of violence, and the civil rights movement was plagued by calls for racial separatism. These kaleidoscopic images have caused some historians to demarcate the early years of the decade as the "good" 1960s, in contrast to the bad years at the end of the decade.[25] This narrative of declension has obscured the overlap between the two major movements and overly simplified a complex array of forces that shaped a tumultuous decade.[26] The struggle for civil rights was a messy campaign comprising an unwieldy coalition of organizations, and it occurred against the backdrop of a political and social milieu dominated by the Cold War. It did not occur in a vacuum. The Americanization of the Vietnam War gave rise to profound forces that divided as well as transformed American politics, society, and culture. More than anything else, the Vietnam War destroyed the post–World War II liberal consensus that facilitated the rise of conservatism—a movement that had historically opposed civil rights legislation. The Vietnam War divided the civil rights movement and African Americans more than any other event in American history, exacerbating preexisting rifts in the civil rights coalition, and it diverted attention away from the struggle for racial justice and toward opposition to the war. All these factors had profound and tragic consequences for the civil rights movement and for black America.

The seeds of the civil rights movement's interplay with the Vietnam War were planted a few decades before the Americanization of the conflict. That is where our story begins.

ongoing war against French imperialism in faraway Vietnam was hardly a salient event for most Americans in 1954, Robeson, a longtime opponent of colonialism, hailed Ho as "the modern-day Toussaint L'Ouverture leading his people to freedom," and he chided African American leaders for their silence in the face of "twenty-three million brown-skinned people" in Indochina struggling for their independence. Robeson queried whether "Negro sharecroppers from Mississippi should be sent down to shoot down brown-skinned peasants in Vietnam—to serve the interests of those who oppose Negro liberation at home and colonial freedom abroad?"[3]

Robeson's musings presciently reflected the dilemma African Americans would confront in the following decade when the Americanization of the Vietnam War coincided with the passage of landmark civil rights legislation that toppled Jim Crow. The suppression of African American activists and artists during the Red scare, including Robeson, W. E. B. Du Bois, Langston Hughes, and journalists Charlotta Bass and William Worthy, as well as the deportation of radical Trinidadian intellectuals C. L. R. James and Claudia Jones—all of whom criticized America's Cold War policy—had a chilling effect on civil rights activists' willingness to speak out against the Vietnam War in the mid-1960s. Their response to the Vietnam War was further complicated by the fact that many of these early dissenters to the Cold War had ties to the Communist Party.[4]

The Vietnam War was an offshoot of the Cold War, and for more than forty-five years, Americans lived under "the shadow of war."[5] This Cold War backdrop inevitably had a racial component and therefore profound ramifications on African Americans' ongoing struggle for civil rights at home, validating historian Mary Dudziak's assertion that "civil rights reform was *in part* a product of the Cold War."[6] When African Americans confronted the explosive issue of the Vietnam War in the 1960s, McCarthyism was only a little more than a decade in the past. This proximity to the Red scare, combined with the Cold War ethos, which too often conflated dissent from American foreign policy with communism, left an imprint on many veterans of the struggle for racial justice, including Roy Wilkins, Whitney Young Jr., and even longtime pacifist Bayard Rustin. They had witnessed the vilification of an illustrious group of African American leftists, intellectuals, and activists like Robeson, who had linked the African American movement for freedom with the anticolonial movement in general and the Vietminh's struggle against French colonialism in particular. Now in the prime of their careers, with many of their cherished goals tantalizingly within their grasp, these wily veterans of the African American freedom struggle feared that speaking out against the Vietnam War would earn them a similar fate. Their reservations about protesting the military escalation in Southeast Asia were reinforced by the presence of Lyndon Johnson in the White House—a close ally whose magisterial efforts on behalf of civil rights endeared him to most African Americans.

The chasm that developed within the African American civil rights coalition over the Vietnam War was rooted in the early years of the Cold War.[7] By the mid-1960s, the more cautious older generation, steeped in the Cold War zeitgeist, was faced with a more emboldened cohort of youthful African Americans who were born in the late 1930s and early 1940s and came of age in the heady years of sit-ins and Freedom Rides. As part of the New Left, they embraced a new politics that transcended Cold War dichotomies, and their critiques of the Vietnam War were linked to black nationalism. Instead of anxiously sidling away from Robeson's and Du Bois's anticolonialism, these younger activists sought to resuscitate their critiques of American imperialism and preached a similar vision of the interrelatedness of the struggle against racism at home and imperialism abroad. For them, the Vietnam War was merely the latest manifestation of the perennial struggle by people of color to liberate themselves from the yoke of colonial oppression. Unlike their Old Left elders, they did not perceive the Vietnam War through the narrow, dichotomous prism of an inevitable struggle between East and West. These differing perspectives laid the groundwork for the acrimonious debates over the Vietnam War that fractured the civil rights movement during the years of the Johnson administration.[8]

A thorough examination of the historical antecedents of the war-related rifts within the civil rights coalition is a necessary corrective to the historiographical trend that developed in the aftermath of the assassination of Martin Luther King Jr. At the time, historians created a facilely narrow template of the civil rights movement that focused on a few charismatic leaders and limited the movement's years to 1954 through 1968.[9] More recently, historians have begun to challenge this narrative of a short, fourteen-year civil rights movement as overly static, claiming that it unduly muddies the longevity, complexity, and radicalism of the movement.[10] This short narrative has been distorted by the New Right in an attempt to reverse the movement's gains and appropriate its legacy. Historian Jacqueline Dowd Hall's challenge to fellow scholars to extend the boundaries of civil rights historiography has generated a host of questions, particularly about the movement's earlier and more radical internationalist bent that flourished in the 1930s and 1940s.[11] The chill of the Cold War tempered

African Americans' internationalist view of race relations and truncated the movement's more radical faction, which likened the fight against racism at home with anti-imperialism abroad. The expansion of the temporal and spatial boundaries of the struggle against Jim Crow, however, sharpened the connections between foreign affairs and domestic racism, which crystallized during the Vietnam War. African Americans' divisive reaction to the Vietnam War was a by-product of this rupture between the peace and freedom movements that arose during the Red scare, which rendered dissent against American foreign policy synonymous with treason.

Scholars focusing on the so-called long civil rights movement have produced a number of influential studies combining the movement and the Cold War, which share a common chronology and "mutually reinforcing ideological and political contexts."[12] Recent works examining the impact of the Cold War on the trajectory of the civil rights movement have reached different conclusions on whether the Cold War hastened civil rights advances or narrowed the parameters of dissent by taking the issues of economic justice and peace off the table in exchange for piecemeal progress on civil rights. Historians who contend that the Cold War limited the trajectory of the civil rights movement claim that the Red scare elicited a vigorous crackdown against the African American Left, thereby destroying the organizations, individuals, and institutions best equipped to mobilize the masses on behalf of human rights, economic justice, and world peace.[13] They also note that the anticommunist hysteria helped segregationists brand the NAACP—the most mainstream civil rights organization—the National Association for the Advancement of the Communist Party. As a result, the movement was put on the defensive and had to showcase its anticommunist credentials.[14]

Other historians, such as Mary Dudziak, Thomas Borstelmann, and Jonathan Rosenberg, argue that because of the United States' focus on promoting a positive image to the Third World in its relentless public relations campaign against the Soviet Union, the Cold War helped spur civil rights after the thaw of McCarthyism in the mid-1950s.[15] They presuppose that elites in faraway Washington engineered the civil rights breakthroughs in the South, and they tend to lessen the impact of grassroots organizing. Although it is undisputable that the United States' concern with its image abroad played a role in ending the embarrassment of segregation, the Red scare split the peace and freedom wings of the African American struggle and truncated the earlier civil rights movement's alliance with pacifism and anticolonialism.[16] There is no question that the Cold War, and the attendant rise of McCarthyism, forced African Americans to be wary of speaking out against Cold War orthodoxy. Historian Adam Fairclough is correct in the following assertion: "On balance, however, the anticommunism of the early Cold War years damaged the cause of racial equality more far than [it] helped," because it cast suspicion on civil rights supporters in the South as communist sympathizers.[17] The legacy of McCarthyism was a major reason why debates over Vietnam were so divisive and created so many ruptures within the civil rights movement and black America.

At the end of World War II, African Americans were generally united in their optimism about the future postwar world. They hoped that the creation of the United Nations would usher in a world free of colonialism and imperialism, and they expected that the fight against fascism would lead to the amelioration of domestic racial problems. For example, on January 2, 1944, Walter White, the executive director of the NAACP, embarked on a tour of the war-ravaged battlefronts of Europe and North Africa as a correspondent for the *New York Post* and *Life* magazine. He later published his observations in a small volume titled *A Rising Wind*, wherein he optimistically spoke of the opportunity for "the have-nots in the world to share in the benefits of freedom and prosperity, which the haves of the earth have tried to keep for themselves."[18] White's sentiments were shared by African American leaders and citizens alike, who tended to view World War II through the prism of anticolonialism. The outbreak of the Cold War only a few years later shattered this vision. Confronted by the strength of the incipient Cold War, White jettisoned his anticolonial rhetoric, and the NAACP embraced Cold War liberalism. While many rank-and-file members disapproved when White and the NAACP hierarchy repudiated their critiques of U.S. foreign policy, this tactic enabled the association to escape the Red scare relatively unscathed.[19] White's conversion from anti-imperialist to Cold War sympathizer is instructive because it forecast the NAACP's and black moderates' support of the Vietnam War during the tumultuous 1960s.[20]

Although historians have recognized the Cold War's destructive legacy for the American Left, it similarly stifled African American political expression and the anticolonial consciousness that had sprouted among a broad coalition of African Americans in the mid-1930s, following Italy's invasion of Ethiopia. With the thaw in McCarthyism in the late 1950s and the emergence of the New Left in the early 1960s, African American activists who demanded an end to the war in Vietnam would find sustenance and inspiration from an earlier generation of African American journalists, intellectuals, artists, and ordinary citizens who found their voices during the Popular Front of the 1930s and in the celebratory aftermath of World War II, when a new world order seemed possible. Only a few years later, however, the brutal repression of the Cold War years would have a chilling effect on political expression. These warring and irreconcilable philosophies were often generational and contributed to the schism in the African American community during the Vietnam War era. In keeping with the intellectual spirit of the long civil rights movement, the origins of these debates over Vietnam must be investigated.

The Rise of Anticolonialism in the 1930s and 1940s

A prominent network of African American intellectuals, political leaders, and journalists forcefully promoted an anticolonial politics that crested at the end of World War II.[21] This color-conscious internationalism developed in the aftermath of World War I, when black military service failed to produce racial reforms.[22] As early as the 1920s, Mahatma Gandhi's nonviolent campaigns against British imperial rule on behalf of the "colored" race in India struck a chord among the African American public.[23] In 1932 the *Chicago Defender* plaintively asked, "Will a Gandhi arise" in America "who will fight for the cause of the oppressed?"[24]

For African Americans, the Italo-Ethiopian war, which began in October 1935, was the critical event that internationalized their struggle for racial justice at home.[25] It laid the groundwork for a rising anticolonial consciousness that would persist until the late 1940s, dissipate under the assault of the Red scare and McCarthyism, and then reemerge with SNCC and the more militant wing of the civil rights movement. African American organizations and individuals that were early opponents of the Vietnam War were the intellectual heirs of this anticolonial sensibility.

African Americans had long venerated the kingdom of Ethiopia as "the spiritual fatherland of Negroes throughout the world."[26] Spurred by the growing African American press that reflected a more cosmopolitan and urban black lifestyle, the Italian invasion of Ethiopia ignited an emotional response and solidified a growing sense of Pan-Africanism that, thanks to black activist Marcus Garvey, had spread beyond a small elite.[27] In 1943 black journalist Roi Ottley opined, "I know of no other event in recent times that has stirred the rank-and-file Negroes more than the Italo-Ethiopian War."[28] John Hope Franklin concurred and noted, "The interest in the Negro in world affairs lagged very little after Italy invaded Ethiopia in 1935."[29] The racist rationale of Mussolini's invasion rankled African American intellectuals who were already predisposed to perceive racism through an international lens. W. E. B. Du Bois remarked that the Ethiopians gave colored peoples all over the world a reason to unite against white oppression.[30]

The African American press whetted the public's appetite for news of the latest developments in Ethiopia by providing a constant drumbeat of coverage and editorial opinion.[31] In spite of the economic depredations of the Great Depression, which struck its sharpest blow against blacks, the 1930s witnessed the expansion of a black intelligentsia, and more than one-third of black families subscribed to the commercial black press.[32] By the beginning of World War II, the United States had 155 African American newspapers that contributed to the increasing interest in foreign affairs.[33] The Spanish Civil War did not reverberate with African Americans to the same extent as the war in Ethiopia ("Mother Africa") did, but approximately ninety African Americans volunteered and fought in Spain, and a handful of them died there. According to historian Robin D. G. Kelly, the African Americans who joined the Abraham Lincoln Brigade "regarded the Civil War as an extension of the Italo-Ethiopian conflict."[34] Robeson traveled to Spain in 1938 and later characterized it as the "turning point" in his life.[35] This newfound internationalism led Robeson to create the rudiments of an organization that would become the Council on African Affairs (CAA) in 1942. During its brief existence, the CAA, which was largely a fund-raising entity that was influenced by communists and "fellow travelers" such as Robeson and Du Bois, sought to educate the African American public and lobby the U.S. government to take part in Africans' struggle against European colonial rule.[36] The academic orientation of the CAA reflected its modest appeal, particularly among young workers, but its influence was far-reaching. Ella Baker, for instance, imbibed this Pan-African current during her years as a young activist in Harlem in the 1930s. Later known as the "godmother" to legions of SNCC activists in the 1960s, her views on the racist nature of the Vietnam War originated in the furor over Ethiopia.[37]

African Americans' increasing engagement in global events occurred against the chilling backdrop of war in Europe, which soon eclipsed the Italian plunder of Ethiopia as the most pressing foreign policy issue of the day. Unable to fathom the extent and scope of the horrors of Hitler's regime, African Americans' animus was still largely directed against the decaying

British and French empires. The specter of another war in Europe did not resonate with African Americans initially, and it eerily reminded them of the Great War, when they had "closed ranks" behind the war effort only to have their manifold sacrifices repaid with an outbreak of lynching, race riots, and repression.[38] The NAACP's *Crisis* queried, "How can a country expect a class of citizens to rally to its defense wholeheartedly when those citizens receive the dirty end of all deals."[39] Trinidadian writer George Padmore evoked the prevailing suspicion of British imperialism shared by many African Americans: "Today the name of England is one of scorn and derision in the market places of Africa and the bazaars of India. British democracy! Why, the very words stink in the nostrils of every coloured subject in the Empire. Those who talk of honour and England will have a big job to retrieve this 'honour' and win back the confidence of blacks!"[40]

This anticolonial sensibility informed African Americans' circumspection about fighting alongside England and France in another war. However, the stunning ferocity of the Japanese attack on Pearl Harbor on December 7, 1941, shocked African Americans, and for the most part, they promptly rallied around the flag. Although recent memories of World War I lingered, the Japanese attack largely dispelled any doubt about whether to support the United States in another world war. On December 8, the day after Pearl Harbor, at its regularly scheduled meeting, the NAACP Board of Directors announced its unequivocal support for the war effort, while underscoring African Americans' ongoing struggle for full citizenship in a land that denied them equal rights.[41] For the duration of the war, most African Americans embraced the "Double V" campaign as their primary rationale for supporting the war: victory against the fascist menace abroad, and victory against Jim Crow and racism at home. Still, a large segment of the African American public chafed at the indignities of the Jim Crow military, such as the segregation of "white" and "black" blood for transfusions.[42] Many black men used ingenious methods to evade the draft. Malcolm Little, who later changed his name to Malcolm X, feigned insanity at his physical examination.[43] Liberal journalist Carey McWilliams recounted that one young African American draftee supposedly said, "Just carve on my tombstone, 'Here lies a black man killed fighting a yellow man, for the protection of the white man.'"[44] Blacks would utter this same lament two decades later during the Vietnam War.

In the meantime, World War II hastened the extension of the anticolonial fever spread by the African American press. *Crisis* produced a flood of articles during the war years highlighting the international racial dimensions of the conflict.[45] In 1944 iconoclastic *Pittsburgh Courier* columnist George Schuyler, who had headed the Negroes against the War Committee just a few years earlier, charged the Caucasian powers with victimizing the colored races of the world.[46] The fate of colored peoples in Asia and Africa gained even more prominence among African Americans and whites alike in the closing months of the war. These sentiments were corroborated by *Negro Digest* polls, which indicated that African Americans believed the war would not completely eradicate racism but would help create a more equitable world order.[47] World War II was a great watershed for blacks because the paradox of fighting against racism and fascism while being consigned to a Jim Crow army stimulated a race consciousness and a confidence to tackle segregation.[48]

White, famously speaking of a "rising wind," warned that the "Allied nations must choose without delay one of two courses—to revolutionize their racial concepts and practices, to abolish imperialism and grant full equality to all its people, or else prepare for World War III."[49] At the time, most Americans, black and white, were unfamiliar with Ho Chi Minh and the Vietminh's quest for self-determination, but Ho confided to an Office of Strategic Services (OSS) agent that he would "welcome a million American soldiers, but no French."[50] In the waning days of World War II, White's exhortation also resonated with African Americans looking forward to a future world order devoid of colonialism and racial subjugation and predicated on international cooperation. Ottley encapsulated this yearning when he wrote that victory on the battlefield "must bring in its train the liberation of all peoples."[51]

This notion was not so far-fetched. The imminent defeat of the fascist powers, along with the enunciation of the Atlantic Charter and President Roosevelt's plan for a new international order based on the United Nations, offered hope to colored peoples around the world. Their confidence was reinforced by Roosevelt's antipathy to colonialism, which he articulated most succinctly in a March 1941 speech before the White House Correspondents' Association: "There has never been, and there isn't now, and there will never be, any race of people on earth fit to serve as masters over their fellow men. . . . We believe any nationality, no matter how small, has the inherent right to its own nationhood."[52] With respect to Vietnam, Roosevelt's well-known disdain for Charles de Gaulle, coupled with his opposition to France's reclaiming colonial control over Indochina after World War II, seemed to bode well for the Vietminh's long-standing battle for independence. Roosevelt's belief in the obsolescence of colonialism never slackened. But when he died on April 12, 1945, the Vietminh's hope of receiving American support in their fight against French imperialism was dashed.

The Emerging Cold War Zeitgeist

Ho Chi Minh had long perceived the United States as a bastion against colonialism. As a young man, Ho visited the United States in 1912 because he was convinced Americans would be willing to help the Vietnamese overthrow French imperial rule. During his short stay, he was impressed by the fact that Asian immigrants on the East Coast seemed to enjoy equal rights, even though they were ineligible for citizenship. He marveled at Abraham Lincoln's courage in ending slavery.[53] Ho's biographer recounted that he attended meetings of black activists such as the Universal Trust in Harlem, an organization founded by Marcus Garvey, and the young Vietnamese revolutionary was moved by the plight of African Americans.[54] The unattractive reality of racism and segregation troubled him, but America's idealistic principles prompted Ho to deliver a message to President Woodrow Wilson, urging him to address self-determination for the people of Vietnam.

Thirty years later, Roosevelt's World War II rhetoric of freedom and self-determination furnished sustenance to Ho Chi Minh, who had been waging a guerrilla war against his country's Japanese occupiers. For a brief period, the U.S. government corroborated Ho's faith in America. At the Tehran Conference in December 1943, FDR needled Churchill over colonial issues and declared that he "was 100% in agreement with Marshall Stalin . . . that France should not get back Indochina." He groused that "after 100 years of French rule in Indochina, the inhabitants were worse off than before."[55] During the last year of the war, American OSS officers who were tasked with gathering intelligence collaborated closely with Ho and other anticolonial factions to fight their common Japanese foe. Much to the chagrin of the French, Ho and his Vietminh convinced many of these young Americans that French colonialism should be relegated to the dustbin of history.[56] On September 2, 1945, shortly after the Japanese surrendered, Ho declared an independent Vietnam fashioned on the U.S. Declaration of Independence, and he pleaded for American support in his long quest to break the yoke of foreign domination. Given the Roosevelt administration's rhetoric of decolonization, Ho and the rest of the colonial world had reason for optimism.[57] Roosevelt failed to impose his policies on either the State Department or the military.[58] A month before Roosevelt's death, the Japanese coup against the French puppet regime in Indochina forced him to support the French. FDR's death marked a change in U.S. policy in Indochina at a crucial time. Harry S. Truman, a relative novice in foreign affairs, assumed the presidency, and his advisers scuttled Roosevelt's notion of a trusteeship for Indochina. Within months, the reconstruction of French imperialism emerged as an imperative of the Cold War.

Meanwhile, only weeks after Roosevelt's death, the world's attention turned to San Francisco, where the United Nations Conference on International Organization (UNCIO) was set to convene and determine the contours for a new entity: the United Nations. As the leading African American organization, the NAACP, whose membership had increased nearly tenfold during World War II, had lobbied for and been granted an invitation from the State Department to work as a consultant at the UNCIO.[59] For the African American leadership, this opportunity to help frame the United Nations Charter provided a unique opportunity to strike a blow at the international color line.[60] In early 1945 Du Bois published his polemic *Color and Democracy: Colonies and Peace*, which reiterated his long-standing view that the so-called democracies were not democratic because of their racist and imperialist policies.[61] In anticipation of the conference, the NAACP and the CAA worked to present a strong case for African Americans and colonial peoples. Hopes for a new world order were ascendant. On the eve of the conference, the NAACP, the CAA, the Ethiopian World Federation, and the West Indian National Council organized a large rally in Harlem, where speakers described the elimination of imperialism and colonial oppression as a cornerstone of international harmony and stability.[62]

The African American press covered the UNCIO proceedings with much fanfare.[63] The *Chicago Defender* typified blacks' expectations of a new postwar order when it concluded that African Americans and colored peoples throughout the world could not expect massive change immediately, but they could anticipate the eventual liberation of colored peoples, as "San Francisco will set the temper of the times to come."[64] On May 2, 1945, W. E. B. Du Bois, Walter White, and Mary McLeod Bethune submitted a formal statement to the U.S. delegation affirming the equality of all races and claiming "that it was the duty of the United Nations to abrogate imperialism and racism."[65] For a brief moment, the African American community was united, and with the world in flux, a new world order devoid of colonialism seemed possible.[66] African American leaders hoped that imperialism and colonialism would be a casualty of the war, which would spur the momentum to end segregation at home.

African Americans' idealism soon succumbed to the reality of power politics and the looming crisis over the Soviet Union's actions in Poland and eastern Europe. According to Anthony Eden, Roosevelt's death "was a calamity of immeasurable proportions" because it weakened the prospects for avoiding, or at least alleviating, the Cold War.[67] Truman took a more belligerent approach to the Soviet Union and would backpedal from Roosevelt's views on decolonization.[68] Truman also lacked his predecessor's interest in ridding Indochina of French colonial rule, as well as his contempt for de Gaulle and the French performance in the Battle of France. The status of the African American delegation to UNCIO as merely advisers to the State Department was another bad omen, which led White to decry their presence as nothing more than "window dressing."[69] The United States' foreign policy establishment was headed by corporate lawyers and businessmen—including Secretary of State Edward Stettinius and future secretaries Dean Acheson and John Foster Dulles—who desired international stability and were loath to upset their British and French allies over colonial issues. Acheson, in particular, was highly skeptical of the United Nations' ability to resolve the critical international issues of the day; he was also a fierce critic of anticolonialism and a supporter of white colonial rule in South Africa.[70] American foreign policy makers believed that reconstruction of the global international economy was paramount and should supersede the project of colonial emancipation.[71] Their deference to commercial stability foreshadowed the U.S. government's support for France when it reclaimed Vietnam as a French colony. Although the U.S. delegation in San Francisco proposed an amendment to the United Nations Charter that prohibited discrimination on the basis of "race, language, and gender," it also included the caveat that this did not authorize the organization to intervene in matters "within the domestic jurisdiction of a state concerned."[72] On the issue of autonomy for colonial peoples, the U.S. delegation did not call for independence but merely supported a UN trusteeship for all colonies that were already under international mandate, which applied to a mere 3 percent of the colonial world. The United States appeared to be intent on propping up the old colonial regimes as a buffer against Soviet expansionism.[73]

This tepid language presaged the Truman administration's abandonment of FDR's vision of ending colonialism. The African American press universally condemned American capitulation to the imperial powers.[74] Metz T. P. Lochard, chief editor of the *Chicago Defender*, noted how the "optimism that permeated the first sessions" was gradually giving way to "pessimistic mutterings" and bemoaned the lack of interest in the colonial question.[75] After the conference adjourned, Rayford Logan, an African American historian at Howard University and one of the most visible blacks writing on colonial issues, castigated the new United Nations as a "tragic joke."[76] Similarly, the NAACP's *Crisis* claimed that by voting against the proposal for colonial freedom, the United States had renounced its own revolutionary legacy. Walter White likewise attacked the timidity of the U.S. delegation, which left the United Nations powerless to intervene against racism and colonial exploitation.[77]

The abandonment of the principle of self-determination for colonial subjects in exchange for the imperial status quo had immediate consequences in Vietnam. By November 1945, the U.S. government, intent on propping up the French colonial regime, ordered the merchant marines to transport 12,000 French colonial troops through the South China Sea. The crew of the ship cabled President Truman to protest. Why, they asked, are "American vessels . . . carrying foreign combat troops to foreign soil for the purpose of engaging in hostilities to further the imperialistic policies of foreign governments when there are American soldiers waiting to come home?"[78] This question went unanswered, but in the emerging ambience of the Cold War, issues of power, stability, and commercial interests trumped earlier concerns for anticolonialism and self-determination. Despite the expectations generated by the OSS's earlier antipathy for the French in Vietnam, Truman ignored Ho's entreaties that the United States abide by the principles of the Atlantic Charter. Ensuring a stable France as an ally against the Soviet Union became the United States' paramount consideration in Southeast Asia. Upon learning of France's plan to restore its empire in Vietnam, White warned that resurrection of the old order would "inevitably lead to another war."[79] Had the United States not forsaken Ho Chi Minh and the Vietminh's quest for self-determination, it likely would have been spared its long and lethal war in Vietnam.

This disappointment over the United Nations notwithstanding, for the next few years, the African American leadership persisted in its determination to expose racism and all its ramifications on the international stage. African Americans, for the most part, looked askance on the escalating crisis with the Soviet Union and continued to insist that racism, not communism, posed the greatest threat to democracy.[80] After all, the Soviet Union's rhetoric of interracial brotherhood had generated goodwill among African Americans.[81] A number of African Americans, including Langston Hughes, Paul Robeson, W. E. B. Du Bois, and Claude McKay, had visited the Soviet Union and regarded it as a racial paradise compared with racist America.[82] Rayford Logan, for instance, lauded the Soviets' "almost complete absence of race prejudice" and opined that the Soviets could be expected to follow a nonracist foreign policy.[83] After Prime Minister Winston Churchill delivered his famous "Iron Curtain" speech on March 6, 1946, Du Bois groused that it was "one of the most discouraging occurrences of modern times."[84] The *Chicago Defender* editorialized that Britain was now hiding behind U.S. military power to "maintain [its] iron dominion over India, Africa, and other colonies densely populated by darker peoples."[85] The *Pittsburgh Courier* titled an editorial "Invitation to Imperialism" and admonished: "Churchill's call for an alliance between the British Empire and the United States would mean that American money and blood would back British imperialism all over the world, and whenever the Indians, Nigerians, East Africans and other subject peoples sought to throw off the British yoke, the American Armed Forces would be Johnny on the Spot with planes, battleships, tanks and atom bombs to help 'restore order.'"[86] African American intellectuals and journalists were upset that the French and British were using American-manufactured arms to oppress colonial peoples in places like Vietnam and Africa. The NAACP continued its diatribes against colonialism. *Crisis* acknowledged that the Soviet Union was not preoccupied with human rights but noted that at least it had never "subscribed to the Anglo-American color line philosophy," and its very presence at the bargaining table of world politics meant that "human rights may now and then get a break." It also observed that the threat of communism paled in comparison to the reality of injustice in Mississippi.[87]

Following the announcement of the Truman Doctrine and the Marshall Plan in 1947, the conflicts between the United States and the Soviet Union that had erupted at Yalta hardened into the Cold War. As historian Melvyn Leffler notes, the Truman administration decided to seek "a preponderance of power" throughout the globe and became convinced that negotiating with the Soviet Union was futile.[88] For American policy makers, "peace" now meant anticommunist stability, and advocates of peaceful coexistence with the Soviets were marginalized as Red. By late 1946, communism became a domestic political issue as Republicans took control of the House of Representatives and accused Democrats of being soft on communism. The House Un-American Activities Committee (HUAC) began investigating the alleged communist penetration of the motion picture industry in the fall of 1947, soon after Truman's initiation of a loyalty oath for federal employees. These events signified the beginning of the second Red scare.[89]

This climate of anticommunist hysteria would have consequences for African Americans and for the vision of a peaceful world devoid of imperial rivalries. Given that many African American individuals and organizations were affiliated with the communist movement dating back to the years of the Popular Front in the 1930s, the incipient Cold War climate placed them on the defensive and forced them to distance themselves from the Communist Party's emphasis on peace. Under the leadership of rabid segregationist John Rankin of Mississippi, HUAC began pursuing black radicalism and conflated civil rights activism with communist subversion. In the ensuing years, southerners used the Red scare to paint the civil rights movement Red.[90] As early as 1946, liberal historian and cold warrior Arthur Schlesinger Jr. published a story in Henry Luce's anticommunist *Life* magazine in which he made unsubstantiated accusations that the American Communist Party was attempting to "sink its tentacles" into the most mainstream civil rights organization—the NAACP.[91]

Such attacks, combined with the emergence of the second Red scare, caused many African American leaders, intellectuals, and journalists to embrace the Cold War and retreat from anticolonialism. By the beginning of 1947, the increasingly repressive climate adversely impacted the African American press's willingness to question American foreign policy. John H. Sengstacke, editor and publisher of the *Chicago Defender*, the nation's largest black newspaper, joined Schlesinger in forming the liberal, anticommunist organization called Americans for Democratic Action (ADA), which led to editorial changes in the paper's coverage of foreign affairs.[92] African Americans' historical weakness and vulnerability made them particularly susceptible to this new period of repression. The African American press was one of the first casualties. Anticolonial journalists such as George Padmore disappeared, and the circulation of the leading black papers plummeted.[93] This new climate of fear caused most of the African American press to jump on the Cold War bandwagon and distance itself from those who questioned American support of British and French imperialism.

Because it was an influential organization with deep ties to the liberal political establishment, the NAACP's leadership was nervous. Walter White feared for the association's future, but he also realized that attacking Truman's Cold War policy was untenable. As a result, White and the NAACP jettisoned their anticolonial rhetoric and embraced the ascendant liberal anticommunism. Gone were White's arguments linking the struggle against Jim Crow in the South with that of Asians and Africans against colonialism. White eventually dismissed Du Bois from the NAACP after the latter insisted that the NAACP present the UN Commission on Human Rights with a petition that accused the United States of denying human rights to African Americans.[94] White's volte-face on the colonial issue was dramatic and signified a broad shift in mainstream African American opinion. Until his death in 1955, White also tried to suppress African American critics on the Left who continued to speak out about the international dimensions of racism and who criticized American support of repressive regimes that happened to be anticommunist, such as the French in Vietnam.[95] White's reversal was not an isolated incident. Mary McLeod Bethune, Adam Clayton Powell Jr., and CAA cofounder Max Yergan were just some of the notable black activists who joined the anticommunist brigade. In his later years, Yergan even became an apologist for apartheid.[96] In 1948 Rayford Logan recanted his earlier views of African self-determination. In spite of American support of the racist regime in South Africa, Logan spoke of the United States as a bastion of democracy, and he now perceived Africa as a prize in the contest against communism.[97] Yergan's and Logan's apostasy exemplified how the broad anticolonial alliances would be one of the earliest casualties of the Cold War.[98]

Truman's auspicious gestures on behalf of civil rights prompted White's gravitation toward the president's foreign policy. Although he was raised in rural Missouri and his grandparents had owned slaves, Truman made some cautious albeit important concessions to the civil rights movement. Biographer Alonzo Hamby argues that Truman's civil rights record "went against everything in his upbringing" and concludes that his "civil rights program was a noble resolution of contradictory impulses."[99] On the other hand, Truman's detractors note that he whittled down the Fair Employment Practices Commission (FEPC) by creating the weak Committee on Government Contracts, and his loyalty oaths rendered black radicals susceptible to charges of disloyalty.[100]

Historical debates over Truman's civil rights policy endure. To his credit, Truman publicly embraced the cause of civil rights, but historians have emphasized that political considerations played an important role.[101] For example, the NAACP prodded Truman to issue an executive order creating a Civil Rights Commission in response to a wave of mob violence that erupted in the Deep South in the summer of 1946. Although the commission was not created until December 1946 (after the November elections), the *Chicago Defender* greeted it as "a portent of good tidings."[102] In June 1947 Truman became the first president to address the convention of the NAACP, where he announced the findings of the Civil Rights Commission before an audience of 10,000 at the Lincoln Memorial and proposed a far-reaching civil rights package that included antilynching and anti–poll tax measures.[103] This cemented the Democratic Party's enduring ties to the NAACP.[104] Truman's crowning achievement was his signing of Executive Order 9981 on July 27, 1948, which mandated "equal opportunity" in the military but avoided language that "explicitly mandated desegregation."[105] Truman's civil rights record was substantial, but disagreement persists on whether he was motivated by political considerations—that is, the desire to get African American votes in his upcoming reelection campaign.[106] However, his record also reflected an unwillingness to wage a decisive assault on Jim Crow. In the end, Cold War imperatives led Truman to be preoccupied with shaping the international perceptions of race in America, and he was unwilling to be too far ahead of American public opinion on the race issue.[107] Barton Bernstein best summed up Truman's civil rights legacy, calling it ambiguous.[108] The same could not be said of Truman's foreign policy, which fundamentally reoriented the United States' role in the world.

The few dissenters from the emerging Cold War consensus coalesced around the presidential campaign of former vice president Henry Wallace. Wallace's long-standing commitment to racial equality and justice earned him the admiration of African Americans.[109] Not surprisingly, Du Bois argued that Wallace's stand on colonialism and his unwavering support for civil rights warranted African Americans' support.[110] The former vice president criticized Truman's militaristic approach to the Soviet Union, and earlier he had characterized the Allies' wartime goals as "The Century of the Common Man," mirroring the views of the CAA and other African American anticolonialists. Wallace and his supporters argued that peaceful coexistence with the Soviet Union was imperative in an age of atomic weaponry. His quixotic run for the presidency in 1948 on the Progressive Party ticket marked the last time an established political figure running for the highest office would question Cold War orthodoxy—until 1968.[111]

The Progressive Party's platform also called for an immediate end to segregation and Jim Crow laws in the South and inspired enthusiasm among African Americans who were tired of Truman and the Democratic Party's compromises with its reactionary southern wing. Du Bois, Robeson, and the dwindling band of African Americans who remained stalwart in their support of anticolonialism flocked to the Progressive Party. Wallace and his running mate, Senator Glen H. Taylor of Idaho, made the courageous decision to speak only before nonsegregated audiences in the South. The violence and harassment with which southerners greeted Wallace and his supporters became front-page news.[112] The physical danger Wallace was exposed to as he spoke of interracial brotherhood and peaceful coexistence with the Soviet Union underscored the intolerance and fear that undermined any resistance to the emerging Cold War consensus.

Wallace's overtures to African Americans, however, did not earn him the endorsement of the NAACP hierarchy. The Communist Party supported Wallace, and the party and fellow travelers played an instrumental role in the Progressive Party.[113] The NAACP leadership and other African American leaders, such as socialist A. Philip Randolph, condemned the communist influence in the Wallace campaign.[114] As the election approached, a series of events, including Alger Hiss's indictment for perjury and the indictment of American Communist Party leaders under the Smith Act, lent an air of credibility to the impression that communism posed a grave danger to America. In view of the Communist Party's history of antiracism and its support of the Scottsboro defendants, the NAACP felt increasingly vulnerable and sought to distance itself from the Left. Furthermore, White and the NAACP leadership recognized that Truman's stinting civil rights initiatives at least offered them an opportunity to mold policy. A seasoned political operator, White recognized that Wallace had no chance of winning the election, and support of his ill-fated campaign would have compromised the NAACP's access to power and influence. This pragmatism informed the association's embrace of Truman's Cold War policies and its abandonment of the anticolonial vision. White's desire for viability was behind his accusation that the "Wallace crowd" was muddying "the political waters of the Negro organizations instead of working to reward" the Truman administration.[115]

Although the African American press and many of the eligible African American voters in the North were sympathetic to Wallace, they voted overwhelmingly for Truman. In the end, Wallace received only 2.38 percent of the total vote and only 10 percent of the African American vote.[116]

Wallace's enlightened views on race could not withstand the charges of Red-baiting, nor could he compete with the political machinery of the Democratic Party in mobilizing black voters in the key urban centers in the North. Roy Wilkins explained African American support for Truman: "See, the Negro is very pragmatic. He isn't worried particularly about whether the bread comes from the devil or from heaven, as long as it's there, and doesn't have too big a price-tag."[117] Wilkins's professed pragmatism best explains the civil rights movement's fidelity to Cold War liberalism. As a result, for the next twenty years, the mainstream African American political establishment would struggle for civil rights within the narrow parameters of the Cold War. They would slough off their earlier views of anti-imperialism and peaceful cooperation with the Soviets and mute their commitment to economic justice. Their adherence to Cold War liberalism would endure and would inform their reluctance to speak out against the Vietnam War two decades later.

McCarthyism and the Eclipse of Anticolonialism

Truman's upset victory over Thomas Dewey in the 1948 presidential election marked the triumph of Cold War liberalism, an ideology based on Arthur Schlesinger's concept of the "vital center": a marriage between the New Deal state and an aggressive anticommunist foreign policy. Schlesinger's ADA was at the forefront of vital center liberalism, and it helped push Truman to support a stronger civil rights platform.[118] The ascendancy of Cold War liberalism further eclipsed African Americans' anticolonial ardor. The prospects for challenging the United States' support of its imperial allies, such as France, suffered a major setback when the Red scare reached a fevered pitch with the emergence of McCarthyism. On February 8, 1950, Joseph McCarthy, a hitherto undistinguished junior senator from Wisconsin, made his debut on the national stage with an infamous speech in Wheeling, West Virginia, in which he accused the State Department and anti-Soviet Secretary of State Dean Acheson of harboring communists. These reckless and unsubstantiated allegations led to a period of national hysteria and fear that suffused the body politic and destroyed careers, reputations, and lives. Coming on the heels of the Soviets' detonation of an atomic bomb and the Chinese Revolution, McCarthyism gripped the nation. As historian Richard Fried notes, Joseph McCarthy gave the age its name, and anticommunism dominated American life until the mid-1950s.[119]

McCarthyism unleashed a witch hunt for communists that infested every aspect of American life. As a vulnerable minority that was already viewed with suspicion if not derision, African Americans were more susceptible to this anticommunist repression, and recent historiography has demonstrated McCarthyism's destructive impact on the struggle for racial equality.[120] African Americans who internationalized the civil rights struggle were some of the chief victims of McCarthyism because they were viewed as tools of the Soviets. Paul Robeson, his wife Eslanda Goode Robeson, W. E. B. Du Bois, W. Alphaeus Hunton Jr., Charlotta Bass, and Lorraine Hansberry were some of the most influential African American intellectuals, activists, and artists who paid dearly for their willingness to speak out on behalf of peace and against Cold War policies that ran afoul of their perception of racism as a global phenomenon. Although the extent of their affiliation with the Communist Party varied, McCarthyism brooked no tolerance for even the most casual fellow traveler. The persecution of the African American Left created a political void and made African Americans leery of protesting U.S. Cold War policy for the next generation. Although Senator McCarthy was censured in 1954, his legacy cast a pall on the Left, and an enduring fear informed the civil rights movement's unwillingness to oppose the Vietnam War.

The NAACP's response to McCarthyism reflected not only its long and antagonistic relationship with the Communist Party but also its desire to remain politically viable in an era when segregationists and racial conservatives tried to discredit the civil rights movement with a Red brush. The association thus cloaked itself in declarations of patriotism and insulated itself from local branches. For example, following the murder of Florida NAACP leader Harry T. Moore and his wife on Christmas Day 1951, local NAACP members wrote to Truman (in language presaging African American protests against the Vietnam War a decade later), "If you can intervene in a civil war in far off Korea," surely "you can intervene in the war . . . against the Negro people in the United States."[121] In public, White shied away from such criticism and instead eulogized Moore as a fighter against communism.[122] Most important, the NAACP swiftly moved to distance itself from its erstwhile leftist allies in the labor, civil rights, and peace movements. Its actions smacked of opportunism. Even a sympathetic chronicler of the NAACP, historian Manfred Berg, concedes that "the early Cold War hardly represents a glorious chapter in the association's history."[123]

White's successor at the NAACP, Roy Wilkins, was a staunch foe of communism, and he quickly mobilized against the Communist Party. For example, the NAACP distanced itself from organizations that were suspected of being communist fronts, such as the Civil Rights Congress (CRC), an organization formed in 1946 as a result of the merger of the National Negro Congress, the International Labor Defense, and the National Federation for Constitutional Liberties.[124] While there is no evidence that the NAACP purged itself of communists, the board of directors implemented a policy obliging local branches to report efforts of communist infiltration to the national office.[125] At its annual convention in Boston in June 1950, the NAACP passed an anticommunist resolution, and Wilkins wrote to White citing the need to "clean out our organization."[126] Wilkins best summed up the association's hostility toward communism: "The comrades were a problem that the NAACP had to face squarely because ever since the twenties the Communists had been in a lather over the ways to seduce Negroes. God knows it was hard enough being black, we certainly didn't need to be Red, too."[127]

The NAACP's abandonment of its left-wing cohorts in the civil rights struggle took a great toll. *Pittsburgh Courier* columnist Marjorie McKenzie pointed out the irony of a civil rights group involved "in acts of exclusion on the grounds of political affiliation" and questioned the "cost to us and the democratic process."[128] Although Berg notes that the association's actions were necessary for self-preservation, the adverse effects on its integrity and ideals were enormous. Furthermore, the NAACP's opposition to communism failed to insulate it from the Red scare. Segregationists and other opponents of civil rights continued to accuse the NAACP and the moderate CORE of being dominated by communists.[129] Once it renounced its attacks on the Cold War and decided to soft-pedal the economic inequities inherent in society, the NAACP confined its activities to litigation and lobbying, thereby limiting the arc of the civil rights movement. As legal historian Mary L. Dudziak explains: "The narrow boundaries of Cold War era civil rights politics kept discussions of broad-based social change, or a lining of race and class, off the agenda."[130] As discussed in chapter 7, Wilkins, who would head the NAACP until the 1970s, remained the African American establishment's foremost supporter of the Vietnam War and defender of Cold War liberalism. He had virtually no interest in international affairs and their connections to racism at home. By the early 1950s, the NAACP's rupture with its previous anticolonialist and anti-imperialist views would be complete.

During the McCarthy period, Du Bois became a target because of his repeated expressions of sympathy for the Soviet Union and his belief in the imperative of peace. In February 1951 the U.S. government indicted the eighty-two-year-old race reformer for allegedly serving as an unregistered agent for a foreign power. This charge was based on Du Bois's involvement with the Peace Information Center, a small organization that printed and circulated a statement calling for the abolition of nuclear weapons.[131] Throughout this ordeal, the NAACP refused to render any assistance to its legendary founder. The mainstream African American press also succumbed to the prevailing hysteria, and the *Chicago Defender* lamented, "Dr. Du Bois has earned many honors and it is a supreme tragedy that he should have become embroiled in activities that have been exposed as subversive in the twilight of his years."[132] Du Bois was acquitted after a five-week trial, but the experience embittered him. The federal government continued to harass him by opening his mail and watching his every move. Prestigious journals, periodicals, and publishing houses no longer solicited his essays. The government revoked his passport from 1952 through 1958, depriving him of the ability to work and travel abroad. Du Bois ruefully acknowledged that he had lost the leadership of his race. He confessed in his autobiography that "it was a bitter experience and I bowed before the storm. But I did not break."[133] Du Bois eventually joined the Communist Party and moved to Ghana, where he became a citizen on his ninety-fifth birthday.

The government similarly singled out Paul Robeson for his attacks on Cold War policy, and he would suffer a tragic fate. The final straw was Robeson's statement at a CRC rally at Madison Square Garden in June 1950, where he urged blacks "to fight for the freedoms at home" and not in Korea.[134] Shortly thereafter, FBI agents notified Robeson that the State Department had revoked his passport, depriving him of the ability to earn a living abroad. Even though Robeson garnered international support, the African American press and leadership abandoned him.[135] In a withering article in *Ebony*, Wilkins wrote, "While ordinary folks in the Deep South were crying for help, Robeson was writing and talking about Africa [and] singing Russian work songs," and this rich movie star traded the leadership position he could have had in the United States for a "circle of international intellectuals" and "causes that [barely] touched the Negro's plight."[136] Nearly a decade later, and after years of litigation and numerous appearances before the HUAC, the State Department finally reissued Robeson's passport in 1958. The entire ordeal exacted an enormous financial, physical, and emotional toll, and Robeson never fully recovered. In the end, he died a broken, isolated man who felt that an entire generation of civil rights activists had failed to give him his proper recognition.[137] Robeson's example inspired a new generation of African American activists who opposed U.S. policy in Vietnam.[138] In March 1966, SNCC leaders John Lewis and James Forman paid homage to Robeson for his pioneering efforts on behalf of civil rights.[139] At the same time, Robeson's persecution would provide a cautionary tale for black leaders contemplating speaking out against the Vietnam War.

Du Bois and Robeson were the most famous African American victims of the Red scare, but they were not the only ones.[140] Indeed, during the McCarthy period, the U.S. government targeted many lesser-known black leftists, leading to the decimation of the anticolonial project. Passport revocation was the government's weapon of choice. When it revoked the passport of Charlotta Bass, publisher of the *California Eagle* and a supporter of Henry Wallace, she was forced to stop publication of the oldest black paper in the West.[141] The State Department also took notice of William Patterson, head of the CRC, who helped draft the petition to the United Nations that accused the U.S. government of perpetrating "genocide" on African Americans. For his attempt to expose American racism on the international stage, the State Department forced him to surrender his passport.[142] Prominent black radicals of foreign descent were most vulnerable to the anticommunist hysteria. For example, the government deported anti-Stalinist Caribbean radicals C. L. R. James and Claudia Jones, after they were incarcerated for nine months in 1955.[143] Even noncommunist Langston Hughes was not immune. In March 1953 McCarthy summoned Hughes to testify before his Senate committee regarding the author's previous communist sympathies. As a result, Hughes lost many of his speaking engagements.[144] W. Alphaeus Hunton Jr., literary scholar and founding member of the CAA, also appeared before Congress, and he served six months at a segregated federal prison in Virginia for contempt of court.[145]

The federal government identified the CAA, the CRC, and the National Negro Congress as communist front organizations. By the early 1950s, the purge of the black Left was virtually complete, and the barbs against colonialism and American imperialism subsided. Even though the Truman administration continued to expend billions of dollars supporting French colonial rule in Vietnam and the ongoing battle against the Vietminh, there were no protests from the NAACP and the mainstream civil rights establishment; they had accepted the imperative of operating within the restrictive channels of the Cold War. Gone was White's "rising wind" rhetoric.

The Red scare of the post–World War II period made critiques of U.S. Cold War policy tantamount to treason.

The outbreak of the Korean War in June 1950 reinforced the repressive climate. Despite the war's unpopularity, it presented unique opportunities for the civil rights movement. To challenge government policies during wartime in this repressive milieu appeared to be an act of folly. After all, African Americans had applauded Truman's Executive Order 9981, in spite of its open-ended timetable. The integration of the military was a cherished goal and represented an important benchmark in the long quest for equality. The African American press encouraged young black men to enlist in the armed services because doing so would allow them to acquire marketable skills, and their patriotism would redound to the benefit of the race. Historian Kimberley Phillips notes that the African American press urged military service as a civil rights imperative.[146] By the end of the 1940s, the need for manpower in the event of war necessitated accepting recruits wherever they could be found. As a result, there were almost 100,000 African American soldiers on active duty when the Korean War began. At first, blacks fought in segregated units, but by the end of the war, these units had been integrated. As a result, the Korean War was instrumental in eliminating the Jim Crow military.[147]

The story of African Americans and the Korean War is a complicated one that should be explored in a more comprehensive fashion elsewhere. Suffice it to say, the integration of the military occurred in a tortuous fashion. During the first months of the war, the largest of the all-black units, the Twenty-Fourth Infantry Regiment, sustained heavy losses when North Korean troops overran the vastly outnumbered UN forces. Massive casualties led to the withdrawal of the UN forces to a small perimeter in the south of the Korean Peninsula. But according to the NAACP and the African American press, an inordinate number of black troops had been charged with cowardice and court-martialed. *Baltimore Afro-American* correspondent James Hicks reported on the poor conditions in the field; he claimed that black soldiers were court-martialed by southern officers and that they lacked adequate legal representation, demonstrating that the military hierarchy was scapegoating African American troops for the fiasco in Korea.[148]

After hearing these reports, Thurgood Marshall, the NAACP's chief legal counsel, decided to go to Japan and Korea to investigate the allegations of disparate treatment of black soldiers. Under pressure from General Douglas MacArthur (a notorious racist who had suppressed the Bonus Marchers in 1932), the FBI denied Marshall's request for a passport on the grounds that he belonged to two groups the HUAC had cited as communist fronts.[149] Truman's personal intervention cleared the way for Marshall's trip to the Far East, and he detailed the military's racial bias in its use of punishment. Marshall attributed the vindictive prosecution of black soldiers to the high rate of casualties sustained under the leadership of white southern officers, and he blamed MacArthur and the southern orientation of the military brass for the racism inherent in the military justice system.[150] Following MacArthur's dismissal as UN commander in April 1951, the armed forces gradually began to comply with Truman's executive order to desegregate the military. Nonetheless, hostility among officers, many of them southern, caused integration to evolve in an erratic fashion, and racial inequities would persist in the ostensibly integrated armed forces until the 1970s.

Not surprisingly, the African American press and the civil rights community focused on the travails of black soldiers, and by the end of the Korean War, the enhanced status of African Americans in the military was cause for celebration. *Ebony*, for example, touted the Korean War for "hastening the complete integration in the Army."[151] Paeans to the virtuous African American soldier fighting against communism would be a trope used by the mainstream civil rights leadership and the African American press until the early years of the Vietnam War, evidencing the civil rights movement's marriage to Cold War liberalism.

Other than the reporting by black soldiers, the African American press's coverage of the Korean War was slight—particularly compared with the robust coverage of events in Asia and Africa during World War II.[152] Because of their preoccupation with the plight of African American soldiers, and the repression of the Red scare, blacks were unwilling to level critiques against the Korean War. A. Philip Randolph, who as a young labor organizer had opposed U.S. entry into World War I, defended America's militarism in Korea as the only language Russia would understand, and he could not imagine any fate worse than "domination of the world by Communist Russia arms and culture."[153] Although Randolph had a bitter and antagonistic relationship with the Communist Party, his full-throated embrace of the Korean War reflected the black leadership's acceptance of Cold War liberalism.[154] African American opponents of the Korean War risked passport revocation and were especially vulnerable to other reprisals.

There were, however, a number of young blacks who spoke out, such as army veteran and civil rights militant Robert F. Williams from Monroe, North Carolina, who "thought it was stupid to lose so many men fighting for nothing."[155] James Lawson, another future civil rights leader, was imprisoned for being a conscientious objector during the Korean War and later spent three years in India imbibing Gandhi's philosophy of non-violence.[156] Instead of enlisting to fight in Korea, young Robert Parris Moses, a pivotal figure in the civil rights and antiwar movements in the 1960s, attended summer peace camps in Europe and Japan.[157] Whereas the NAACP and leading civil rights activists used the Korean War as a cudgel to force American policy makers to live up to their ideals and promises, for many future civil rights leaders, the war exposed the hypocrisy of fighting for freedom in Korea when Jim Crow persisted at home. Many of these young people, like Lawson and Moses, would later reestablish the links between the peace and the freedom movements once the Red scare dissipated in the late 1950s. In the meantime, they were small, lonely voices in the margins.

The French war against the Vietminh garnered the attention of Paul Robeson and William Worthy. As early as 1954, the young Malcolm X compared the situation in Vietnam to the Mau Mau rebellion in Kenya.[158] For the time being, however, the crisis in Vietnam was a peripheral concern. But the dangers of dissent against the Cold War culture were manifest; they muzzled assaults against the Korean War and would force civil rights leaders to be cautious about protesting the Vietnam War in the 1960s.

Cold War Civil Rights

The exigencies of the Red scare caused the civil rights establishment to abandon its previous concern for anticolonialism and peace. The presence of communists in peace organizations created major problems for the pacifist movement and silenced African American demands for both peace and racial justice.[159] Moreover, attacks on economic inequities were muted because they were redolent of Marxist critiques of capitalism.

At the same time, the Cold War created opportunities for the civil rights movement to dismantle segregation. It enabled activists to leverage their rhetoric to demonstrate that U.S. racial policies undermined the country's international standing and its ongoing propaganda campaign against the Soviet Union. In the late 1940s, the NAACP's legal staff had waged a frontal assault on the white primary, restrictive racial covenants, and segregation in graduate schools, which brought them within striking distance of overturning the ignominious "separate but equal" precedent.[160] This was a protracted campaign that culminated on May 17, 1954, with the Supreme

Court's issuance of its landmark decision in *Brown v. Board of Education* that declared Jim Crow unconstitutional. The Justice Department had filed an amicus brief emphasizing the international embarrassment of segregation in the nation's capital.[161] *Brown* underscored the benefits of the civil rights movement's alliance with Cold War liberalism, and it foreshadowed the triumphs achieved with the help of the liberal political establishment in the mid-1960s. These civil rights successes were partially reinforced by Cold War incentives to support military conflicts abroad. In choosing sides in the debate over Vietnam, the civil rights movement would take into consideration the benefits of its marriage to Cold War liberalism, and mainstream groups would be reluctant to challenge U.S. policies.

In spite of *Brown*, the link between the civil rights movement and Cold War liberalism had its limitations until the presidency of Lyndon Johnson. Civil rights and race rarely concerned prominent white intellectuals and politicians outside of the South.[162] The NAACP and much of the African American establishment cast their lot with liberalism, but the Democratic Party was still beholden to its segregationist wing and therefore failed to make African American equality a paramount objective.[163] *Brown* may have buoyed the spirits of racial activists, but it signified only piecemeal progress. Although it outlawed segregation in schools, *Brown*'s ameliorative impact was shrouded in ambiguous language that precipitated years of additional litigation. It also unleashed a reign of renewed terror and obstinacy in the South that placed the movement on the defensive. On the whole, the civil rights movement of the 1950s belied a certain cautiousness that was informed by the repressive domestic political climate. It would take a new generation of young African American activists to break through the frigid Cold War climate and renew the sense of urgency for racial justice.

Until the presidency of Lyndon Johnson, the executive branch displayed a lamentable timidity on civil rights. Other than his precatory order about desegregating the military, Truman's sympathetic rhetoric, though symbolic, did not translate into decisive action against Jim Crow. His successor, Dwight D. Eisenhower, was even worse. When Arkansas governor Orval Faubus encouraged riots to prevent the integration of Little Rock's Central High School, Eisenhower dispatched federal troops only after the international press pilloried the United States.[164] Ike's mantra was "gradualism," and he famously called his own decision to appoint Earl Warren as chief justice of the Supreme Court "the biggest damnfool mistake" he ever made.[165] His tributes to the martial virtues of the South were legendary, epitomizing his comfort with the southern racial caste and his moral indifference to segregation.[166] The presidencies of Truman and Eisenhower, and even that of John F. Kennedy, were informed by their obsession with the Cold War and their fear of the Soviet enemy. If the issue of civil rights caught their interest, it was usually based on a desire to avert international embarrassment. They frequently derided civil rights leaders and segregationists as equal opportunity extremists.

Until the mid-1960s, African Americans' success occurred outside the realm of politics. But shortly after *Brown*, twenty-six-year-old Martin Luther King Jr. emerged and rose to prominence as the leader of the successful Montgomery bus boycott. This event was of major importance because it ushered in a new chapter of nonviolent protest that differed from the NAACP's near-exclusive focus on litigation, lobbying, and legislation and helped puncture the complacency of the 1950s civic culture. But it would not be until the early 1960s, under the leadership of a new generation removed from the fratricidal wars of the Old Left, that the civil rights movement accelerated the pace of change. SNCC embodied this resurgent spirit, and many of its members took their inspiration from Robeson, Du Bois, and other figures from that era. The destruction of their anticolonial predecessors, however, forced this new generation—loosely dubbed the "New Left"—to take up the fight in a vacuum.[167] Their successes in the domestic sphere and their renewed claims of the international nature of the race problem occurred against the backdrop of the United States' growing engagement in distant Vietnam. In a new era characterized by the waning of the Red scare and McCarthyism, SNCC's new spirit foreshadowed its early opposition to the Vietnam War, which would eventually tear the civil rights coalition asunder. In the early 1960s, the attempt to reunite the struggles for civil rights and for peace would begin anew. But the vitality of the Cold War zeitgeist and the lingering impact of McCarthyism would make this a fitful and arduous endeavor.

2

African Americans and the Long Cold War Thaw, 1954–1965

Most liberals think of Mississippi as a cancer, as a distortion of
America. But we think Mississippi is an accurate reflection of
America's values and morality. Why can't the people who killed
Andrew, James, and Mickie be brought to justice, unless a majority
of the community condones murder? Sheriff Rainey is not a freak; he
reflects the majority. And what he did is related to the napalm bombing
of "objects" in Vietnam.

—Robert Moses, 1965

The Geneva Accords of 1954 signified the end of France's colonial empire in the Far East. Among other things, it temporarily divided Vietnam at the seventeenth parallel and called for free elections by 1956. Wishing to distance themselves from the taint of compromise with the communist forces, President Eisenhower and Secretary of State John Foster Dulles refused to sign the accords; they perceived the French withdrawal as a fresh opportunity to create an independent capitalist bastion in South Vietnam, free of the stench of colonialism. The Eisenhower administration breathed a sigh of relief when the election that would have unified Vietnam never occurred—an election that Ho Chi Minh would have won. Starting in 1956, U.S. assistance to South Vietnam's government, led by avowed Catholic and anticommunist Ngo Dinh Diem, totaled more than $300 million annually, most of which went to buy military goods. Eisenhower's decision to invest millions of dollars to create an anticommunist buffer in South Vietnam was rooted in his adherence to the domino theory, and it would contribute to the massive military involvement a decade later.[1]

Like most Americans, civil rights leaders did not consider events in faraway Vietnam a pressing matter. During the second week of the conference at Geneva, the U.S. Supreme Court handed down the *Brown* decision, which seemingly validated the NAACP's strategy of litigation and its partnership with Cold War liberalism. *Brown* was also predictive of a diminution in anticommunist hysteria, opening up a small crevice for dissent by African Americans and other opponents of America's hawkish foreign policy. Meanwhile, cracks in the pall of American conformity began to surface in the period following *Brown* and the Geneva Accords. With the end of the Korean War, the passing of McCarthyism, and the relaxation of Cold War tensions following Stalin's death (which lessened the likelihood of nuclear confrontation), forums for expressing dissent against the prevailing zeitgeist occurred with greater frequency.[2] As early as 1955, Paul Robeson (still without his passport) observed this new spirit when he addressed students at Swarthmore College, which had maintained its commitment to peace and disarmament during the height of the Red scare. Robeson said he was buoyed by the "stirring of new life among the students" and relieved that "the Ivy Curtain of conformity, which for a decade has shut them off from the sunlight of independent thinking, is beginning to wilt."[3]

Robeson was also heartened by attempts to reconstitute the pacifist movement around the issues of world peace and nuclear disarmament, another sign of a thaw in the Cold War. In 1956 David Dellinger, a long-time pacifist and World War II conscientious objector, founded a radical bimonthly newspaper called *Liberation*, which signaled a new moment in American political and cultural dissent.[4] In addition to Dellinger, *Liberation*'s editorial board comprised prominent individuals who would play crucial roles in the antiwar and civil rights movements of the 1960s, including Staughton Lynd, Howard Zinn, Bayard Rustin, Lorraine Hansberry, James Baldwin, and Robert Williams. *Liberation* published one of the first articles touting the leadership skills of a young minister in Alabama named Martin Luther King Jr., who was gaining notoriety for leading the Montgomery bus boycott.[5]

Only a few years later, Albert Bigelow, a World War II veteran turned civil rights activist and Quaker pacifist, generated publicity when he was arrested for attempting to sail his thirty-two-foot boat, the *Golden Rule*, into the U.S. bomb-test site at Eniwetok atoll in the Pacific.[6] Although the peace movement remained largely on the periphery, the abatement of the Red scare and the government's lessened interest in prosecuting and harassing suspected communists provided small openings for opposition to the Cold War. These small forums enabled a few African American leftists to reestablish the connections between the peace and freedom movements. It would be an arduous and fitful process, but by the time the Vietnam War erupted, many on the Left, including African Americans, would identify with Ho Chi Minh's struggle for independence from white imperialism, and they would not be silent.

As the country crept out of the haze of McCarthyism, Bayard Rustin played a critical role in reviving the moribund pacifist movement and mentoring young Martin Luther King Jr., thereby revitalizing the civil rights movement's connection with pacifism. A conscientious objector during World War II, Rustin was one of the most prominent and controversial African American crusaders for peace and civil rights from the 1930s until his death in 1987.[7] He briefly joined the Young Communist League in the 1930s and was arrested for homosexual behavior during the height of McCarthyism, when homosexuality was viewed as a facilitator of communist subversion. As a result, Rustin would be stigmatized throughout his life and forced to operate from the shadows. In 1956 Rustin not only helped create *Liberation* but also traveled to Montgomery to give twenty-seven-year-old Martin Luther King Jr. a tutorial on Gandhian nonviolence. At the same time, Rustin headed the War Resisters League (WRL), and he was the linchpin between the pacifist movement and the civil rights movement. The Cold War and the Red scare had debilitated the pacifist movement and fractured the alliance between peace groups and civil rights organizations. Membership of the WRL, for example, plummeted during the Red scare.[8] Nonetheless, the resurgence of the WRL, along with the formation of two anticommunist peace organizations in 1957—Committee for Non-Violent Action (CNVA) and Committee for a Sane Nuclear Policy (SANE)—helped spur a peace movement renaissance based on the nuclear threat.[9] Although the connections between radical pacifists and the civil rights movement were tenuous prior to the 1960s, veteran war resister Dellinger exhorted white pacifists to devote some of their passion to civil rights activism.[10]

The slackening of anticommunist hysteria coincided with propitious developments in the civil rights movement. By the mid-1950s, African American impatience with segregation quickened. The brutal lynching of fourteen-year-old Emmett Till in Mississippi in the summer of 1955 provoked international and national outrage and sparked a renewed urgency for racial justice. Gruesome photographs of Till's deformed face accompanied news reports of the crime, and they had a visceral impact on a generation of future civil rights leaders who would become shock troops of the movement. Years later, congressman and SNCC leader John Lewis recounted his reaction to the Till murder: "As for me, I was shaken to the core by the killing of Emmett Till. I was fifteen, black, at the edge of my own manhood just like him. He could have been me. *That* could have been me, beaten, tortured, dead at the bottom of a river."[11]

A few months later, the Montgomery bus boycott introduced the concept of "nonviolent direct action," which transformed the nature of the civil rights struggle. Montgomery also brought to the fore Martin Luther King Jr., who reignited the freedom struggle and described the battle against segregation as part of a global struggle to end colonialism and imperialism.[12] Whereas the NAACP's strategy of focusing on litigation, legislation, and lobbying had reaped *Brown v. Board of Education* and other victories, it did not resonate with ordinary African Americans. King, however, articulated the yearnings of the common people whose lives revolved around church, community, and family. As a minister of the Gospel based in the South, King also embodied a certain palatability that made him less threatening to the American public as a whole. Anne Braden, a progressive white activist who, along with her husband Carl Braden, waged a lonely and dangerous battle against segregation in the South in the late 1940s and 1950s, recalled that the prevailing aura of fear began to dissipate by 1957, when "there was beginning to be a much more organized fight-back against the repressive atmosphere of the 1950s." Braden credited the black freedom struggle in the South with breaking through the "silence of the fifties and the whole McCarthy period," which led to a "feeling of real motion in the South.[13] In spite of these auspicious developments, segregationists still deftly branded the struggle for civil rights in the South as a communist-inspired movement, and a harsh period of repression stymied civil rights activists in the late 1950s.[14] Historian Thomas F. Jackson characterized the three years following the Montgomery bus boycott as "fallow" for King's newly formed Southern Christian Leadership Conference (SCLC) and for the civil rights movement in the South.[15]

The rise of King and the success of the Montgomery bus boycott overshadowed African Americans' interest in foreign affairs. Nonetheless, events abroad also resulted in slight fissures in the Cold War monolith. In the aftermath of the French defeat in Vietnam, the United States created the Southeast Asia Treaty Organization (SEATO) and attempted to incorporate all nations in the region under its military umbrella, thereby blocking further communist gains. India, Burma, Ceylon, Pakistan, and Indonesia opposed inclusion in this Western ambit and vowed to be neutral. In December 1954 these five nations called for a conference of twenty-four other nonaligned African and Asian states to convene in Bandung, Indonesia, in April 1955.[16] The Bandung Conference signaled the desire of these nonaligned nations to advance their "common and mutual interests" as they grappled with their own issues of racism, decolonization, and diplomacy in a nuclear world.[17] Not surprisingly, Secretary of State John Foster Dulles, a hawkish cold warrior who had vowed to construct South Vietnam as a capitalist bulwark, was wary of the prospect of an independent bloc comprising more than half the world's population existing outside the authority of the West, especially after the five nations invited China to attend the conference.[18] Conversely, even though W. E. B. Du Bois and Paul Robeson were still without their passports and unable to attend, African American anticolonialists had a more sanguine view of Bandung. According to historian Penny Von Eschen, Bandung generated excitement among African American intellectuals and opened up new vistas for discourse on foreign affairs "after the most repressive years of the Cold War."[19] Organizers of the conference invited African American expatriate Richard Wright, who was exultant about the possibility of a new international alliance and hailed Bandung as "the last call of Westernized Asians to the moral conscience of the West."[20] Bandung's recognition of people of color as autonomous political actors infused African American intellectuals with a sense of pride and gave them a glimpse of the future in a postcolonial world. It also reignited interest in colonial issues beyond Cold War typologies. While Harlem congressman Adam Clayton Powell, a visitor at the Bandung Conference, shocked attendees with his declaration that "racism in the United States is on the way out" and that Washington, D.C., had become "a place of complete racial equality," the black press lauded the entrance of perennially subjugated colored people onto the world stage.[21] The African American reaction to Bandung demonstrated excitement over potential new platforms to discuss the international dimensions of racism in an age of decolonization.

In an era when it was still perilous to criticize American foreign policy, African American journalist William Worthy was notable for publishing a slew of articles in the 1950s for the *Baltimore Afro-American* and *Crisis* that questioned American imperial designs in Asia and Africa. Later, Worthy would be a staunch supporter of Fidel Castro. Like Rustin, Worthy had been a conscientious objector during World War II and wrote contemptuously about the Korean War, which he derided as racist. He was equally critical of the NAACP and Walter White for encouraging blacks to fight in Korea, accusing them of complicity in the European colonial powers' subjugation of colored peoples in Asia.[22] Only weeks before the French surrendered to the Vietminh at Dien Bien Phu, Worthy branded the war in Vietnam a racist "dirty war" and called it "a potential colonial prelude to a World War III of color."[23] For the most part, Worthy's jeremiads on the racial implications of U.S. foreign policy in Africa and Asia fell on deaf ears. While Robeson and a smattering of African American intellectuals and activists lamented the United States' support of repressive regimes that opposed national liberation movements in what was now being called the Third World, most African Americans were oblivious to the potential perils in distant Southeast Asia. Indeed, Eisenhower's decision not to get bogged down in a land war in Asia relegated Vietnam to a tertiary concern until the early 1960s.

Worthy was the most influential black foreign correspondent of the 1950s. He traveled to Malaysia, Algeria, the Belgian Congo, and South Africa, where he lambasted apartheid. In 1955 he went to the Soviet Union, where he became the first American journalist since 1948 to broadcast a live interview with Nikita Khrushchev.[24] Worthy's 1956 trip to China, where he interviewed Premier Cho En-lai, defied a travel ban and caused the U.S. government to revoke his passport. The State Department's harsh treatment of Worthy illustrates that black internationalism's radical bent remained largely a peripheral consideration until the early 1960s.[25] Worthy and a few other African American journalists, such as Eugene Gordon, had trouble finding an interested readership for their stories criticizing American Cold War policy.[26] It would take the nation's plunge into Vietnam to rivet blacks' attention to foreign policy. Meanwhile, Worthy's views foreshadowed the African American Third Worldism that would erupt a decade later.

On June 16, 1958, the Supreme Court's ruling in *Kent v. Dulles* invalidated passport revocation as a means of punishing citizens for their political affiliations.[27] This landmark decision, along with the government's greater concern about the ramifications of segregation on international public opinion, engendered some hope of uniting the fragments of African American anticolonialism. Although direct assaults against U.S. foreign policy were still dangerous, this changed atmosphere gave blacks the ability to shape the narrative of decolonization if it furthered American interests in influencing the Third World. African Americans' celebration of Ghana's independence on March 5, 1957, is a case in point. Ghana, under the leadership of Pan-Africanist Kwame Nkrumah, became the first sub-Saharan country to achieve formal independence from colonial rule. This feat aroused such interest among African Americans that Martin Luther King Jr., A. Philip Randolph, Ralph Bunche, Lester Granger of the NUL, Congressman Adam Clayton Powell Jr., and White House aide E. Frederic Morrow traveled all the way to West Africa to attend the celebration.[28] African American journalists also made the pilgrimage to Ghana, but their coverage was colored by Cold War realities, causing them to gloss over Britain's long history of oppression and colonialism.[29] For instance, the *Chicago Defender* editorialized independence as a "glorious day for Africa," but it also lauded England for adding a "new chapter to the history of modern civilization" and for "removing the yoke of colonialism from the necks of the oppressed natives of West Africa."[30] Vice President Richard Nixon also attended the ceremonies as part of a three-week goodwill tour of Africa, and he hoped to steer the newly independent sub-Saharan state in a pro-Western and capitalist direction.[31] In subsequent years, Ghana would be a destination for African American radical expatriates like Du Bois, who could not attend the ceremonies in 1957 (he still had no passport) but would spend his final years there. Other notable African American writers such as Du Bois's wife Shirley Graham Du Bois, Julian Mayfield, Maya Angelou, Richard Wright, and Malcolm X would either work in Ghana or spend significant time there.

Nkrumah was the first head of state whom King met, and King's experiences in Ghana reinforced his belief that Western imperialism and racism had an international structure based on racial and economic oppression. However, he hewed to Cold War niceties and tread a delicate line between publicly expressing his views about the importance of Ghanaian independence for African Americans and the world and attempting to inoculate the civil rights movement from any taint of communist influence.[32] King's balancing act on Ghana portended the muting of his antipathy to the Vietnam War in the mid-1960s and reflected the Red scare's lingering impact on African Americans' willingness to express their opinions on Cold War policy. In a few years, King's caution would be tested by a group of young activists who were more willing to question Cold War verities. More than anything else, the birth of SNCC emboldened and reoriented the civil rights movement, giving it an anti-imperialist and pacifist sensibility and prompting King to speak out more forcefully on the connections between racial justice and world peace.

The 1960s: The Birth of SNCC and the Rise of the New Left

Events in the early 1960s quickened the pace of change and finally brought the issue of civil rights to the forefront of the nation's consciousness. The civil rights movement would inspire a biracial group of activists known as the New Left. They would oppose Cold War liberalism, repudiate the Old Left's fixation with Marxism, and call for young intellectuals to be the new agents of revolutionary change.[33] The rise of the New Left, with its fidelity to nonviolence, would furnish the most militant wing of the civil rights movement with the intellectual ammunition and courage to perceive the links between Jim Crow at home and imperialism abroad in the form of U.S. military aggression in Vietnam.[34]

The 1960s was only a few weeks old when four African American students at North Carolina Agricultural and Technical College in Greensboro staged a sit-in at a Woolworth's lunch counter and inaugurated the most turbulent decade of the twentieth century.[35] Within the next two months, the student sit-in movement spread like wildfire throughout the South, and by the end of the spring semester, there had been 2,000 sit-ins. As a consequence of this ferment, veteran civil rights activist Ella Baker organized a conference of young African American student activists in April at her alma mater, Shaw College in Raleigh, North Carolina, which eventually resulted in the formation of SNCC.[36] Nonviolence was the mainstay of SNCC's ethos, and it would shape the group's opposition to U.S. military action abroad. At the end of the conference, Baker exhorted the students to go beyond the integration of lunch counters and strive to transform the entire southern social structure.[37] Baker, who had recently befriended accused communists Anne and Carl Braden, told the students that their sit-ins were part of an international struggle against injustice, and her antipathy for Red-baiting influenced SNCC's policy of not excluding individuals or organizations with ties to communism.[38] This dictum would shape SNCC's later willingness to criticize U.S. foreign policy and revive the links between the peace and freedom movements that had been fragmented during the early years of the Cold War.[39] In their struggles and travails against white dominion in the South, these activists identified with anticolonial struggles in Asia, Africa, and the Middle East and celebrated the courage of Du Bois, Robeson, and other notables who had been marginalized during the Red scare.

The sit-ins, the formation of SNCC, and a rejuvenated CORE that sponsored Freedom Rides in the spring and summer of 1961 all ignited a revolutionary grassroots movement in the South comprised predominantly of young African Americans. Their courage, their willingness to get arrested, and their commitment to transforming the racial caste system in the South prompted historian and SNCC adviser Howard Zinn to gush, "For the first time in our history, a major social movement, shaking the nation to its bone, is being led by youngsters."[40] As their commitment deepened, the young SNCC activists developed an alternative perspective that differed from what they perceived to be the alienating and numbingly materialistic quality of American middle-class life. The notion of racism's internationalism, which transcended Cold War shibboleths, was one aspect of this sensibility. Future civil rights and antiwar activists Diane Nash, James Bevel, and John Lewis arose from the Nashville wing of SNCC and came under the spell of James Lawson, a charismatic African American pacifist who had been imprisoned as a conscientious objector during the Korean War and had been influenced by Gandhi while working as a missionary in India.[41] Beginning in 1959, Lawson led seminars on Gandhian practices of nonviolence for his group of young disciples and future SNCC leaders.[42] As the keynote speaker at the Shaw University conference in April 1960, Lawson mesmerized the students when he characterized sit-ins as a "judgment upon the middle-class conventional, half-way efforts to deal with radical social evil."[43] The civil rights movement's commitment to nonviolence would reestablish the ties between the peace and freedom coalitions, which would resurface as major constituencies of the New Left during the civil rights protests of the early 1960s and the subsequent antiwar movement.

As part of the New Left, the young activists in SNCC and CORE were liberated from the internal debates over Marxist dogma that had devastated the Old Left and the African American anticolonial activists of the 1930s and 1940s.[44] They rejected the dominant cultural and political mores of American society; they were intent on transcending the narrow prism of Cold War America and railed against the violence inherent in the arms race.[45] The nation's fixation on communism in places like Vietnam was risible to SNCC activists, who would endure months of terror as they waged war against Jim Crow in the Deep South. As SNCC executive director and air force veteran James Forman stated, "We decided that the so-called fights of the Thirties and the Forties were not really our fights, although some tried to impose them on us."[46] Casey Hayden, a young white woman from Texas who worked with SNCC, recalled that communism was a "dead" issue. "I didn't know any communists, only their children, who were just part of our gang."[47] While the newly inaugurated John F. Kennedy instituted a muscular foreign policy and sent a fresh crop of military advisers to Vietnam, SNCC and CORE perceived events in Southeast Asia as remote from the real struggle for racial justice at home.

The accelerated pace of the civil rights movement of the early 1960s electrified a cohort of young white students from Berkeley to Ann Arbor to Cambridge who were struggling to articulate their grievances against the stultifying, middle-class mores of their youth. SNCC's courageous examples of nonviolent direct-action campaigns furnished them with inspiration as they searched for their own authenticity.[48] For example, twenty-year-old Tom Hayden's life was transformed when he interviewed Martin Luther King Jr. while covering the 1960 Democratic Convention in Los Angeles for the *Michigan Daily*. King told the young University of Michigan undergraduate, "Ultimately, you have to take a stand with your life."[49] Shortly thereafter, Hayden attended the National Student Association's annual convention at the University of Minnesota and recalled meeting about twenty-five representatives from SNCC who "were in many ways like myself—young, politically innocent, driven by moral values, impatient with their elders, finding authentic purpose through risking their lives, their fortunes, and their sacred honor—in short, a genuinely revolutionary leadership."[50] Hayden called that meeting of the SNCC leaders "a key turning point, the moment my political identity began to take shape," which spurred him to go down to Mississippi and assist with the voter registration project there.[51] Historian Wesley Hogan notes that in the early 1960s, "SNCC became a magnet for northern white students" like Hayden who were "trying to do something, yet unsure how to proceed."[52]

SNCC's youthful style of grassroots activism, its fidelity to nonviolence, and its policy of not excluding alleged communists or fellow travelers provided a template for Students for a Democratic Society (SDS), which Hayden helped form. Within a few years, SDS became the most influential New Left organization of the 1960s, and it was the first organization to mobilize Americans against the Vietnam War. SDS hosted a conference on "Human Rights in the North" on May 5–7, 1960, at the University of Michigan. A number of civil rights leaders—Bayard Rustin, James Farmer from CORE, and Herbert Hill from the NAACP—attended the conference, which solidified SDS's ties to the civil rights community. For the next two years, SDS continued to speak out on behalf of civil rights. By December 1961, hoping to create a mass movement, SDS decided that it needed to articulate its values and political objectives in a manifesto that would encapsulate the goals of a new generation of activists. The task of crafting that manifesto fell to Hayden.[53]

In the fall of 1961, Hayden had moved to Atlanta to become SDS's field secretary in the South, and his experiences on the front lines of the civil rights movement totally changed his life.[54] On October 9, 1961, Hayden and Paul Potter, a white student and future SDS chief from Oberlin College, arrived in McComb, Mississippi, to publicize the vigilante violence that was imperiling SNCC's voter registration drive there. Less than forty-eight hours later, two assailants dragged them from their vehicle and nearly clubbed them to death. A photographer from the Associated Press snapped a picture of a helpless and bloody Hayden cowering on the ground, and it was splashed across the wires, contributing to his growing fame among the New Left.[55] Hayden's harrowing experience in Mississippi did not deter him from participating in SNCC's ongoing campaign in Albany, Georgia, where he was jailed a few months later for trying to integrate a railroad terminal.[56] While imprisoned in Albany on December 11, 1961, his twenty-second birthday, Hayden wrote a dramatic letter to his SDS colleagues "on a smuggled piece of paper with [a] smuggled pen." From his cell, "which is perhaps seven feet high and no more than ten feet long," he wrote of the need for "SDS to become a national organization, a counterpart to SNCC in the rest of the country."[57] It was against the backdrop of his searing experiences in the Deep South that Hayden began to formulate the intellectual blueprint for the SDS manifesto that would be known as the *Port Huron Statement*.

On June 12, 1962, fifty-nine activists, mostly students, attended a conference in Port Huron, Michigan. There, they agreed to ratify Hayden's manifesto, which became the anthem for the New Left.[58] SNCC and the civil rights movement shaped Hayden's views of domestic and international affairs. Taking its cue from SNCC's style of grassroots activism and nonviolence, the *Port Huron Statement* touted the virtues of "participatory democracy" and called on individuals to take part in the fundamental decisions affecting their lives. Similarly, it mirrored SNCC's critique of the single-minded obsession with the purported communist menace when segregation made a mockery of American ideals of freedom and liberty. Hayden strove to transcend the stale typologies of mid-twentieth-century American political dialogue. He indicted U.S. foreign policy for continuing the Cold War and for hypocritically supporting some of the most ruthless despots, such as Diem in South Vietnam, in the name of preserving democracy. Hayden was no less charitable to the Soviet Union, which, he argued, was "becoming a conservative status quo nation-state." Like the Bandung Conference, Port Huron sought an alternative to the suffocating debates between capitalism and communism that obscured the glaring paradox of Jim Crow in the South. With respect to the Third World revolutions raging in Vietnam and throughout much of Africa in the wake of decolonization, the statement called for the United States to provide sustenance and "critical support" and not to moralize. In words that presaged the New Left's opposition to the Vietnam War, Hayden argued that the cause of democracy would be enhanced by working to keep such revolutions independent, rather than viewing them through the narrow prism of Cold War competition. Implicit in the *Port Huron Statement* was an anti-anticommunism, reminiscent of SNCC's view that communism was irrelevant. In the years prior to escalation of the Vietnam War, SNCC's and SDS's shared sensibilities on racial issues and foreign policy opened up the possibility of an interracial coalition of young people oriented toward peace and racial justice.[59]

Early on, SNCC members and their white counterparts in the New Left chafed at the Kennedy administration's torpor on civil rights and its bellicose Cold War rhetoric.[60] Kennedy's reservations about alienating the powerful southern bloc in Congress caused him to renege on his campaign promise to end racial discrimination in federal housing with a "stroke of the pen."[61] Harris Wofford, Kennedy's adviser on civil rights, recalled that the president's primary concern about racial segregation was its effect on America's image abroad, especially the potential fallout from any mistreatment of African diplomats stationed in Washington, D.C.[62] Nonviolent direct action was anathema to most members of Kennedy's inner circle. As a result, the Kennedy administration was instrumental in creating the Voter Education Project (VEP), intended to get SNCC activists off the streets and channel their energies toward voter registration. This created divisions within SNCC because it received less funding than other civil rights organizations, and many members perceived this as a self-interested policy designed to weaken civil disobedience and nonviolent direct action.[63]

In addition, much to the chagrin of civil rights leaders, Kennedy, an aggressive cold warrior, was preoccupied with the Soviet Union and the tensions in Cuba, Berlin, and especially Vietnam, which was becoming a focal point in the struggle between the superpowers. The Freedom Rides coincided with JFK's first European summit, where he was anticipating a tense meeting with Soviet premier Nikita Khrushchev.[64] Kennedy's first instinct was to pressure the Freedom Riders to cancel their protests out of fear of handing Khrushchev a public relations victory.[65] Although the Kennedy administration dispatched U.S. marshals to the University of Mississippi and the University of Alabama, proposed a voter registration campaign, and was more welcoming to African Americans, it was not until the spring of 1963, when Birmingham authorities' brutal tactics against protesters ignited a public outrage, that the Kennedy administration gave civil rights a higher priority. Robert Kennedy later conceded, "I did not lie awake at night worrying about the problems of Negroes."[66] The president's statements on civil rights were tempered with caution, lest he roil the segregationist wing of the Democratic Party and upset his upcoming reelection campaign. In particular, Kennedy castigated SNCC and referred to members as "sons of a bitches" who "had an investment in violence."[67] Throughout his short tenure, Kennedy frequently chided both sides for their extremism. Historian Nick Bryant rebuked Kennedy for being a bystander on civil rights and stated that his policy of inaction "unintentionally set in motion a chain reaction that had a radicalizing effect" on southern extremists and agitators.[68] For all these reasons, there was animosity between SNCC and CORE and the Kennedy administration. Nothing dramatized this bitterness more than a tumultuous meeting between Robert Kennedy and civil rights activists, arranged by novelist James Baldwin, in the aftermath of Birmingham in May 1963. There, a Freedom Rider from CORE shocked the attorney general by saying he could never imagine fighting for the United States.[69]

Kennedy's temporizing on civil rights notwithstanding, the early 1960s was a groundbreaking era in the African American freedom struggle. The wellspring of change was not the highest office in the land but the high-profile grassroots campaigns engineered by SNCC, CORE, and SCLC in the streets, parks, beaches, bus terminals, and lunch counters of some of the most benighted hamlets and cities in the Deep South. Particularly noteworthy was 1963, a year that witnessed an array of iconic events and images that captured the imagination of the national and international public. In the spring, the campaign to end segregation in Birmingham led to a public relations coup for the civil rights movement when the media disseminated disturbing images of vicious dogs attacking defenseless African American children and southern policemen clubbing and turning high-pressure fire hoses on innocent bystanders.[70] A few months later, on August 28, 1963, the March on Washington confounded its skeptics by its peaceful and rarefied nature, culminating in King's majestic "I Have a Dream" speech. The public success of the March of Washington belied the internal controversy over the censorship of John Lewis's proposed speech, wherein he castigated the Kennedy administration and the Democratic Party for their sluggishness on the issue of racial justice.[71] The ebullient mood was broken only a few weeks later when a bomb exploded at the Seventeenth Street Church in Birmingham, killing four young girls. Most important, though, this grassroots activism catapulted civil rights to the forefront of the nation's agenda, forcing Americans to recognize the imperative of rectifying the country's original sin: slavery. It would retain its status as America's most pressing issue for the next two years, until a secret war simmering in distant Indochina erupted into a conflagration and consumed most of the nation's energy, zeal, and resources for the next decade.

The Black Left and Foreign Policy, 1959–1964

The unfolding, often electrifying saga of the civil rights movement consumed Americans in the late 1950s and early 1960s. Foreign affairs, for the most part, was a peripheral concern. Until Lyndon Johnson Americanized the conflict in Vietnam in 1964 and 1965, most blacks—and, for that matter, most Americans—were not focused on the civil war raging in Vietnam. In fact, news of the conflict in distant Indochina was buried beneath headlines of the intensifying struggle for racial justice in the South and developments in other Cold War hot spots such as Cuba and Berlin. Nonetheless, the resurgent spirit embodied in the revitalized civil rights and pacifist movements spilled over to African American views of foreign affairs, rekindling a sliver of the anticolonialism of the pre–Cold War years. Beginning in the late 1950s, African American interest in the decolonization of African countries such as Ghana, coupled with the birth of Third World neutralism at the Bandung Conference, sparked a revival of criticism of U.S. Cold War policy among a small group of left-wing African American journalists, activists, and intellectuals that included Malcolm X, James Baldwin, and Robert Williams. Dissent remained on the margins, but the Warren Court's outlawing of passport revocation and other egregious aspects of McCarthyism opened up opportunities for renewed critiques of U.S. policy abroad.

Between 1959 and 1962, a number of prominent African American leftists focused their passions on the revolution that erupted on the neighboring island of Cuba on January 1, 1959.[72] Though the Cuban Revolution engendered less interest than the invasion of Ethiopia had in the 1930s, their identification with Fidel Castro's regime foreshadowed the groundswell of African American support for Ho Chi Minh and other Third World nationalist figures. Many African Americans initially lauded Castro for his early vow to integrate the army.[73] Months after the revolution, even mainstream *Ebony* published an article by veteran correspondent Simeon Booker touting Castro's avowed intention to bring racial justice to Cuba.[74] The strong support for the revolution among the large population of black Cubans cemented African American solidarity with Castro. While most of the civil rights establishment remained wedded to the Cold War liberal consensus, Robert Williams, head of the NAACP in Monroe County, North Carolina, felt an affinity for Castro's youthfulness, toughness, and charisma, and he marveled at Castro's commitment to making Afro-Cubans part of the revolution.[75] In addition to Williams, Malcolm X, young writers Maya Angelou, LeRoi Jones, and James Baldwin, and journalist William Worthy were all beguiled by Castro's courage and his professed fidelity to racial equality. For a brief moment, they were suffused with hope that the Cuban Revolution would fulfill Bandung's vision of Third World neutrality and scramble the Cold War dichotomy. According to historian Peniel Joseph, among a small cohort of African American leftists based in Harlem, "Cuba became a repository of black American support for the Third World during the civil rights movement."[76] Castro's vision of racial justice and his image of military heroism also found a receptive audience among the battered remnants of the Old Left and the rebellious and restless younger generation that was coalescing around the New Left. Historian Van Gosse notes that Castro "became their rebel with a cause on a grand scale."[77]

Once the U.S. government spurned the revolution after Castro began expropriating and nationalizing Cuban assets belonging to U.S. corporations, Castro's American supporters created the Fair Play for Cuba Committee (FPCC) to support the revolutionaries in the event of a U.S. attack. Within six months, the FPCC had approximately 7,000 members, most of them on college campuses on both coasts and in the Midwest. Of the thirty founders of the FPCC, nearly a third of them were African American. The black founders included novelists James Baldwin, Oliver Killens, and Julian Mayfield; Pan-Africanist historian John Henrik Clarke, who would later help edit the radical journal *Freedomways*; foreign correspondent William Worthy; and fiery Robert Williams.[78] In the summer and fall of 1960, the FPCC invited a number of black writers, artists, and activists to visit Cuba, and several wrote rapturous accounts of their experiences, comparing Castro's treatment of blacks with America's intransigence on the race issue.[79] In words reminiscent of Robeson's initial encounter with the Soviet Union in the 1930s, Robert Williams called his Cuba adventure the most profound experience of his lifetime.[80] Williams was so intoxicated by the sense of freedom he felt in Cuba that he fled there in 1961, after North Carolina and federal authorities falsely charged him with kidnapping after a riot erupted in his hometown of Monroe during the Freedom Rides. Beat poet LeRoi Jones, who later changed his name to Amiri Baraka, published an essay called "Cuba Libra" wherein he refers to his Cuban experience as a "turning point in his political consciousness."[81] Baraka would eventually become an important figure in the black arts movement. Other African Americans who accepted the FPCC's invitation included writers Julian Mayfield and John Henrik Clarke, who would publish favorable accounts of their visits in the new left-wing journal *Freedomways*, which provided a forum for fresh perspectives on anticolonialism and placed the civil rights movement in an international perspective.[82] In the coming years, *Freedomways* would also publish some of the first articles by African Americans questioning the morality and wisdom of the Vietnam War.

Fidel Castro's ten-day trip to New York City in September 1960, during which he addressed the UN General Assembly, received widespread coverage and earned him favorable reviews from the black press.[83] After initially checking into the luxurious Shelbourne Hotel in Midtown Manhattan, Castro and the Cuban delegation relocated to the historic Theresa Hotel in the heart of Harlem after a misunderstanding between Castro's entourage and hotel management caused the bearded thirty-four-year-old revolutionary to charge the tony hotel with racism. Castro's stay in Harlem, where he hosted radicals Malcolm X and Robert Williams as well as Khrushchev, was a source of immense pride among blacks there, who were thrilled by the presence of such an important foreign dignitary. Columnist James L. Hicks of the *Amsterdam News* expressed this sentiment: "Though many Harlemites are far too smart to admit it publicly, Castro's move to the Theresa and Khrushchev's decision to visit him gave the Negroes of Harlem one of the biggest 'lifts' they had had in the cold racial war with the white man."[84] The *New York Times* was more cynical, reporting that Castro had been contemplating the move to Harlem even before the dispute because he believed "Negroes would be more sympathetic to the Cuban Revolutionaries."[85] Whatever his motives, an estimated crowd of 5,000 cheered as a beaming Castro emerged from the Theresa Hotel with his arms wrapped around Khrushchev, and Castro exulted in the warm reception. Even Malcolm X lauded Castro as the "only white person he ever liked."[86] Castro's charisma and brazenness in flouting conventional racial practices earned him the enduring admiration of the coterie of mostly New York–based black radicals who would become the vanguard of the Black Power movement. Castro's historic trip to New York was punctuated by his September 26 speech at the United Nations, where he wowed his African American supporters with expressions of solidarity with colonial subjects in Africa and Negroes in South Africa.[87] In an era of decolonization, Castro's trip to America and his warm reception by blacks reflected the activists' hopes of the possibility of an ideological and racial reconfiguration of Cold War relations that had begun with Bandung.

Most African American politicians and statesmen, along with the mainstream civil rights organizations, took pains to distance themselves from Castro and his radical followers in the FPCC. Harlem congressman Adam Clayton Powell Jr. acknowledged Castro's charisma but denounced his stay in Harlem as "sheer hypocrisy," and he admonished Castro that the "Negro people of Harlem were not communist dupes."[88] The late Senator McCarthy may have been repudiated, but Castro's visit to Harlem occurred against the backdrop of the close presidential race between Senator John F. Kennedy and Vice President Richard Nixon. Their exchange of barbs over who was the most hawkish candidate testified to the intractability of anticommunism in mid-twentieth-century America. Robert Williams, Castro's most vocal supporter in the southern civil rights movement, was a marginal figure, having been expelled from the NAACP in 1959 for his advocacy of armed self-defense.[89] The other African American members of the FPCC were artists and writers based largely in New York; they were not intimately involved in the civil rights struggles in the South, which was the movement's primary focus in the early 1960s. As Cuba became the United States' major adversary in the Western Hemisphere in early 1961, following the Bay of Pigs fiasco and the Cuban Missile Crisis, the civil rights movement generally steered clear of any taint of collusion with America's Caribbean archenemy.

By the spring of 1962, the travails of *Baltimore Afro-American* reporter William Worthy became a cautionary tale of the perils of being too cozy with Castro's regime. The peripatetic Worthy had traveled to Cuba without his passport, and during his stay he published favorable articles on Castro and the Cuban Revolution, going so far as to remark that he could understand "why the proud people of Cuba marvel out loud every day that this giant of the Twentieth Century should have been born on their little island."[90] After his activities with the FPCC surfaced, federal officials indicted Worthy on April 24, 1962, in Miami for returning from Cuba the previous autumn without his passport.[91] In August 1962 a federal judge convicted him of violating the McCarran-Walter Immigration Act, a statute passed at the height of the Red scare that gave the federal government broad discretion to regulate travel, which was directed mainly at suspected communists. Until a federal court overturned his conviction in 1964, Worthy had the distinction of being the only U.S. citizen to be arrested for leaving and then reentering the country.[92] African American activists and newspaper editors rallied to Worthy's support, but by that time, the Bay of Pigs and the Cuban Missile Crisis had placed the FPCC on life support. Its final breath occurred only weeks after Kennedy's assassination, with the news of Lee Harvey Oswald's alleged distribution of FPCC literature.[93]

In early 1963, only months after the Cuban Missile Crisis, Brad Lyttle, head of the CNVA, proposed the Quebec-Washington-Guantanamo Walk for Peace in an attempt to unite the goals of the pacifist and civil rights movements. Taking his cue from the Freedom Rides, the plan was for an integrated group of peace and civil rights advocates to march through the heart of Dixie.[94] Ella Baker and white southerners Anne and Carl Braden were optimistic that the walk would succeed in reassembling the fragmented peace and freedom movements.[95] Barbara Deming, a pacifist stalwart who would later travel to Hanoi with SNCC's Diane Nash, was one of many who felt "that the two struggles—for disarmament and Negro rights—were properly parts of one struggle."[96] The hopes of the planners vanished, however, when violence erupted as soon as marchers crossed the Mason-Dixon line. White pacifists resented the fact that civil rights eclipsed peace as soon as the marchers entered the South. For their part, civil rights activists were riveted on the South in 1963, rendering all other issues subsidiary. Nevertheless, the walk highlighted the divergent aims and cultural differences that would hamper the two movements' attempts to form a cohesive coalition during the Vietnam War.

In the weeks before President Kennedy's fateful trip to Dallas, Vietnam may not have been of primary interest to activists in the black freedom struggle, but the deteriorating situation on the ground in Southeast Asia propelled it to the epicenter of Cold War politics. The crisis had reached an impasse. Ever since the Truman administration's decision to support France's attempt to reestablish its colonial rule in Indochina, the U.S. government had spent billions of dollars opposing Ho Chi Minh and his revolution for national liberation. After the Vietminh's defeat of the French at Dien Bien Phu in 1954, Cold War imperatives led the Eisenhower administration to create and nourish a noncommunist bastion in the South headed by Ngo Dinh Diem. Eisenhower's articulation of the domino theory, predicting that the communists would control all of Southeast Asia if the South Vietnamese government collapsed, became an article of faith among the American national security establishment. By the late 1950s, no one questioned the maxim that Ho Chi Minh could not prevail in uniting Vietnam.[97]

With respect to Vietnam, Kennedy was endowed with a greater sensitivity than most of his contemporaries. As a thirty-four-year-old congressman seeking to augment his foreign policy bona fides, Kennedy had visited South Vietnam in 1951 and noted in his diary, "We are more and more becoming colonialists in the minds of the [Vietnamese] people," and he noted their lack of support for the puppet government in the South.[98] He told his constituents shortly after his return that action "in defiance of innately nationalistic aims spells foredoomed failure."[99] In spite of his earlier reservations, Kennedy campaigned for the presidency as an aggressive cold warrior, and in his first months in the White House, he accelerated support to the floundering South Vietnamese government but resisted calls for military escalation.[100] Notwithstanding Kennedy's reluctance to become embroiled in another Asian conflict less than a decade after Korea and his recognition of Ho's support among the Vietnamese, international and domestic political pressures convinced him of the necessity of averting a defeat in Vietnam. Beginning in late 1961, the U.S. government shipped vast quantities of high-quality American weapons along with a new crop of military advisers to try to save South Vietnam.[101] The number of American advisers in Vietnam reached 8,000 by mid-1962, increased to 11,000 by the end of the year, and totaled almost 16,000 at the time of Kennedy's assassination.[102] It was apparent to veteran *New York Times* columnist Homer Bigart in February 1962 that a secret war was under way in Vietnam, and he concluded that "American troops will stay until victory."[103]

By the end of the summer of 1963, as most African Americans were preoccupied with the March on Washington, Vietnam loomed as Kennedy's greatest foreign policy challenge.[104] The increasing American commitment could not save Diem's faltering regime. Even though Kennedy presented a façade of toughness, he bristled at the dire reports of Diem's continued corruption and incompetence. To stop them, he urged Arthur Sulzberger, publisher of the *New York Times*, to remove journalist David

Halberstam from the Vietnam beat.[105] To complicate an already thorny sit-uation, Diem's reprisals against Buddhists had further eroded his support among the South Vietnamese people following public acts of self-immo-lation by Buddhist monks in Saigon.[106] All these factors forced Kennedy to conclude that events in Vietnam were reaching a critical phase, neces-sitating a reappraisal of his policy. After weeks of temporizing, Kennedy authorized a coup against the Diem regime on November 2, 1963.[107] In the meantime, Kennedy's doubts about the wisdom of getting bogged down in a full-scale war in Vietnam persisted, but the upcoming election forced him to defer a final decision on whether to withdraw U.S. forces, maintain the status quo, or escalate the conflict.[108] His assassination passed the issue of Vietnam to his successor, Lyndon Johnson.

Freedom Summer and Vietnam

Until the beginning of 1964, the civil rights movement and other domes-tic and international issues monopolized the American public's attention, eclipsing news of the smoldering albeit aggravating conflict in Vietnam. For African Americans and civil rights leaders in particular, the high drama in the Deep South rendered other issues peripheral, and matters of foreign policy caught the attention of only a few dissenters on the fringes of the political spectrum. Robert S. Browne, for example, was an African Ameri-can who had served as an economic adviser in Vietnam from 1958 through 1961 and had married a Vietnamese woman. A renowned expert on Viet-nam, Browne wrote a series of editorials and letters warning against a rush to war in South Vietnam on the grounds that an "incipient anti-American-ism," fueled by a corrupt and decadent government, made military success unlikely.[109] In 1965 Browne would revisit Vietnam after a four-year hiatus. He also helped inaugurate the teach-in movement on U.S. college cam-puses and wrote an editorial in *Freedomways* urging civil rights leaders to speak out against U.S. involvement in Vietnam on the grounds that Afri-can Americans have an affinity with struggles for national liberation.[110]

For the most part, however, news of the Vietnam War did not pen-etrate the civil rights movement until Freedom Summer of 1964, when coverage of the Gulf of Tonkin Resolution coincided with news that the decomposed bodies of three missing civil rights workers had been discov-ered beneath an earthen dam in Mississippi. The intensification of hostili-ties in Vietnam brought that conflict into greater focus for SNCC activists, whose confrontation with terror in Mississippi and their profound disillusionment after the Democratic Party's convention in Atlantic City, New Jersey, sharpened their earlier reservations about liberalism and the viability of American institutions. Freedom Summer and SNCC's experiences in Mississippi, the citadel of white supremacy in the Deep South, would forge the most activist wing of the civil rights movement's early opposition to the Vietnam War. Accordingly, Freedom Summer marked a turning point for SNCC, the civil rights movement, and the nation.

Freedom Summer brought approximately 1,000 idealistic white students to Mississippi to assist in SNCC's project to register African Americans to vote and to teach in "Freedom Schools." These students exhibited the youthful idealism of the early 1960s and a willingness to risk their lives for the cause of racial equality. In the end, the grisly murder of three civil rights workers and the bitterness over the compromise at the Democratic National Convention punctured much of their innocence and turned the summer into a radicalizing experience. Freedom Summer spawned a host of studies and firsthand accounts.[111] Freedom Summer also had an important Vietnamese subtext that warrants further explication.[112] The disheartening experience of Freedom Summer combined with the debacle in Atlantic City and the Gulf of Tonkin Resolution laid the groundwork for the youthful wing of the black freedom struggle to become disillusioned with the promise of American liberalism. These events also aggravated the cleavages between the nonviolent branch of the civil rights movement and the liberal pragmatists who coalesced around the NAACP and the Democratic Party. If the Vietnam War was a prime cause of the demolition of the civil rights coalition, Freedom Summer, Atlantic City, and the Gulf of Tonkin were the sparks that lit the fuse.

Back in 1960, Robert Moses, a young, idealistic African American pacifist from Harlem, caught the attention of Ella Baker. Moses displayed courage when he moved to McComb, Mississippi, in an effort to register African American voters in the Magnolia State.[113] These early attempts to register black voters sparked a wave of violence and terror.[114] While the U.S. government was sending advisers and weapons to Vietnam, purportedly to bring democracy to that country, democracy was absent in Mississippi. Less than 7 percent of adult African Americans were registered to vote; in rural areas like the Delta, the figures were much lower.[115] But by the summer of 1963, after two bloody years of effort culminating in the murder on Mississippi NAACP leader Medgar Evers, SNCC's campaigns had not increased these woeful numbers. In large part, SNCC workers' frustration was rooted in the federal government's failure to intervene and blunt the violent resistance by die-hard segregationists. Early on, they resented the contrast between the federal government's inaction in Mississippi and its aggressiveness in faraway Vietnam.

The constant death threats, violence, and ridicule were exacting an emotional and physical toll on young SNCC workers in the Deep South. James Forman, SNCC's thirty-five-year-old executive secretary and a military veteran, nearly died in 1963 from a bleeding ulcer, which he attributed to the stress of the movement.[116] Many, like young SNCC worker Anne Moody from rural Mississippi, were beginning to experience what would later be referred to as "burnout" or "battle fatigue." This led Harvard psychiatrist Robert Coles to observe: "In many ways these young civil rights workers are in a war and exposed to the stresses of warfare," including "exhaustion, frustration, and rage."[117]

By the summer of 1963, the stalemate in Mississippi impelled SNCC leaders to conclude that bold action was necessary. In early July, propelled by the demonstrations that consumed Jackson in the weeks following the assassination of Medgar Evers, Allard Lowenstein drove to Mississippi and was immediately introduced to Moses. Lowenstein, one of the youngest of the generation of Cold War liberals, had cultivated an extensive network of ties with the Democratic Party and students. He suggested to Moses that African Americans in Mississippi should vote not at official election sites but at public places, such as African American schools and churches, where they were less likely to be subjected to harassment and intimidation.[118] Moses, who had been contemplating drastic measures to break the logjam in his voter registration project and rivet the nation's attention on Mississippi, was amenable to the suggestion. This was the genesis of Freedom Summer.[119]

Moses's enthusiasm surged on August 6, 1963, after approximately 700 African Americans were mobilized to vote in the Democratic primary. In the gubernatorial runoff three weeks later, more than 27,000 unregistered African Americans voted in special polling venues established by black churches and businesses. Even though the Mississippi authorities threw out the votes, Moses regarded it as a triumph in political theater, and it prompted him to ask SNCC's Executive Committee in Atlanta to organize another voting rights campaign for the upcoming November election.[120]

In anticipation of Election Day 1963, which soon became known as the "Freedom Vote," Lowenstein left Mississippi and traveled to the West

Coast and New England to tap his extensive contacts at Stanford University, where he had recently worked as an undergraduate dean, and at Yale University, where he had attended law school in the mid-1950s. By mid-October, Lowenstein had recruited approximately 100 white volunteers, and they fanned out across the state of Mississippi and exhorted African Americans to vote in mock elections. In the first week of November, more than 80,000 African Americans cast their votes, rendering the Freedom Vote a triumphant experiment.[121] The *Southern Patriot*, a radical monthly newspaper published by Anne Braden's Southern Conference Education Fund (an interracial group dedicated to integration), observed that the Freedom Vote demonstrated that Mississippi blacks "would vote if they could—and had someone decent to vote for."[122]

Following the success of the Freedom Vote, SNCC became embroiled in a contentious debate over whether to bring large numbers of whites into the organization.[123] On the one hand, Ella Baker and James Forman were dubious of Lowenstein's motivations and suspicious of his determination to Red-bait longtime SNCC allies such as the National Lawyers Guild.[124] Many veteran SNCC workers worried that the young, well-educated, skilled whites would take over the organization.[125] On the other hand, Robert Moses and others realized that the federal government would not tolerate violent reprisals against white youths; they argued in favor of creating a crisis that would force the federal government to intervene. The Freedom Vote had demonstrated that "wherever those white volunteers went, FBI agents followed."[126] In the end, the murder of Louis Allen on the evening of January 31, 1964, convinced Moses that SNCC needed outside help.[127] (A few years earlier, Allen, a black man from Mississippi, had witnessed the murder of SNCC member Herbert Lee by E. H. Hurst, a segregationist state senator. Under pressure, Allen falsely testified that Hurst had shot Lee in self-defense, and the senator was cleared of any wrongdoing. But when Allen approached the FBI and the U.S. Civil Rights Commission with the real story, he received a number of death threats. Allen was murdered the day before he was scheduled to move with his family to Milwaukee.) Having already assumed mythical status among his coworkers for his charisma, courage, and quiet leadership, Moses convinced them that it was imperative to bring in white reinforcements: the movement in Mississippi could not succeed without them.[128]

The decision in favor of Freedom Summer highlighted SNCC's desperation over its inability to crack Mississippi. Most of the young white participants were oblivious to the terror in the Deep South, but their idealism was quickly shattered by the disappearance of three young civil rights workers—Michael Schwerner, James Chaney, and Andrew Goodman—on June 21, 1964. The fact that two of the young men were white riveted media attention on Mississippi. Over the years, scores of blacks had disappeared in the Delta without fanfare, but President Johnson ordered at least 200 navy men and more than 100 FBI agents to search for the missing men.[129] Johnson met personally with the parents of the two missing white workers, Schwerner and Goodman. By contrast, his assistant, Lee White, merely telephoned the mother of Chaney, the missing African American man. LBJ also dispatched former CIA director Allen Dulles and FBI director J. Edgar Hoover to Mississippi to coordinate the intelligence efforts.[130] The fact that it took the disappearance of two white boys to arouse federal action and to focus national attention on Mississippi was not a surprise, but it embittered those who had long witnessed whites killing blacks in the Deep South with impunity. Sally Belfrage, a white volunteer, captured SNCC's outrage when she described how the northern media handled the story: they showed pictures of the two whites, Goodman and Schwerner, but for Chaney, "no picture, no name. His mother's grief was recognized, but it had a she-ought-to-be-used-to-it note beside that of the white parents, decent martyrs to gratuitous Southern savagery."[131]

Amid the national uproar over the disappearance of the three civil rights workers, the situation in Vietnam was beginning to seep into the collective national consciousness. Until President Johnson's announcement of the Gulf of Tonkin Resolution on August 4, 1964, the American public remained largely uninformed about and disinterested in the deteriorating situation in Southeast Asia. A Gallup poll released on May 27, 1964, showed that two-thirds of the American public had either "not followed" or had no opinion about the United States' "handling [of] affairs in South Vietnam."[132] For most African Americans, who were captivated by the historic passage of the Civil Rights Act on July 2, 1964, and the drama in Mississippi, Vietnam was even less of a concern. The searing experience of Freedom Summer radicalized SNCC workers. As Belfrage remarked, Freedom Summer volunteers "became unusually contemptuous of the threat of red-baiting and attuned to hypocrisy in the government power they had, only that spring, by and large unquestionably respected."[133] Consequently, SNCC and its New Left allies developed a profound skepticism of the inviolability of American institutions, which manifested in their early opposition to the Vietnam War in the mid-1960s.

Johnson's announcement of the Gulf of Tonkin Resolution occurred

on the same day that the bodies of the three missing civil rights workers were discovered near Philadelphia, Mississippi. Both stories appeared
on the front page of the next day's edition of the *New York Times*. SNCC
workers were particularly distressed at the disparity between the federal
government's passivity in Mississippi and the alacrity with which it was
willing to intervene in a conflict 8,000 miles away. In their minds, they
were fighting on the real front lines for freedom in Mississippi. Stokely
Carmichael summed it up by remarking, "In 1964 the country's best and
brightest were headed for Mississippi, not Southeast Asia."[134] At a memorial service in Neshoba County for the three slain civil rights workers,
Howard Zinn recalled that Moses held a copy of the morning's newspaper with the headline "LBJ Says Shoot to Kill in the Gulf of Tonkin," and
he castigated a government that refused to protect civil rights workers but
was ready to send its armed forces halfway around the world for a cause
nobody could reasonably explain.[135] The mourners were visibly moved
when Moses added, "This is what we're trying to do away with—the idea
whoever disagrees with us, must be killed."[136]

Years later, Pat Watters, a reporter and columnist for the *Atlanta
Journal*, recalled his first sighting of an anti–Vietnam War poster at the
headquarters of the Council of Federated Organizations (an umbrella organization of major civil rights groups) in Jackson during Freedom Summer.[137] Many white volunteers were also struck by the parallels between
the violence against African Americans in Mississippi and the violence
against the Vietnamese. Only eight days after passage of the Gulf of
Tonkin Resolution, Radcliffe College student and Freedom Summer volunteer Ellen Lake wrote a plaintive letter to her parents: "The people we're
killing in Vietnam are the same people whom we've been killing for years
in Mississippi. True, we didn't tie the knot in Mississippi and we didn't
pull the trigger in Vietnam—that is, we personally—but we've been standing behind the knot-tiers and the trigger-pullers too long."[138] The shooting
of Silas McGhee, a young African American soldier who tried to sit in the
whites-only section of a movie theater in Greenwood, Mississippi, provoked similar outrage.[139] One white civil rights volunteer remembered: "A
group of us were waiting at the hospital and Silas' family comes including
one of his brothers, or a cousin or something: and this guy is huge; and
he's in uniform. Turns out he's on leave from the Army! . . . That was it.
I remember thinking that any war in which blacks are fighting Asians for
the benefit of whites while their brothers are being murdered back home is
not worth supporting."[140] In the coming years, this lament would resonate

with legions of African Americans, particularly those on the front lines of the battle for racial justice, and it would provide a compelling rationale for their opposition to the war in Vietnam. Mississippi would be a crucible for SNCC's early opposition to the war.

The Mississippi Freedom Democratic Party and the Betrayal in Atlantic City

The primary thrust of Freedom Summer was to challenge the hegemony of the all-white Mississippi delegation at the 1964 Democratic National Convention in Atlantic City.[141] By dint of the efforts of volunteers and SNCC staff, approximately 80,000 African Americans had registered to vote as members of the Mississippi Freedom Democratic Party (MFDP), thus creating a viable political apparatus to challenge the regular segregationist Democratic Party's slate.[142]

By mid-August, the hundreds of white volunteers had returned home to cities and campuses in the North—radicalized by their experiences in Mississippi. Some, like University of California–Berkeley student Mario Savio, would take the lessons of Freedom Summer and translate them into a new style of political activism that would transform college campuses into hotbeds of dissent.[143] In the meantime, the bus carrying the MFDP delegation arrived in Atlantic City on Friday, August 21. Most of the delegates had never been outside the state of Mississippi, and their unshakable belief that "the law was on our side" made the weary travelers buoyant.[144] Victoria Gray cited a spirit of optimism among the MFDP delegates, recalling, "we were still idealistic enough to believe that the constitutional rights were all there to be ours."[145] The *New York Times* agreed with her and published an editorial in favor of seating the MFDP delegation. It queried: "Who still believes the nation can placidly accept what Mississippi calls normal?"[146]

The outcome of events in Atlantic City is an oft-told tale. Suffice it to say that President Johnson, fearing that his political coronation would be marred by a walkout of the southern delegations if the predominantly black MFDP delegation was seated, masterminded a covert campaign to deny it recognition that included FBI surveillance, wiretaps on MFDP offices, FBI agents masquerading as journalists, and his legendary political arm-twisting. Throughout the week, Johnson ordered his confidants to deny his involvement in the stratagems. This raw exercise of political power staggered the MFDP. The convention's failure to seat the entire

MFDP delegation aggravated the bitterness that had been brewing against the Kennedy and Johnson administrations and the Democratic Party over the past few years. In the end, Atlantic City left the MFDP, SNCC, and the young activists with an antipathy for the party and for the American political process itself. Their firsthand experience with the political machinations of Johnson, Democratic Party leaders, and their liberal allies fueled the activists' cynicism about the ability to effectuate change within the context of the liberal power structure. This disillusionment, in turn, fueled SNCC's early opposition to the Vietnam War.[147]

Sharecropper Fannie Lou Hamer's televised prime-time testimony on August 22, 1964, was mesmerizing and elicited tears from members of the convention's Credentials Committee. In her peroration, Hamer remarked, "If the freedom party is not seated now, I question America."[148] This sentiment epitomized the high stakes involved in the MFDP's quest to be seated, and Hamer's moving testimonial generated euphoria among MFDP supporters at the convention. Veteran reporter Mary McGory commented in the *Washington Star* that before Hamer's speech, the "opinion around the convention hall was that they [MFDP] had no chance and would be given short shrift."[149] However, Hamer's speech changed the calculus. With the parties seemingly deadlocked, the White House proposed the following compromise on Tuesday, August 25: The Democratic Party would allow two MFDP delegates to be seated—the Reverend Edwin King and Aaron Henry—and any state delegation that discriminated against African Americans would be barred from the 1968 convention. This offer insulted the MFDP delegation, particularly the party's designation of which two delegates would be seated. Hamer, the symbol of grassroots activism, best articulated its paltriness: "We didn't come all the way here for no two seats."[150]

Hamer's speech caused President Johnson to ratchet up the pressure, and he used every tool in his arsenal to avert a crisis. At the last minute, Johnson summoned United Auto Workers (UAW) president Walter Reuther to Atlantic City to notify Martin Luther King that the UAW would withdraw funding for the SCLC unless King pressured the MFDP to accept the compromise.[151] King's aide, Andrew Young, remembered that King was torn by his "disappointment in Lyndon Johnson" as well as "SNCC's unrealistic expectations."[152] King urged the MFDP to accept the compromise, but he stressed that if he were an MFDP delegate, he would refuse the offer, which confirmed the Mississippians' suspicions that King was an unreliable ally.[153] Other civil rights leaders, including Bayard Rustin, Allard Lowenstein, and Roy Wilkins, all implored the MFDP to be pragmatic and accept the compromise. At one point during the convention, Wilkins patronizingly scolded Hamer: "You people have put your point across. You don't know anything, you're ignorant, you don't know anything about politics. I have been in this business over twenty years. . . . Now why don't you pack up and go home?"[154] Wilkins's condescending tone enraged SNCC, and his complicity in the arm-twisting spurred SNCC's resentment of the moderate wing of the civil rights movement. That outrage would manifest in bitter disagreement over Wilkins's steadfast support of Johnson's Vietnam policies.

Above all, the process whereby the administration's minions shoved the compromise down the throats of the MFDP delegation left the deepest scars—far surpassing the enmity over the outcome itself. James Forman branded it "Profiles in Treachery."[155] While last-ditch negotiations between representatives of the MFDP and the White House were still going on behind closed doors, Hubert Humphrey confidant and Minnesota attorney general Walter Mondale announced on television that the parties had, in fact, agreed on the two-seat compromise. In keeping with the spirit of participatory democracy, Robert Moses, the principal negotiator for the MFDP, had wanted all sixty-eight delegates to ratify any agreement, and they unanimously agreed that no compromise had been accepted.[156] Upon hearing Mondale's announcement, a furious Moses shouted, "You cheated!" and stormed out of the room, taking a cab back to the hotel to assure the MFDP delegation that he had not accepted the compromise.[157] Edwin King, a white minister from Tugaloo College, remembered that Humphrey told them, "This is going to be done," so "accept it and make the best of it."[158] The MFDP delegation was incensed by this duplicity and overwhelmingly rejected the compromise.[159] They returned to Mississippi with their faith in the political process and the Democratic Party shattered.

James Forman characterized Atlantic City as a watershed in the civil rights movement "for SNCC and many other people as well. No longer was there any hope, among those who still had it, that the federal government would change the situation in the Deep South."[160] Forman's younger colleague, future draft resister Cleveland Sellers, recalled that after Atlantic City, SNCC realized that "the struggle was not for civil rights but for liberation," and it recognized the "need for alternative or parallel political structures."[161] The failure to seat the MFDP corroborated Fannie Lou Hamer's impulse to "question America." She and her comrades in SNCC questioned America's commitment to democracy, including its claim to be fighting for the liberation of the Vietnamese people. Their firsthand encounter with the unseemly side of democracy—raw power exercised with arrogance to perpetuate itself—resulted in their refusal to accept any of the government's claims at face value. After Atlantic City, SNCC abandoned hope that the political process could effectuate meaningful change, perceiving it as hopelessly corrupt and sordid. "We must stop playing the game of accepting token recognition for real change," Moses wrote in a postmortem memorandum to the MFDP. He added: "Until then [Atlantic City], despite every setback and disappointment and obstacle we had faced over the years, the belief still prevailed that the system would work, the system would listen, the system would respond. Now, for the first time, we had made our way to the very center of the system. We had played by the rules, done everything we were supposed to do, had played the game exactly as required, had arrived at the doorstep and found the door slammed in our face."[162] For SNCC and its allies, their belief in democracy and in the nostrums equality, liberty, and freedom vanished in the shoals of Atlantic City.

After the convention, an exhausted and disgruntled SNCC returned to Mississippi and the Deep South, knowing things could never be the same. Years later, John Lewis characterized Atlantic City as a "disaster" and a "turning point for the civil rights movement."[163] Edwin King recalled that after the convention, SNCC "simply did not know what to do."[164] A few weeks later, ten veteran SNCC leaders, including John Lewis, Robert Moses, James Forman, Julian Bond, and Fannie Lou Hamer, accepted an invitation to accompany singer Harry Belafonte to Africa.[165] Belafonte, a longtime SNCC supporter whose political vision had been inspired by Paul Robeson, had been blacklisted himself in the 1950s and possessed an anticolonial mind-set unmoored to Cold War verities.[166] Belafonte was sensitive to the fact that many young people in SNCC were suffering from "burnout," and he thought it would behoove them to become acquainted with the work of Guinea president Sekou Toure, whose construction of an independent nation "held great promise for Africa's future."[167] This African sojourn contributed to a shift in SNCC's collective ideological orientation. While at the New Stanley Hotel in Nairobi, Kenya, the group unexpectedly encountered Malcolm X, who had recently broken with Elijah Muhammad's Nation of Islam. Malcolm's ideas of self-determination and racial pride dovetailed with SNCC's long-standing belief in local empowerment and reinforced the international dimensions of the racial struggle. They discussed the looming problem of Vietnam and its similarity to the plight of African countries struggling for independence.[168] After ten weeks abroad, the delegation returned home with a deepening Pan-African perspective. Their experience in Africa would be another factor in their opposition to the Vietnam War.

Meanwhile, SNCC's Executive Committee in Atlanta announced a weeklong retreat to be held in the second week of November at the resort town of Waveland, Mississippi, for the purpose of discussing the organization's future, goals, and programs.[169] Throughout the week, discussions (some of which were heated) covered a range of subjects, including SNCC's future direction, the role of women and whites in the movement, and the intensifying crisis in Vietnam. Casey Hayden and Mary King drafted an anonymous paper entitled "SNCC Position Paper: Women in the Movement," bemoaning the subordinate status of women in the organization (an early expression of the grievances that would inform second-wave feminism). But the most salient issues debated at Waveland involved the organization's structure and interracial participation. Forman argued that SNCC's rapid growth and complexity necessitated a more hierarchical and coherent organization with clear lines of authority. Others, led by Moses (who had become uncomfortable with his own iconic status in the movement), disagreed and harked back to Ella Baker's vision of horizontal leadership, arguing that Forman's proposal contradicted SNCC's original mission. For the first time in its brief history, SNCC began to fracture into different factions characterized as "anarchists," "floaters," and "hardliners." After an emotionally wrenching week at Waveland, the participants adjourned in a dispirited mood. In this fragile state, SNCC would have to confront the issue of the mushrooming conflict in Vietnam.

Early Rumblings: Vietnam

Lyndon Johnson had inherited a deteriorating situation in Vietnam. The coup that had toppled Diem and his family on November 1, 1963, failed to ameliorate the disintegration of South Vietnamese society that had left his government with virtually no popular support. Trapped between several unattractive options, Johnson continued to pursue Kennedy's policy, but as noted by historian Fredrik Logevall, "a subtle but crucial shift" occurred when Johnson assumed the presidency, "in the form of a greater presidential insistence on preventing defeat in Vietnam."[170] Most Americans who were familiar with the war supported it, and the vitality of the Cold War consensus caused the public and policy makers to embrace the domino theory as dogma. As early as 1962, faint ripples of dissent had occurred among the New Left and older pacifist organizations such as the Fellowship of Reconciliation (FOR) and the WRL.[171] By the beginning of 1964, Walter Lippmann, the doyen of foreign correspondents, realized the daunting challenges in Southeast Asia and agreed with French president Charles de Gaulle's dire prognostications that the Vietnam War was not winnable. De Gaulle counseled the U.S. government to seek a negotiated settlement, but the "best and the brightest," holdovers from the Kennedy administration, were imbued with hubris and were determined to succeed where the French had failed.[172]

By early 1964, the crisis in Vietnam was beginning to percolate the New Left's consciousness. On February 29, 1964, SDS's Richard Flacks drafted a memorandum entitled "New Crisis in Vietnam," wherein he suggested that President Johnson was planning a major expansion of the war. He observed, "The decisions being made at this point have to do with *what kind* of military operation is to be undertaken—whether to extend the war to North Vietnam, or to increase American participation in the South, or some variant of this." Flacks urged that the inchoate peace movement take a stand on Vietnam.[173] By 1964, although the effects of McCarthyism lingered, antiwar dissenters exhibited a more emboldened spirit. A showdown was brewing.

As noted, participants in Freedom Summer saw their first antiwar slogans in Mississippi. Their suspicions of the federal government and their affinity for Third World struggles against racial domination led historian Clayborne Carson to note, "Most SNCC workers opposed the U.S. involvement in Vietnam as soon as they became aware of it."[174] Compared with other civil rights activists, members of SNCC and the MFDP were more conscious of the hypocrisy of the U.S. policy in Vietnam, as a consequence of their intimate encounter with terror in the Deep South.[175] Nevertheless, until early 1965, Vietnam remained on the periphery as the civil rights movement focused its attention on Freedom Summer, passage of the Civil Rights Act, the MFDP challenge, and the 1964 presidential campaign. With the civil rights movement at its apogee, the distant conflict in Vietnam did not appear to be a menacing problem. In fact, a University of Michigan survey released in December 1964 revealed that one in four Americans were oblivious to the fighting in Vietnam.[176]

As for the presidential campaign, Johnson's efforts on behalf of civil rights earned him the overwhelming support of the civil rights movement, which called for a moratorium on demonstrations against the president for the duration of the campaign.[177] When the issue of Vietnam arose, Johnson used it to cudgel his opponent, Senator Barry Goldwater, as a dangerous warmonger. Avoiding a bloodbath in Vietnam was a cornerstone of Johnson's campaign, which was displayed most dramatically by his famous mushroom-cloud television commercial. African Americans by and large celebrated Johnson's rout of the hapless Goldwater, who opposed the Civil Rights Act of 1964 as an unconstitutional expansion of federal power. African Americans exulted over LBJ's triumph as a validation of his civil rights agenda.[178]

Given Johnson's landslide victory, the American electorate delivered a mandate to continue his policies, both at home and abroad. A beneficiary of Kennedy's martyrdom, Johnson's large margin of victory was also attributable to "the simple fact that he was not Barry Goldwater," whose bellicose speeches on the need to force a military confrontation in Vietnam scared the American people, who were still haunted by the Cuban Missile Crisis.[179] Throughout the campaign, Johnson had promised to keep the United States out of a full-scale conflict in Vietnam and presented himself as the peace candidate, vowing he was "not about to send American boys 9 or 10,000 miles away from home to do what Asian boys ought to be doing for themselves."[180] In spite of his trouncing of the hawkish Goldwater, Johnson, a product of the Cold War political culture, feared that his presidency would be destroyed if he lost Vietnam. Determined not to be the first U.S. president to lose a war, LBJ shed his peaceful persona and took decisive steps to escalate hostilities.[181] Within a matter of weeks, Johnson moved closer and closer to Goldwater's position on Vietnam—the man he had so recently and so dexterously caricatured as a trigger-happy hawk.[182]

These steps toward war roused the SDS and further embittered SNCC and CORE. In the weeks after the election, Vietnam started to eclipse the civil rights movement as the New Left's primary focus. By late 1964, SDS leader Todd Gitlin spoke of the growing reaction against the war as his group's "main motive."[183] Even though formal opposition to the war would not coalesce until the beginning of 1965, a significant base of dissent gathered momentum after the Gulf of Tonkin Resolution. In addition to the older pacifist organizations, SNCC, MFDP, CORE, SDS, the Freedom Summer volunteers, and other elements of the New Left, many of whom had been foot soldiers in the African American freedom struggle, would constitute the vanguard of the nascent antiwar movement. The success of the Free Speech movement in Berkeley was emblematic of the untapped political ferment among young white students.

Perhaps more than anyone else, Robert Moses embodied SNCC's

transformation. By all accounts, he returned from Africa a noticeably changed man. Like his predecessors who were active in the CAA in the 1930s and 1940s, Moses's trip to Africa broadened his horizons, furnishing an international perspective on the United States' role in world affairs. His bitterness over Atlantic City, combined with SNCC's rancorous debates over whether to expel his white comrades, caused him profound anguish and triggered a sinking feeling that all the sacrifices of the last four years had been in vain.[184] On top of all this, he was growing weary of his deification among the New Left. In early 1965 he announced that he would no longer go by the name Robert Moses—instead, he would be Robert Parris (his middle name).[185] He would leave Mississippi shortly and, like Du Bois, move to Africa. But first, Parris would shift his efforts to protesting the war in Vietnam—which he saw as a logical continuum of the violence in the Deep South. In a 1965 interview with journalist Jack Newfield, he explained: "Most liberals think of Mississippi as a cancer, as a distortion of America. But we think Mississippi is an accurate reflection of America's values and morality. Why can't the people who killed Andrew, James, and Mickie be brought to justice, unless a majority of the community condones murder? Sheriff Rainey is not a freak; he reflects the majority. And what he did is related to the napalm bombing of 'objects' in Vietnam."[186]

Parris was endowed with insights that were not yet discernible to most contemporary observers. His angst over the direction of the civil rights movement was predictive of the discontent that would engulf the movement, but it was the antithesis of the sanguine mood that pervaded the African American community at the dawn of 1965. Whitney Young Jr., executive director of the National Urban League, best captured this spirit in a column he wrote for the *New York Amsterdam News*: "The nation has more reason for optimism for the prospects of eradicating racial injustice as the New Year begins than ever before."[187] By all objective standards, Young's views were unassailable. Since February 1960, when Robert Moses's life had been dramatically transformed by a picture of the Greensboro sit-inners, the civil rights movements had achieved unforeseen and unprecedented accomplishments.[188] Most important, SNCC and its white allies in the New Left had stirred the sympathies of large segments of the American public and finally forced political action at the highest levels of the U.S. government. For a few years, the notion of a "beloved community" exemplified the glimmering hope of an interracial and intergenerational alliance between SNCC and the predominately white New Left, with civil rights as the animating cause—that is, until the Vietnam War deflated the struggle for racial justice in the South.

Parris may have been an idealist, but he was also a perspicacious observer of current events, and his trepidations were not without justification. Whereas the tragic dimensions of the Vietnam War were still unfathomable to Johnson loyalists Whitney Young Jr. and Roy Wilkins, its early rumblings pained Parris and SNCC. According to Freedom Summer volunteer Sally Belfrage, SNCC's early opposition to the Vietnam War occurred "not because they understood so much about foreign policy, but because they understood so much about the United States."[189] Throughout the fall of 1964, the escalating crisis in Vietnam cast a dark shadow over SNCC. Mary King and Jane Stembridge, two longtime white members of SNCC, were so stricken by the sight of African American families meeting aluminum caskets bearing bodies from Vietnam that they decided to collaborate on a short film about the war's impact on African Americans in Mississippi.[190] Tom Hayden paid a visit to his old SNCC friends in the winter of 1964 and was struck by how "the memory of Atlantic City—as well as the shadow of Vietnam—hung over the future menacingly."[191] On New Year's Eve, SNCC dispatched a delegation of McComb, Mississippi, teenagers to Harlem, where they met with Malcolm X. Malcolm delivered a diatribe against the U.S. government as "the most hypocritical since the world began" because "it was supposed to be a democracy, supposed to be for freedom . . . but they want to draft you . . . send you to Saigon to fight for them," while blacks at home still had to worry about being able to vote without being murdered.[192] While Malcolm was making his eloquent plea, SDS was meeting in Lower Manhattan and heeding Flacks's earlier call to protest the war and stage a major demonstration in early 1965. Parris would participate in this march, and he would devote the spring and summer of 1965 to mobilizing his fellow civil rights workers to protest the Vietnam War.[193]

By the end of 1964, approximately 23,000 young Americans were serving in Vietnam, and hundreds had already paid the ultimate price: their lives. Many of these young men were African Americans seeking to escape the limited opportunities in the urban ghettos of the North or the rural villages of the South. By the end of 1965, the number of Americans troops in Vietnam would increase fivefold. The military buildup in Vietnam would be matched by the growing turmoil at home. From Selma to Watts, violence would grip the nation. But this was merely the beginning. For the civil rights movement and African Americans, the Americanization of the Vietnamese conflict would aggravate tensions within the civil rights coalition and attenuate its links with the New Left. They would now be fighting on two fronts, even though they barely had enough strength for one. The Vietnam War would supplant civil rights as the nation's most pressing issue and polarize the struggle for racial justice at home.

3

Vietnam and Civil Rights

The Great Diversion, 1965

My own feeling was that the anti-war movement took the wind out of the sails of the civil rights movement. To put it another way—one of the many victims of Vietnam was the southern civil rights movement, if because the country's attention was turned away from the South and the movement to a war.

—Danny Lyon, SNNC photographer

The Vietnam War . . . has practically pushed the civil rights movement off the center page of American history.

—A. Philip Randolph

On August 6, 1965, approximately six months after transforming the conflict in Vietnam into an American war, Lyndon Johnson signed the Voting Rights Act in a solemn ceremony at the Capitol. Approximately seventy years since African Americans were systematically disenfranchised in the South, this historic piece of legislation guaranteed voting rights to all African Americans. As Dr. Martin Luther King Jr., Rosa Parks, Roy Wilkins, James Farmer, Bayard Rustin, and other luminaries of the civil rights community sat nearby in seats of honor, President Johnson addressed the nation and proclaimed the act "a triumph for freedom as huge as any victory that has ever been won on any battlefield." Later that day, King spoke for virtually all African Americans when he praised the president's speech as "eloquent and persuasive" and touted the law for its removal of "all the obstacles to the right to vote."[1] Coming on the heels of Johnson's extraordinary commencement speech at Howard University and the passage of key elements of his Great Society, the president's signing of the Voting Rights Act marked the apogee of the civil rights movement. After decades of struggle, both ordinary African Americans and civil rights leaders were justifiably imbued with an unprecedented degree of optimism and felt an abiding fidelity to the president.[2]

For David Dellinger and Bayard Rustin, who had been allies in the fight against militarism and segregation for decades, this historic event should have been an occasion for celebration. In spite of their different racial and socioeconomic backgrounds, Dellinger and Rustin were part of the same cohort that had gravitated to left-wing politics and pacifism during the Great Depression and World War II. Coincidentally, they both served lengthy prison sentences at the Lewisburg Federal Penitentiary in Pennsylvania for being conscientious objectors in the "good war" against fascism. Dellinger, born into a prominent white family and reared in an affluent Boston suburb, graduated from Yale in 1936. As a young man, he forsook his parents' affluent lifestyle and dedicated himself to the struggle against racism and militarism—he even undertook a near-fatal hunger strike to protest racial segregation while imprisoned at Lewisburg.[3] Dellinger and Rustin bore similar scars from the repressive years of the Cold War and McCarthyism, and by the early 1960s, they represented an important bridge between the Old Left and the New Left. Rustin was a coeditor of *Liberator*, Dellinger's left-leaning bimonthly publication, and it was influential among the new generation of political activists who materialized in the early 1960s. In the months leading up to the signing of the Voting Right Acts, however, the two men had been embroiled in an increasingly acrimonious controversy over the spiraling war in Vietnam. Rustin's reluctance to take an unequivocal stand against the war earned him the enmity of Dellinger and his colleague Staughton Lynd, who accused Rustin of betraying "the essential moralism which you have taught myself and others over the years."[4]

In the early morning of August 6, 1965, Dellinger was at LaGuardia Airport in New York to catch a flight to Washington, D.C., where he and Robert Parris (formerly Robert Moses) were scheduled to lead an anti–Vietnam War protest to commemorate the twentieth anniversary of the bombing of Hiroshima and Nagasaki. As Dellinger was boarding the plane, he saw that Rustin was on the same flight, beaming with joy because President Johnson had personally invited him to witness the signing of the Voting Rights Act. Dellinger needled Rustin to "be sure to get one of the pens Johnson uses to sign it so you could come out, cross the street into Lafayette Park and use the pen to sign the Declaration of Conscience" in support of draft resistance. "Then," Dellinger added, "you can say a few words linking Black rights and opposition to the war."[5] Rustin, however, was loath to protest Johnson's war on the same day as the signing of the Voting Rights Act, and he uncomfortably demurred. Having been marginalized after his arrest for homosexual conduct, Rustin believed the current political milieu afforded him a rare opportunity to influence policy from within, and he also feared that Johnson would crush the incipient antiwar movement.[6] After their flight touched down in Washington, the two awkwardly went their separate ways—Rustin attended the signing of the Voting Rights Act, and Dellinger, along with Parris, Lynd, and Rustin's mentor A. J. Muste, stood mutely outside the White House and held a vigil protesting the administration's policies in Vietnam. Three days later, on the twentieth anniversary of the bombing of Nagasaki, Dellinger, Parris, and Lynd led a march of more than 800 people. Moments before he was arrested, Parris shouted into a bullhorn, "Negroes better than anyone else are in a position to question the war. Not because they understand the war better, but because they understand the United States."[7] A group of right-wing extremists wearing Nazi uniforms doused Parris, Lynd, and Dellinger with red paint, and the next issue of *Life* magazine carried a dramatic picture of the splattered trio.[8]

The inability of erstwhile comrades Dellinger and Rustin to rejoice in such a landmark event as the Voting Rights Act was an ominous sign for the future of the civil rights movement. Indeed, by the middle of 1965, the tiff between the two was emblematic of the clefts in the coalition between the New Left and the civil rights movement and within the civil rights movement itself, caused by the mushrooming Vietnam War. In addition to Vietnam, Rustin and others were concerned about the rising tide of Black Power, which was engulfing SNCC and impacting blacks in the northern ghettos who were chafing over their limited opportunities and issues of police brutality. The war, however, was deflecting much of the fervor from the struggle for racial justice and further fraying the civil rights coalition. Whereas SNCC's sense of betrayal by the Democrats in Atlantic City had been an embittering experience and caused substantial rifts among SNCC leaders and the mainstream civil rights movement, the overall damage was limited to a marginal sector of the movement that had already concluded that American politics and culture were increasingly "depraved." But the unwieldy coalition of African American civil rights organizations, the New Left, and liberal elites could not withstand the strains of the escalating Vietnam War.

The early protests against the war in 1965, only a decade removed from the height of McCarthyism, unleashed a paroxysm of anger, bitterness, and frustration. Johnson's ill-fated decision to Americanize the Vietnam War diverted much of the New Left's reformist zeal away from the civil rights movement, further radicalized SNCC and CORE, and thereby exacerbated preexisting schisms within the civil rights coalition. As the Vietnam War supplanted the civil rights movement as the most pressing issue confronting the American public and dominated the political discourse, the civil rights movement began to flounder.[9] By the end of 1965, the war consumed the Johnson administration and polarized the nation. The passions the war engendered within the radical community were so potent that Rustin and Dellinger would not speak to each other for years. For the most militant wing of the civil rights movement, 1965 would be the year of reckoning.

Crossing the Rubicon: The War and Initial Views of African Americans

When Lyndon Johnson assumed the presidency, he earned near-unanimous plaudits for healing the wounds of the nation after the shocking assassination of his youthful predecessor. Even his adversaries marveled at his masterful legislative prowess in advancing his ambitious domestic agenda. His unshakable determination to fulfill Kennedy's legacy and shepherd his civil rights legislation through Congress particularly endeared Johnson to civil rights activists.

In the realm of foreign affairs, however, the president was a relative novice. Surrounded by Kennedy's hawkish Ivy League advisers, the graduate of Southwest Texas Teachers College felt on shaky ground.[10] In late 1964 and early 1965, President Johnson and his advisers faced a rapidly deterioration situation in South Vietnam, which was largely a by-product of the chaos following the U.S.-sanctioned coup against Diem. Although Secretary of Defense Robert McNamara correctly pointed out that Johnson had "inherited a mess," the president felt trapped by events.[11] On one hand, he was reluctant to risk his presidency for an indeterminate foreign venture in that "damn little pissant country," as he called Vietnam. Perhaps his campaign promise in the fall of 1964—that he intended to keep the nation out of war—was not disingenuous; Johnson did not eagerly seek war in Southeast Asia, and he regarded it as a distraction from his grander ambitions. On the other hand, Johnson was a victim of the Cold War mentality that gripped most of American society.[12] He was haunted by vivid memories of the spurious allegations that Truman had lost China, and Johnson feared that losing Vietnam would destroy his own presidency, along with his cherished Great Society. Lacking Kennedy's nuanced understanding of and sensitivity to the nationalist strivings of Ho Chi Minh and the Vietcong, Johnson was unwilling to question the premise of the domino theory, which had become dogma among the natural security cognoscenti.[13] For President Johnson and his team of advisers, the Munich analogy and their reluctance to be perceived as "appeasers" became a central premise of their foreign policy. As the situation in South Vietnam became increasingly dire in the months following his reelection, Johnson refused to even consider the alternatives of neutralization and withdrawal. In the end, Johnson's fears overcame his skepticism.[14] Years later, he explained to Doris Kearns:

> I knew from the start that I was bound to be crucified either way I moved. If I left the woman I really loved—the Great Society—in order to get involved with that bitch of a war on the other side of the world, then I would lose everything at home. All my programs.
> . . . All my dreams to provide education and medical care to the browns and blacks and the lame and the poor. But if I left that war and let the Communists take over South Vietnam . . . there would follow in this country an endless debate—a mean and destructive debate—that would shatter my presidency, kill my administration, and damage our democracy.[15]

By early February 1965, Johnson chose war to save South Vietnam from communism and, in the process, invested the nation's blood and treasure.[16] Ironically, his decision for war was motivated in part by the desire to preserve his power, but it ended up destroying his administration and ultimately left him a broken man. The war was an unmitigated disaster. George Kennan summed it up best, calling the Vietnam War "the most disastrous of all America's undertakings in the whole 200 years of its history."[17]

For a number of reasons, the escalation of the war in the spring of 1965 initially failed to penetrate the consciousness of most African Americans. First, the government's obfuscations and secret deliberations lent an aura of mystery to the entire campaign.[18] David Halberstam, who covered the war in Vietnam as a correspondent for the *New York Times*, aptly stated that U.S. decision makers "inched across the Rubicon without even admitting it," and the task of their press secretaries was "to misinform the public."[19] Second, in the beginning of 1965, the future impact of the conflict in such a faraway, remote country was unfathomable to nearly all experts. Even the war's most vocal critics could not have foreseen the scope of the ensuing calamity. Third and most important, the attention of most African Americans was riveted on Selma, Alabama, and the epic campaign for voting rights. On the whole, African Americans were basking in a rare ray of optimism, and their sanguinity received widespread coverage in the African American press.[20] The inception of Operation Rolling Thunder—the massive aerial campaign against Hanoi—and the dispatching of the first land troops to the beaches of Vietnam coincided with the apex of the civil rights movement. The African American press's coverage of the war was scant, and despite the numerous reporters in Vietnam, few were black.[21] For instance, the *Chicago Defender* rarely mentioned the war, except when it published a photograph and a cursory biography of some local soldier whose service reflected the achievements of African Americans in the newly integrated armed forces. Therefore, in the early months of 1965, the Vietnam War was not a preoccupying concern for most African Americans.

Amid the atypical buoyancy that permeated the African American public, there was a smattering of anxiety over the rumbles of war in distant Southeast Asia. Even before the initiation of Rolling Thunder, on January 2, 1965, the *Pittsburgh Courier* editorialized that, in light of the statement by Lieutenant General Nguyen Khan of South Vietnam that his military would not fight "to carry out the policy of any foreign country," it made no sense for the United States to pour millions of dollars into that remote Asian country, and the paper recommended that the Johnson administration find "some face-saving way to get out—yesterday."[22] Veteran columnist P. L. Prattis echoed similar concerns when he questioned why the United States was fighting in Vietnam, given reports that the Vietnamese in the South were supporting the Vietcong.[23] A few months later, following the introduction of ground troops, the *Chicago Defender* chided the U.S. government for failing to inform the American public "why we are at war and why our soldiers are dying on the battlefields that have no clear lines of military demarcation."[24]

These editorials raised important questions, but they were anomalous, given African Americans' overall support of the Johnson administration and its domestic and foreign policies. The conventional wisdom was reflected in the *Pittsburgh Courier*'s May 15 editorial, which warned that a unilateral withdrawal from Vietnam would cause the "Communists from the North" to overrun "not only South Viet Nam" but also "non-Communist countries in the area."[25] In addition to the legacy of McCarthyism and their fondness for the president, the presence of large numbers of African American men in the newly integrated military cemented African American support for the war. For the next few years, mainstream African American leaders and the black press gave Lyndon Johnson's war the benefit of the doubt. Most important, they believed it would be detrimental to the cause of civil rights to challenge Cold War orthodoxy.

Among African American organizations, the Vietnam War penetrated SNCC's collective consciousness most profoundly.[26] Yet, in spite of their instinctive opposition to the war, prior to 1965, most SNCC members deemed the war not irrelevant but remote. James Forman recalled, "Its importance to black people had not come home to us."[27] SNCC had always possessed a post–Cold War mind-set, and after Atlantic City, it was even more inclined to view the liberal establishment with contempt. Weary of the national obsession with communism and tired of Red-baiting, SNCC had less compunction than other civil rights organizations when it came to criticizing the war. After all, the notion of nonviolence had been a cornerstone of SNCC's philosophy since its inception in 1960.

In the early weeks of 1965, SNCC executive director John Lewis was deluged with letters from pacifist organizations seeking his organization's support in the embryonic antiwar movement.[28] In view of its long-standing pacifism, SNCC was sympathetic to the objectives of the antiwar groups, and Lewis harbored a visceral antipathy for the war. On the same day that 3,500 marines first waded ashore to defend the Da Nang air base, Alabama state troopers fractured Lewis's skull in Selma, Alabama, on Bloody Sunday (March 7, 1965). Just before he went to the hospital, a stricken Lewis bellowed to a crowd of his fellow marchers: "I don't know how President Johnson can send troops to Vietnam" but "he can't send troops to Selma, Alabama," to protect his own citizens.[29] SNCC's New Left allies were beginning to publicize the discrepancy between Johnson's inaction in quelling segregationist violence in the South with his alacrity in dispatching troops to Vietnam.[30] These entreaties from the New Left notwithstanding, in early 1965, SNCC's primary preoccupation continued to be the civil rights struggle in the South, specifically the ongoing campaign for the right to vote. Even though some individual members, such as Robert Parris, voiced their opposition to the war, as an organization, SNCC considered an official proclamation against the war premature. However, its patience was wearing thin.[31]

SNCC and the Peace Movement: Early 1965

The Johnson administration's decision for war in early 1965 sparked an antiwar movement that, within months, would establish a framework for dissent among the divergent peace organizations. Spurred by the hordes of baby boomers just entering college, a vocal but chaotic antiwar movement existed by the mid-1960s. For the first time since the beginning of the Cold War, a mass movement would publicly protest the government's Cold War policy.[32] Within months of the escalation in Vietnam, SDS membership swelled on college campuses, which had already been roused by the Free Speech movement in Berkeley the previous autumn. The military buildup necessitated an infusion of manpower in the armed forces, and in colleges across the United States, thousands of young men brooded over their futures as they watched the nation plunge into war. The war's immediacy resonated among young white students. Although they may have condemned the outrages inflicted on African Americans, the war affected them personally and posed an imminent threat to their own futures. Given the affinities between the more radical wing of the civil rights movement and the New Left, many white New Left figures, notably Tom Hayden, Todd Gitlin, Staughton Lynd, and Howard Zinn, had harbored high hopes of a merger, or at least collaboration, between the two movements.[33] SDS's Carl Ogelsby summed it up best: "I see SNCC as the Nile Valley of the New Left, and I honor SDS to call it part of the delta that SNCC created."[34] By the spring of 1965, SNCC and its allies in the civil rights movement would be enmeshed in the antiwar movement.

In December 1964 SDS's proposal for a massive antiwar rally had not generated much interest.[35] Interest spiked, however, after the initiation of Operation Rolling Thunder, and SDS scheduled the rally for Easter Sunday, April 17, 1965, in Washington, D.C. SDS president Paul Potter relocated to Washington to coordinate the march, and member Paul Booth noted that "every day's mail brings word of a demonstration or two we'd never heard of."[36] Using SNCC's Freedom Schools as a model, antiwar activists and prominent academics instituted the first "teach-ins" on March 24 at the University of Michigan, and they spread to thirty-five campuses within a week.[37] SDS made a concerted effort to appeal to its longtime allies in SNCC and the civil rights movement, and in view of its resentment over the government's willingness to use force in Vietnam but not in the American South, SNCC was a likely ally in the emerging antiwar movement.

This groundswell of antiwar activity on the part of the white New

Left was beginning to influence its commitment to civil rights. To complicate matters, this initial stirring of antiwar protest occurred just months after Freedom Summer, and given SNCC's brewing resentment over white participation in the civil rights movement, many whites felt compelled to turn their attention to the war. Helen Garvy, who helped establish the SDS chapter at Harvard, recalled that the war "totally distorted the movement, and made us drop a lot of other things that were important," such as civil rights. "But it had to be done."[38] Civil rights had been a paramount issue for SDS, but after 1964, its direct engagement with the movement waned.[39] Like other white activists, Sue Thrasher was beginning to feel burned out by 1965. Years later, she recalled that the war "and the draft were fast encroaching on the Freedom Movement, demanding an analysis of U.S. society that went beyond the southern system of segregation."[40] For other longtime white civil rights activists such as Tom Hayden, Howard Zinn, Dennis Sweeney, Mary King, and Staughton Lynd, their concern for racial justice continued unabated, but for the next decade, the Vietnam War was their primary obsession, and civil rights receded to the background.[41]

The war was not the sole reason for the New Left's disengagement with the civil rights movement. By the mid-1960s, the end of de jure segregation in the South; the outbreak of racial unrest in the cities; the spread of Black Power in SNCC, CORE, and large segments of the African American population in the North; and the emergence of a counterculture all encouraged young whites to pursue other avenues of engagement. These events did not happen overnight, but they coincided with the onset of the Vietnam War. SDS had always been concerned with issues other than civil rights. As early as 1963, SDS had established the Economic Research and Action Project (ERAP), modeled after SNCC's grassroots work in the South. SDS envisioned ERAP as an interracial organization of the poor and unemployed, and it established programs to alleviate poverty in the slums of Newark, Chicago, and Chester, Pennsylvania.[42] However, because of SNCC's concern that whites had become too powerful and that too many of them had remained in Mississippi after Freedom Summer, Forman introduced a resolution that SDS and whites should orient their campaign toward poor white communities, and blacks should work in black communities. As a result, ERAP shifted its focus to combating white poverty.[43] Consequently, by early 1965, many white civil rights workers left the South because they no longer felt welcome in SNCC, and antiwar activity provided them with an outlet for their political commitment. Despite these other factors, the war in Southeast Asia was the critical catalyst for the New Left's increasing withdrawal from the civil rights movement.

Within the African American community itself, the war was beginning to siphon energy from the struggle for racial justice. The psychic wounds from years of harrowing work on the front lines of the civil rights movement had finally taken its toll, and Robert Parris became a victim of burnout. Sensing that his usefulness in Mississippi was over, he and his wife, Dona Richards, left the Magnolia State for good. By the beginning of 1965, Parris was becoming obsessed with the Vietnam War.[44] In fact, he and his wife became so embroiled in disagreements over the extent to which the civil rights movement should invest in antiwar activity that it contributed to the unraveling of their marriage.[45] Parris's departure from SNCC was a blow to his many admirers, who had hoped he might help unite the civil rights and antiwar movements. His quiet charisma and economy of expression cast a spell over his cohorts. Years later, SNCC's Cleveland Sellers wrote of Parris: "There was something about him[,] the manner in which he carried himself, that seemed to draw all of us to him. He had been where we were going. And more important, he had emerged as the kind of person we wanted to be."[46]

Throughout 1965 Parris acted as a crucial liaison between the antiwar and civil rights movements. In May he gave a powerful speech before 10,000 at a Berkeley teach-in, where he related the Vietnam War to the overall pattern of racism in America and pointed out that if the audience understood the differing reactions "to the deaths of James Reeb and Jimmy Jackson in Mississippi, they could begin to understand this country in relation to Vietnam and the Third World, the Congo and Santo Domingo."[47] But by the end of the summer, he told Staughton Lynd that he just couldn't "seem to find solid ground under my feet in the anti-war movement."[48] After the federal government ordered him to report for induction into the armed forces, the thirty-one-year-old moved to Montreal, Canada, where he spent two years working at an assortment of jobs before moving to Tanzania, where he lived for the next decade.[49] His departure was a loss to the movements for peace and justice.

The reasons for Parris's early and passionate involvement in the antiwar movement are instructive. First, his bitter exposure to the nature of politics at Atlantic City inoculated him from any desire to operate within a system he viewed as morally compromised. In a speech he had delivered the previous November, Parris stated that the lesson of Atlantic City was "that the destiny of America was not in their hands, that they should seek their own objectives. Let the chips fall where they may."[50] A committed pacifist since he had first encountered Quaker ideology as an undergraduate at Hamilton College in the mid-1950s, Parris would not be mute. For Parris, Rustin's vision of coalition politics smacked of elitism, whereby self-appointed elites usurped power from ordinary people.[51] The Vietnam War corroborated his view that America was hopelessly irredeemable. He wanted no part in it.

Second, and perhaps more important, Parris's and SNCC's work in the Deep South had exposed them to the hypocrisy of American rhetoric about promoting freedom in South Vietnam.[52] His views were best embodied in an October 1965 interview with *Southern Patriot*, where he addressed the question of whether civil rights organizations should take formal positions on the Vietnam War. Having witnessed firsthand the U.S. government's complicity in perpetuating Jim Crow and denying fundamental liberties to African Americans, Parris argued that those who had participated in the civil rights struggle in the South were skeptical of the government's righteous claims about Vietnam. This experience allowed civil rights activists to discern the "sickness in America regarding the way it viewed the world," and he mused that "those that have been part of the agonies of the South in recent years" were endowed with a deeper understanding. He likened oppression in the South to U.S. oppression in Vietnam.

> The rationale this nation uses to justify war in Vietnam turns out to be amazingly similar to the rationale that has been used by the white South to justify its opposition to the freedom movement.
>
> The South has said its civilization is being attacked by people—outsiders—who want to overthrow it, and that's what this country says in Vietnam.[53]

In response to those who feared that venturing into the antiwar movement would threaten the recent gains in civil rights, Parris said: "Certainly one of the most basic rights we have been seeking in this country is the right to participate fully in the life of this country. Now if by participating—that is, taking part in the discussions of the great issues that face the country—we threaten the right to participate, we have to begin to wonder whether the right is real. . . . In addition to the right to take a stand on the peace issue, however, civil rights forces may also have the responsibility to do so."[54]

The antiwar issue revived the thorny debate over African American support of Cold War policy and anticolonialism. Its reemergence in the mid-1960s presented stark dilemmas for African Americans. Although Parris's open dissent against the Vietnam War was predictive, it was not the norm among civil rights leaders. Malcolm X, Robert Williams, James Baldwin, and those who had been active in the FPCC were among the few who expressed early opposition to the war. Two weeks before his untimely death, Malcolm X dismissed the idea that Americans "can win in South Vietnam" when the French "couldn't stay there," even though they had been "deeply entrenched in Vietnam for a hundred years or so" and had the "best weapons of warfare, a highly mechanized army, everything that you would need."[55]

In spite of Malcolm's fighting words, the vast majority of the civil rights establishment was unwilling to risk the taint of pacifism. Most importantly, the mainstream civil rights movement's implicit compromise with Cold War liberalism was finally paying dividends, such as passage of the Civil Rights Act in 1964. After enduring years in the political wilderness, African American leaders, mostly moderates, were being offered unprecedented access to power. This older generation had long viewed Parris and his SNCC colleagues as parvenus who were oblivious to the consequences of associating with leftists. They also harbored legitimate concerns that an antiwar stance would dilute Lyndon Johnson's support for civil rights and the Great Society. Conversely, Parris and his contemporaries who grew up in the 1950s and attended college in the early 1960s had not directly experienced the collapse and political defeat of the Old Left. As former SDS president Todd Gitlin noted, because the New Left "rose from the ashes of the American left, the movement was inclined to feel that it had given birth to itself—and came to overvalue the power of sheer will, which had apparently created something from nothing."[56] They shared the belief that America was rotten to the core, and the removal of legal barriers was a cosmetic effort that did not address the deeper, more intractable problems of poverty, violence, war, and racism. The Vietnam War indicated the poverty of the American spirit, and the New Left did not wish to be accomplices in this violence against the "darker" peoples of Vietnam. They wanted to forge a massive social movement with the goal of radically restructuring American society. In early 1965 these disagreements were limited primarily to elites, but the escalation of the war would bring the dispute into sharper focus, presaging a looming crisis.

African Americans and the SDS March on Washington

The Johnson administration's decision for war dramatically increased the significance of SDS's march on Washington to oppose American foreign policy in Vietnam. On February 8, 1965, the day U.S. planes began to bomb North Vietnam, SDS placed a full-page ad in *Liberation* that publicized the April 17 march and indicted the war as "hideously immoral," charging that the United States was "committing pointless murder."[57] The early months of 1965 were heady times for the antiwar movement, and the military escalation engendered a series of small demonstrations throughout the country reminiscent of the spontaneous civil rights actions that took place in 1960 and 1961.[58] Many observers hoped the New Left could capitalize on the ties between the civil rights movement and the peace movement and forge a powerful coalition. On March 15 the *New York Times* published a front-page story on the student Left and its aim to create an "alliance between the millions of American whites and Negroes who have no economic or political power."[59] According to Fred Halstead, a longtime socialist and trade union activist, "Following these early demonstrations, the SDS march became the national focus for the entire protest movement."[60] SDS hoped that its April 17 march for peace would arouse the nation's conscience, just as the 1963 March on Washington had done for racial justice.[61] Ultimately, it hoped to tap this energy to build a mass movement. But for civil rights leaders, this posed a problem because the black struggle was not yet finished. Many queried whether there was enough space for both peace and freedom.

The possibility of communist involvement in the upcoming march plagued the organizers and worried civil rights activists. With the nation at war, many civil rights leaders were leery of being tarred with a Red brush. But SDS had decided at its National Council meeting in December that it would be the sole sponsor of the march, and it made the tactical decision that all organizations, including those with communist ties, were welcome to participate. In doing so, SDS conformed to its anti-anticommunism and maintained its fidelity to "participatory democracy" without adhering to Cold War niceties. Just as SNCC had been dogged by charges of communist subversion, the issue of communist involvement in SDS's proposed march immediately led to divisions within the peace movement. The newly mobilized activists fueled concerns by voicing incendiary rhetoric, such as: "If the Vietnamese want Ho Chi Minh, they should have him."[62] Like their youthful counterparts in SNCC and CORE, members of SDS represented the younger generation of the New Left that believed racial injustice, political powerlessness, economic inequality, and the threat of nuclear destruction demanded immediate attention. The scattered remnants of a few thousand old communists were hardly a concern to them.

When SNCC and SDS navigated the welter of civil rights and pacifist politics, they encountered pressures from older groups that had been scarred by McCarthyism. Accordingly, within a matter of weeks after calling for a march on Washington, the issue of the inclusion of organizations with ties to communism posed a challenge to the embryonic peace movement. It reflected the challenges faced by the civil rights movement in critiquing U.S. policy in Vietnam. It also illustrated the enduring efficacy of anticommunism well into the 1960s.

SDS's nonexclusion policy raised the ire of the leaders of more traditional peace movements, such as famed socialist Norman Thomas, venerable pacifist A. J. Muste, Bayard Rustin, and the organizers of the Committee for a Sane Nuclear Policy (SANE). They feared that the march would be taken over by communists, which would obscure the demonstration's message and thereby undermine the peace movement at its inception. Muste, Thomas, and Rustin were longtime anticommunists and considered SNCC's and SDS's nonexclusion policy naïve. They also criticized SDS's failure to present a clear alternative to the Johnson administration's Vietnam policy and worried that its call for an immediate unilateral withdrawal would give credence to right-wing critics' charges that SDS was less concerned with peace than with ensuring a communist victory.[63]

For their part, in the weeks leading up to the planned April 17 march, SDS and other left-wing student organizations accused their elders of practicing a form of McCarthyism. SNCC members and African Americans opposed to the war were privy to these ideological skirmishes. Taking their cue from their friends in SNCC, the leaders of SDS perceived these pressures as eerily reminiscent of the Mississippi Freedom Democratic Party's recent experience in Atlantic City and were determined to remain true to their principles. These disputes underscored the peace movement's struggle to gain traction when the country was still recuperating from McCarthyism, and it sent a message to the civil rights movement about the danger of protesting against the Vietnam War. After a series of behind-the-scenes deliberations, the older, more established peace groups released a statement stressing that they were "not soft on Communism," and the march proceeded according to schedule.[64] But even within the anticommunist wing of the peace movement there were disagreements. Muste and Thomas opposed Rustin's plan to torpedo the march "because he thought communists had taken it over in some places."[65] Eventually, the various peace groups temporarily put aside their differences, but the situation highlighted the difficulties of forging a unified antiwar movement that was erupting almost overnight.

This atmosphere posed challenges for SNCC. With the exception of Parris, Forman, and a few others, SNCC members had thus far muted their antipathy for the war. Still preoccupied with Selma and the voting rights campaign, and still grieving over Malcolm X's assassination, most SNCC members resisted taking a headlong antiwar stand. Additional concerns included SNCC's precarious finances and its internal disarray.[66] In the weeks leading up to the April 17 demonstration, the Red-baiting, which had intensified against SNCC after Atlantic City, reached a fevered pitch. As hard-core segregationists had known for years, Red-baiting was a potent tool that placed the civil rights movement on the defensive.[67] The major culprits this time were *Washington Post* columnists Rowland Evans and Robert Novak, who wrote a series of articles smearing SNCC with unsubstantiated allegations of communist infiltration. Days after the heralded civil rights march from Selma to Montgomery, Evans and Novak spuriously stated, "There is no doubt that SNCC is substantially infiltrated by beatnik left-wing revolutionaries, and—worst of all—by Communists." They went on to say: "SNCC and its leaders aren't really interested in the right to vote or any other attainable goal, but in demanding the unattainable as a means of provoking social turmoil. As revolutionaries, they aren't about to stop demonstrating and pitch into the hard task of actually registering voters."[68]

Evans and Novak were not finished. A few weeks later, they channeled Joe McCarthy in alleging that the National Lawyers Guild's role in the MFDP's legal affairs, combined with SNCC's long-standing ties to "leftist" Ella Baker, proved that "it would be a miracle if Communists had not attached themselves to SNCC."[69] *Newsweek* joined the chorus, running a story highlighting the "expressions of anxiety" by SNCC's liberal allies in the civil rights movement over potential communist involvement. While the article stressed the tenuous nature of such a connection, it gave the whispers greater salience, and the overall tenor of the piece reified the impression that a communist takeover of SNCC was a legitimate concern.[70] The *New York Post*'s James Weschler, an apostle of liberal anticommunism, was convinced that militants were "staging an uprising against the major civil rights blocs . . . encouraged by a fragment of Communists (Chinese rather than Russian in orientation)."[71] These provocative allegations prompted John Lewis to reply that Evans and Novak were engaged in "a systematic conspiracy . . . to discredit [the] work of SNCC in the civil rights movement."[72] Amid these cries of subversion, Andrew Kopkind's thoughtful piece in the *New Republic*, noting that SNCC's penchant for inflammatory rhetoric belied its programmatic approach of empowering the masses, was buried beneath the avalanche of smears.[73] This cavalcade of attacks in the mainstream press cast a pall on SNCC and other opponents of the war as April 17 approached, and it elevated the stakes of participating in antiwar activity.

In the early-morning hours of April 17, 1965, the first picketers appeared outside the White House. By noon, thousands of protesters packed the Sylvan Theatre on the grounds of the Washington Monument and listened to the melodies of Joan Baez, Judy Collins, and a SNCC trio, the Freedom Voices, sing "We Shall Overcome." Speeches by SDS president Paul Potter, Senator Ernest Gruening of Alaska, and Freedom Summer veterans Staughton Lynd and Robert Parris followed. Afterward, the demonstrators paraded in the balmy spring sunshine down the Mall to the Capitol, singing freedom songs and bearing a petition demanding that "Congress immediately end the war." The demonstration was by far the largest antiwar rally in the United States since the beginning of the Cold War—triple the size of the last major peace march in January 1962—and by most accounts, it was a success.[74] While opinions varied, Fred Halstead estimated that as many as 20,000 people marched, and the *New York Times* reported that 15,000 showed up. In any case, the number of demonstrators exceeded SDS's expectation of 10,000.[75] Writing in 1966, journalist Jack Newfield characterized the march as the day the Silent Generation found its voice.[76]

Paul Potter's keynote speech won the most applause and generated the most headlines. As mentioned earlier, Potter had attracted national attention when he and Tom Hayden were attacked by a crowd of segregationists at a SNCC voter registration event in McComb, Mississippi, back in October 1961. Potter had been particularly frustrated that the media had refused to cover the event until two young whites (he and Hayden) were assaulted.[77] Now twenty-five and the head of SDS, Potter exhorted the audience to use the "razor" of the war to fashion a new social movement to purify America. Like Martin Luther King's later critiques, he condemned the Vietnam War as "a symptom of a deeper malaise within America."[78] He even stated that SDS would support the growing number of young men who were refusing to fight in Vietnam. Without explicitly mentioning capitalism (because SDS leaders feared it would provoke further Red-baiting), he enumerated a litany of capitalism's sins, including its "disenfranchisement of peoples in the South." Potter repeatedly asked the audience to "name the system," and he blamed the American system, not the Pentagon, for the war. Potter suggested that the war stemmed from problems within America's borders, which he had witnessed firsthand in the South. According to Todd Gitlin, Potter's "speech was to become an inspiration for the movement: a way to think about the war and the movement against it."[79] At the end of his speech, the biracial and intergenerational audience rose to its feet, overcome by emotion. Twenty-five-year-old Ralph Featherstone, an African American SNCC member from Howard University, summed up the mood of the demonstration: "The people here are the ones who move in this country."[80]

Potter's eloquence overshadowed another important aspect of the march: approximately 10 percent of the audience was African American. In his address at the base of the Washington Monument, Parris, whose legendary status extended beyond the civil rights movement, pointed out that the leaders conducting the war for the freedom of the South Vietnamese were the same ones who refused to guarantee the fundamental rights of African Americans in the South. The singing of freedom songs and the conduct of SNCC workshops provided further evidence that the spirit of the civil rights movement pervaded the rally. A group of African American high school students drove all the way up from Indianola, Mississippi, to participate in the march. Sixteen-year-old Otis Brown explained that they had come to Washington "because we have to look beyond just Negro freedom. We don't want to grow up 'free' at home in a country which supports this kind of war abroad."[81] According to William A. Price of the *National Guardian*, an unidentified SDS leader commented that the "breadth and urgency of the march could never have been achieved without the life instilled in the student movement by the Southern civil rights struggle." The most important new liaison was that between the young, vibrant "freedom workers of the South and the peace-oriented students of the North." As Price noted, there were high hopes of "a joining of forces."[82] Of course, these bonds had been forged in the crucible of the civil rights struggle in the South. Parris was not alone in perceiving the antiwar movement as an extension of the civil rights movement.[83]

For a fleeting moment in the spring and summer of 1965, a coalition between the fledgling antiwar movement and the radical wing of the civil rights movement, with the goal of changing the "system," seemed possible.[84] President Johnson's decision to invade the Dominican Republic on April 28, 1965, to thwart a possible communist takeover reconfirmed their view of the moral bankruptcy of American imperialism and fueled their mutual animus against the system. The generational frictions over communist exclusion notwithstanding, the commonality of interests among the dominant youth bridged many of the differences that would later split the movement. At this juncture, the antiwar movement had not yet turned into a mass movement—which would lead to a proliferation of sects and expose the chasm between radicals and liberals. Black Power was percolating, but its effects had not yet permeated the movement. Most African Americans who opposed the war were still in favor of working with Johnson on passing the Voting Rights Act and other legislation. The SDS-sponsored march on Washington highlighted the possibility of cooperation between the peace and freedom movements.

James Farmer's receptivity to the civil rights movement's engagement in peace activity reflected this auspicious climate for cooperation. Although Farmer, the influential national director of CORE, was not present at the march, he endorsed it. Situated on the left wing of the civil rights movement, CORE, like SNCC, had become increasingly disdainful of American society and cynical about liberals and liberalism. Farmer's recent disillusionment had been fueled by his opposition to the compromise at Atlantic City, as well as the civil rights movement's moratorium on demonstrations until after the 1964 elections.[85] Farmer's relationship with President Johnson, a fellow Texan, soured after CORE's opposition to the moratorium.[86] Appearing on CBS's *Face the Nation* days after the march, Farmer stopped short of taking a firm antiwar stance. A towering presence more than twenty years older than most SNCC and SDS members, Farmer had a long history of pacifism. A conscientious objector during World War II, Farmer had managed to survive the Red scare, but it nearly destroyed his beloved CORE.[87] He was more circumspect than his younger subordinates, but he could identify with their abiding interest in foreign policy: "Well, I think that as American citizens, persons who participate in the civil rights movement have not only a right, but a duty to be interested in all activities of our government—domestic policies outside of the civil rights area and foreign policy. One thing that has happened is that the civil rights movement has motivated youngsters, both white and black, has given them an interest in current events, has made them read the press, the newspapers and so forth. And this has created an interest in the whole scope of foreign affairs."[88]

The issue of Vietnam, of course, did not elude Martin Luther King Jr., the titular head of the civil rights movement. King's torturous decision on whether to break publicly with the Johnson administration over the war is the subject of chapters 5 and 6. For now, suffice it to say that as early as the winter of 1965, King had issued a number of statements expressing his disapproval of the war. He had recently become the youngest recipient of the Nobel Peace Prize, so his antiwar sentiments were not surprising, given his visceral hatred of violence. On March 2 King publicly voiced his feelings about the war for the first time, telling an audience at Howard University that the "war in Vietnam is accomplishing nothing."[89] These words, expressed during the frenzied days of Selma, largely escaped public scrutiny. A few months later, however, King provoked the ire of the FBI when he spoke at Virginia State College and said, "The time has come for the civil rights movement to become involved in the problems of war. . . . There is no reason why there cannot be peace rallies like we have freedom rallies. . . . We are not going to defeat Communism with bombs and guns and gases. We will do it by making democracy work. The war in Vietnam must be stopped. There must be a negotiated settlement with the Vietcong. . . . The long night of war must be stopped."[90]

This statement encapsulated King's belief in the futility of the war. But the ferocity of the attacks leveled against him by the mainstream liberal establishment astonished him. FBI director J. Edgar Hoover was convinced that King was a communist, and the Red-baiting was relentless. The attacks reached a crescendo in September after King called for the United States to halt the bombing of North Vietnam and negotiate with the Vietcong. President Johnson unleashed his attack dogs, including the powerful Senator Thomas Dodd of Connecticut, who eviscerated King for his "arrogance" and questioned his competence to speak out on complex matters of foreign policy.[91] The weight of these criticisms overwhelmed King and forced him to confront the bitter reality that he did not have the strength to fight for both civil rights and peace. For the next eighteen months, King muted his disapproval of the war and demonstrated his reluctant pragmatism when he admitted, "There is a possibility that the more we stand up on the peace questions, the more we're going to lose people who are not prepared to go that far with us."[92] The vicious nature of the personal attacks against such a revered figure as Dr. King foretold the challenges ahead in crafting a civil rights and antiwar coalition.

Summer 1965: The War Escalates, Watts Burns, and Fissures Surface

On July 28, 1965, Lyndon Johnson announced his intention to increase the number of American troops in Vietnam by 50,000, with the goal of having

125,000 soldiers there by the end of 1965. Speaking at a noontime press conference, the president said, "We cannot be defeated by force of arms. We will stand in Vietnam." He had never officially declared war, but the president stated, this "is really war."[93] For the rest of his presidency, Johnson would be consumed by Vietnam. Accordingly, his ability to implement additional civil rights legislation would be compromised.

Like the rest of America, African Americans had to accept the reality of a long-term U.S. military commitment in Southeast Asia. By the summer of 1965, Vietnam was beginning to curtail the primacy of civil rights on the domestic agenda. At the same time, Jim Crow was crumbling, which gave the illusory impression that the long campaign for racial justice was over. Meanwhile, the preeminence of the war was beginning to command the energy of the New Left. Prominent whites such as Staughton Lynd, who had been a foot soldier in the civil rights movement and the director of SNCC's Freedom Schools in Mississippi in 1964, were now migrating to the antiwar movement. Lynd, whose refusal to pay taxes made him a legend in civil rights circles, now emerged as a pivotal figure in the antiwar movement.[94] On December 21, 1965, Lynd and Tom Hayden flew to Vietnam in a quixotic attempt to negotiate between the U.S. government and Hanoi. At the same time, the government was beginning to siphon billions of dollars from the Great Society to pay for the war.[95]

The question of whether the civil rights movement should join the burgeoning antiwar fray was emerging as a fractious issue. In the summer of 1965, the Vietnam quandary shook CORE, which was in the midst of an ideological transformation similar to the one occurring in SNCC. Given CORE's pacifist strain—dating from its spin-off in the early 1940s from the Fellowship of Reconciliation, the oldest interfaith peace and justice organization in the United States—its unease with the war was not unexpected.[96] Days after King's July antiwar diatribe at Petersburg, Virginia, the Vietnam issue arose at CORE's annual convention in Durham, North Carolina. In his keynote address, James Farmer declared that it was impossible for the U.S. government "to mount a decisive war against poverty and bigotry while it is pouring billions down the war against people in Vietnam."[97] His personal antipathy to the war notwithstanding, at this point, Farmer was opposed to CORE's formal involvement in the antiwar movement. His fighting words, however, sent an erroneous message to the delegates. On the last day of the convention, CORE's peace bloc pushed through a resolution condemning "the United States intervention in the Dominican Republic and Vietnam" and called for the immediate withdrawal of American troops from these nonwhite countries. Farmer was absent when the resolution was approved, and he did not even know it was pending. After his staff informed him of its passage, Farmer stormed to the floor and requested that the convention reconsider the matter, precipitating a heated debate. At the end of the day, CORE agreed to overturn the resolution by a five-to-one margin. Years later, Farmer recalled, "I did not let CORE adopt a resolution calling for unilateral U.S. withdrawal from Vietnam, [but] it in no way softened my anger at my personal opposition to Vietnam policy." Not surprisingly, Farmer also cited the omnipresent specter of communism and noted that "CORE had always had a problem of attempts at Communist infiltrations." He reasoned, "For us to pass that resolution at this time would tend to open that door."[98] The shift within CORE was also dramatized by the first appearance of a Black Muslim speaker at the convention, who conveyed this simple message: "All whites are evil."[99] The growing frustrations over the war were affecting CORE's unity, forecasting troubles down the road. In part because of his caution on the war, Farmer's long tenure as the head of CORE was drawing to a close.[100]

As the leaders of major civil rights organizations, Farmer, King, and SNCC's John Lewis all attended Lyndon Johnson's historic signing of the Voting Rights Act on August 6, 1965. The jubilance surrounding the passage of this landmark legislation belied an undertow of anxiety over the war and the future of the civil rights movement—an anxiety that their moderate allies Roy Wilkins of the NAACP and Whitney Young of the Urban League did not yet fathom. Many liberals and middle-class whites touted the passage of the Civil Rights Act of 1964 and the Voting Rights Act of 1965 as the culmination of the civil rights movement, creating the erroneous impression that the civil rights issue had been resolved. They believed that it was now the responsibility of African Americans alone to improve their plight. The euphoria over the eradication of de jure segregation in the South would be short-lived and would give way to confusion over how to tackle the more tenacious issues of poverty, despair, and illiteracy in the northern ghettos. Ella Baker's warning to young SNCC students, during the heady days of the first sit-ins, that the struggle involved "more than a hamburger" seemed more prophetic than ever. Back in 1960, however, Baker could not have envisioned that the transition to combating de facto discrimination would be transpiring against the confusing backdrop of an escalating war.

More than any individual, Baker's protégé Robert Parris was the symbolic force in the early years of the voting rights campaign in the Deep South. But as mentioned earlier, Parris was not alongside his fellow African American dignitaries applauding the realization of his death-defying efforts in Mississippi. Instead, Parris, David Dellinger, and Staughton Lynd were a few blocks away attending an interracial demonstration against the war organized by the Assembly of Unrepresented People (AUP), a group formed to link the civil rights and antiwar movements. A busload of African Americans from Mississippi, two delegations from New Orleans, and small groups from other southern communities came to Washington as part of the AUP.[101] According to Jack Newfield of the *Village Voice*, the demonstration was marred by tension between "mindless militancy and reflective radicalism" and even "between black and white," when African Americans spontaneously organized "an all-black workshop that was closed to white participation."[102]

The tensions at the AUP demonstration contrasted with the spirit of harmony displayed during the April 17 march on Washington. The changed ambience was in part rooted in SDS's preoccupation with internal problems. It was experiencing "growing pains" and rebelling against a strong centralized authority. At its annual convention at Kewadin, Michigan, in June, confusion within SDS's ranks was evident. A new generation, or what Todd Gitlin derisively termed "prairie-power," had assumed control of the organization. According to historians Nancy Zaroulis and Gerald Sullivan, the Kewadin conference "foundered in endless debates unable to agree on a position on any issues."[103] Fearing that the war would turn it into a single-issue organization, SDS decided not to assume leadership of the antiwar movement—even refusing to organize or support a national campaign for draft resistance. As a result, SDS radicalism became more of a hodgepodge of individual acts rather than an organized, collective structure for social revolution. SDS, like SNCC, was becoming more anarchic, which would hinder efforts to create a biracial coalition of peace and justice. Paul Booth, a longtime SDS member, explained the implications: "We really screwed up. We had the opportunity . . . to make SDS the organizational vehicle of the anti-war movement. It was ours. We had achieved it. Instead, we chose to go off in all kinds of different directions. . . . The main thrust of anti-war activity was left unorganized by us."[104]

The cooperative spirit between SDS and SNCC—so painstakingly nourished since the early 1960s—was now jeopardized by the unrest swirling within both organizations. The war's diversionary impact on these groups was compounded by the violence that detonated in Watts, an

African American ghetto in Los Angeles, California.[105] Prior to the mid-1960s, the issue of black rage in the urban centers of the North and the West had been an undercurrent, but it was subsumed by coverage of and interest in combating Jim Crow in the South. In 1963 the *New Yorker* serialized James Baldwin's inflammatory essay on race relations, "The Fire Next Time," which predicted that chaos and destruction would ensue at the hands of the oppressed unless the nation confronted the grisly problem of black poverty.[106] Baldwin appeared on the cover of *Time* magazine and became America's most esteemed black writer.[107] He agreed with much of Malcolm X's apocalyptic vision of white society, and his grim prognostications came true in Harlem during the summer of 1964. Riots ensued after an off-duty New York City police officer shot and killed an African American teenager—a harbinger of the future unrest that would engulf America for the rest of the decade.[108] Harlem was the most prominent uprising, but Philadelphia, St. Louis, and Rochester also erupted in flames.[109] Although President Johnson and most white Americans were shocked at the devastation that rocked Watts the following year, the seeds of the urban crisis had been planted in previous decades, when redlining real estate practices in the North had confined blacks to ghettos, and public policy and other market practices had relegated them to second-class citizenship.[110] Watts was a wake-up call for the liberal establishment, which finally came to the realization that race was not merely a southern issue; it was a national issue.

On the surface, the tree-lined, unlittered streets of Watts, with its comely single-family cottages, was an unlikely place for the ferocious explosion of riots and looting that occurred in August 1965 after police arrested a young black man for drunk driving. The previous year, the National Urban League had conducted a national survey that ranked Los Angeles as the best place for African Americans among sixty-eight American cities.[111] Despite Watts's halcyon façade, it burned for six days, leaving a trail of personal and physical destruction. In the end, the riots took thirty-four lives, left more than a thousand injured, and cost approximately $35 million in property damage. Most of the dead and injured, and almost all of the approximately 4,000 people arrested, were African American. It was the largest riot to date in U.S. history, far exceeding the disturbance in Harlem the previous summer. Over the next few years, urban riots would erupt with almost quotidian regularity, and the disturbing images broadcast into middle-class homes would fray white Americans' patience with the War on Poverty and efforts to rectify racial inequality.

The conflagration in Watts not only consumed the residences and businesses of the African American ghetto but also seared the consciousness of the liberal establishment. Igniting less than a week after Johnson signed the Voting Rights Act, the riots shocked the president. Joseph Califano, LBJ's principal coordinator for domestic affairs, recalled that in the aftermath of the Watts riots, Johnson felt compelled to mute his public commitment to African Americans and assigned garrulous Vice President Hubert Humphrey to be the administration's point man on civil rights. From now on, Johnson felt comfortable dealing with only the most conservative elements of the civil rights establishment.[112] On a personal level, the thinskinned president regarded the riots as a rebuke that indicated African Americans' lack of gratitude. Despite his anger and confusion, Johnson had no intention of abandoning inner-city African Americans. Nevertheless, he brooded over the political ramifications of a white backlash and predicted that one of the riot's beneficiaries would be Ronald Reagan, who would almost certainly run for governor of California in 1966.[113]

Meanwhile, at the annual SCLC convention in Birmingham, Alabama, Martin Luther King Jr. bemoaned that the war in Vietnam had "stirred my conscience and pained my heart" more than almost any event "in my lifetime."[114] Only hours later, bulletins on the fatalities in Watts spread from Los Angeles across the nation. Devastated by the news, King flew with Bayard Rustin to Watts on August 17, where he personally witnessed the devastation. Touring the charred remains of the neighborhood, Rustin and King accosted residents on street corners. Rustin recalled one memorable exchange he had with an unemployed, twenty-year-old African American who told Rustin, "We won." Rustin posed the question: "How have you won? Homes have been destroyed, Negroes are lying dead in the streets, the stores from which you buy food and clothes are destroyed, and people were bringing you relief." His reply was significant: "We won because we made the whole world pay attention to us. The police chief never came here before; the mayor always stayed uptown. We made them come."[115] Not surprisingly, Watts appalled King, and the wanton destruction threatened to undermine his message of love and nonviolence. In Rustin's view, King "was absolutely undone" by Watts. But Rustin attributed King's understanding of "the centrality of economics to the movement for racial equality" to his wrenching and visceral reaction to Watts. King was starting to see the correlation between the violence raging in the ghettos over poverty, unemployment, and despair and the violence the U.S. military was perpetrating on innocent civilians in North Vietnam. Although the Watts riots were not a direct response to the war, for King, they illuminated the violence ingrained in the fabric of the American system.[116]

SNCC was less surprised by the devastation in Watts. It substantiated SNCC's belief that the focus of the struggle for racial justice was shifting away from the familiar terrain of the rural Deep South to the poverty, hopelessness, and racism endemic in the urban ghettos of the North and West. The denizens of Watts perceived the police as an occupying force, a "white gang," which helped set the stage for the rise of the Black Panther Party in the coming years.[117] One young African American man standing on a street corner in the heart of Watts told an interviewer, "I've got my 'stuff' [gun] ready, I'm not going to die in Vietnam, whitey has been kicking ass too long,"[118]

The confluence of events in the summer of 1965—including Vietnam, Watts, and debates about Black Power—presented a daunting array of challenges to SNCC, which was still searching for new strategies to adapt to the changing landscape. One of SNCC's pilot programs was Stokely Carmichael's effort to establish a completely autonomous African American political party in Lowndes County, Alabama, with the goal of empowering African Americans and proving, according to Cleveland Sellers, "that blacks could handle political affairs without the assistance of whites."[119] The Lowndes County Freedom Organization adopted a snarling black panther as its official symbol, which would inspire the Black Panther Party that emerged in California a few years later. Since Freedom Summer, SNCC had been flirting with the idea of becoming an exclusively black organization, and it had already ordered some of its white workers to organize on behalf of poor whites. This turn to racial separatism was another impediment to an alliance with SDS and the white New Left. Furthermore, SNCC's evolving views on Black Power were colliding with King's, Rustin's, and the NAACP's long-standing belief in integration. SNCC was becoming internally fragmented and isolated from both its white and black allies.

In the summer and fall of 1965, the question of whether SNCC should take a formal stand against the Vietnam War was becoming more salient. In a televised press conference on July 28, President Johnson announced an increase in the number of draft calls. The war was starting to come home. Due to their limited educational opportunities, African Americans were ineligible for the exemptions granted to millions of white college students. Many young African American men actually viewed military service as a path to upward mobility and an escape from their stultifying rural hamlets or dangerous urban ghettos. Accordingly, African Americans were enlisting, fighting, and dying in disproportionate numbers—a trend that would continue for the next few years.[120] The SNCC community was not immune from the human cost of the war. In July 1965 young Mississippian John Shaw, who had participated in the demonstrations in McComb back in 1961, was killed in Vietnam. The news of his death sparked a protest among the African American community in Mississippi.[121] Shaw was the first person in the larger SNCC community to die in Vietnam, but he would not be the last. Approximately 85 percent of SNCC's members were eligible for the draft. John Lewis poignantly remembered: "There were SNCC volunteers who were drafted and eventually died in Vietnam. Some were from Selma, young black men who had stood on those courthouse steps with me in '64 and '65. I can't remember their names, but I can remember their faces. They went to Vietnam and did not return."[122]

On the heels of Shaw's untimely death, Joe Martin of McComb and Clint Hopson, a law student from Neptune, New Jersey, circulated a leaflet throughout McComb's African American community that was reprinted in the MFDP's newsletter on July 28, 1965—the same day that Johnson called for additional troops. Martin and Hopson had been classmates of Shaw, and his death outraged them. They listed five compelling reasons why African Americans "should not be fighting in Vietnam" and advocated the controversial course of draft resistance:

No Mississippi Negroes should be fighting in Vietnam for the White Man's freedom, until all Negro people are free in Mississippi.

Negro boys should not honor the draft here in Mississippi. Mothers should encourage their sons not to.

We will gain respect and dignity as a race only by forcing the United States government and the Mississippi government to come with guns, dogs, and trucks to take our sons away to fight and be killed protecting Mississippi, Alabama, Georgia, and Louisiana.

No one has a right to ask us to risk our lives and kill other Colored People in Santo Domingo and Vietnam, so that the White American can get richer. We will be looked upon as traitors by all the Colored People of the world if the Negro people continue to fight and die without a cause.

Last week a white soldier from New Jersey was discharged from the Army because he refused to fight in Vietnam; he went on a hunger strike. Negro boys can do the same thing. We can write and ask our sons if they know what they are fighting for. If he answers Freedom, tell him the truth—we don't know anything about Communism, Socialism, and all that, but we do know that Negroes have caught hell right here under this American Democracy.[123]

In its newsletter, the MFDP raised the ante by encouraging its members to take a public stance on the war, and it bemoaned the national press's failure to cover the many activities it had initiated. Forecasting the inevitable attacks on its patriotism, the MFDP pointed "to the great sacrifices made by our members toward bringing true freedom and democracy to Mississippi." It went on to say: "It is easy to understand why Negro citizens of McComb, themselves the victims of bombings, Klan-inspired terrorism, harassment, and arrests, should resent the death of a citizen of McComb while fighting in Vietnam for 'freedom not enjoyed by the Negro community of McComb.' However, the Mississippi Freedom Democratic Party does not have such a position."[124] Ruthie Reed of Issaquena County, Mississippi, agreed with the MFDP and added that Negroes "don't have any business over there because how in the world can [they] fight for someone else when they don't have it [freedom] themselves."[125] Vietnam had always been less remote to SNCC than to other civil rights organizations. Tragically, by mid-1965, Vietnam had reached SNCC's doorstep.[126]

The MFDP's newsletter, particularly its rather brazen call to defy the draft, precipitated a fusillade of attacks from friend and foe alike. Charles Evers, brother of the slain Medgar Evers and head of the Mississippi NAACP, said, "For Negro citizens to ignore the draft can only destroy that which they have fought so hard to achieve."[127] Draft evasion smacked of disloyalty, and segregationists smelled blood. The executive committee of Mississippi's American Legion called for a federal investigation of the MFDP, demanding that it be vigorously prosecuted if such treasonous statements had been made.[128] What gave the MFDP pause was the dispatch with which moderate African Americans distanced themselves from the party. Representative Charles C. Diggs Jr., an African American Democrat from Michigan and usually a reliable ally of SNCC, called the newsletter's statement "ridiculous and completely irresponsible." Charles Evers and Aaron Henry, Mississippi's two top NAACP officials, issued this powerful rejoinder: "We strongly urge all citizens Negroes and whites to support our country in this major crisis. It is the duty of every American to give unstinted support to the fight for freedom abroad and step up the pace in the fight for democracy at home."[129]

These criticisms dispirited MFDP officials, and the negative publicity threatened to undermine the party's challenge to the seating of five Mississippi congressmen elected in 1964 on the grounds that African Americans had been systematically excluded from voter rolls.[130] MFDP leaders immediately set out to do damage control. Only days after the newsletter's publication, Lawrence Guyot, the MFDP's executive secretary, did an about-face. He personally disavowed the call for defiance of the draft and stated that he would serve if called. "I have a draft card," he said. "I am not prepared to encourage open defiance of any Federal statute." But Guyot also found "it fantastic that the most patriotic people in this country would have their patriotism questioned."[131] Although he was the MFDP's leader, Guyot stressed that he was refuting the newsletter's statement in an individual capacity; his views did not represent official MFDP policy. While most MFDP leaders personally opposed the war, they agreed that it was not the right time to officially come out against it. They believed the press was aiding their enemies by distorting their views and preferred to make their feelings known on their own terms.[132] In retrospect, Guyot, Farmer, and other civil rights leaders who personally opposed the war had difficulty envisioning its eventual scope, duration, and cost.

Still, the question of Vietnam simmered among civil rights activists throughout the summer of 1965. Now that the war was displacing civil rights as the most burning issue of the day, members of the civil rights community were increasingly torn over whether to plunge into the antiwar movement. As late as the fall of 1965, even SNCC's John Lewis, who was working on the upcoming White House Conference on Civil Rights, urged SNCC to avoid a complete rupture with the Johnson administration, lest the organization divert its precious resources by merging domestic and international issues.[133] A devoutly religious man endowed with indomitable physical courage, Lewis (a future congressman) struck many of his SNCC contemporaries as too politically cautious and overly concerned with ingratiating himself with the liberal establishment. Like CORE's Farmer, Lewis was facing an insurrection within his own ranks led by a group of younger firebrands. The tide was beginning to turn.

Howard Zinn, a radical historian who taught at Spelman College, also served as an informal SNCC adviser. The forty-two-year-old Zinn had just published *SNCC: The New Abolitionists*—his warmly received and flattering inside account of SNCC's brief history. Zinn was among

the many SNCC members who were becoming impatient with the organization's temporizing on Vietnam.[134] In the August 30 issue of SNCC's
monthly publication the *Student Voice*, Zinn penned an editorial calling for
civil rights workers to take a stand on Vietnam. In language reminiscent of
Robert Parris's recent speech at the AUP in Washington, Zinn argued that
SNCC's organizing tradition in the Deep South, where it endured "beatings,
bombings, and murders," provided a unique context for comprehending the
disturbing events in Vietnam, where a similar "uprising against an oppres-
sive system" was occurring. Zinn posited an evocative analogy between
the plight of African Americans in the South and the crisis in Vietnam. In
both cases, he argued, two explosive words "arouse hatred and distort reality: the use of 'nigger' in the South, and 'communist' in American foreign
policy."[135] Zinn took on the Red-baiters for using the epithet "communist"
as a blanket smear to obscure the "complexity of the world and the indi-
viduality of human beings." Addressing the misgivings of Whitney Young
Jr., John Lewis, and Martin Luther King Jr., Zinn declared that there was no
reason why civil rights groups could not continue to focus on fighting racial
inequality while simultaneously turning their attention not only to the violence in Vietnam but also to the injustice and oppression in the Dominican
Republic and the apartheid regime of South Africa. Zinn, along with fellow
radical white historian Staughton Lynd, retained a revered status among
the younger SNCC workers, even when African Americans were beginning
to embrace Black Power. Although Zinn's opinion was not the final word
on the matter, it carried weight within SNCC and reflected the prevailing
opinion within SNCC's rank and file.[136] Julian Bond remembered that by
the summer of 1965, SNCC members were overwhelmingly in favor of the
organization coming out against the war, and they were growing weary of
"dissociating themselves from the organization" when stating their opposition to the war.[137]

As Martin Luther King and Lawrence Guyot were learning, there were
practical costs to taking a stand on the war that threatened their work as
civil rights leaders. Aside from John Lewis, there were other SNCC members who resisted taking a precipitate antiwar stand. Dona Richards argued
that doing so would create more Red-baiting and erode their already weakened fund-raising efforts. Richards, whose marriage to Robert Parris was
reeling as a result of their disagreements over antiwar activism, argued:
"While we care a great deal about both Vietnam and civil rights, we can't
do anything to help the Vietnam situation, and we can hurt ourselves by
trying."[138]

Other longtime SNCC workers shared Richards's reservations about being too vociferous on the issue of the war. One of them was Mitchell Zimmerman, a native of the Bronx and one of the few whites left in the organization. Zimmerman, who was working for SNCC's Arkansas Project, felt so strongly that he wrote a long letter to the *Student Voice* responding to Zinn.[139] At the outset, Zimmerman acknowledged that there was a general "level of agreement within SNCC on Vietnam," and he ruefully conceded that "the war in Vietnam is going to go on for a long time." He argued that Zinn's position, though noble, needed to be tempered by a pragmatic consideration of SNCC's long-term interests. Taking such a rash antiwar stand, Zimmerman argued, would weaken SNCC because the public's generally low regard for the antiwar movement would "doom it to ineffectiveness." Fund-raising, which was already anemic, would be reduced to a mere trickle. Just as important, he cited the ubiquitous fear that an antiwar stand would "hand our enemies the means of effectively red-baiting us. And we can be hurt by such red-baiting."[140] Indeed, a Gallup poll released on November 19, 1965, substantiated Zimmerman's concern, revealing that an overwhelming number of Americans believed that communists had infiltrated both the civil rights and the antiwar movements.[141] Zimmerman was one of many young activists who were dedicating their lives to the cause, and his concerns were heartfelt. Years later, Zimmerman acknowledged that he had been wrong.[142] But lacking the benefit of historical hindsight, Zimmerman's concerns reflected the civil rights movement's vexing predicament in the early months of the war.[143]

These persistent debates over Vietnam were occurring in the context of an expanding war and a burgeoning, albeit rudderless, antiwar movement. With public opinion polls indicating that most Americans approved of the war, the Johnson administration intensified its military commitment. A Harris poll conducted in September indicated that two-thirds of the American public now supported the administration's position in Vietnam.[144] By the fall of 1965, more than 180,000 American troops were fighting in Vietnam, a ninefold increase since the beginning of the year. This extraordinary upsurge inevitably meant that more young men would be drafted, which was beginning to radicalize college campuses and was prompting a flurry of antiwar protests, most of them spontaneous in nature. The widespread public support for the war and its objective of containing communism, coupled with the mainstream media's often patronizing characterization of antiwar activists as "unshaven and unscrubbed Vietniks," was irksome to the antiwar forces and gave civil rights activists reason to keep their distance.[145] At first, the grassroots antiwar demonstrations were confined to college campuses and the more cosmopolitan and progressive enclaves of the San Francisco Bay Area and New York City, but they generated publicity and galvanized the disparate strands of the antiwar movement. In the following months, the movement would grow exponentially.[146]

Fall 1965: Groping for a Strategy

By the fall of 1965, the war, the urban riots, and the resonance of Black Power were fracturing the civil rights movement along ideological and generational lines. The end of segregation in the South was the capstone of decades of struggle, but it provided little solace to the millions of blacks mired in the urban ghettos and dealing with the lingering issues of poverty and discrimination in education, employment, and housing. With these challenges abounding, the civil rights movement was fitfully groping for a strategy to address the more intractable issues of institutionalized racism in the North. The bitter experience of SNCC, CORE, and the Young Turks in the more radical wing of the movement had made them contemptuous of politics, and they were becoming receptive to Black Power and, like their SDS brethren, increasingly anarchic. SDS's renunciation of a leadership role in the peace movement had resulted in an unwieldy coalition of religious pacifists, disenchanted liberals, young New Leftists, and a smattering of hard-line members of the Trotskyite Young Socialist Alliance.[147] By contrast, the passage of the Civil Rights Act and the Voting Rights Act had validated the NAACP, the Urban League, and the moderates' fidelity to Cold War liberalism and the Democratic Party. Meanwhile, Martin Luther King Jr., stung by Watts, was contemplating a move to Chicago to tackle northern racism. The civil rights movement was at a crossroads, and the insertion of the war into the calculus only heightened the confusion and accentuated the cracks. Most important, the burgeoning antiwar movement was siphoning the passion and energy from the civil rights movement.

The spike in antiwar activity during the fall of 1965 accentuated the drama. On the weekend of October 15–16, 1965, the National Coordinating Committee to End the War in Vietnam (NCCEWVN), comprising thirty-three separate groups, organized the International Days of Protest. The largest demonstrations occurred in Berkeley and New York City, but approximately 100,000 people demonstrated in more than eighty cities and several European capitals—by far the largest antiwar protest thus far. In Berkeley, where antiwar protesters tried to blockade trains carrying U.S. soldiers bound for Vietnam, the *New Republic* estimated that 10,000 marched from the campus of the University of California to a vacant lot adjacent to the Oakland army base.[148] Three thousand miles away in New York City, Norma Becker, a veteran of the civil rights movement, organized a march down Fifth Avenue that drew an estimated 10,000 participants, along with some jeering hecklers and occasional egg throwing.[149] Perhaps the weekend's most notable occurrence took place on a small side street in Lower Manhattan when David J. Miller, a Catholic pacifist, became the first person to burn his draft card since Congress had passed, by a vote of 329 to 1, a draconian law making draft-card burning a felony punishable by a maximum sentence of five years and a $10,000 fine.[150] Passions became even more inflamed in late October when Attorney General Nicolas Katzenbach announced his intention to investigate the antidraft movement.[151] Perceiving conscription as a powerful symbol of the war, a number of New York pacifists scheduled the first draft-card burning ceremony at Manhattan's Foley Square for October 28. A few days later, on November 2, Norman Morrison, a thirty-two-year-old father of three, stood before the entrance of the Pentagon and, in an act reminiscent of the monks in Saigon, burned himself to death. A week later Roger LaPorte, another pacifist, burned himself to death at the United Nations.[152] Amid this surge of antiwar activity, the protesters were swimming against the tide of public opinion. "The problem of peace now lies not in Washington but in Hanoi," claimed James Reston, the reigning dean of the national press core; he criticized the demonstrations as "lawless" and accused them of "not promoting peace," only "postponing it."[153] Unlike African Americans' substantial participation in the SDS march on Washington the previous April, their involvement in the October International Days of Protest was negligible.[154]

The draft-card burnings, the disruption of trains, and the suicides of Morrison and LaPorte stunned the American public and were signs of the tumult that would rock the country in the coming years. For the civil rights leadership, divided over whether to veer into antiwar activity, these symbolically charged tactics gave them pause. After all, most Americans opposed the antiwar movement, and the mainstream press derisively caricatured the peace movement as comprising "hippies," "Vietniks," and "pinkos."[155] With the exception of the younger, more radical wing of the movement, most civil rights activists looked askance at the tactics and culture of the antiwar movement and took pains to prove their patriotism.[156]

In particular, the mainstream African American press touted the virtues of the patriotic African American soldiers who were proving themselves worthy of their newly acquired civil rights by fighting against the communist menace in Southeast Asia.[157] SNCC's and SDS's policy of not excluding communists, which had caused rifts between the Old Left and the New Left since the early 1960s, worried most civil rights leaders. Bayard Rustin agreed with socialist Michael Harrington's insistence that the peace movement disassociate itself from "any hint of being an apologist for the Viet Cong."[158]

SANE, the bastion of antiwar liberalism, scheduled another march on Washington for Thanksgiving weekend. Taking Rustin's advice, SANE attempted to maintain a veneer of respectability and moderation and thereby distanced itself from charges of communist and hippie infiltration. In a letter to SNCC, for example, SANE refused to call for an immediate U.S. withdrawal from Vietnam.[159] Sanford Gottlieb, the organizer of the march, even cabled Ho Chi Minh and demanded that he cease hostilities.[160] In keeping with this public relations tack, SANE tried to keep the radicals at bay by establishing a dress code, urging demonstrators to carry American flags, and omitting so-called radicals Staughton Lynd, Robert Parris, and David Dellinger from its list of sponsors.[161] SANE's Thanksgiving rally was the major antiwar event in the fall of 1965, and it attempted to replicate the enthusiasm surrounding SDS's rally the previous April.[162]

SANE's tone was intended to appeal to liberals. CORE's James Farmer and Bayard Rustin were sponsors of the march, and SANE invited Coretta Scott King to be one of the speakers. All of them personally opposed the war but were reluctant to criticize the president, who had just shepherded the civil rights legislation through Congress. Rustin's commitment to the antiwar movement was lukewarm, and his fidelity to coalition politics made him wary of alienating the Johnson administration.[163] Farmer's evolving stance on the war demonstrated the shifting currents of opinion. Just a few months earlier, he had led the charge to overturn the antiwar resolution at CORE's summer convention. Farmer was the epitome of maturity—the image SANE wanted to convey to an American public disdainful of the Vietnik-laden antiwar movement. A few weeks prior to the march, Farmer articulated a view of the war that was closely aligned with that of SANE and the more moderate wing of the peace movement. In an editorial in the *New York Amsterdam News*, Farmer expressed his dismay at the ferocity of the criticism directed at the antiwar demonstrations, but he would not "sanctify the Vietcong, the North Vietnamese, or the

Chinese Communists." Farmer added that he did not "support immediate withdrawal" and thought "that many of the demonstrators don't acknowledge Johnson's efforts to try for a settlement."[164]

Only a few weeks later, however, Farmer's tone had changed markedly. In a follow-up editorial, he expressed weariness over the carnage in Southeast Asia. Conceding that he had "no answers" to the war, Farmer was now less concerned with the movement's controversial endorsement of the Vietcong and increasingly frustrated with the Johnson administration's lack of negotiation. He fretted, "We are slipping into a nightmare of a patriotic war which can only be commemorated at the grave."[165] Within a matter of weeks, Farmer's shift from irritation at the antics of the more vocal elements of the antiwar movement to outright frustration over the government's handling of the war reflected a growing impatience that was shared by many in the civil rights movement. Meanwhile, Farmer was also feeling pressure from a younger and more militant generation of CORE activists who found him increasingly out of step with the times. He did not attend the SANE march, even though he was listed as a sponsor. Farmer's days at the helm of CORE were numbered.[166]

For the civil rights movement, the Thanksgiving march was a disappointment. Overall, a sense of ennui infused the event, where an estimated 30,000 people turned out under cloudless skies for the November 27 demonstration in Washington, D.C.[167] Even the presence of Coretta Scott King, who claimed to be attending "as a mother who is concerned about *all* of the children in the world," could not buoy the spirits of the few African Americans who dotted the throngs of well-dressed, largely middle-aged citizens carrying American flags.[168] A small group of young SNCC members tried to encourage the crowd to sing freedom songs at the northeast corner of the White House but soon gave up, saying, "There's too many white folks here."[169] The *New Republic*'s Andrew Kopkind remarked on the "uncommon pessimism" pervading the weekend—a view shared by most observers.[170] This negative attitude was traceable to two factors. First, in contrast to the idealism of the April march, by November, few of the marchers retained any illusions that they could influence the intensifying war.[171] Second, the NCCEWVN had scheduled its inaugural convention over the Thanksgiving weekend in Washington, D.C., heightening the friction between the liberal and radical contingent of the peace movement and exposing the racial tensions that alienated the civil rights community from the antiwar movement.

The NCCEWVN's convention drew thousands of antiwar leftists representing its thirty-three autonomous organizations spanning the ideological spectrum. The diversity of these organizations turned the workshops, seminars, and discussions into an exercise in futility as factional infighting on procedural and organizational matters eroded any semblance of civility. As a result, the convention did not devise a comprehensive plan of action to end the war.[172] The simmering tensions between radical leftists and African Americans noted at the AUP demonstration in August resurfaced. For instance, this motley assortment of white leftist organizations and their non-stop wrangling over ideology riled the small MFDP delegation, which had traveled hundreds of miles to Washington. MFDP members resented the political infighting and bristled at the heavy dose of political indoctrination administered by the Young Socialist Alliance (YSA) on the first night of the convention. They were feeling not only unwelcome but also *used*, and they threatened to leave. An unidentified woman from the MFDP wondered why she had even made the trip. "I didn't come to meet people, and listen to the YSA interpret ideology for the ones who don't know where they're at. You college people messed up again. I tell you that, brother." Although the MFDP delegation decided to stay, they resented the directives emanating from the top. At issue was a clash of cultures between the MFDP, with its emphasis on the emotional and experiential element of revolutionary action, and the scholasticism of the unwieldy collection of peace groups that could not even agree on a course of action. Their experiences in Mississippi had made the MFDP receptive to the idea that revolution can originate from the sufferings and experiences of the rank and file. Al Johnson, an African American MFDP delegate, said to Steve Weissman of the Vietnam Day Committee and a veteran of Freedom Summer: "I'm not sure what this convention has to offer to the movement in the South—we had it all in SNCC, and look where it led. No more local autonomy. Every worker has to file a weekly *report*. Man, that's what I'd call a co-*erc*ive structure."[173]

From their head office in Atlanta, leaders of SNCC viewed the farcical proceedings with an air of bemusement. In the fall of 1965, their frustration over the war was reaching a crescendo. Paul Lauter, one of the few white members left in SNCC, recalled that the slogan "No Vietnamese Ever Called Me Nigger" was mounted on the bathroom wall at SNCC's headquarters.[174] On Veterans Day, fifty people, mostly students from Tougaloo College, had staged the first integrated peace demonstration protesting U.S. involvement in Vietnam in Jackson, Mississippi.[175] This growing passion over the war thawed John Lewis's innate prudence, and he began to sprinkle his speeches with analogies between Selma and Saigon.

In November SNCC convened a staff meeting at the Gammon Theological Seminary in Atlanta, with the purpose of coming to an official reckoning on the war in Vietnam. Marion Barry was one of the few members who cautioned against making a public statement, on the grounds that SNCC would be singled out for increased repression. But Barry was in the minority. Cleveland Sellers recounted, "The majority of the organization's members were thoroughly convinced that we had no alternative [but] to condemn the war and the American government."[176] After long hours of deliberation, the staff resolved to make a public statement on the war. The one they drafted was nearly identical to the statement SNCC ultimately issued after Sammy Younge's murder a few weeks later. Their unabashed sympathy with draft evaders was mixed with a scathing indictment of American foreign policy gleaned from their travails in the South:

> We have been involved in black people's struggle for liberation and self-determination in this country for the past five years and our work in the South and the North has taught us that the United States government has never guaranteed the freedom of oppressed United States citizens, and is not prepared to end the rule of terror and suppression within its borders.
>
> We know the extent to which certain elections in this country are not free.
>
> We recall that numerous persons who have been murdered in the South because of their efforts in the struggle and their murderers have gone free.[177]

Lewis hoped to make SNCC's position public as soon as possible, but the organization's laissez-faire style rendered an expeditious disposition of any important matter problematic. He requested members' input by December 13, 1965, and they chimed in, voicing their dissatisfaction with the proposed statement. Like the NCCEWVN, SNCC was paralyzed by confusion.[178]

What made 1965 a watershed year for both the antiwar and the civil rights movements was the dizzying sequence of events that altered the terms of the debate. The liberal hour had arrived, but the euphoria over passage of the Voting Rights Act quickly dissipated under the weight of the looming war and the divergent stratagems for addressing de facto discrimination outside the South. In addition, the escalating war had converted the embryonic antiwar campaign into a large political movement. Many of the original cadre were steeped in the nonviolent traditions of the civil rights movement, but many of the newcomers were unmoored to this peaceful heritage. The intense passions the war engendered suffused the movement with a more militant edge, and the unrest that erupted in 1965 would roil the nation until the early 1970s and beyond.[179]

Consequently, the end of 1965 witnessed divergent pronouncements that indicated the depth of the racial and cultural breach in America. The vast majority of white Americans wanted a reprieve from the problems of African Americans. The moderate *U.S. News and World Report* ran a cover story on the recent advances in civil rights and the economic gains of African Americans, reporting that, for the first time, blacks were "entering the American middle class."[180] Therefore, the publication intimated, the objectives of the civil rights movement had been achieved, and no more sacrifices were necessary. Representing the mainstream African American opinion, the *Chicago Defender* observed, "Though all of our dreams did not come to fulfillment, 1965 leaves a legacy which gives a bright outlook to the New Year."[181] In contrast, in the view of SNCC and CORE, American life, culture, and political institutions were still tainted by racism and materialism, and they saw no silver linings in the clouds on the horizon. On December 30, two days after Staughton Lynd and Tom Hayden flew to South Vietnam, John Lewis, searching in vain for consensus on the proposed Vietnam War statement, circulated an internal memorandum stating that "the gains of 1965 can only be called the lessons of the losses of '65." Without mentioning the war, Lewis noted the failure to seat the MFDP slate in Congress and acknowledged the "futility of further legislation when we have laws that are not being enforced in Congress."[182]

These varying verdicts on 1965 could not obfuscate the fact that more than 180,000 American troops were now stationed in Vietnam. A merger between the peace and freedom movements, a long-standing dream of the Left, was still unresolved. And it was becoming clear that the war was exacerbating the divisions within the civil rights movement. The problem would only worsen in 1966.

4

The Vietnam War and Black Power

The Deepening Divide, 1966

What does we have again the Vietnams
Why are we fighting them?
Who are really the enemy?
Are Vietnam the enemy or we
Americans enemies to ourselves,
If we are the same as Vietnams
Why should we fight them?
>—Ida Mae Lawrence, African American plantation worker
>from Mississippi

The murder of Samuel Younge in Tuskegee, Alabama, is no different than the murder of peasants in Vietnam, for both Younge and the Vietnamese, sought, and are seeking, to secure the rights guaranteed them by law.
>—SNCC statement, January 6, 1966

After its crowning legislative accomplishments in 1964 and 1965, the civil rights movement floundered in 1966. With the Vietnam War now sucking the life from the Great Society and the civil rights agenda stalled in Congress, African Americans' impatience and anger mounted. This was best reflected in a spike in militancy among black activists, which had surfaced most prominently in Watts. By mid-1966, SNCC and CORE moved further toward Black Power, which alienated them from white liberals and riled the moderate wing of the civil rights movement. While the struggle for racial justice continued, the nonviolent interracial phase that had crested in early 1965 was over. The war not only polarized the nation; it also drew a fault line across the civil rights movement and black America. Less than six months after SNCC's John Lewis called the Voting Rights Act "the nation's finest hour," the civil rights movement became embroiled in a protracted crisis over the war.[1]

Just three days into the New Year, shots pierced the crisp winter air outside a Standard Oil station in Tuskegee, Alabama, killing a twenty-one-year-old African American college student named Sammy Younge Jr. Marvin Segrest, the sixty-nine-year-old owner of the gas station and a stalwart segregationist, killed Younge because he was attempting to use the station's whites-only restroom.[2] The murder enraged the local African American community. Younge was not only a veteran of the U.S. Navy but also a student activist in SNCC's Tuskegee chapter. In the preceding months, he had worked on SNCC's voter registration projects in Alabama and Mississippi.[3] Younge's murder immediately sparked a wave of protests, as more than 3,000 angry demonstrators, many of them young African Americans opposed to the war, marched through the town where Booker T. Washington had established the famed Tuskegee Institute as a model southern community in the early 1880s.[4] Only recently, Tuskegee and Macon County had earned the praise of racial progressives for having the first biracial local government in the Deep South since Reconstruction.[5] The cold-blooded murder of Younge shattered this veneer of racial tranquility and pushed the students at Tuskegee Institute in a more militant direction.[6] The following December, an all-white jury in Macon County took just one hour and ten minutes to acquit Segrest, prompting further demonstrations and vandalism in the Tuskegee town square.[7]

Sammy Younge's childhood in the staid, middle-class African American town of Tuskegee had been unremarkable. After graduating from Tuskegee Institute High School in 1962, Sammy chose not to go straight to college—the usual path taken by the sons and daughters of Tuskegee's middle class. Instead, he enlisted in the navy to see the world. He was one of thousands of young African Americans on the threshold of manhood who joined the armed forces, the most integrated institution in American society. For them, military service furnished vocational opportunities and slaked their thirst for adventure. But Sammy's stint in the navy was short-lived; he fell ill, and navy physicians diagnosed a congenital malfunctioning of the kidneys, necessitating the removal of one of them and leading to his medical discharge in July 1964. Shortly after his return to Alabama, he enrolled in Tuskegee College, where he found his passion in the civil rights movement. His participation in the famous march from Selma to Montgomery on March 10, 1965, represented a turning point in his life. Sammy cut ties with his past and with his bourgeois friends and dedicated the last months of his life to the movement, where he was emerging as a major player in the raging battle between SNCC and the conservative Tuskegee Institute administrators. His childhood friend Wendy Paris recalled, "The only thing that could keep him still was the movement."[8]

Sammy's murder rocked the civil rights movement, not only inciting riots in the ordinarily placid town of Tuskegee but also creating a national sensation.[9] According to Stokely Carmichael, the fact that Sammy was a veteran made his death even more galling.[10] Longtime SNCC activist Cleveland Sellers remembered, "More than anything else," the murder of Sammy Younge Jr. "turned SNCC inward, and we began to look at, the realities we were dealing with." Sellers explained:

And that's where the statement comes, the statement against the war in Vietnam. We just figured that our efforts to focus primarily on civil rights were no longer valid, and we needed to move to another level, and that area was the whole issue of human rights. We needed to broaden our scope. We didn't need to look at just America and Alabama. We needed to be looking at Cape Town and Sharpsville [South Africa]. We needed to be looking at other kinds of progressive movements and countries around. That our struggle was a much larger struggle than we had all anticipated in the beginning.[11]

In death, the twenty-one-year-old military veteran, student, and civil rights activist wielded an influence that would have been unfathomable to him in life.[12]

Along with the rest of SNCC, chairman John Lewis was stunned when he received the news of Younge's murder from the group's Atlanta headquarters. The next day, as Lewis, Carmichael, and James Forman (Younge's mentor and future biographer) stood looking at the American flag draped over his casket, Lewis recalled, "The irony hit me hard. Here was a man who had served his country, and what had it gotten him?"[13] Forman's belief that Sammy's murder "marked the end of tactical nonviolence" is not as far-fetched as it appears because it ended SNCC's vacillation over whether to speak out against the war.[14] An outraged and grieving SNCC membership mustered enough composure to conduct an arduous debate. Finally, on the afternoon of January 6, 1966, Lewis held a solemn news conference at SNCC's headquarters and read a statement that was virtually identical to the one drafted earlier, but with the following tribute to their fallen comrade: "The murder of Samuel Younge in Tuskegee, Alabama, is no different than the murder of peasants in Vietnam, for both Younge and the Vietnamese sought, and are seeking, to secure the rights guaranteed them by law. In each case, the United States government bears a great part of the responsibility for these deaths." The most explosive element of SNCC's antiwar statement was the avowal of "sympathy and support for the young men in this country" who resisted "the tide of United States aggression" by defying the draft. Proclaiming that civil rights work constituted a valid alternative to the draft, Lewis queried: "Where is the draft for the freedom fight in the United States?"[15]

SNCC's blistering attack on the war was the lead story the next day. The reaction to the statement was so intense that Alabama's selective service director announced that he was considering reviewing Lewis's draft status.[16] The moderate *Atlanta Journal*, which had long purported to be a friend of the movement, opened a full-scale assault on SNCC, observing that its statement "treads far beyond dissent and doubt about policy" and implying that SNCC's comments were treasonous.[17] Withering denunciations of the statement thundered from the African American establishment. It took the NAACP only forty-eight hours to issue a strong rejoinder disassociating itself from SNCC's attack on the war.[18] The African American *Atlanta World* harshly condemned Lewis's statements as "most deplorable, misleading and incorrect."[19] After the NAACP distanced itself from SNCC and pointed out that its statement did not represent the views of other groups in the movement, the *New York Amsterdam News* polled a representative group of African Americans to find out where they stood on the matter. Although most of the interviewees supported SNCC's endeavors in the South, Agnes Haywood, a middle-aged African American woman from the Bronx, typified the respondents' unease about opposition to the war. Acknowledging the difficulty of the issue, Haywood said that, as a mother, she was concerned about "my son and the boys who grew up with him. But a neighborhood boy just died in Vietnam and you won't find anybody in the neighborhood who will say anything against the government."[20] Her neighbor Lillie Niblick went further: "This is our country. This is the country we love. We want to keep it safe for ourselves and our children. Serving one's country when called to duty is no more than a good citizen can do. My son volunteered for the Marines and he's leaving tomorrow. He wants to keep this country safe for all of us. One day he'll get married and he wants our country safe for his children."[21]

News of the disturbance in Tuskegee set off a flurry of activity inside the Oval Office as the Johnson administration sought to defuse the crisis.[22] Clifford Alexander Jr., the top-ranking African American in the White House, fired off a series of memos to President Johnson requesting an increased federal presence in Tuskegee to keep order there.[23] In response, the president merely instructed his aides to call Sammy Younge's father on his behalf.[24] With respect to the SNCC statement, Alexander assured the president that White House officials had already taken steps to mobilize the African American community to "negate the impact of the story" and present a countervailing message of support for the administration's policy in Vietnam.[25] The question of how Martin Luther King Jr. (who was currently in Chicago, launching his campaign against economic exploitation) would react to SNCC's statement caused anxiety in the White House.[26] After all, King's stature in the African American community was unparalleled. And despite King's complex and often tortured relationship with SNCC, they shared a common history and a vision of a nonviolent society. The Johnson administration feared King's possible influence on African American public opinion. Evidence of the sharpening cleavages within the civil rights movement occurred a few days later when Roy Wilkins of the NAACP sent the president a warm telegram lauding Johnson's commitment to Vietnam as the "right call."[27]

The Bond Affair

Within a few hours, preoccupation over King's reaction to SNCC's antiwar statement was eclipsed by a new bombshell involving Julian Bond, SNCC's twenty-five-year-old communications director who had recently been elected to the Georgia legislature and was due to be sworn in on January 10. The scion of a distinguished African American family and a graduate of the Quaker-run George School in Bucks County, Pennsylvania, Bond had shocked his family by dropping out of Morehouse College and joining SNCC in 1961.[28] Bond was attending a YMCA meeting when Lewis held his press conference, and the newly elected representative from Georgia's 136th District returned to his office to find a spate of telephone messages from reporters. The furor erupted when Ed Spivia of the state-owned radio station WGST asked Bond whether he endorsed Lewis's statement in its entirety and Bond answered, "Yes, I do."[29] Adding to the firestorm was Bond's expression of admiration for "the courage of draft-card burners."[30] His approval of such tactics was particularly galling to white southerners, who were still reeling from the "ignominious" passage, against their will, of the civil rights legislation.

Bond's election, along with that of six other African Americans, marked the first time since Reconstruction that an African American would be seated in the Georgia House of Representatives. That Bond was a member of the despised and purportedly communist-ridden SNCC aggravated the festering wounds of stalwart segregationists. Sensing an opportunity for revenge, Bond's opponents pounced, threatening to deny him his seat on the grounds that his comments were traitorous and demonstrated a patent unfitness for office.[31] Reaction to Bond's statement was swift, as newspapers, particularly those in Atlanta, plastered their front pages with the latest denunciations of his alleged perfidy, converting the well-groomed and articulate father of two into a villain. Lieutenant Governor Peter Zack Geer spoke for the majority of white Georgians, calling Bond's statement a "glaring, sad and tragic example of a total lack of patriotism to the United States of America. Wittingly or unwittingly, this position exactly suits the Kremlin."[32] This upsurge in anticommunist hysteria marked one of the "last flickers of red scare politics," testifying to McCarthyism's vitality well into the 1960s.[33]

The Bond affair created such a commotion that it superseded stories of SNCC's antiwar statement and the Younge murder.[34] Henry Luce's *Time* chastised Bond for not knowing "when to keep his mouth shut," referring to his statement about the prickly issue of the draft.[35] Bond's opponents quickly seized on that statement to Red-bait him, which resonated powerfully in the South. SNCC, still grief-stricken over Younge's murder, was unprepared for the onslaught as the Georgia legislature announced its intention to bar Bond from taking his seat the following Monday. A besieged John Lewis convened a press conference, alongside SCLC spokesman Junius Griffin, and read a statement denying that "Julian Bond or anyone in SNCC called for a violation of federal law." Lewis went on to rebut the notion that SNCC had suggested that people burn their draft cards.[36] King, who had been irritated with SNCC for months, interrupted a vacation in Los Angeles to write a statement that was read by Griffin: "Our nation is approaching a dangerous totalitarian policy when dissent becomes synonymous with treason." And King pointed out the irony "that so many of Mr. Bond's political colleagues and critics did not feel that they were violating the United States Constitution when they sought to perpetuate racial discrimination from their vaunted position."[37]

In addition to the expected attacks from the NAACP and the National Urban League, the African American press mostly distanced itself from Bond.[38] His hometown African American daily, the *Atlanta World*, stopped short of condoning the actions of the Georgia House of Representatives in barring Bond, but it affirmed that some form of censure was an appropriate remedy because no "elective official should be permitted to take the position embraced by young Bond."[39] The *Pittsburgh Courier* took a more charitable view, supporting Bond's right to speak his mind and ascribing the actions of the Georgia legislature to racial animus.[40] The *Courier*'s assessment of the racist rationale was indisputable, but the draft issue furnished Bond's foes with a sharp cudgel, and their racism was camouflaged by the legislature's unwillingness to challenge the credentials of the other five African American representatives-elect. Bond's alleged crime was committing an act of independence from white politicians without their consent. The brouhaha created a spiraling crisis that veered out of control and turned into a public relations nightmare. The splintered reactions within the African American community, as reflected by the divergent editorials in the *Courier* and the *World*, testified to the disturbing fragmentation of the civil rights movement. The issue of the war was only sharpening these cleavages, and SNCC's and Bond's antiwar views were running afoul of the deep support for the war within black America. With the exception Howard Zinn, who wrote a letter to the editors of the *Atlanta Constitution* in which he personally vouched for Julian Bond's intelligence and talent, his white comrades in the New Left were silent.[41]

On the morning of January 10, 1966, Bond, who had received numerous death threats, nervously climbed the steps of the Georgia statehouse in Atlanta, flanked by his lawyers. Even before the legislature convened, the atmosphere of hysteria made Bond's seating an exceedingly remote possibility. When the other members of the Georgia house, many of them elected in districts where African Americans were still not allowed to register to vote, stood up to be sworn in, the clerk instructed Bond to step aside because "several challenges have been filed to his right to be seated here."[42] Bond left the chambers and walked down the corridors, surrounded by throngs of reporters. He read the following statement: "I have not counseled burning draft cards, nor have I burned mine. I have suggested that Congressional outlined alternatives to military service be extended to include building democracy at home. . . . As to the current

controversy, because of convictions that I have arrived [at] through examination of my conscience, I have decided that I personally cannot participate in the war."[43]

Before a packed chamber, Bond's accusers, led by avowed racist
James Lane, who had recently invited Alabama governor George Wallace
to address the Georgia house, alleged that Bond's comments on the war
and the draft were treasonous, rendering him unfit to serve.[44] The chamber overwhelmingly concurred and, by the staggering margin of 184 to
12, denied Bond his seat.[45] After staring at the tally board through a veil
of tears, an unrepentant Bond marched out of the statehouse in a defiant mood, vowing to appeal the unconstitutional proceedings and telling
Newsweek's Marshall Frady that he intended to "do everything I can to
take that seat."[46] Just after midnight, James Forman issued a SNCC bul-
letin: "Everybody including Julian is in a state of shock."[47] The Georgia
house's near-unanimous vote to expel Bond indicated the overwhelming
support for the war, particularly in the South.

In swimming against the tide of public opinion, SNCC and Bond left
themselves vulnerable to assaults from their segregationist enemies. As
late as 1966, many southerners still considered the civil rights movement
a communist-inspired plot.[48] Given that the antiwar movement was still
held in low regard by the American public, SNCC and Bond could count
on little support from the liberal establishment. Seemingly oblivious to the
racial overtones of the affair, the *New York Times* condemned both Bond
and the legislature for their "misguided" conduct.[49] The conservative *Wall
Street Journal*, not surprisingly, lambasted Bond's position as "puerile and
repugnant."[50] Former SNCC supporter Lillian Smith, a southern liberal
whose novel *Strange Fruit* exposed the human cost of racism, wrote a letter to the *Atlanta Constitution* suggesting that SNCC had been overrun by
communists.[51] The establishment's lack of support for SNCC's and Bond's
opposition to the war highlighted the danger of moving too far ahead of
public opinion on the Vietnam War.

The end of segregation had altered the terms of the debate. Ironically,
the passage of civil rights legislation came with a cost: the fight against
racial injustice had lost its sense of urgency among the national press,
which was now riveted by the escalating war in Vietnam. A smattering of
letters from twenty-four U.S. congressmen excoriating the Georgia legislature's actions could not obviate SNCC's growing sense of isolation.[52]
Public opinion polls revealed that 85 percent of blacks approved of the
government's policy on Vietnam, and the views of Roy Wilkins and other

moderates reflected this widespread pro-war sentiment.[53] Already weakened by internal disarray, and with its coffers running dry, SNCC released a statement reaffirming its unflagging support for Bond. In an interview, Lewis blamed the press for fomenting the climate that allowed Bond to be denied his seat, and he noted that the culture places "more emphasis and a greater price on symbols, on the American flag, than on the souls, the bodies and the minds of millions of people, young and old, black and white"[54] Even as late as 1966, the fierceness of the attacks and the rapidity of the legislature's actions testified to the enduring legacy of the Cold War culture that would brook no dissent from U.S. foreign policy.[55]

At the same time, Bond's and SNCC's pioneering role in the peace movement, though controversial and unpopular at the time, was the most passionate and public resuscitation of the linkages among imperialism, war, and racism. It rekindled the anticolonial critiques of U.S. foreign policy and energized and expanded the scope of the antiwar movement. Bond garnered a lot of sympathy from civil libertarian groups, such as the American Civil Liberties Union (ACLU), and from some liberals who otherwise might have been alienated by SNCC's turn to separatism.[56] For instance, New York City's Republican mayor John Lindsay said that he would have represented Bond if he still practiced law.[57] Appearing on NBC's *Meet the Press*, Bond situated his pacifism in his Quaker education, and his eloquent defense of his right to dissent impressed many observers.[58] Bond's case highlighted the maelstrom of dissent within the civil rights movement in 1966. In the coming years, the movement would take a more global perspective whereby the war was seen to reflect problems inherent in American society and capitalism writ large.

Outraged and shocked by Bond's ejection from the Georgia legislature after receiving 82 percent of the vote, SNCC, with its characteristic élan, vowed to fight back in the streets and in the halls of justice. Bond's attorneys waited only three days before filing an injunction in federal district court seeking to force the legislature to seat him.[59] As will be discussed in greater detail in chapter 6, almost as soon as the firestorm over Bond ignited, Martin Luther King Jr. returned to Atlanta and injected himself into the swirling controversy. Preoccupied with his campaign in Chicago, King was annoyed by this new crisis caused by his unruly SNCC allies. While supporting Bond's right to speak out, King, still reeling from the negative response to his own recent foray into the Vietnam issue, danced around the topic of the war. In early 1966 King was not yet ready to break with the Johnson administration.[60]

In the meantime, Julian Bond spent almost a year in litigation until the U.S. Supreme Court unanimously ruled on December 5, 1966, that the Georgia house had violated his right to free expression guaranteed under the First Amendment.[61] In January 1967 Bond officially took the oath of office. The ordeal transformed the soft-spoken Bond into a national celebrity, and his multifaceted communication skills were displayed when he crafted a cartoon that evinced the African American critique of the Vietnam War.[62] On the whole, Bond's tribulations elevated the public consciousness of the war's racial inequities and demonstrated the "authoritarian mindset of some of its supporters."[63]

Bond, who had been on a leave of absence from SNCC during the tumultuous months of his appeal, officially resigned from the organization in September 1966.[64] By the time of his departure, SNCC had undergone a wholesale transformation, expelling all but a few whites. Its turn to racial separatism discomfited Bond and the dwindling band of interracialists, such as longtime SNCC activist Bob Zellner and his wife Dottie, who remained firmly wedded to the original dream of creating a "beloved community."[65]

SNCC, CORE, and Black Power

Along with the Vietnam War, Black Power surged to the forefront of the civil rights movement's national consciousness in 1966 and contributed to its implosion along generational and ideological lines. Contrary to the first wave of civil rights scholarship, Black Power did not emerge sui generis in the mid-1960s.[66] Indeed, Black Power, with its emphasis on African American racial pride, economic self-sufficiency, and racial separatism, can be traced to nineteenth-century abolitionist Martin Delaney.[67] In 1916 Marcus Garvey, a Jamaican immigrant, formed the United Negro Improvement Association (UNIA), which advocated black-owned businesses and urged African Americans to recapture their African identity and establish a black homeland in Africa. In the post–World War I era, Garvey and his UNIA embodied an early-twentieth-century iteration of Black Power, and he remained a heroic figure to future black nationalists and others, such as Ho Chi Minh, even after his conviction for mail fraud in 1923.[68]

In the 1930s Wallace Fard, a Detroit peddler, founded the Nation of Islam, which sought to develop black separatism and economic autonomy under the ambit of a new variant of Islam that branded Caucasians "white devils."[69] After Fard disappeared in 1934, his disciple, Elijah Muhammad, became the leader of the sect and furnished solace and inspiration to many African American men struggling with poverty and racism in northern cities such as Detroit, Chicago, and Boston. However, it was not until the emergence of the charismatic Malcolm X in the late 1950s that the Nation of Islam moved from the margins to the center of the discussion on race and civil rights.[70] Throughout his short life, Malcolm X attracted a host of young men who were dissatisfied with the gradualism of the mainstream civil rights movement and its alliance with Cold War liberalism. Malcolm X and his allies, such as North Carolina firebrand Robert Williams, privileged black political empowerment and maintained their commitment to the global dimensions of the freedom struggle. As noted earlier, their fidelity to Fidel Castro's Cuban Revolution, with its dedication to ending racial hierarchies, reflected their belief in the link between imperialism abroad and racism at home. Most of Malcolm's acolytes and admirers were northerner militants who had grown increasingly bitter and cynical about their status as second-class citizens; many were mired in poverty and despair and were frequently victims of police brutality.[71] The long (and long neglected) struggle in the North in the 1940, 1950s, and early 1960s for equality in housing, education, and employment led to the postwar version of Black Power that challenged the nonviolent, interracial civil rights movement in the mid-1960s.[72]

By the early 1960s, Williams's and Malcolm's fiery critiques of the civil rights movement inspired Max Stanford and a few other students from Cleveland to form the Revolutionary Action Movement (RAM), which envisioned African Americans as the vanguard of Third World revolutions sweeping Asia, Africa, and South America.[73] Like Malcolm X, Stanford and RAM venerated Mao and the Chinese revolutionaries and argued that African Americans were living under domestic colonialism.[74] Vietnam, of course, became a focal point of the global revolutionary struggle against racism, and on July 4, 1965, RAM wrote an open letter to the Vietnamese National Liberation Front declaring its solidarity in the struggle against American imperialism.[75] Although RAM was never a large organization, Stanford, a tireless networker, found a number of young black men in the North who were receptive to his strategy of discrediting white and black liberals as "Uncle Toms." In 1964 RAM activists worked with SNCC in the South, and their message of self-defense and anti-imperialism resonated with many civil rights workers. Stokely Carmichael, who would soon become the face of SNCC, and Huey Newton and Bobby Seale, future leaders of the Black Panther Party, were captivated by RAM's vision of armed revolutionary struggle, anti-imperialism, and black separatism.[76] This revival of anti-imperialism by Malcolm X, Carmichael, and the Black Panther Party during the height of the Vietnam War transformed the dialogue and highlighted the international dimensions of racism in a way that resonated with young blacks, thereby challenging King's message of nonviolence. Black Power advocates presented a perceptive, penetrating critique of the Vietnam War that was anathema to Cold War liberals but highlighted the connections between racism at home and imperialism abroad.

Prior to the mid-1960s, the growing band of racial separatists had little support among the African American public, and they were confined to the fringes of the civil rights movement. For instance, a *Newsweek* poll conducted at the end of 1963 showed that only 13 percent of African Americans had a positive view of the Nation of Islam.[77] The civil rights movement overwhelmingly repudiated Malcolm X's derision of the March on Washington as the "Farce on Washington." But as we have seen, after Atlantic City, the tenets of Black Power began to penetrate the civil rights movement. SNCC and CORE were beginning to combine civil rights activism with aspects of Black Power militancy, even though SNCC workers de-emphasized any racial rhetoric in the Lowndes County campaign of 1965.[78] It was no accident that SNCC's shift to Black Power occurred only four months after the torrid attacks over its indictment of the Vietnam War and the uproar over the seating of Julian Bond. SNCC had been trending toward racial separatism since Atlantic City, but the war radicalized it, expanded its vision to encompass a global movement for racial justice, and engendered an affinity for the peoples of the Third World, especially the Vietnamese peasants. Carmichael summed it up best with the following quip: "This Vietnam War ain't nothing but white men sending black men to kill brown men, to defend, so they claim, a country they stole from red men."[79]

The apotheosis of the Vietnam War as the preeminent issue in America dovetailed with a sharp erosion in public support for the civil rights movement. After passage of the Civil Rights Act of 1964, CORE's James Farmer ruefully recalled the emergence of the following sentiment: "Well, it's all over now. We have done it. We have succeeded."[80] Stokely Carmichael summed it up best: "It was easier to get support when we were just going after the right to eat at lunch counters. Now what we're going after is political power for the poor and the stakes are much higher."[81] As the public's preoccupation with the Vietnam War increased, all the major civil rights organizations, with the exception of the NAACP, experienced a financial crisis.[82] In fact, a month prior to the issuance of SNCC's antiwar statement, Gene Roberts of the *New York Times* reported that the organization's $100,000 debt had caused it to miss its paltry payroll for the past three weeks. Likewise, CORE's annual budget dropped from a high of close to $1 million in 1962 to only about $300,000 in 1965, and it reported a debt of $200,000.[83] SCLC contributions, which had spiked during Selma, also plummeted in early 1966 after King embarked on his Chicago campaign.[84] The flagging passion for civil rights was partially attributable to the movement's success in ending segregation in the South. Moreover, dealing with the panoply of problems related to de facto segregation in the North did not create the kind of high drama generated in Montgomery, Little Rock, Birmingham, and Selma. As early as July 1964, a Harris poll demonstrated that 58 percent of whites feared that African Americans wanted to take their jobs, and 25 percent feared that blacks wanted to take their women.[85] The insertion of the war into this morass only compounded the problems. Given this scenario, frustration and impatience in SNCC and CORE reached the breaking point. They were groping for new strategies.

Malcolm X had been dead for less than a year, but his canonization among the militant wing of the civil rights movement happened virtually overnight. His ideas on the international dimension of the struggle for human dignity, which harked back to Du Bois and Robeson, as well as his belief in the creation of African American institutions, profoundly influenced a new generation of activists, including twenty-one-year-old Cleveland Sellers, one of Carmichael's deputies.[86] Sellers, a longtime SNCC member, would later gain notoriety for refusing to be inducted into the U.S. Army. Only months after SNCC came out against the war, its views were ascendant. John Lewis recalled that SNCC members now dismissed him as an anachronistic "Christ-loving damn fool," and instead of the writings of Gandhi, Camus, and Thoreau, they were now reading the works of Frantz Fanon, a psychiatrist from Martinique who had moved to Algeria and fought against French colonialism.[87] Their reading of Fanon's *The Wretched of the Earth*, *Black Skin*, and *White Masks* shaped their view of the civil rights movement as part of a worldwide struggle against colonialism, and it informed their belief that black America was a colonial nation within the greater white-dominated United States.[88] By the beginning of 1966, SNCC's views on imperialism closely mirrored those of the anticolonialists and the recently defunct FPCC. Just before the murder of Younge, the bloc urging racial separatism circulated an internal memorandum stressing Lewis's fatigue and the need to inject fresh blood into the leadership to meet the new challenges.[89] Bill Ware, another newcomer to SNCC who had developed a Pan-Africanist perspective, formed the Atlanta Project, a grassroots campaign to promote "economic justice" that, according to historian Clayborne Carson, "promoted black separatism with a singular fervor."[90]

SNCC's turmoil over Vietnam and racial separatism was echoed in CORE, which had also been mired in acrimonious debates over the war and over whether to expel whites.[91] With the departure of James Farmer on March 1, 1966, CORE was moving in a parallel direction with SNCC on African American nationalism, and the organization's position on Vietnam had evolved considerably since the previous summer. Until the end of his tenure, Farmer, in spite of his personal opposition to the war, asserted that civil rights organizations should not take positions on the war in Vietnam.[92] In contrast, Farmer's successor, North Carolina attorney Floyd McKissick, urged CORE to come out against the war. In January, CORE's National Action Committee called the war in Vietnam a drain on the fight against poverty and warned that "we as a nation are faced with a choice of priorities": guns or butter.[93] Following Farmer's departure, CORE's changing attitude on the war was evident. In April its Northeast Regional Council blasted the war as an intentionally "racist" ploy designed to undermine civil rights activity.[94] At the June White House Conference on Civil Rights, McKissick and CORE representatives repeatedly cited the impossibility of devoting the necessary resources to the Great Society while waging a costly war in Vietnam.[95] When the conference failed to consider an antiwar resolution, McKissick charged that it had been "rigged."[96]

Not surprisingly, one year after Vietnam had roiled CORE at its convention in Durham, the war was again on the minds of CORE delegates as they gathered for the twenty-third annual convention in Baltimore on the first weekend of July.[97] Following SNCC's lead, the delegates unanimously adopted a resolution calling for the withdrawal of U.S. troops from Vietnam. It passed another resolution stating that the selective service system "places a heavy discriminatory burden" on minority groups. It also pledged to support anyone who refused to serve in the armed forces because of the Vietnam War, and it vowed to explain the "immorality of the war to African American youths."[98] In spite of McKissick's more militant rhetoric, the majority of CORE members still considered him too integrationist, and his short tenure was marred by perpetual clashes with the ascendant African American separatists. Meanwhile, the NAACP and the National Urban League drew closer to the Johnson administration.

The war was increasing the centrifugal forces within the civil rights movement and adding to the appeal of Black Power. By early July 1966, the civil rights coalition was increasingly embroiled in internecine warfare. It would only get worse with the meteoric rise of the glamorous Stokely Carmichael, who would combine the strands of Black Power, antiwar protest, and civil rights in a potent message and become a global icon.

Stokely Carmichael and the Rebirth of Anticolonialism

For several years, Stokely Carmichael had been the leader of a highly intellectual, self-possessed, and articulate SNCC subgroup that was dissatisfied with the trajectory of the civil rights movement. Since the spring of 1965, he had headed the effort to forge separate African American political institutions in rural Lowndes County, Alabama.[99] By 1966, the twenty-five-year-old Carmichael's charisma, wit, and courage had already made him a legend in the civil rights community. As a young child, Carmichael had emigrated from Trinidad to Harlem, where he acquired an invaluable political education listening to the stepladder orators extolling the legendary African revolutionaries on the famed 125th Street strip. His exposure in Harlem to the great Pan-African thinkers George Padmore and C. L. R. James informed his later views on the international dimensions of the racial struggle. These anticolonial sensibilities also reflected the views of his boyhood idol, Paul Robeson.[100] After enrolling in Howard University in the fall of 1960, he became a leading activist in the campus's chapter of the Nonviolent Action Group, an affiliate of SNCC. Carmichael joined the Freedom Rides in the summer of 1961 and was jailed in Mississippi's infamous Parchman Penitentiary, where his persistence and courage drove his captors crazy.[101] His time in Parchman exposed him to the gamut of ideologies, experiences, and philosophies that constituted the civil rights movement. It was also where he became acquainted with the cohort of original SNCC members, such as John Lewis, James Bevel, and Marion Barry, whose orientation in the African American religious culture of their native South differed so markedly from his own upbringing.[102] Carmichael joined SNCC in 1964, and his firebrand style inspired his fellow civil rights workers. By the spring of 1966, the voluble Carmichael was poised to become the public face of SNCC.[103]

Cleveland Sellers called SNCC's staff meeting at the beautiful resort of Kingston Springs, Tennessee, in May 1966 "the most important meeting in its history."[104] Despite changes in SNCC's personnel and policy, James Forman had served as executive secretary since 1961, and John Lewis had been chairman since 1963. In the frenzied aftermath of the antiwar statement, Lewis managed to alienate both the moderate wing of the civil rights movement and SNCC militants, who criticized his participation in planning the White House's much ballyhooed conference on civil rights entitled "To Fulfill These Rights."[105] A consummate integrationist, Lewis was also out of step with SNCC's embrace of racial separatism, and his continued involvement with the board of the SCLC became a source of irritation to those urging a different direction. In March 1966 the staff of the Atlanta Project drafted a position paper arguing that white participation in the movement was obsolete. The document stated, "If we are to proceed toward liberation, we must cut ourselves off from the white people." It advocated the formation of "our own institutions, credit unions, co-ops, [and] political parties" and the writing of "our own histories."[106] The notion of expelling whites was anathema to Lewis.[107] Carmichael, too, harbored reservations about excluding whites from SNCC; during his years in the movement, he had cultivated a host of enduring friendships with whites and was also sensitive to SNCC's reliance on white northern support. Nonetheless, Carmichael's tenure in Lowndes County made him more receptive to the ideas expressed in the Atlanta Project paper, and his affinity for Third World revolutionary struggles factored into his eventual decision—which he made on the eve of the Kingston Springs staff meeting. Carmichael decided to take the unprecedented step of challenging Lewis's position as the chairman of SNCC.[108]

Since its inception, SNCC had been opposed to factions and eschewed strong, charismatic leaders. In the spring of 1966, the beleaguered organization had a slew of enemies, and most members were averse to a fight over leadership. Accordingly, when the conference convened at Kingston Springs on May 8, SNCC was inclined to keep its leadership intact. After all, John Lewis's quiet dignity, commitment, and courage had endeared him to many members. However, there were others who believed that the changing times called for fresh leadership and considered Lewis's religiosity and soft-spoken demeanor out of step with the times. In the end, after an emotionally wrenching and contentious debate that lasted until the dawn of May 14, the staff elected Stokely Carmichael to be SNCC's next chairman. James Forman voluntarily stepped aside as executive secretary and was replaced by Ruby Doris Smith Robinson. A visibly shaken

Lewis refused to say whether he would remain with the organization.[109] Some members felt guilty about their treatment of Lewis. Worth Long, one of the insurgents, expressed a great deal of ambivalence about his role in Lewis's ouster. Years later, Long said, "John was the most courageous person that I have ever worked with in the movement. John would not just follow you into the lion's den; he would lead you into it."[110] After the vote, Carmichael reassuringly told the media, "We will not fire any of our white organizers, but if they want to organize, they can organize white people. Negroes will organize Negroes."[111] Carmichael's coronation ushered in an era of increasing stridency for SNCC that further distanced it from the mainstream civil rights organizations.[112] His attacks on the Vietnam War as a racist, imperialistic affair became even more vociferous and further polarized the civil rights coalition.

Not long after Carmichael assumed leadership of SNCC, he became a national celebrity—a folk hero to radicals and a villain to others.[113] The national press seized on Carmichael's declaration of support for Black Power in June, at the Meredith march in Mississippi, as an indication of a new, even sinister African American militancy. Aided by media coverage that focused on the sensational, Black Power reverberated across the collective national consciousness in the summer of 1966. Carmichael made great copy, and some of his detractors in SNCC dubbed him "Stokely Starmichael." *Time* spoke for the white press when it indicted "Black Power as a racist philosophy that preached segregation in reverse."[114]

Coming on the heels of its antiwar statement, SNCC's more radical tone frightened away donors and made established civil rights organizations unwilling to share resources with it. Indeed, moderate, mainstream civil rights organizations like the NAACP, already seething at SNCC's antiwar position, were aghast at SNCC's Black Power turn.[115] The notion of biracialism had undergirded the NAACP since its founding in 1909. At the 1966 NAACP convention in Los Angeles, Roy Wilkins denounced Black Power as "the father of hatred and the mother of violence."[116] The National Urban League's Whitney Young said Black Power was "indistinguishable from the bigotry of Bilbo, Talmadge, and Eastland."[117] By contrast, Carmichael's rhetoric and his call for racial pride resonated with the masses of African American youths who were entering the workforce with their dignity under assault and their horizons restricted by virtue of their blackness. Many were fodder for the swelling draft rolls. Their anger was not confined to the white power structure; it extended to the mainstream civil rights organizations. African American delegates to the Philadelphia convention of the National Urban League had to make their way past a jeering picket line manned by young African Americans shouting Black Power slogans.[118] Carmichael's appeals to racial pride filled the void left by Malcolm X's untimely death. Appearing on CBS's *Face the Nation* on June 19, 1966, Carmichael explained his opposition to the draft:

> My own feeling is that there is no reason why black people should be fighting for free elections in Vietnam for some other people to get free elections when they don't have it in their own country. I feel that they should have free elections in their country, and then decide whether or not they in fact want to participate in that war.
>
> All of those black soldiers from Mississippi did not even decide whether or not they want to participate in that war.[119]

Carmichael's diatribes riled the civil rights establishment. When SNCC scheduled an antiwar demonstration at the wedding of President Johnson's daughter Luci on August 6, 1966 (the twenty-first anniversary of Hiroshima), King, Wilkins, Young, and the venerable A. Philip Randolph sent a telegram criticizing SNCC's incivility. Carmichael responded with a withering missive accusing them of displaying "more backbone in defending Luci than you have shown for our colored peoples of Vietnam being napalmed by Luci's father [and] for our black soldiers being exterminated in Vietnam." Carmichael then scathingly noted: "As far as we are concerned your messengers can tell your boss that his day of jubilation is also the day his country murdered many in Hiroshima. In addition, we believe that your boss-man selected this day to divert the news coverage from Vietnam and Hiroshima, which is a national day of protest, to a special wedding." He signed it, "Yours for Black power."[120] This strident rhetoric alarmed King, who had only recently acknowledged that the civil rights movement was very close to a permanent split over the war and the issue of Black Power, and he proposed that the civil rights leadership hold a meeting to patch their differences.[121] The meeting never happened.

Carmichael was not all talk. Only days after his election, SNCC announced that it was withdrawing from the White House Conference on Civil Rights scheduled to begin on June 1.[122] From its headquarters in Atlanta, Ruby Doris Smith Robinson branded the conference a "useless endeavor" and declared that SNCC "cannot in good conscience meet the chief policymaker of the Vietnam War to discuss human rights in this country when he flagrantly violates the human rights of colored people in

Vietnam." The organization was also perturbed by the conference's focus on the "troubled" state of the African American family, in the wake of the highly touted Moynihan report, and it resented white America's attempt "to shift responsibility for the degrading position in which blacks now find themselves away from the oppressors to the oppressed."[123] Appearing on *Face the Nation*, King expressed his sorrow that SNCC had decided to boycott the conference.[124]

SNCC's absence failed to alleviate the internal tensions plaguing the movement, which surfaced immediately when a band of militants picketed the conference and attempted to dissuade African American delegates from attending, calling them "Uncle Toms." CORE's Floyd McKissick, who charged that the conference's "fixed agenda" made it seem "rigged," was outraged that the antiwar resolution was completely ignored.[125] After the high hopes generated by LBJ's soaring words at the Howard University commencement where he had announced the conference, McKissick and other civil rights activists departed in a sour mood.[126] The confusion and disorder that characterized the conference highlighted the deepening fragmentation of the civil rights coalition less than a year after passage of the Voting Rights Act.[127]

The cries of Black Power and the talk of violence and separatism that permeated the discussion on civil rights was too much for John Lewis. For years, he had been the spiritual leader of SNCC, on a par with the revered Robert Parris. But by 1966, Lewis's advocacy of love, nonviolence, and brotherhood had fallen on deaf ears. Admitting that Carmichael's election "hurt more than anything I'd ever been through," Lewis suspected that James Forman was one of those who wanted him out, because Forman had never accepted the notion of a biracial society.[128] Nobody was surprised when, on June 11, 1966, Lewis resigned from the organization he had once loved.[129] After much soul-searching, he decided to move to New York City "to put some space between what was behind" him and "what lay ahead."[130] From his small apartment in the Chelsea section of Manhattan, he watched in horror as SNCC imploded and the carnage in Vietnam continued unabated. After his unceremonious dismissal as SNCC chairman, he felt adrift.

SNCC, meanwhile, was also floating in a sea of confusion. The passing of the torch to a new generation under the leadership of Carmichael was virtually complete. But Black Power and separatism marked the beginning of the end for SNCC. Over the next few years, SNCC would wither in the face of internal dissent and vicious reprisals from its enemies. Its fund-raising, which had always been anemic, was now on life support.[131] Lewis's resignation was followed by a spate of additional departures, including such SNCC stalwarts as Julian Bond, Charles Sherrod, Marion Barry, and Diane Nash Bevel.[132] Bevel, who had been a pillar of strength and courage during the early years of the sit-ins and the Freedom Rides, left for Hanoi in December 1966 via Moscow and Beijing as part of a small contingent of American women. She had been so incensed by a magazine cover depicting a brown Vietnamese woman holding her dead or wounded baby that she proclaimed "she was willing to give up her passport."[133] Upon her arrival in Hanoi, Bevel sent a telegram to friends in Chicago noting the large amount of cotton grown and observed that "the Vietnam War is being fought for the same reason slavery was maintained in Mississippi— cotton."[134] She was impressed by the resilience of the ordinary Vietnamese people, and their plight reminded her of the struggles in the South. She documented the war's carnage, including her own harrowing experience of hiding in a hotel cellar during a bombing raid, in an article she wrote for *Freedomways*, a quarterly African American journal that had become a platform for antiwar and Pan-African views.[135] At the end of their trip, Bevel and her group spent an hour with Ho Chi Minh, who spoke to them in English and reached into a vase by his chair and handed each women a red rose.[136] When she returned home, Bevel spoke at a press conference in Chicago and attacked the Vietnamese conflict as an "economic war with racial overtones" and added that "Negroes are going to have to decide whether they want to be the murderers of other colored people."[137] Although her responsibilities as a single mother limited her involvement in the antiwar movement, Bevel's experience on the front lines fighting segregation in the Deep South informed her views that Vietnam was a racist and imperialist war. However, her antipathy to Black Power caused her to sever all ties with SNCC.[138]

These conflicts enveloping the freedom struggle by the summer and fall of 1966 occurred against the backdrop of a deteriorating political landscape. The expanding war diminished resources for the Great Society, fueled inflation, and jeopardized the bold vision LBJ had enunciated at his Howard University commencement address. In addition to Vietnam, the spate of urban uprisings and the sensational reports of Black Power, which aroused whites' fear of an imminent race war, were roiling President Johnson's vaunted coalition. In his State of the Union address in January, the president had introduced new civil rights legislation that included provisions to ensure impartial jury selection, eliminate housing discrimination, and protect civil rights workers.[139] From the outset, Johnson recognized that passage of this new legislation would be an uphill battle. A July 1966 congressional survey revealed that 90 percent of respondents opposed additional civil rights legislation, and a September 1965 Gallup poll of whites found that 88 percent believed blacks should improve their own lot by self-reliance rather than government help.[140] Not surprisingly, the civil rights legislation stalled in the Senate. Throughout the rest of his presidency, Johnson's obsession with Vietnam vitiated his ability to implement further civil rights legislation.

The biggest test of Johnson's political standing, of course, was the midterm elections in November 1966. A month prior to the elections, the Republican national chairman announced that his slate would emphasize racial issues, citing polls indicating that 58 percent of Republicans considered urban unrest the paramount issue.[141] In October the *Wall Street Journal* editorialized that "every legislative enactment seemed to incite more mob activity, more mob violence, more demonstrations, and bloodshed."[142] The turbulence over the war, unrest in the ghettos, and a revitalized Republican Party aroused fear among Democrats that they would have difficulty holding on to their wide majority in Congress and winning statewide races.[143] Their fears were justified. Although the Democratic Party retained its majority, it lost forty-seven seats in the House and three in the Senate, signaling the retreat of the Great Society. Moreover, the election results seemingly validated the dreaded "white backlash." Actor Ronald Reagan, who opposed the Civil Rights Act of 1964, won a stunning victory against incumbent Pat Brown in the gubernatorial race in California. During the campaign, Reagan preached against the excesses of the Great Society, exploited white fears of African American gains, and pilloried the "mess" created by the treacherous New Left students at Berkeley.[144] Governor Brown's support of the Rumford Fair Housing Act, prohibiting racial discrimination in the sale or leasing of property, was opposed by most whites, and that played a role in his defeat.[145] The electoral losses dispirited the civil rights movement as it pivoted toward economic issues. A mere fifteen months after the signing of the historic Voting Rights Act, Bayard Rustin's vision of a grand political coalition was now a chimera—and the war was a major culprit. The midterm losses signaled the beginning of the end of the reigning New Deal liberal order.[146]

A few weeks later, SNCC met in upstate New York, at the secluded estate of African American entertainer Clayton "Peg Leg" Bates, to vote on whether to exclude whites. By that time, only a handful of whites remained in the organization.[147] With the ascendancy of the separatists now secure, Danny Lyon, SNCC's official photographer and one of the last whites remaining, realized that the days of interracial brotherhood born in the heady days of the sit-ins were over.[148] Although the outcome seemed certain, the emotional meetings lasted for an entire week. Robert Zellner, a native of Alabama whose grandfather had been in the Ku Klux Klan, and his wife Dorothy Miller Zellner were longtime members whose years of courageous, selfless devotion to the movement had inspired whites and blacks alike. They were present at the proceedings and watched with a sense of bemusement. Carmichael deemed the motion to expel whites a diversionary matter, and he was unwilling to sunder long-standing relationships with old friends and sincere white progressives like the Zellners. He proposed a division of labor, with whites organizing in white areas under SNCC auspices. The debates turned nasty. After the revered Fannie Lou Hamer called the separatists "cold and unloving," the African American militants claimed that she was "no longer relevant" and not at their "level of development."[149] James Forman was so disgusted that he put forth a resolution to dissolve the organization and send its surplus funds to Guinea to support liberation movements in Africa.[150] The eventual outcome was a narrowly passed compromise (the vote was nineteen to eighteen) that allowed whites to remain in fund-raising and administrative work but excluded them from policy, organizing, and other leadership roles. This vote did not end the internal dissent. For the rest of SNCC's brief history, it struggled to develop a coherent strategy to turn its separatist rhetoric into a viable program. In the following months, its intrepid support of the Vietcong led to government repression.[151] With the rise of the antiwar movement, SNCC passed from the national consciousness and was soon supplanted by the Black Panther Party in California, preaching armed revolution. A key phase in the civil rights struggle had passed.[152]

Likewise, CORE embraced racial separatism at its 1966 convention in Baltimore, where it also formally opposed the war.[153] Inspired by the southern sit-ins, CORE had been infused with younger, more militant African American activists in cities throughout the North, Midwest, and West, and they brought a new urgency to the campaign for open housing and school desegregation.[154] CORE's embrace of racial separatism was only a matter of time, and most close observers were not surprised when it also abandoned its longtime adherence to nonviolence.[155] Its new rhetoric alarmed moderates. In announcing CORE's break from the integrationist wing of the civil rights movement, McKissick declared, "The cup is running over the ghetto, and when it runs over, we're not going to start condemning anyone. . . . There is no possible return to non-violence."[156] CORE's leader referred to President Johnson as the "great white father" to whom the "Toms" always appeal for help, and other speakers repeatedly assailed the African American bourgeois and the white middle class.[157] James Farmer, whose support of McKissick had been instrumental to his ascension in CORE, charged that the "Black Power" cry had sparked the so-called white backlash and the defeat of the 1966 civil rights bill.[158] Whites, such as novelist Lillian Smith, were turning away from CORE.[159] By the end of the 1960s, CORE, like SNCC, was in decline. CORE historians August Meier and Elliott Rudwick assert that, with "its embrace of separatism," CORE, like SNCC, "was no longer at the cutting edge of the black revolt."[160]

Black Soldiers and the Civil Rights Movement

As the civil rights movement grappled with the issue of Vietnam, the plight of African American soldiers on the front lines of battle and the inherent inequities in the draft drew increased scrutiny. In view of the rising rate of African American enlistment in the armed forces and the historic view that military service hastens the pace of racial reform, the movement had to consider these factors as it decided whether to support or oppose the war in Vietnam.[161]

In the late 1950s and early 1960s, the African American press and the civil rights movement lauded the integrated military as one of the most important accomplishments of the "post–Korean War civil rights struggle."[162] As a result of their limited opportunities, many young African American men volunteered for military service and perceived it as their Harvard—an opportunity to escape the urban ghettos or the impoverished rural hamlets of the South. For example, Robert L. Daniels, a nineteen-year-old from a tough neighborhood on Chicago's South Side, joined the army because he thought the "GI Bill of Rights would enable him to go to college."[163] A 1965 survey found that nearly 40 percent of African Americans cited self-advancement as their major reason for enlisting.[164] Young African American men had the additional incentive of proving that they were worthy of their newly acquired civil rights. Just months after President Johnson escalated the war in Vietnam, *Ebony* touted the "valor, honor, strength, and determination of the Negro GI honorably fighting to stave off the communist menace."[165] This stereotype of the African American as a "good soldier" was also disseminated in the white press and echoed throughout the military establishment.[166] Even General William Westmoreland, a native South Carolinian whose ancestors had served in the Confederacy, lavished praise on the African American soldier, declaring, "The performance of the Negro serviceman has been particularly inspirational to me. They have served with distinction. He has been courageous on the battlefield, proficient, and a possessor of technical skills."[167]

By the end of 1966, there were approximately 60,000 African American troops stationed in Vietnam—a disproportionately large number. A critical factor explaining the inordinately high percentage of African American soldiers in Vietnam was Project 100,000, a program designed by Secretary of Defense Robert McNamara to admit 100,000 men into the military each year, many of whom had initially failed the Armed Forces Qualification Test.[168] (The most notable was none other than Muhammad Ali.) Project 100,000 was the brainchild of Daniel Patrick Moynihan, the author of a controversial 1965 report on the "Negro family" in which he argued that "military service is disruptive in some respects" but, on balance, was a great advantage to African Americans. Moynihan viewed the military as a surrogate family, particularly for young African American men from fatherless homes: "Given the strains of disorganized and matrifocal family life in which so many Negro youth come of age, the armed forces are a dramatic and desperately needed change; a world away from women, a world run by strong men and unquestioned authority, where discipline, if harsh, is nonetheless orderly and predictable, and where rewards, if limited, are granted on the basis of performance."[169]

Moynihan's views gained traction when the rapid troop buildup in Vietnam necessitated drastic measures to increase military manpower. He inundated the White House with statistics demonstrating that because such a high percentage of blacks failed the Armed Forces Qualifying Test (AFQT), the armed forces were "the single most important and dramatic instance of the exclusion of Americans from employment opportunity in the United States."[170] Moynihan's vision inspired McNamara to launch Project 100,000 on August 23, 1966, which he outlined in a speech to the Veterans of Foreign Wars that had been written by Albert B. Fitt, a counsel to the army.[171] McNamara disclosed that 40,000 draft rejects and substandard volunteers, most of them from "poverty-encrusted backgrounds, would be 'salvaged' for military duty in the next 10 months"; the number of "salvaged" would increase to 100,000 in the "next fiscal and in succeeding years."[172] McNamara promised that this program would "rehabilitate the nation's subterranean poor" as well as "cure them of the idleness, ignorance, and apathy" that characterized their lives. Manpower experts at the Department of Defense acknowledged that as many as 30 percent of the 40,000 draft rejects and substandard volunteers who would be salvaged were African American, but they denied that this would make Vietnam a "poor man's war."[173] Project 100,000 was rife with paternalism and reflected the military's view that young African American men would appreciate the opportunity to be used as "cannon fodder."

In the ensuing years, most African Americans would come to concur with Floyd McKissick's harsh assessment that the war was "a cynical method to punish black youths for the social ills imposed on them by the major society." Some would even concur with Stokely Carmichael's accusation that it was "clear that the [white] man is moving to get rid of black people in the ghettos."[174] For the most part, the large numbers of African American soldiers initially resulted in support for the war from a broad segment of the civil rights movement. An integrated military, after all, had been a perennial goal of the movement. Not surprisingly, the NAACP, the Urban League, and other moderates in the civil rights movement rallied around the flag. After all, they had embraced Cold War liberalism since the early 1950s. World War II veteran and National Urban League president Whitney M. Young Jr. summed it up best when he claimed that in Vietnam, for "all intents and purposes, race is irrelevant"; there, "colored soldiers fight and die courageously as representatives of all America."[175]

This notion that blacks should support the war because of the large number of African American soldiers in harm's way in Vietnam began to weaken by the end in 1966. A flurry of reports that blacks were fighting and dying in disproportionate numbers in the jungles of Southeast Asia was beginning to raise questions and arouse concerns throughout black America. Toward the end of 1965, African Americans constituted only 11 percent of the population, but their death rate in Vietnam approached 25 percent.[176] Anger over the high black casualty rate was aggravated by a spate of articles in both the white and the African American press deriding the racial inequities of the draft.[177] As of October 1966, only 1.3 percent of draft board members in the entire country were African American; tiny Delaware was the only state where the number of African American board members was equal to the proportion of blacks in the population.[178] Overall, the mounting draft notices, inductions, and funerals lent an immediacy to the war that was experienced in neighborhoods and communities throughout black America. The gnawing anger over the injustice of the war was magnified by disturbing stories in the African American press. For instance, the community of Wetumpka, Alabama, refused to bury fallen African American GIs in unsegregated cemeteries.[179] By 1966, African Americans' opposition to Vietnam exceeded that of whites, and this intensifying antiwar sentiment was attracting the attention of the NAACP and other African American organizations that had thus far opposed the antiwar movement but were also wary of straying too far from public opinion. The murder of Sammy Younge Jr., a veteran, had been the event that forced SNCC to cross the Rubicon and issue its antiwar statement. By 1966, Martin Luther King Jr. realized that he generated the greatest emotional response when he talked about the Vietnam War. The spiraling casualty rate in Vietnam, especially among blacks, was an important factor in his decision to oppose the war.

The crucible of Vietnam radicalized many African American soldiers, and scores of them returned home angry and committed to reshaping the civil rights movement into an antiwar movement.[180] African American soldiers developed a race consciousness that informed their view of Vietnam as an imperialistic war.[181] For example, Reginald "Malik" Edwards from rural Phoenix, Louisiana, had volunteered for the Marine Corps in 1963 because, he said, "I knew I couldn't go to college because my folks couldn't afford it." After being discharged for participating in a race riot at Quantico in 1970, Edwards joined the Black Panther Party. After serving almost seven years in the Marine Corps, Edwards was disillusioned. "I left one war and came back and got into another one. Most of the Panthers then were veterans. We figured if we had been in Vietnam fighting for our own country, which at that point wasn't serving us properly, it was only proper that we had to go out and fight for our own cause."[182]

Elmer "Geronimo" Pratt from Morgan City, Louisiana, returned from Vietnam with a chest full of medals, including two Purple Hearts. He immediately joined the Black Panther Party in Southern California, where he rose to a major leadership position.[183] Black Panther leader Bobby Seale observed that a lot of African American veterans joined the Black Panthers and noted, "They're angry because they fought for the man and black people are still being messed over."[184] This anger did not fully crystallize within the African American community until the late 1960s and early 1970s, but the travails of black soldiers made blacks in general more sympathetic to SNCC's view that Vietnam was a racist and imperialist war. As the carnage continued unabated in Vietnam, the experiences and treatment of black soldiers fueled African American opposition to the war. By 1966, the fate of these tens of thousands of black men complicated the civil rights movement's reaction to the war. With each passing month, the mounting casualties forced the civil rights movement, especially King, to choose sides. Over the weeks, months, and years, the scales tilted toward peace.

By the middle of 1966, the potent mixture of the Vietnam War and Black Power hampered cooperation between the predominantly white antiwar movement and the civil rights movement.[185] It is perhaps too simplistic to label the entire antiwar movement as racist, but SDS and many white New Leftists felt that they were the vanguard of social change in America, and they resented African American leadership in the antiwar movement.[186] For their part, African American civil rights leaders criticized the largely white antiwar movement for being oblivious to the concerns of African Americans. CORE's McKissick, for example, charged that antiwar activists found "it too easy to look thousands of miles away from home and with much indignation, see the extermination of the Vietnamese. On the other hand, they cannot see ten blocks away, where many Black People are Walking Dead—dead in mind and spirit, because of the lack of hope and lack of chance."[187]

Nevertheless, there were fitful attempts to broaden the antiwar movement by forging an alliance between the civil rights movement and the white peace activists on the issue of Vietnam.[188] In the fall of 1966 the University of California–Berkeley chapter of SDS invited Stokely Carmichael to speak at a conference on Black Power. Addressing "the white intellectual ghetto of the West," Carmichael called the "peace movement a failure because it hasn't gotten off the college campuses where everybody has a 2S and is not afraid of being drafted anyway," and he implored white Americans to resist the draft.[189] Carmichael electrified the Berkeley students by thundering against the war. He likened the plight of African Americans to the Vietnamese: "Any time a black man leaves the country where he can't vote to supposedly deliver the vote to somebody else, he's a black mercenary. Any time a black man leaves the country, gets shot in Vietnam on foreign ground, and returns home and you won't give him a burial place in his own homeland, he's a black mercenary."[190]

Throughout 1966, their revulsion against the war prompted SNCC and CORE representatives to march in antiwar rallies, cooperating with the coalitions headed by white organizations. One of these groups, the Fifth Avenue Vietnam Peace Parade Committee, held a large antiwar protest in Midtown Manhattan on August 6, 1966, to commemorate the bombing of Hiroshima. Susan Goodman, a reporter for the *Village Voice*, observed that the large number of African American antiwar demonstrators was quite a contrast to the "nearly lily-white crowd of 5,000 antiwar demonstrators" who had "paraded down Fifth Avenue the previous March." The participation of African American protesters did not mask the tension, as many of them carried "Black Power" placards. The difficulty of retaining a semblance of harmony was revealed when New York SNCC director Ivanhoe Donaldson erupted in anger when asked about SNCC's role in the antiwar movement: "We're not inside the peace movement. It's basically all-white. There's no way to relate to that."[191]

White paternalism, the appeal of Black Power, and African American rage over the racial subtext of the war combined to negate any possibility of a union between black civil rights leaders and the white New Left on the issue of Vietnam. Donaldson's tirade evidenced the inhospitable environment for interracial cooperation in the era of Black Power. The SDS newspaper *New Left Notes* applauded Black Power and shared SNCC's view that the Vietnam War was "a logical extension of racism abroad," but it wondered whether white peaceniks could relate to the violence inherent in SNCC's antiwar tirades and whether such violence would "undermine much of the moral basis of middle-class anti-war ferment."[192] SNCC's and CORE's expulsion of whites dramatized the problem. Even though thousands of white men had been drafted, Carmichael still spoke of the draft as nothing more than "white people sending black people to make war on yellow people in order to defend the land they stole from red people."[193]

Many whites who were committed to civil rights resented Black Power. James Peck, a scion of the Peck & Peck clothing company, was a particularly revered white figure in the civil rights movement. His first act of revolt occurred in 1933, when he escorted an African American woman to Harvard's freshman dance. He was an iconic veteran of the 1947 Journey of Reconciliation and was nearly beaten to death in 1961 during the Freedom Rides. Peck angrily denounced "Black Power" as a racist slogan after he was ousted from CORE in the summer of 1966.[194] Peck continued to be active in the antiwar movement and wrote a letter to Martin Luther King Jr., expressing his continued support and his admiration for King's fidelity to nonviolence and equality.[195] Like many longtime activists, Peck was distressed over the chaos and drift within the peace and freedom movements, and he was looking for a leader of maturity and stature to heal the rancor. Peck, along with many antiwar adherents in SNCC and CORE who had had their differences with King, now viewed him as an indispensable leader who could bridge the widening divide.

David Dellinger passionately disagreed with Peck's dour assessment and admired the young militants' moxie. However, he concurred with Peck's view that it was imperative to bring King into the antiwar movement. Dellinger had become obsessed with ending the war in Vietnam. In 1966 he argued that the peace movement "has an historic opportunity to move from its perpetually repeated beginnings to a new stage of historical relevance," and he urged a "close alliance with the black-power militants as a necessary prerequisite."[196] While his old colleagues Rustin and Peck excoriated Black Power as lacking "any real value for the civil rights movement," Dellinger was more sanguine.[197] He empathized with African Americans' need to slough off their reliance on the liberal establishment, and he admired the nationalists' fiery critiques of the war. He believed that the peace movement had to carve out its own base of power, and he worked with Carmichael to protest the case of the Fort Hood Three—a trio of soldiers, one of them African American, who refused to serve in Vietnam. James Johnson, the twenty-five-year-old African American, refused to serve in Vietnam for the following reasons: "In my case, the fact that I am a Negro makes the fact of U.S. involvement more acute. The Negro in Vietnam is being called upon to defend freedom that in many parts of this country does not exist for him."[198]

Despite the low morale afflicting the antiwar movement, Dellinger glimpsed a silver lining. After returning from a trip to North Vietnam in November 1966, he helped form the Spring Mobilization Committee to End the War in Vietnam (MOBE) and announced that two major rallies would be held on April 15, 1967—one in San Francisco and the other in New York.[199] A few weeks after MOBE's formation, Dellinger approached the Reverend James Bevel, a former SNCC worker and King confidant who was working to forge an alliance between peace and civil rights organizations, in the hope that Bevel could convince King to join the antiwar movement.[200] Dellinger was certainly not alone in believing that King, the putative leader of the civil rights movement and the most widely esteemed African American in the world, offered the best prospect of forging a coalition between the rudderless antiwar movement and the increasingly fractious civil rights movement.[201] While Dellinger and others in the New Left struggled to enlist King in the antiwar movement, many of King's closest supporters, such as Andrew Young, Stanley Levison, and Bayard Rustin, steadfastly opposed his involvement and cautioned him that an unbridled attack on American foreign policy could cost him the support of the federal government and mainstream America.

Rustin and King had been close ever since Rustin had sojourned to Montgomery during the early days of the bus boycott to give the then-unknown young minister a tutorial on Gandhian nonviolence. Now, more than a decade later, King was moving away from his mentor's pragmatism, caution, and commitment to coalition politics. It was agonizing for King to watch his country plunge into the abyss of war and siphon funds from antipoverty programs and the Great Society. Perhaps King's greatest frustration was that by the end of 1966, the number of American troops in Vietnam had risen to almost 400,000—more than 60,000 of them African American. He told a Mississippi audience, "I'm tired of violence. I'm tired of the war in Vietnam. I'm tired of selfishness. I'm tired of evil. I'm not going to use violence, no matter who says it."[202] Thus, there were reasons for Dellinger and others to be optimistic that King could be persuaded to break with the Johnson administration. In addition to being in accord with King's nonviolent philosophy, opposing the war in Vietnam offered the hope of gaining the support of embittered youths in the ghettos who were turning away from nonviolence, reinvigorating the African American freedom struggle, and uniting the antiwar and civil rights movements.

In the waning days of 1966, the emotionally drained King engaged in haunting meditations on the war. According to King's chief lieutenant, Andrew Young, James Bevel's psychotic ramblings about God telling him "we've got to stop" the war only added to King's consternation.[203] In spite of the transformations that had occurred over the past few years, the near-unanimous consensus among the American ruling class that the Vietnam War was necessary testified to the continuing domination of the Cold War zeitgeist. The corrosiveness of the war belied the enormous cost that King's public break from the Johnson administration would entail. The Democratic Party's defeat in the midterm election, which Johnson privately blamed on African Americans, had no doubt weakened the administration, but King realized that most Americans still held the antiwar movement in low esteem.[204] Besides, what U.S. president had done more for the cause of African American advancement than Lyndon Baines Johnson? The powerful NAACP, the mainstream African American press, and luminaries such as Ralph Bunche, A. Philip Randolph, Jackie Robinson, and Carl Rowan all revered Johnson. King's visceral hatred of war notwithstanding, these countervailing factors were too potent to be dismissed so cursorily. King mulled his options at the beginning of 1967 as he went to Jamaica for a well-deserved sabbatical to work on his next (and final) book, fittingly entitled *Where Do We Go from Here: Chaos or Community?*[205]

5

Dr. King's Painful Dilemma

I don't really have the strength to fight this issue [of Vietnam] and keep
my civil rights fight going.
                    —Martin Luther King Jr., September 15, 1965

On the evening of Monday, March 15, 1965, Martin Luther King Jr. was
emotionally and physically drained. He huddled with a few close aides
in front of a small black-and-white television in a living room in Selma,
Alabama, anxiously awaiting President Johnson's address to Congress on
the issue of civil rights. For the past two months, the civil rights movement had made a stand for voting rights in Selma, a former slave market
in the heart of the Black Belt. Although African Americans made up 57
percent of Selma's population, less than 1 percent were eligible to vote.[1] It
had been a vicious campaign. Southern vigilantes had recently murdered
James Reeb, a white Unitarian minister, and Jimmie Lee Jackson, a young
African American. More murders would follow. Throughout the ordeal,
King had maintained his usual whirlwind schedule—what Andrew Young
called King's "war on sleep."[2] Along with nearly 3,500 other civil rights
workers, including 700 teenagers, King had been jailed for attempting to
register to vote. In Dallas County, Sheriff Jim Clark and his "posse" of
white citizens patrolled the streets of Selma, determined to control African
Americans by sheer physical intimidation (including the use of electric
cattle prods).[3] Earlier, King had remarked, "We'll have some funerals to
deal with in the Black Belt of Alabama and we won't just be burying segregation, we'll be burying some of us."[4] King's closest friend Ralph Abernathy recalled, "Martin had been receiving an excessive number of death
threats as a result of the Selma campaign, perhaps more than any other
time in his career."[5]

Only eight days earlier, on March 7, the violence had climaxed when Alabama state troopers clubbed, trampled, and tear-gassed approximately 500 unarmed protesters who had just begun a highly publicized march to Montgomery to present a petition of grievances to Governor George Wallace. Images of helmeted officers clubbing demonstrators who were kneeling in prayer, shrouded in an eerie fog of tear gas, were captured by television cameras and shown on the evening news, sparking a national and international furor. It soon became known as "Bloody Sunday." To make matters worse, the long-standing friction between SNCC and King resurfaced. SNCC had spent months organizing a grassroots movement, but King had just come to Selma and seized the spotlight. SNCC excoriated him for refusing to disobey a federal court injunction forbidding the march. Upon learning that King had made a deal with federal officials not to march, a livid James Forman denounced King's "trickery" and angrily declared that "SNCC would no longer work with the SCLC."[6]

The bloodbath in Selma outraged Lyndon Johnson, who that same weekend made the critical decision to dispatch the first battalion of ground troops to South Vietnam to protect the U.S. air base at Da Nang. After Bloody Sunday, the ongoing saga in Selma seized the president's attention, and he interrupted a number of sensitive meetings on the situation in Vietnam to deal with the brewing crisis in Alabama.[7] More than a thousand civil rights demonstrators flocked to the White House, denouncing Johnson's failure to send troops to quell the police riot in Selma. They carried placards that said, "LBJ, just you wait . . . see what happens in '68."[8] After a particularly contentious meeting with Governor Wallace, the president requested permission to address a joint session of Congress to present a voting rights bill—the first time in nineteen years that a president had addressed Congress on a domestic matter.[9] The president had been apprehensive and moody since his decision to send ground troops to Vietnam, but the First Lady noted that his mood brightened at the prospect of delivering a major speech on civil rights.[10] As Johnson walked into the chamber to thunderous applause, King nervously pulled his armchair closer to the TV in the living room of Selma dentist James Jackson, who had opened his home to King during the tumultuous weeks of the voting rights campaign. The tension was palpable as Johnson began his address.

Johnson's prime-time speech, delivered live to more than 70 million viewers, was one of the greatest presidential addresses in American history, and it lifted King from his doldrums. Sitting next to King, SNCC chairman John Lewis, recovering from a serious head wound he had sustained on Bloody Sunday, later enthused that it was "not only the finest speech of his career, but probably the strongest speech any American president has ever made on the subject of civil rights."[11] In his slow, measured southern accent, the president began on a powerful note: "At times, history and fate meet at a single time in a single place to shape a turning point in man's unending search for freedom. So it was at Lexington and Concord. So it was a century ago at Appomattox. So it was last week in Selma, Alabama." Having established the historical significance of Selma in the long struggle for freedom, Johnson got down to the issue of voting rights. Never before had an American president pressed the cause of equality for African Americans with such moral fervor. After a hushed silence, he continued:

> But rarely in any time does an issue lay bare the secret heart of America itself. Rarely are we met with a challenge, not to growth or abundance, or our welfare or our security, but rather to the values and the purposes and the meaning of our beloved nation. The issue of equal rights for American Negroes is such an issue. And should we defeat every enemy, and should we double our wealth and conquer the stars, and still be unequal to this issue, then we will have failed as a people and as a nation. For, with a country as with a person, "What is a man profited if he shall gain the world, and lose his own soul." There is no Negro problem. There is no Southern problem. There is no Northern problem. There is only an American problem.

Johnson then introduced a comprehensive bill "designed to eliminate illegal barriers to the right to vote." He briefly paused and claimed, "Their cause must be our cause, too." After placing his hands on the lectern, he slowly intoned, "Because it is not just Negroes, but really it's all of us, who must overcome the crippling legacy of bigotry and injustice." In perhaps the most poignant moment of the speech, he raised his arms over his head, slowly and emphatically uttering the rallying cry of the civil rights movement, "And—we shall overcome."[12] While *New York Times* columnist Tom Wicker noted that the president's words elicited an array of reactions from Congress and official Washington, Lewis remembered that King wiped away a tear following Johnson's invocation of the anthem of the civil rights movement. This was the first and only time King's closest associates ever saw him cry.[13]

In the days following the president's historic speech, African Americans were overcome with euphoria. The *New York Amsterdam News* praised the speech as "the most forceful and eloquent approach to civil rights ever shown by a chief executive of the United States" with respect to the "Negro's 300 year struggle for first class citizenship." It extolled President Johnson as "one of the greatest humanitarians of his time" and "one of our greatest presidents."[14] The day after the speech, King sent the following telegram to Johnson: "Your speech to the Joint Session of Congress last night was the most moving, eloquent, and passionate plea for human rights ever made by any President of the Nation. You evidenced amazing understanding of the depth and dimensions of the problems we face in our struggle. Your tone was sincere throughout and your persuasive power was never more forceful. We are ready to join with you in a quick passage of the voting bill. Please know that we are deeply encouraged by your support and leadership."[15] The effusive praise for the president's address was not confined to African Americans. The Democratic National Committee circulated excerpts from editorials and columns from across the country hailing the speech. Even the conservative *Houston Post* lauded Johnson for making "the case for Federal legislative action to ensure all American citizens the right to vote," adding that it could not have "been stated more forcefully and more fervently."[16] Forman, who had already turned against the Vietnam War and had never forgiven the president for the "treachery" in Atlantic City, quipped that Johnson's reference to "We Shall Overcome" was a "tinkling empty symbol" that "ruined a good song."[17]

Forman's ire could not dispel the buoyant mood of civil rights activists and proponents of racial reform in the weeks following the March 15 speech. A Gallup poll conducted from March 18 to 23 indicated that 76 percent of Americans, including 49 percent of southerners, favored the voting rights bill.[18] The spring and summer of 1965 represented the pinnacle of the civil rights movement as President Johnson mobilized congressional and public support behind the pending legislation. Despite the violence, Bloody Sunday in Selma had galvanized public opinion and the federal government behind the cause of civil rights.

President Johnson delivered another seminal address at Howard University on June 4, reaching new heights of political courage by proposing steps to remedy racism: "Civil rights laws are not an end. It is not even the beginning of the end. But it is, perhaps, the end of the beginning. That beginning is freedom; and the barriers to that freedom are tumbling down."[19] Three days later, King sent another telegram to the White House:

"Please accept my belated thanks for your magnificent speech at the Howard University commencement. Never before has a president articulated the depths and dimensions of the problems of racial injustice more eloquently and profoundly. The whole speech evinced amazing sensitivity to the difficult problems that Negro Americans face in the stride toward freedom. It is my hope that all Americans will capture the spirit of this great statement."[20]

King's fulsome praise belied the fact that the African American preacher from Georgia and the white politician from Texas had a strained working relationship that was fraught with ambiguity.[21] Harry McPherson, a close White House adviser who attended meetings between the two, noted that Johnson was much closer to Roy Wilkins of the NAACP and Whitney Young of the Urban League; the president was suspicious of King because he "was out there on the streets."[22] Louis Martin, a prominent African American journalist and politician who served as the president's emissary to African Americans, recalled that Johnson thought King "was bullheaded and arrogant in the fact that he did not respond to his blandishments." For his part, King initially gave the president the benefit of the doubt but eventually concluded that "LBJ was selling soap oil."[23] The goodwill between King and Johnson, which crested in mid-1965, proved to be short-lived in the wake of the president's subsequent obsession with the Vietnam War. King's initial criticisms of the war in the summer of 1965 provoked an irate Johnson to complain to African American journalist Carl Rowan, head of the U.S. Information Agency, that the preacher was "making me look like a fool. He's got a goddam nest of spies around him."[24]

By the summer of 1965, King's conflicted response to the Vietnam War had blemished his productive relationship with President Johnson. The Vietnam War exacted an enormous psychic toll on King. Given that nonviolence was the touchstone of his philosophy, he harbored grave reservations about the conflict in Southeast Asia. Racism, poverty, and hatred were festering amid unparalleled plenty at home, and King feared that the war would undermine Johnson's ambitious domestic agenda. An astute student of history, King had traveled throughout Africa and India in the late 1950s, giving him with a profound awareness of the anticolonial impulses of the Vietcong and other insurgents fighting against white imperial dominion in the Third World.[25] To King, the convergence of anticolonialism in Asia and Africa and the black freedom struggle in the United States was not fortuitous; both represented an assault on white supremacy.

Moreover, he scoffed at the domino theory and the simplistic notion of a monolithic communist conspiracy, and he found the idea that communists posed a threat to America preposterous. Throughout the summer and fall of 1965, King voiced his dissent over the escalating conflict in Vietnam, which earned him the opprobrium of the White House and withering criticism from white and African American liberals alike. Accustomed to criticism from segregationists, King was staggered by the ferocity of these attacks from the White House and its Cold War liberal allies. The unbearable pressure of simultaneously leading the antiwar movement and taking the civil rights movement to a new stage of protest in the North impelled King to mute his opposition to the Vietnam War. Only months after passage of the Voting Rights Act, King was unwilling to risk a complete break with the president over Vietnam, but their relationship soured. By the end of 1965, however, the relationship between King and Johnson became another casualty of the war in Vietnam.

King's Nonviolent Philosophy and Early Views of the Cold War

In many respects, the myths surrounding King in the years after his assassination have obscured the historical reality of his remarkably short and exceptional life.[26] The apotheosis of King to national sainthood has created a sanitized version of him. These misconceptions have led many contemporary observers to gloss over King's more radical critiques of American capitalism and the Vietnam War.[27] King's tortured response to the Vietnam War reflected his complexity as he engaged in an inner struggle between pragmatism and idealism. In the end, his unflinching denunciation of the Vietnam War, capitalism, violence, and poverty was a culmination of his decade-long dissent against the folly and militarism inherent in American Cold War policy, which found its ultimate expression in the Vietnam War.

A prime example of this myopic view of King is the proclivity to perceive his notion of nonviolence in an overly static fashion. This is understandable in view of his eminence as America's principal exponent of nonviolence in the twentieth century. Unlike Bayard Rustin and David Dellinger, who were conscientious objectors during World War II, and Coretta Scott King, whose association with the peace movement went back to her student days at Antioch College, King had not always been a strict pacifist. As a nineteen-year-old student at Crozer Theological Seminary in Chester, Pennsylvania, King imbibed the works of eminent theologian Reinhold Niebuhr, whom King described as a prime influence on his life.[28] The publication of Niebuhr's *Moral Man and Immoral Society* in 1932 shocked the theological establishment with its heretical view that the seemingly inexorable march of reason and progress was poorly equipped to eradicate social ills. Niebuhr argued that human nature was such that individuals could respond to reason, but large social groups such as nations, corporations, and labor unions would always be selfish. As such, the creed of the Social Gospel was too chaste to combat the powerful forces of evil, and Niebuhr contended that violence was sometimes an appropriate means of resisting oppression. While Niebuhr praised Gandhi and yearned for an American Gandhi to lead African Americans out of the wilderness, he argued that Gandhi's nonresistance was a form of "physical coercion" because it entered "the field of social and physical relations" and thereby imposed "physical restraints upon the desires and activities of others."[29] In the early 1950s the young King "devoured Niebuhr almost uncritically, swallowing all of his 'social ethics.'"[30] Having repudiated pacifism after Hitler's rise to power, Niebuhr's apostasy now vindicated him, and by the time King fell under his spell, Niebuhr had become a Cold War liberal and espoused containment of the Soviet Union. Even after King embraced nonviolence, Niebuhr's pessimistic view of human nature would continue to temper King's outlook, making him realize that too many pacifists had an "unwarranted optimism concerning man and leaned unconsciously toward self-righteousness."[31]

When the Montgomery bus boycott vaulted the twenty-six-year-old King to fame in December 1955, he received the first of a harrowing series of death threats that would plague him throughout his life. These initial attempts to intimidate him had a transformative impact on King's evolving leadership. He began his career as a reluctant leader from a privileged background, and the flurry of threatening phone calls to his home and office deepened his faith and fortified his spirit during the early days of the boycott.[32] On January 30, 1956, segregationists bombed King's house in retaliation for his leadership in the Montgomery bus boycott. When Bayard Rustin traveled to Montgomery in February 1956, he was shocked to find that King had armed guards and loaded firearms in his home.[33] Rustin was disappointed when King told him that he was doing his best to practice nonviolence under these difficult circumstances, but he did not adhere to the precepts of pacifism espoused by Rustin's mentor A. J. Muste because "no just society could exist without at least a police power."[34]

Under Rustin's tutelage, King's commitment to nonviolence deepened.

A few months later, he divested himself of the security detail and the guns. Yet there was always a pragmatic element to King's nonviolence: he realized that African Americans were far outnumbered by whites and that violence would only invite white repression. In his interpretation of Gandhian philosophy, King drew a distinction between "aggressive violence" and "defensive violence." According to Andrew Young, King approved of a young African American woman who fired on Ku Klux Klan members who were about to break into her home but disapproved of violence by protesters during a demonstration and condemned "any retaliatory violence."[35]

King's receptivity to Niebuhr's dark view of human nature did not, however, extend to unquestioned fidelity to Niebuhr's support for the United States' aggressive Cold War policy against the Soviet Union. By the late 1950s, King was moving away from Niebuhr's realpolitik and losing patience with Cold War liberalism. On the cusp of victory in Montgomery, King declared, "The struggle of the [American] Negro was also part of an international struggle of non-white people to throw off the colonialism."[36] King's travels to Africa and Asia in the late 1950s spurred his interest in decolonization in the developing world. In March 1957 King and his wife traveled to Africa to attend Ghana's independence ceremony and visited with Prime Minister Kwame Nkrumah.[37] Nkrumah, who had been jailed repeatedly by the British, was the embodiment of the Gandhian struggle.[38] King's trip to Africa and his talks with Nkrumah made a profound impression and caused King to remark, "There is no basic difference between colonialism and racial segregation."[39] On the way home from Ghana, King stopped in London for a few days, where he spent an afternoon talking with West Indian anticolonial writer C. L. R. James, who had been expelled from the United States in 1953.[40] James likened King's nonviolent campaign in Montgomery to Nkrumah's independence struggle in Ghana.[41] Two years later the Kings went to India, where they encountered the problems of massive poverty and became more acquainted with the notion of Third World nonalignment, which had come to fruition at the Bandung Conference in 1955. The Cold War, which viewed the developing world as a pawn in the "irrepressible" rivalry between the two superpowers, struck King as arrogant, racist, and blind to historical forces and native cultures. His questioning of the Cold War was rooted not in pacifism but in his belief that it had a corrosive impact on national liberation movements, which policy makers conflated with communist aggression. This realization would inform his view of the Vietnam War as essentially a civil war for national liberation and not a fight for world supremacy against the monolith of communism.

During the early 1960s, and on more than one occasion, America's obsessive preoccupation with the purported communist menace rankled King. Although he was too preoccupied with the civil rights struggle in the South to be involved with the Fair Play for Cuba Committee, the Kennedy administration's botched invasion of the Bay of Pigs incensed King, and his high hopes for the new administration quickly turned into frustration over its single-minded obsession with the Cold War and its lukewarm support for civil rights. Writing to a supporter shortly after the Bay of Pigs, King angrily noted that the United States did not comprehend "the meaning of the revolution taking place in the world . . . against colonialism, reactionary dictatorship, and systems of exploitation." He lamented that unless America quickly revived its revolutionary heritage, it would become "a second class power" lacking any internationally respected "moral voice."[42] King believed that, in its determination to overthrow Fidel Castro, the United States was swimming against the tide of progress.[43] The arms race, which had brought the world to the brink of nuclear Armageddon during the Cuban Missile Crisis, was another source of consternation to King. As early as the spring of 1958, King had stated, "The development and use of nuclear weapons should be banned."[44]

For King, American support of apartheid and the racist regimes in South Africa and Rhodesia epitomized the hypocrisy and racism of U.S. Cold War policy. A few months after King expressed his disgust at the Kennedy administration's hawkish policy toward Cuba, he discussed the parallels between the American South and black Africa at a forum convened by the American Negro Leadership Conference on Africa. In both cases, he argued, there existed a similar set "of complex politico-economic forces," and the Kennedy administration had "done no better when faced with the choice between advantageous economic aid and military alliance, versus the establishment of racial and political justice" in South Africa, than it had in dealing with the problems in the South.[45] Unlike the more provocative and controversial Malcolm X, King's status as the titular head of the movement made him more circumspect when speaking out against Cold War policy. Much to the dismay of King's friends in the peace movement, these restraints would influence King's early reaction to the escalation of the war in Vietnam.

King and the Americanization of the Vietnam War

The stirrings of war in Vietnam were more remote to King and the SCLC than they were to SNCC and its members, whose connections with the

New Left and collective disillusionment following Freedom Summer had largely destroyed their faith in the Johnson administration and the American political process. Furthermore, the draft had personally impacted many young SNCC activists, who were intimately acquainted with many young black men who had served and even lost their lives in Vietnam. By contrast, Martin Luther King Jr. traveled in more rarefied circles than the younger, more ideologically oriented SNCC. His role in attempting to persuade the MFDP to accept the compromise in Atlantic City evinced his more pragmatic approach. On the whole, and particularly prior to passage of the Voting Rights Act, King tempered his disapproval of U.S. Cold War policies to avoid losing support for the civil rights struggle. The initiation of Operation Rolling Thunder and the broadening of America's involvement in Vietnam coincided with the most amicable period in the uneasy and tortuous relationship between King and President Johnson. The stream of reports from FBI director J. Edgar Hoover on King's ostensible ties with communists notwithstanding, King and Johnson had forged a fruitful alliance to expedite passage of the Civil Rights Act on July 2, 1964.

On February 9, 1965, only days after his release from the Selma jail, King flew to Washington, D.C., for a private meeting with the president and other federal officials. King praised the meeting as "successful" and touted Johnson's "deep commitment to obtaining the right to vote for all Americans."[46] Although the relationship between Johnson and King was never personally close (King had a warmer rapport with Kennedy), King was heartened by Johnson's earnest stance toward civil rights—a refreshing change from the Kennedy administration's more cautious approach. For the time being, King was grateful to have a partner who was willing to expend political capital for the cause of civil rights.

Back in Selma, the first reports of the broadening war in Southeast Asia managed to catch King's attention. On March 2, 1965, King flew back to Washington to deliver the principal speech at the ninety-eighth anniversary of the founding of the predominantly African American Howard University. The assassination of Malcolm X only nine days earlier heightened security precautions. Speaking before a heavily guarded capacity crowd of nearly 2,000 students and faculty, King said, "Love for all mankind can overcome the 'towering evils' of racial injustice, poverty, and war." Following the speech, King made his first public statement on Vietnam, in response to reports of the initiation of U.S. air strikes on North Vietnam. He told reporters that his belief in nonviolence convinced him that the United States must negotiate with the other participants to end the war.

While he acknowledged the president's difficult predicament, King none-theless bluntly stated, "The war in Vietnam is accomplishing nothing."[47]

The following day, King returned to Selma and delivered a eulogy for Jimmie Lee Jackson, a twenty-six-year-old black pulpwood worker who had been shot in the stomach by an Alabama state trooper in the nearby town of Marion. Charles Fager, a white civil rights activist from Kansas who had joined the SCLC, was among the many mourners who braved a rainstorm to attend Jackson's funeral. Fager recalled that King enumerated a litany of reasons for Jackson's death, including the contention that he had been "murdered by the timidity of a Federal Government that is will-ing to spend millions of dollars a day to defend freedom in Vietnam but cannot protect the rights of citizens at home."[48]

Events in Selma did not block early reports of increased hostilities in Vietnam. The day after Bloody Sunday, for instance, SCLC member and future antiwar leader James Bevel denounced the president for overreact-ing in Vietnam "and underreacting in Selma," where there were "two mil-lion white savages here in Alabama."[49] For the time being, however, in the minds of King and the SCLC, the disturbing rumbles in distant Vietnam were muted by the ongoing travails of the campaign in Selma and the quest for voting rights.

King's early misgivings about Vietnam raised eyebrows at the White House, which was especially sensitive to domestic criticism of its foreign policy. In FBI director Hoover, who waged a personal vendetta against King, the civil rights movement had a powerful nemesis. Hoover had long regarded the African American struggle for civil rights as a communist-inspired plot to destabilize American society, and he hewed to old racial stereotypes.[50] For example, he told a group of newspaper publishers in 1965 that "colored people are quite ignorant, mostly uneducated and I doubt they would seek an education if they had an opportunity."[51] For several years, Hoover had been sending reports to the White House, the Department of Justice, and the State Department accusing King of con-sorting with communists.[52] Hoover's antipathy to King intensified after the March on Washington, which convinced the FBI director that the civil rights movement was gaining momentum and he would have to destroy it.[53] King's condemnation of the Bureau's laxity in investigating vio-lence against civil rights workers and his characterization of FBI agents as comfortable with the mores of the segregated South incensed Hoover. According to former associate William C. Sullivan, "Hoover was jeal-ous of King's national prominence and the international awards that were offered him."[54] Livid over King's receipt of the Nobel Peace Prize, Hoover famously told a group of women reporters that King was "the most notorious liar in America."[55]

By early 1965, Hoover's campaign to destroy King was becoming more intense and more personal, and the FBI director's obsession with King's sex life reflected the racist stereotype of the sexual prowess of black males and the perils posed to white society. For the remaining days of his life, King was continuously under FBI surveillance. Any expressions of opposition to Johnson's war only gave Hoover more ammunition in his vendetta against King and the civil rights movement. For instance, in preparation for a meeting with King in early March 1965, Hoover sent a report to White House assistant Marvin Watson, which was passed on to the president, detailing a wiretapped conversation between two King advisers in which one said, "It is a mockery to talk about freedom in South Vietnam when the one man who is defending [freedom] in Selma is in jeopardy."[56] At the time, King was not as preoccupied with the war as were his younger colleagues in SNCC, many of whom were becoming active in the incipient antiwar movement. He was focused on working with President Johnson in support of voting rights legislation, but Hoover was ready to exploit any negative comment about the Vietnam War. Hoover's war against King sullied King's relationship with Johnson. But according to historian and special consultant to the president Eric Goldman, "Johnson was no great admirer of Martin Luther King and opposed the whole program of mass demonstrations."[57] Johnson, the consummate politician, distrusted King's ability to speak directly to the American people.

King's fixation on the right to vote did not mitigate his alarm over the turn of events in Vietnam. Indeed, the expanding conflict disquieted King, and he expressed his dismay over the apparent willingness of world powers to escalate hostilities. A few days after the first major antiwar rally in Washington, D.C., King arrived in Boston on April 17, 1965, for the first mass civil rights demonstration in the North.[58] In response to a shouted question from a reporter about the shift of energy in the New Left from civil rights to peace issues, King bluntly claimed, "I have no objection to civil rights leaders speaking against war as against segregation."[59] He added, "One cannot just be concerned with civil rights. . . . It is very nice to drink milk at an unsegregated lunch counter—but not when there's Strontium 90 in it." This offhanded remark generated a headline from the *New York Herald Tribune* and a flood of telegrams from peace leaders such as Dr. Benjamin Spock and A. J. Muste, urging King to join the burgeoning antiwar movement.[60] Unwilling to brook any dissent against his policy in Vietnam, these remarks reinforced President Johnson's suspicions of King.

King's most forceful statement against the war prior to passage of the Voting Rights Act in August occurred at an SCLC rally at Virginia State College on July 2, when he called for the end of violence in Vietnam and supported holding "peace rallies just like we have freedom rallies."[61] A few days later, King explained to an interviewer, "I'm much more than a civil rights leader."[62] These statements garnered widespread press coverage and prompted a concerned president to ask Hoover to prepare a classified paper on the extent of King's involvement in the peace issue.[63] Hoover was only too happy to oblige, realizing that any involvement by King or his associates in the antiwar movement would further the FBI's director's objective of destroying King.

The midsummer of 1965 was a particularly wrenching time for President Johnson as he anguished over the decision to send thousands of ground troops to Vietnam. According to Richard Goodwin, the president's chief speechwriter, the cumulative stress of Vietnam and attacks on his foreign policy were causing him to exhibit "paranoid behavior."[64] Bill Moyers, another longtime Johnson aide, shared Goodwin's concerns. Goodwin recalled the president saying on July 5 (three days after King's statement), "You know, Dick, the communists are taking over the country."[65] Years later, Moyers told the Church Committee, "Johnson, as everybody knows bordered on paranoia about his enemies."[66] While it is difficult to substantiate recollections of conversation that occurred decades ago, *New York Times* columnist Tom Wicker corroborated Goodwin's observations in mid-July, writing, "The news out of Washington these days is that Mr. Johnson is irascible, moody, high-handed, peeved at his critics, and generally hard to deal with."[67] It was in this tense atmosphere that Hoover fed the overwrought president reports of King's involvement in antiwar and other "communist" activity.

On July 7, an apprehensive King initiated his first telephone call to the president in an attempt to defuse the situation. At the outset, King reassured Johnson that he had only been speaking generally as "a minister of the gospel," and he conceded that his call for "a unilateral withdrawal was unreasonable." A chastened King informed the president that the press had taken his statements out of context. In response, Johnson politely said he was aware of King's recent criticisms, but instead of challenging them, LBJ indulged in a guilt-ridden confession about the unbearable pressures from the Republicans. He told King he hoped to find a resolution to the conflict and welcomed an opportunity to speak with King about it. "If I pulled out," the president said, "I think our commitments would be no good anymore . . . and God knows what we would have in other places in the world." At the end of the conversation, King reiterated his gratitude for everything the president was doing on behalf of African Americans.[68] Thus, during the height of the legislative battle to pass the voting rights bill, the two leaders awkwardly danced around the Vietnam issue in the interest of maintaining their alliance. While the war was exploding onto the national consciousness, King was loath to alienate the president at a time when Johnson was supporting a flurry of civil rights legislation and liberalism was at its apogee. In the first half of 1965, Johnson's secretiveness on Vietnam tended to obfuscate his foreign policy objectives. As a result, King, like most Americans, could not envision the calamity that lay ahead.

In spite of Hoover's relentless campaign to destroy King and King's intermittent grumblings over the president's Vietnam policy, the relationship between King and Johnson, though never intimate, was most fruitful in the months leading up to the signing of the Voting Rights Act on August 6, 1965. Johnson perceived the historic opportunity to bestow the full rights of citizenship on African Americans as the cornerstone of his legacy. The president's soaring rhetoric that had moved King in Selma was equaled by his willingness to expend political capital to get the legislation passed. When Johnson signed the Voting Rights Act in a solemn ceremony, King stood alongside the president and extolled the new law as going "a long way toward removing all obstacles in the right to vote."[69] Despite his concerns about the war, King refused to endorse the antiwar demonstration led by David Dellinger, Staughton Lynd, and Robert Parris in nearby Lafayette Park. Passage of this landmark legislation marked a pivotal accomplishment that could not be dimmed by a distant war that, for the moment, enjoyed the overwhelming support of the American public. King exulted in the triumph of the Voting Rights Act, but his celebration was short-lived.

Fall 1965: It Is Time for a "Cease-Fire"

According to King confidant Vincent Harding, King could have retired from the movement after August 6, 1965, secure in the knowledge that his efforts had been indispensable in dismantling Jim Crow in the South.[70]

More than any other civil rights figure, King had been instrumental in the two crowning legislative achievements of the 1960s: the Civil Rights Act of 1964 and the Voting Rights Act of 1965. His eloquence, integrity, and grace had made the civil rights movement respectable in the eyes of the majority of white Americans, too many of whom had been oblivious to the plight of African Americans for generations. It would have been understandable if the thirty-six-year-old King had stepped back from the constant pressures of heading the movement and taken a quiet academic job teaching theology that would have allowed him to devote more time to his growing family. But for King, retirement was not possible. Although the Voting Rights Act may have ended de jure segregation in the South, King could not rest as long as racism, poverty, and economic injustice continued in the North and militarism and war raged unchecked. So an exhausted King returned home to Atlanta to contemplate his next move. Many Americans agreed with James Bevel's observation that by signing the Voting Rights Act, the president had signed the civil rights movement out of existence.[71] In the days and months ahead, King, the SCLC, and the entire civil rights movement would grapple with the question of what their next strategy would be in the ongoing assault on racial discrimination.

In August 1965 the SCLC gathered in Birmingham, Alabama, for its annual convention. Fresh from their recent victories in the South, Andrew Young recalled, "We really didn't know what our direction should be after Selma."[72] King had recently undertaken a tour of the North, but there was no program in place. Despite the strenuous objections of two of his closest colleagues, Young and Bayard Rustin, King had already decided to take the movement North and tackle the more intractable problems of racism in housing, education, and employment. Johnson's July 28 announcement that he was increasing the number of troops in Vietnam from 75,000 to 125,000 was another source of vexation.[73] In addition, the disturbing news of the Watts uprising coincided with the SCLC's Birmingham convention, blunting the participants' celebratory mood over the Voting Rights Act. James Bevel was in no mood to bask in the movement's accomplishments, even though he and his wife, Diane Nash Bevel, were being award the SCLC Freedom Medal. An angry Bevel suggested that an international peace army be sent into Vietnam and proclaimed the need for a "nonviolent movement of the world."[74]

After pinning the medals on the Bevels, King, in his most visceral and personal comment on the war to date, proclaimed his repugnance for the conflict in Vietnam: "Few events in my lifetime have stirred my conscience and pained my heart as much as the present conflict, which is raging in Vietnam. The day-by-day reports of villages destroyed and people left homeless raise burdensome questions within my conscience." Instead of blaming the Johnson administration or the people of Vietnam, the "real enemy," King proclaimed, was "war" itself, which has trapped "people on both sides" in "its inexorable destruction." As a minister of the gospel, he prayed "for the earliest possible peace for the tormented peoples of Vietnam" and confessed that his prayers were made "more fervent by the fearful recognition that the conflict in Vietnam is pregnant with the risk of an ever-widening war that may imperil the existence of whole continents." At the end of his statement, King called for negotiations to end the hostilities:

> Therefore, I would like to take this opportunity to make an urgent plea for all sides to bring their grievances to the conference table. In order to do this, both sides must go all out to demonstrate their desire for good faith negotiations, and the United States should effect a new diplomatic machinery without giving the impression of appeasement and which would in no way mitigate its national aims in seriously considering bringing to a halt the bombings in North Vietnam.
>
> On the other hand, Ho Chi Minh and Chou En-Lai must express unequivocally their desire to alter their position in demanding the unilateral withdrawal of American forces from South Viet Nam.[75]

Later that evening, King addressed a rally at the Civic Auditorium in Birmingham and announced his intention to send letters to the leaders of all the governments embroiled in the conflict, urging them to end the war. But he made "it clear that President Johnson has demonstrated a greater desire to negotiate than the Hanoi and Peking governments." His criticism of the president was confined to Johnson's "failure to express readiness to talk peace with the Vietcong." King also said that although he had been advised to leave the war to experts, he was "not going to follow this advice."[76] His intention to appeal directly to Ho Chi Minh, President Johnson, the Vietcong, and the Saigon government encouraged antiwar activists to believe that King might join their movement.[77] Their hopes were raised when the SCLC passed a resolution authorizing King to become more involved in international affairs because he was a Nobel Prize winner, even though the SCLC conceded that "our resources are not sufficient to assume the burden of two major issues in our society."[78]

In view of King's entry into the debate on Vietnam, the *New York Times* requested that he answer twelve questions about the war.[79] On August 13, FBI wiretaps recorded a conversation in which King sought Stanley Levison's assistance in preparing the replies. At this point, King told Levison, his closest white confidant, he had no specific plans for mediating the conflict, but he stressed his commitment to devising a strategy to facilitate its resolution. He stopped short of blaming either party for the violence and noted that he was encouraged by Johnson's restraint, but he thought both sides were too willing to flex their military muscle.[80] The contents of the conversation were relayed to the White House. At the conclusion of the SCLC convention, King told reporters that he did not envision "the development of a peace army right now."[81]

The furor over King's appeal to halt the war was temporarily eclipsed by the disturbing reports of the Watts uprising in Los Angeles. Beginning only days after the president signed the Voting Rights Act, the detonation in Watts sent tremors throughout the political landscape and sharpened divisions between King and the White House. King and Rustin flew to Los Angeles and toured the charred remains of the ghetto, where they decried the socioeconomic conditions that had fueled the upheaval. King was shaken by Watts and was profoundly disturbed when throngs of disaffected African American youths assailed his philosophy of nonviolence and jeered him for being out of touch with the reality of life in the ghetto.[82] Cries of "Burn, baby burn!" filled the scorched streets of Watts. The *Los Angeles Times* likened Watts to the "holocaust of rubble" that was Berlin "after allied forces finished their demolition" at the end of World War II.[83] The miserable conditions in South-Central Los Angeles, including rampant unemployment, brutality by a nearly all-white police force, and grinding poverty, led to a hopelessness that would hasten the appeal of Black Power. King lamented local white officials' obliviousness to the desperate plight of the ghetto dwellers in Watts and their tendency to blame African American inferiority, communists, or even the civil rights movement for the destruction. Watts was a searing event for King, and Young recalled that soon after, the SCLC began to seriously consider "the possibility of undertaking a major campaign in Chicago."[84] A month later, King told the United Auto Workers' District 65 in New York that the explosion in Watts mandated "a shift in the focus of [the] struggle [that] is not going to abate until root causes are treated."[85]

The burning, looting, and deaths in Watts paralyzed Lyndon Johnson, who was baffled by the timing of the most destructive urban conflagration in U.S. history, coming only days after his historic legislative victory.

Joseph Califano, one of president's top aides, recalled that a distraught Johnson withdrew "into the bosom of his family and intimate friends" at his Texas ranch and did not return Califano's numerous phone calls—"the only time in the years I worked for Lyndon Johnson that this occurred."[86] Roger Wilkins, thirty-three-year-old nephew of NAACP president Roy Wilkins, was serving in the Justice Department and went to Los Angeles with Ramsey Clark to help quell the disorder. He recalled that "Watts hit Washington like a thunderstorm."[87] Historian Allen Matusow did not exaggerate when he asserted, "No man in America was more stunned by Watts than the President himself."[88] In the wake of Johnson's highly public embrace of civil rights, he had become closely associated with African Americans, and the president feared that the violence in Watts would provoke a white backlash that, along with Vietnam, would imperil his beloved Great Society. The uprising provided a political opening for his Republican opponents, who were still reeling from their landslide defeat in 1964. House Minority Leader Gerald R. Ford and other top Republicans echoed former president Dwight Eisenhower's views of the "disgraceful riots."[89] Californian Jack Shell, who had lost the Republican gubernatorial nomination to Richard Nixon in 1962, was planning another run against incumbent Edmund Brown in 1966; Shell announced that Watts had "amazing political implications" and said the likelihood of his candidacy was "far weighted on the affirmative side."[90] Other Republicans hoped that Watts would prompt Ronald Reagan, whose speeches on behalf of Barry Goldwater had electrified conservatives, to run for governor. Johnson perceived Watts as a personal rebuke, and he likened the African American rioters to the Ku Klux Klan, declaring that they were both "lawbreakers, destroyers of constitutional rights and liberties."[91] Enraged over the rioters and the ungrateful "peaceniks" protesting his war, the president subsequently muted his public commitment to African Americans to forestall a white backlash.

The Watts insurrection complicated the already strained relationship between Johnson and King.[92] It was against this tense backdrop that King called the president from the Los Angeles airport on August 20, 1965, to report on the crisis in Watts and express his concern over African Americans' anger and fear of white reprisals. In response, Johnson warned King that the specter of a white backlash after Watts had changed the political calculus, necessitating that he speak in a different political idiom that King might find offensive. For instance, Johnson did not want King to misinterpret the president's recent statement that "a rioter with a Molotov cocktail was no different than a Klansman with a bomb." The president stressed that the success of his poverty program mandated that he appear tough on the rioters, but he reiterated his enduring commitment to the cause of civil rights.

It was not until the end of the conservation that Johnson broached the subject of Vietnam. He began by noting that King's recent statements made it appear "that you're against me in Vietnam," and he admonished that King "better not leave that impression." Raising his voice, the president continued, "I want peace as much as you do, and more so, because I'm the fellow that had to wake up this morning with fifty Marines killed." In response, King claimed that his recent statements had been "misinterpreted, because as I have mentioned it is just as unreasonable to talk about the United States having a unilateral withdrawal." But, he pointed out to the president, "you have called fourteen or fifteen times for unconditional talks and it is Hanoi—" Whereupon, the Johnson interrupted him and said, "That's right." He proposed that King meet with the newly appointed ambassador to the United Nations, his close political ally and former Supreme Court justice Arthur Goldberg, to discuss what was going on "behind the scenes" to effectuate a settlement in Vietnam. King informed the president that he had received a call from Goldberg a few days ago and looked forward to meeting with him.[93] Although Johnson's recent decision to increase the number of troops in Vietnam and his bellicose rhetoric seemingly belied any intention to negotiate a settlement, King got the impression that Johnson was open to resolving the war. King also avoided expressing his true feelings about the war. In short, both parties were reluctant to engage in a frank discussion on the issue of Vietnam. After their conversation, White House aides leaked spurious reports that the president had sharply rebuked King on Vietnam.[94]

Hoover's flood of reports to the president on King's private conservations in which he admitted his repugnance for the Vietnam War, along with boilerplate on the alleged communist backgrounds of top King aides Stanley Levison and Bayard Rustin, fed the president's legendary paranoia. Unwilling to attack King directly, Johnson left the task to proxies. In a veiled reference to King, George Weaver, the African American assistant secretary of labor, spoke before the Federation of Masons of the World and warned that "criticisms of America's policy in Vietnam by civil rights groups could lead the Communists to make disastrous miscalculations in American determination." Weaver bristled at James Bevel's suggestion that King ought to go abroad to resolve international problems and charged that it might be "more appropriate and effective for prominent American leaders who call for peace talks in Vietnam to suggest how these talks might be brought about when the aggressors refuse to participate."[95] Meanwhile, scientist Linus Pauling announced that King and seven other Nobel Peace Prize winners had signed an appeal to international leaders urging them to take action to resolve the war.[96] King's antiwar statements were beginning to attract greater national attention.

The controversy over King's antiwar utterances was magnified by his August 29, 1965, appearance on CBS's *Face the Nation*. Instead of opening the telecast with questions about riot-shattered Watts, correspondent Martin Agronsky asked whether King had followed up on his intention to appeal personally to the leaders involved in the Vietnam conflict. King replied that he had not yet "had a chance to do it" because of his preoccupation with Watts, but he said he was willing "to use whatever concern I can muster at this point to express my desire along with numerous people all over the world to bring an end to this conflict." Agronsky next asked King whether his involvement in the peace movement would weaken and divide the civil rights movement. King responded:

> Well, I would certainly say I don't think this is true. First, I must make it clear that my expressions on the war in Vietnam grow out of something much larger than my participation in the civil rights movement. I happen to be a Minister of the Gospel and I take that ministry very seriously. . . and I happen to feel that war is obsolete and that it must be cast into unending limbo and that if we continue to escalate this war, we move nearer to the point of plunging the whole of mankind into the abyss of annihilation, and I will continue to speak when I deem it timely and necessary on this issue, not as a Civil Rights leader. I have no intention to urge my organization at this point, for instance, to enter into the peace struggle. I don't think we have the resources nor the energies.

On the subject of Undersecretary Weaver's recent criticisms, King reminded Agronsky that "freedom of speech is part of our sacred heritage" and articulated the need for "creative dissent." King avoided attacking the president personally and said he understood "the moral dilemma of those" in favor of escalating the war. He admitted, "I don't feel that I can stand with any pretense to omniscience and say that I have the answer." King also reiterated his admiration for President Johnson's "great job in the area of civil rights" and announced his plans to meet with Ambassador Goldberg to discuss the administration's efforts to end the conflict.[97] While providing a detailed explanation of his opposition to the war, King took pains not to alienate the White House. He was aware of the pitfalls surrounding the issue of Vietnam, particularly in view of the public's overwhelming support of the Johnson administration and the danger of attacking U.S. foreign policy.[98] Furthermore, King hoped for the passage of additional civil rights legislation related to housing and yearned for a vast infusion of money into the nation's largest cities to ameliorate the crisis in the African American ghettos.

King and Goldberg's meeting, scheduled for September 1 at the latter's office at the United Nations in New York City, was postponed until September 10. The president hoped that Goldberg, a renowned labor negotiator, would be able to convince King that the United States was doing everything in its power to bring the North Vietnamese to the negotiating table. In the days leading up to the meeting, King took a respite from his usual frenetic schedule to immerse himself in the history of the conflict in Vietnam. He consulted an array of sources, from the writings of Buddhist exile Thich Nhat Hanh to those of eminent French military scholar Bernard Fall. King also enlisted the services of his friend and neighbor Spelman College professor Vincent Harding, who had become a Mennonite peace pastor. In addition, Swedish journalist Sven Oste, who had just returned from Vietnam, briefed King thoroughly on the unfolding situation on the ground.[99] Young recalled that King was extremely "well versed on the facts and issues relating to the Vietnam conflict."[100] In keeping with his long-standing criticism of Cold War dogma, this tutorial reinforced King's view that the conflict was essentially a national liberation movement against imperialism. King perceived Ho Chi Minh as a Vietnamese nationalist with maverick tendencies who had the potential to be an Asian Tito. In spite of King's knowledge of international relations, the media, the political establishment, and large segments of the American public clung to the notion that foreign affairs was the exclusive province of the elite, not civil rights activists. This precluded many Americans from taking King's views on Vietnam seriously.

King, accompanied by his advisers Andrew Young, Bayard Rustin, Bernard Lee, and Harry Wachtel, met with Ambassador Goldberg at the United Nations on September 10. King cogently synthesized the history of U.S. involvement in Vietnam and emphasized that Ho was essentially a nationalist, not a communist.[101] He recommended that the Johnson administration expeditiously resolve the conflict through negotiation. Goldberg reassured them that the administration was moving toward peace talks, but he failed to convince King and his aides. According to Young, "We were not sure Goldberg even believed what he was saying."[102] After the meeting, King and Goldberg separately stated that the talks had been amicable, but they both acknowledged they had vastly different perspectives on the situation in Southeast Asia. King called Goldberg "a man of peace" who was searching for solutions, and he expressed gratitude for the opportunity to discuss the "distressing" situation in Vietnam. Once again, he urged the U.S. government to make "an unequivocal and unambiguous statement of its willingness to negotiate with the Vietcong to end the fighting" and halt the bombing.[103] In response to a reporter's question about China, King made the blockbuster statement: "Eight hundred million people are not going to disappear because we refuse to admit their existence," and he urged the United States to reconsider its opposition to having China in the United Nations.[104] This statement questioning Cold War orthodoxy would embroil King in controversy for the next few weeks and stymie his efforts to regenerate the civil rights struggle. For his part, Ambassador Goldberg told reporters the conversation had been cordial, and he had not tried to dissuade King from sending letters to the communist leaders. The ambassador emphasized that even though the United States did not seek permanent military bases and remained committed to obtaining an honorable peace by negotiation, "We will not be forced out of South Vietnam."[105]

The White House immediately pounced on King's comments about China and embarked on a campaign to silence and discredit him. The tense mood turned hostile when Senator Thomas Dodd of Connecticut issued a harsh broadside against King's views on Vietnam and China. Dodd, a member of the Foreign Relations Committee, was a staunch ally of Johnson's and a frequent attacker of those who criticized the president's policies; he was also one of the Senate's strongest supporters of J. Edgar Hoover. Dodd suggested that King's proposed letter-writing campaign violated the Logan Act, which made it a crime for a private individual to carry out foreign policy. Dodd also expressed his regret that "the leader of the civil rights movement, by his intemperate alignment with the forces of appeasement in foreign policy, has alienated much of the support which he previously enjoyed in Congress."[106] Praising King as "a man of unquestioned competence in the field of civil rights," Dodd nonetheless fulminated: "He has absolutely no competence to speak about complex matters of foreign policy. And it is nothing short of arrogance when Dr. King takes it upon himself to thus undermine the policies of the President and of the United States and to enter into personal negotiations with heads of hostile governments."[107]

More barbs ensued, and they spanned the ideological spectrum. Predictably, segregationist senator Strom Thurmond of South Carolina criticized Goldberg for even receiving King and thundered, "A whole new sphere of trouble-making for the United States was launched yesterday."[108] An editorial in the conservative *Washington Evening Star* lampooned King as a "home-made foreign policy expert" and suggested that if he wanted to venture into fields other than civil rights, he might choose to critique the "Broadway stage" or "the rising hemlines on women's dresses" or any of "a hundred fields of human endeavor in which he can do less harm and in which he is at least as well qualified [as] in foreign policy."[109] Fellow African American civil rights leader Whitney Young Jr., head of the National Urban League and a close friend of President Johnson's, piled on by publishing an editorial in the *Chicago Defender* that castigated King for linking civil rights with the war.[110] In the midst of this firestorm, King was overwhelmed and paralyzed. The heated response to his extemporaneous remarks on China was a testament to the perils of speaking out against Cold War dogma. Moreover, the reaction illuminated the persistence of the anticommunist climate, which was an important factor in Johnson's belief that the American people would not tolerate surrender in Vietnam. All the parties were trapped in a stifling Cold War mind-set.

These assaults from friend and foe alike stung King. He bemoaned to his aides that "the press was being stacked against" him.[111] Fearing that further attacks would cripple his effectiveness as a civil rights leader, King arranged a conference call with Stanley Levison, Harry Wachtel, Clarence Jones, and Andrew Young to plot strategy. The FBI wiretaps of their September 12 conversation revealed King's agony. Gone were any illusions that Johnson was amenable to negotiations that would lead to a peaceful resolution of the war.[112] In a statement the FBI relayed to White House aide Marvin Watson, a distraught King expressed his certainty that Johnson had persuaded Dodd to attack him because he had gone too far in urging the cessation of bombing of North Vietnam and the seating of China in the United Nations. A frustrated King acknowledged that, at least for the short term, he was not strong enough to participate in both the civil rights and the antiwar movements. King asked his advisers for their opinions on three things: "how to get across to the public that he is not alone on the Vietnam issue, how to deal with the Dodd statement, and how to conceive of some graceful means whereby he can withdraw from writing the letters to the leaders of the countries involved in Vietnam."[113] Ironically, Levison (whom the FBI never tired of characterizing as "a longtime communist") actually counseled King to abandon the Vietnam issue and get back to his "regular work" of leading the civil rights struggle.[114]

The following day, the group conferred again on how to stanch the avalanche of criticism over Vietnam. Once again, the FBI was listening in. In tune with his pragmatism, Levison called King's statement on China "insane," particularly after he had taken such a strong stance on Vietnam.[115] For the time being, they acknowledged that King had ventured too far ahead of public opinion. According to his wife, Coretta, King was particularly perturbed that his comments on the war were causing disunity within the ranks of the civil rights movement.[116] As a consequence, the group agreed that King should abandon his letter-writing campaign and would be best served by finding influential surrogates to voice their support for his right to dissent. An exhausted King concurred and acknowledged that his "star is waning." He confessed, "I really don't have the strength to fight this issue and keep my civil rights fight going," and he asked his aides to "find out how I can gracefully pull out."[117] He decided to heed Levison's advice to lay low on Vietnam and thereby stem the negative publicity so he could focus on civil rights. The parties agreed that Wachtel should try to persuade the *New York Times* to print an editorial supporting King's right to speak out on Vietnam, and Rustin would ask liberal senator Paul Douglas of Illinois to issue a similar statement supporting King's right to express his opinion.[118]

Two days later, September 17, 1965, White House assistant Marvin Watson released the details of King's face-saving gambit in a typed memo to the president.[119] The president's attempt to muzzle King had succeeded, but Johnson's suspicions were fueled by a flurry of new memos from Hoover linking King to communists. For his part, King was shaken by Johnson's willingness to pick up the telephone and instruct his allies to issue such harsh and disabling attacks. The concerted drive to diminish King's standing was taking its toll. For instance, William Josiah Drummond of Brooklyn, one of King's supporters, expressed his disapproval of King's foray into foreign policy by stating, "Surely, it would seem, much remains in the field of civil rights to which Dr. King could devote his energies." Drummond went on to attack King for failing "to see that politics is a matter which requires a technical skill and a trained judgment."[120]

With thousands of young African American men enlisting in the newly integrated military, and with President Johnson's approval rating among African Americans at an all-time high, King was swimming against the tide of public opinion—and he knew it. Although African American opposition to the Vietnam War outpaced that of their white counterparts, at this point, most blacks still supported the war. In the African American press, the disparaging editorials and letters far outnumbered those in support of King. For example, the *Chicago Defender*, ordinarily a reliable ally, supported King's right to dissent but highlighted the prevailing view that "veering toward the crisis in Vietnam" would "siphon energy from our main objective" of civil rights.[121] The *Baltimore Afro-American* agreed and argued that King's prescriptions for peace were not necessarily "the right solutions," but it derided Dodd's criticism of King's limited competence as "sheer arrogance."[122]

Throughout this brouhaha, King remained convinced of the rightness of peace. It pained him that circumstances compelled him to mute his opposition to the war. He resented the liberal establishment's campaign to muzzle him. He reminded his aides that he was also a man of God and a Nobel Prize winner and had an obligation to be an apostle for peace. In a private conversation with his aides on September 28, King insisted that he should continue to point out "the immorality of United States policy in Vietnam."[123] Again, it was Levison who disagreed. Referring to their previous consensus that King was not "the person to do this," Levison reiterated, "Martin should remain a civil rights leader and not a peace leader."[124] While Levison's opinion carried great weight, other influential people were imploring King to speak out against the war. His wife Coretta, a committed pacifist who planned to speak at the upcoming SANE-sponsored march on Washington, urged him not to relent on his opposition to the war.[125] Dr. Benjamin Spock, the famous pediatrician and antiwar activist, told King that if he joined the peace movement, "he could become the most important symbol for peace in this country, as well as for world peace."[126] Rabbi Everett E. Gendler of Princeton, New Jersey, pacifist A. J. Muste, and fellow Nobel Prize winner Linus Pauling were among those who praised King's antiwar statements.[127] The *New York Amsterdam News* interviewed six local clergymen, two of whom were white, and five of them thought King was eminently qualified to expedite a resolution to the Vietnam War.[128] A Japanese survivor of the U.S. firebombing in World War II wrote to King about the "terrible war of fire" the Americans were raining down on the Vietnamese.[129] These sentiments appealed to King's pacifist sensibility, but none of these individuals was involved in the civil rights movement. By the end of September, King was deeply torn between his disgust for the war and his desire to remain a viable civil rights leader.

In the end, King was overwhelmed by the powerful array of forces condemning his views on the war. Levison's exhortations to cease his anti-war activity seemed to be the only viable option. King's advisers were unanimous in their belief that he needed to drop the Vietnam issue, and a *Newsweek* poll showed that only 18 percent of blacks advocated a with-drawal from Vietnam.[130] Moreover, his moderate allies in the civil rights movement, such as Roy Wilkins and Whitney Young, were pressuring him to avoid further alienating the president. Finally, financial contributors were threatening to cease their donations to the SCLC unless King stifled his antiwar statements. After a few days of reflection, King issued a terse statement on October 5 announcing that he no longer intended to "com-municate by mail with the major powers involved in the conflict" because "the rapidly changing events surrounding the Vietnamese situation indi-cated to me that it is no longer necessary at this time to do so." In reality, there had been no change in Vietnam, and King was dubious about the sincerity of the Johnson administration's claims that it was seeking peace. In his cryptic statement, King alluded to the revitalization of the United Nations and its "extremely creative role" in handling the recent crisis in Kashmir. He added that "free debate" is the "cornerstone" of our democ-racy, and he vowed to fight for the preservation of that great American tra-dition within the context of the nation's foreign policy.[131] King knew that this was not his finest hour. A couple years later he observed, "My name wouldn't have been written in any book called 'Profiles in Courage.'"[132] Weakened and angered by attacks from friend and foe alike, King devoted the final weeks of 1965 to laying the groundwork for the struggle against poverty and racism in Chicago.

By the end of 1965, the number of U.S. troops in Vietnam had soared to 185,000, and the Johnson administration was intimating an increase in 1966. With the war poised to continue indefinitely, a troubled King brooded over its adverse impact on the War on Poverty and feared that the accelerating conflict in Southeast Asia could lead to nuclear annihi-lation.[133] He was particularly disheartened over the widening rifts that Vietnam was creating within the civil rights movement and African Amer-icans.[134] Trapped between his pragmatic advisers, who continued to coun-sel silence on the war, and his wife, his allies in SNCC, and ecumenical circles, which encouraged him to join the antiwar movement, a discon-solate King continued to struggle with his conscience.[135] Reports of the disproportionate number of African American casualties in Vietnam only added to King's resentment. He also bristled over an imperialistic war that was costing billions of dollars while millions of African Americans remained mired in poverty. Only days after his October 5 statement, FBI agents listened to a telephone call between King and New York attorney Clarence Jones in which King said, "The position of our Government is wrong and it is getting wronger every day."[136] King's frustration grew over the ensuing weeks. Speaking before the Synagogue Council of America in New York on December 5, King remarked, "Prospects for peace in Vietnam are growing dimmer" because those who would "question it are being subjected to intensified attack" in the form of "an ugly repressive sentiment to silence peace-seekers."[137] Appearing on the back pages of the *New York Times*, this statement failed to attract much attention.[138] This reflected King's strategy of restricting his criticism to carefully chosen venues where he would highlight his constitutional right to speak out against U.S. foreign policy. This was a tactic he would pursue throughout 1966.

In the waning days of 1965, the triumphs of the Civil Rights Act and the Voting Rights Act could not dispel the gloom that hovered over King and the civil rights movement. Only months after its inspirational Selma campaign, few could have predicted the dissension, confusion, and discord that now rent the civil rights coalition. In November, Charles Silberman, editor of *Fortune* magazine, summed it up best: "The civil rights movement is not dead . . . [but] the movement is at a dreadful impasse; its leaders . . . are estranged from their rank and file and divided and uncertain where to turn."[139]

Above all else, the war continued to haunt King. He was annoyed that while he had painstakingly avoided blaming the president for the conflict, his civility had been repaid with a barrage of personal attacks. The administration's hardball tactics hurt King, and he was coming to the realization that Johnson and Goldberg had duped him into believing they were serious about negotiating an end to the war. In the final days of 1965, King collected his thoughts to write an editorial in the *Chicago Defender.* In this forum, beyond the glare of the national spotlight, King spoke of his overriding desire to assume a public responsibility "to sue for a war-less world." He queried, "What shall it profit the Negro to avail himself of an integrated sandwich or quality education or a good job or a desegregated home—in the midst of horrible death and falling bombs?"[140] King's prayers for 1966 included peace in Vietnam, but no matter how hard he prayed, hopes of ending the war would continually be dashed because the

6

The Second Coming of
Martin Luther King Jr., 1966–1968

In a real sense, the Great Society has been shot down on the battlefields
of Vietnam.
—Martin Luther King Jr.

The war in Asia had as one of its unintended consequences the
dismembering of the civil rights alliance and the destruction of
the consensus for racial reform. As the United States disgorged its
firepower into Vietnam and the ghettos burst into flames, the hopes of
the blacks went up in smoke, and King's dream turned into ash.
—Harvard Sitkoff

By 1966, King's prayers had not been answered, and the military escalation in Vietnam continued unabated. LBJ was consumed by the war, and
civil rights leaders discerned a diminution in his passion for civil rights.[1]
Vietnam would cast its shadow on American life well into the 1970s and
beyond. Writing in the *New York Review of Books* in October 1966, journalist Ronald Steel described Washington as "a city obsessed by Vietnam."
According to Steel, "It eats, sleeps, and particularly drinks this war. There
is virtually no other discussion worthy of the name, and no social gathering or private discussion that does not inevitably gravitate toward the
war." One outspoken journalist griped to Steel, "Were it not for this Vietnam thing, I'd be able to write about the real crises—about poverty, and
civil rights, and the cities."[2] Far from the Georgetown salons, King was
engrossed in his Chicago campaign and the Black Power controversy, and
he avoided the mushrooming antiwar rallies. He tried to eschew discus-

sion of the war, but like the rest of the country, he could not escape the vortex of Vietnam. Like everything else, its whirling currents would envelop King and the civil rights movement. By 1966, King's inner war over Vietnam was reflected in the larger civil war within the American body politic. The war had come home.

As previously mentioned, 1966 was barely a week old when SNCC's denunciation of the war and the controversy over the seating of Julian Bond in the Georgia house created a firestorm.[3] The hysteria unleashed when Bond refused to repudiate SNCC's support of draft resistance seemed to corroborate the wisdom of keeping a low profile on Vietnam. There was ample justification for caution. First, the war was still popular among King's northern liberal donors, and now that he had launched his first campaign against the racist practices embedded in the North, financial contributions were dwindling.[4] Second, LBJ's recent extension of the Christmastime bombing halt against North Vietnam, though more of a public relations gambit than a sincere peace initiative, afforded the administration additional breathing space. Even more problematic for King, the mainstream press continued to brand antiwar protesters "Vietniks." The pillorying of the telegenic and clean-shaven Bond only months after King's similar treatment substantiated King's need for caution.

King, Andrew Young, and Bernard Lee had just left Chicago for a well-deserved vacation in Los Angeles when the furor over Julian Bond's condoning of SNCC's antidraft statement threatened to traumatize the already fragmented civil rights movement. From the West Coast, King watched the exploding story with a sense of foreboding, reinforcing his fear that the nation was approaching a dangerous point at which dissent would be synonymous with treachery. An exasperated King conferred with his aides, and they decided to return to Atlanta to subdue the crisis and speak out in support of Bond's right to free expression.[5] Realizing that the entire ordeal was largely self-inflicted, King resented the drain on his time and energy caused by SNCC's penchant for recklessness. Ever since the brouhaha over the seating of the MFDP in Atlantic City in the summer of 1964, King had chafed at SNCC's lack of discipline and discretion. As fellow foot soldiers for civil rights, however, they had all been called "nigger" as they marched in the Deep South, they had all been jailed in the same fetid cells, and they all dreamed the same dreams. James Forman may have had a lot of harsh words for King, but over the years, King and a number of SNCC leaders, especially John Lewis, Cleveland Sellers, and Stokely Carmichael, had developed warm personal relationships.[6]

Years later, Sellers said he had "fond memories" of the "long, hot hours" he and King spent trudging through the Deep South, and he remembered King as "a staunch ally and true brother."[7] Fearing that freedom of speech was hanging in the balance, King distanced himself from the NAACP's assaults on SNCC, returned to Atlanta, and placed his prestige on the line in an effort to calm the boiling tempest.[8]

On January 12, 1966, the day after the Georgia legislature's near-unanimous decision to deny Julian Bond his seat, King met privately with Bond and then convened a press conference, where he announced his intention to lead a protest march the following Friday, Bond's twenty-sixth birthday.[9] When a reporter asked if King endorsed SNCC's antiwar statement, King cautioned, "This is not the time to endorse or reject the statement." On the issue of the draft, King equivocated:

I have never encouraged evading the draft, and I am not prepared at this point to encourage evading the draft. On the other hand, if persons on the basis of conscience feel that they cannot serve in the armed services or not follow through on the call to be drafted, then on the basis of the Selective Service Act, they have a right to be a conscientious objector and have alternative service. I do think it would be a wonderful thing for the nation to recognize that the civil rights movement is important enough for the nation and for its survival, to be one of those alternatives services that can be rendered.[10]

King realized that the American public, including most African Americans, did not share SNCC's antidraft stance.[11] As proof, two prominent African American ministers from Chattanooga resigned from the SCLC to protest King's support of Bond.[12] Nonetheless, King remained adamant in his conviction that freedom to dissent was at risk, and he feared the swirling controversy would derail the prospects for racial justice.

Two days later, King addressed a rally for Bond in front of the Georgia statehouse. The crowd was smaller than King and SNCC had hoped for. Only about 1,000 people braved the cold to hear King denounce the Georgia legislature and reaffirm his support for "the sacred right of freedom of speech and the right to dissent."[13] Amid a chorus of voices denouncing SNCC, King praised its "heroic activity" in fighting for equal justice and extolled the conspicuously absent Julian Bond "as a man of peace" who has the "inalienable right to speak his mind." He emphasized that "Julian

Bond never said he would burn his draft card, and there was nothing in the SNCC statement that called for burning of draft cards." Paraphrasing the SCLC's motto, he lauded SNCC's efforts "to save the soul of our nation." King skirted the issue of Vietnam and emphasized his belief in freedom of speech, particularly during wartime. King buttressed his First Amendment argument by citing Abraham Lincoln's opposition to the Mexican-American War as a young congressman. He quoted John F. Kennedy, who, as a young sailor, wrote, "War will never cease until that distant day when the conscientious objector enjoys as much respectability and prestige as the warrior enjoys today." King was all too aware of the racist overtones of the firestorm against SNCC and Bond. He pointed out the hypocrisy of the Georgia legislature: it wanted to oust Bond for violating the U.S. Constitution, but the same legislature had invoked nullification and states' rights to flout the Constitution for more than a century.[14]

After King spoke, a scuffle broke out when Willie Ricks, one of SNCC's more militant members, urged about fifty people to break through a police barricade and enter the capitol. One unidentified African American man screamed, "You ain't got nothing but bullets. We're going to sit up there in the Georgia Legislature and make some decent laws." The handful of overwhelmed Georgia troopers requested reinforcements and restored order. Nonetheless, the fracas generated more unwelcome publicity from the already hostile Atlanta press, leading an exasperated King to reiterate his long-standing commitment to nonviolent protest and deny his involvement in "breaking through police lines."[15]

On Sunday, January 16, Vietnam was on his mind as King delivered a sermon to his Ebenezer congregation on how nonconformity and dissent represent the true essence of Christianity. He likened Bond to Ralph Waldo Emerson. On Vietnam, he said, "We aren't doing enough to end the war." He presented a brief history of the conflict and indicted the United States for failing to recognize Vietnam's independence in 1945 and for spending billions of dollars to help France in its imperialistic war against Vietnam. He then reiterated, "However much people write editorials about our policy, we aren't doing enough to end the war in Vietnam." With the repressive climate of the past week in mind, King derided "the press and others for trying to brainwash people and letting us feel that there are no issues to be discussed in this war." In his sharpest broadside to date on American foreign policy, he exhorted America to showcase its moral power, not its military power, and he told his parishioners, "We will not stop communism with bombs and guns and bullets and napalm," but "we will stop communism by letting the world know that democracy is a better government than any other governments, and by making justice a reality for all of God's children." King invoked the words of the Old Testament prophet Isaiah, who said, "Your hands are full of blood." In perhaps his most eloquent defense of Bond, King said: "America must hear the truth, if we are going to survive as a nation, somebody has got to have vision, somebody must be willing to stand up and be criticized and called every bad name, out of love for this country. Nobody should be considered disloyal because they dissent, because it is done out of love."[16]

On the one hand, King's outrage at the "screaming editorials" and the Georgia legislators' "vituperative words" mitigated his pique at SNCC. On the other hand, the likelihood that another ill-considered comment by the organization would provoke another hullabaloo tempered his outrage. He was caught between his pragmatism and his hatred of the war. It was a knotty predicament that seared his conscience. Although he doubted that Johnson's temporary bombing halt indicated a sincere effort to jump-start peace talks, he remained determined to work with Johnson's War on Poverty to maximize funding to the impoverished ghettos. For his part, Johnson was determined to maintain his commitment to the Great Society in the midst of the war in Vietnam.[17]

On January 12, the same day that King announced his "principled" support for SNCC's antiwar position, the president delivered his much-anticipated State of the Union address, the first since the Americanization of the war ten months earlier. Aides remembered that preparations for the speech were frenzied.[18] The gravity of the occasion prompted Johnson to ask former White House speechwriter Richard Goodwin, who had resigned in disgust over the president's Vietnam policy, to help draft the speech.[19] The president who strode into the Senate that evening was more harried and less confident than the one who had spoken so forcefully for civil rights ten months earlier.[20] Sitting with his aides in Atlanta, King watched another prime-time presidential address with great anticipation.

At the outset, the president reaffirmed his pledge to stay in Vietnam "until aggression has stopped," but he expressed the hope that his bombing halt would bear results. Johnson spent the lion's share of the speech vowing to carry forward with "full vigor" the programs on health and education and to "speed up the war on poverty." The address, later referred to as the "guns and butter" speech, proposed new civil rights laws to prohibit discrimination in the sale or rental of private housing, to end discrimination in jury selection, and to make the murder, attack, or intimidation of civil rights workers a federal crime.[21] Although many administration stalwarts were skeptical of the government's ability to pay for both guns and butter without raising taxes or fueling inflation, the speech reassured moderates in the civil rights movement of the benefits of working with the administration, even if the furor over the war was eroding support for more civil rights initiatives.[22] Goodwin was so incensed that the president had watered down pledges for domestic programs and inserted more militant statements on the war that he never spoke to Lyndon Johnson again.[23]

King was pleased with Johnson's reiteration of his commitment to the Great Society and his pioneering civil rights proposals. Despite their frayed relationship, he sent a telegram to the president commending him for his "eloquent and far reaching" address. "It was reassuring to hear you emphatically affirm that the Administration will not allow the continued existance [sic] of the war in Viet Nam to cause a let up in the great domestic and welfare programs that you have so creatively generated through your concepts of the Great Society," King added. He then expressed his hope that Johnson would "continue the quest to bring the whole conflict to the conference table."[24] King's warm words belied his frustration with the war, but Johnson's steadfast commitment to civil rights reinforced King's pragmatic tendencies.

A few days after his Sunday sermon on nonconformity, King returned to Chicago. He was anxious to resume his campaign to address discrimination in housing in the northern ghetto—even vowing to rent an apartment in a slum to highlight the abject squalor of African Americans' existence in the North.[25] The Bond affair had cast him in the role of reluctant savior, but for the remainder of 1966, King muffled his opposition to the war. Parsing his words carefully, King drew a line—albeit a narrow one—separating his defense of Bond's right to dissent and his tacit agreement with SNCC's antiwar position. Even so, these boundaries sometimes blurred, most often in private settings beyond the glare of the national spotlight.

Early 1966: The Pressure Mounts

The Bond affair subsided, and a semblance of normalcy returned to Sammy Younge's hometown of Tuskegee, Alabama, after his murder. King headed north and immersed himself in the struggle against entrenched racism and poverty. He even took up residence in a rat-infested flat on the West Side of Chicago to publicize the plight of slum dwellers.[26] Unfortunately, the carnage in Vietnam was never far from his mind. Johnson resumed the bombing of North Vietnam on January 31, 1966, which shattered any hope of a negotiated settlement and precipitated renewed dissent that spilled into the political establishment.[27] An enraged Senator William J. Fulbright of Arkansas demanded that the Senate conduct open hearings on the war.[28] In due course, the Fulbright hearings were televised and entered the collective American consciousness, just as the Army-McCarthy hearings had done in 1954 (and the Watergate hearings would do seven years later). They convinced many Americans that antiwar activity was not tantamount to disloyalty. George Kennan, the architect of the containment doctrine, was a star witness at the Fulbright hearings and raised eyebrows when he questioned the Johnson administration's justifications for the war. "If we were not already involved as we are today in Vietnam, I would know of no reason why we should wish to become so involved, and I could think of several reasons why we should wish not to," Kennan testified.[29] The daily headlines on Vietnam threatened to submerge Johnson's entire domestic agenda and his upcoming conference on civil rights. Fulbright became the darling of antiwar activists, but Whitney Young reminded African Americans of the Arkansas senator's abysmal record on civil rights.[30] One of the signers of the Southern Manifesto, Fulbright had voted against the 1964 and 1965 civil rights legislation. Though no admirer of Fulbright, King assayed the ominous events in Vietnam with a sense of horror. Addressing his Ebenezer congregation on February 6, 1966, King stated, "It is just as evil to kill Vietnamese as it is to kill Americans."[31]

By early 1966, dissent over the war was crystallizing among King's fellow clergymen. *Christianity and Crisis*, a journal cofounded by Reinhold Niebuhr in response to the belief that pacifism and isolationism posed a threat to the United States, published a series of editorials critical of the war.[32] The journal did not ascribe to the "assumptions of Christian pacifism," but coeditor John C. Bennett argued that "the circumstances under which military power is being used in Vietnam are sufficiently different from those under which it was used to defeat Hitler."[33] Christian realists such as Niebuhr, the Cold War liberal whose work had had such a profound influence on King, broke with the administration over Vietnam. Niebuhr cautioned, "We are making South Vietnam into an American colony by transmuting a civil war into one in which Americans fight Asians while China, the presumed enemy, risks not a single life." He added that continuing the current war policy would result in "physically ruining an unhappy nation in the process of 'saving' it."[34] Other distinguished theologians, such as Robert McAfee Brown of Stanford University and Rabbi Abraham

Heschel, began to voice their moral opposition to the war. Their eminence and moderation lent an air of respectability to an antiwar stance. These reputable theologians, many of whom King held in high esteem, caused large segments of the American public to reassess their view that the antiwar movement was a fringe group composed of hippies and miscreants.[35]

The liberal wing of American Christianity began to mobilize against the war. William Sloane Coffin, the distinguished Yale chaplain whose highly publicized role in the Freedom Rides had catapulted him to fame, formed Clergy and Laymen Concerned about Vietnam (CALCAV) in January 1966 and sent a telegram to LBJ urging an end to the conflict.[36] Among the other notable founders of CALCAV were King's friends Rabbi Abraham Heschel, Father Daniel Berrigan, and John Bennett. CALCAV was primarily a moderate organization that distanced itself from SDS and other radical groups, but it was building a strong antiwar network across the nation.[37] In particular, Coffin's participation was a coup for the antiwar movement because, other than King, Coffin was arguably the most influential liberal Protestant in the United States.[38] Many antiwar activists hoped this new coalition with ties to the political center would prompt King to join his fellow theologians in the antiwar movement. Although the majority of Americans still supported the war, when a respected statesman like Fulbright and Cold War liberals like Niebuhr cast their dissent, it was becoming increasingly problematic to paint all critics of the war with the "Vietnik" brush. By the end of 1966, there were more than sixty CALCAV chapters throughout the United States. The antiwar movement was starting to flourish beyond the college campuses.[39]

King's withdrawal from the Vietnam debate mystified many white supporters. Twenty-three-year-old Charles Fager, King's cellmate in Selma, had just left the staff of the SCLC to become a leader in the antiwar movement.[40] Fager was one of many who pined for King to break with the Johnson administration over the war. Having worked closely with King, he was sensitive to the unique pressures confronting the leader of the civil rights movement. In March 1966 Fager published a penetrating piece in the *Christian Century* analyzing King's predicament: "Dr. King is not known as a man of vacillation," he noted, but with respect to Vietnam, King "seems curiously circumspect, almost tame." He pointed out that King was "trying to walk a tortuous middle path: opposing the war as a matter of form but doing so as quietly as possible." Fager called "the Vietnam War the greatest challenge of King's career—and conceivably its culmination," and speculated "it is possible that Dr. King simply doesn't yet know what to do." In conclusion, Fager asked, "Who among us today could blame him if faced with this dilemma he agonizes over this course of action? No one, surely: but Martin Luther King, Jr., is not only answerable to us today: he must walk with history as well. And if in his agony he should fail to act, it must be asked: can history forgive him?"[41]

In the coming weeks, King continued to confine his antiwar opinions to carefully chosen venues. In early March he made the following comment in his regular *Chicago Defender* column: "A war in which children are incinerated by napalm, in which American soldiers die in mounting numbers . . . is a war that mutilates the conscience."[42] Such passionate pleas encouraged Fager and others to hope that King's break with the administration was imminent. Much to their dismay, however, King and his advisers still considered it the wrong time to do so. Rustin, in particular, admonished King that his allies in the labor movement would "viciously attack" him in their zest to protect their Democratic patrons.[43] With few exceptions, he continued to eschew public statements on the war. In particular, King held out hope that the upcoming White House Conference on Civil Rights, scheduled for June 1 and 2, would lead to some relief for the millions of African Americans subsisting on the edge of poverty. Meanwhile, a Harris poll indicated that four out of ten Americans were unfavorably disposed toward civil rights groups that opposed the Vietnam War, and 41 percent were less inclined to favor civil rights for African Americans when a civil rights group came out against the war.[44] Fager was correct: King was walking a tortuous path.

In late March, King took a trip to Europe, with stops in Paris and Stockholm. He met with Swedish scholar Gunnar Myrdal and King Gustav VI, and a benefit concert put on by Harry Belafonte raised $100,000. King was struck by the dearth of poverty in Sweden, accentuating his affinity for a Scandinavian-style social democracy.[45] His spirits were lifted during his brief stay in Paris, where he was feted by the press and Parisian society. But everywhere he went, Europeans were baffled by King's curious silence on Vietnam, causing one diplomat to comment, "King wears a muzzle on Vietnam."[46]

Heartened by his warm reception overseas, King returned home on April 10 and turned his attention to the SCLC's executive board meeting in Miami. Prior to his trip, King had acknowledged that other than the SCLC's flagging finances, the Vietnam issue would be the most difficult topic of discussion.[47] His own reluctance to enlist in the antiwar movement did not stop him from pressuring the SCLC Board of Directors to draft a stronger antiwar declaration than the one passed the previous August in Birmingham. Speaking at a news conference on April 13, King announced that the SCLC had adopted a resolution calling for the U.S. government to cease aiding the South Vietnamese military junta "under such manifestly vigorous popular opposition." He alleged that the war was "rapidly degenerating into a sordid military adventure" and that it was time "to reassess our position and seriously examine the wisdom of a prompt withdrawal." Roy Reed of the *New York Times* cited Andrew Young, who said that passage of the resolution did not mean the SCLC "would participate in peace demonstrations or support them financially."[48] Back in Chicago, however, King declared his intention "to intensify my personal activity against this war" but ruefully added, "We are more concerned as a nation about winning the war in Vietnam than we are about winning the war against poverty here at home."[49] A few days later, King flew to Washington, D.C., to meet with President Johnson to discuss his new civil rights legislation and the upcoming White House Conference on Civil Rights. The short meeting was perfunctory, and it marked King's final appearance at the White House.[50]

SNCC had announced at its Kingston Springs meeting in May that it planned to boycott the White House conference scheduled for June, signaling an even more militant turn. Among the reasons for not attending the conference was Stokely Carmichael's statement that "integration is irrelevant."[51] After the violence in Watts, such pronouncements fueled fear of another "hot" summer of urban uprisings. Three days before the beginning of the conference, and for the second time in eight months, King appeared on CBS's *Face the Nation*. He first fielded questions about SNCC, distancing himself from its "unrealistic" embrace of separatism and stating that he regretted its decision to boycott the conference.[52] Then the questioning turned to King's views about the war's effect on the Great Society. After calling for the federal government to earmark $10 billion a year over the next decade as part of an urban renewal project, King blasted the war for making it impossible "to implement the Great Society Programs" and stated, "We have got to find a good faith way out" of Vietnam as soon as possible.[53]

These were not new criticisms, but this high-profile attack on television enlarged the rift between King and the Johnson administration. The much-publicized White House Conference on Civil Rights began on a sour note when the *New York Times* reported that an African American soldier had been refused burial in his hometown cemetery in Wetumpka,

Alabama, because the Negro section was full.[54] The situation worsened when Johnson relegated King to spectator status. White House officials stage-managed the conference, allowing close allies and war supporters Roy Wilkins, Whitney Young, and Solicitor General Thurgood Marshall to address the meeting, where they endlessly praised the president.[55] By contrast, King was virtually invisible. Columnists Rowland Evans and Robert Novak speculated that the Johnson administration marginalized King "out of a realistic fear that he could eloquently invoke opposition to Vietnam."[56] According to Andrew Young, this shabby treatment incensed SCLC officials, and they implored King to withdraw from the conference after the first day.[57] A chastened King left Washington without complaint, knowing that his antiwar statements had diminished his standing with the White House.[58]

The snubbing at the conference bolstered King's view that the war was seizing the emotions of the American public. His earlier hopes for Johnson's Great Society—a major factor in his restraint on Vietnam—were now vanishing under the weight of the war. The relationship between King and Johnson would steadily deteriorate during the explosive summer of 1966, furnishing hope to those who were aching for King to lead the antiwar movement. Among his manifold challenges would be the emergence of the Black Power movement, which burst onto the scene and threatened the principles of both nonviolence and integration.

June–December 1966: The Meredith March, Chicago, and the Unremitting War

The second half of 1966 was an especially trying period for King: the Great Society was becoming a casualty of the war, the civil rights struggle reached an impasse, the number of American troops in Vietnam neared 400,000, the popularity of Black Power challenged his long-cherished principles of integration and nonviolence, his campaign to bring political and economic change to Chicago ended in frustration, and the Democratic Party suffered a devastating defeat at the polls that was partially attributed to "white backlash." For the rest of his life, King would see chaos and confusion everywhere as he searched in vain for a way to revitalize the civil rights movement and mend its fraying coalition. These frustrating developments and the sense that King's constituency was ahead of him in opposing the war were instrumental in his eventual break with the Johnson administration.

As the war was supplanting civil rights as the paramount concern of Americans, the Black Power movement exploded onto the national scene during the summer of 1966. It all began on June 6, 1966, when James Meredith, the thirty-two-year-old air force veteran who had become the University of Mississippi's first African American student in 1962, was shot by an unemployed white man. At the time, Meredith was on just the second day of his planned 222-mile trek through Mississippi, which he hoped would inspire African Americans to register to vote.[59] Only hours later, an irate King, along with SNCC's Stokely Carmichael and CORE's Floyd McKissick, flew to Memphis and gathered around Meredith's bed at Bowld's Hospital, vowing to continue the march from the exact site of the ambush in Hernando, Mississippi.[60] They called Roy Wilkins and Whitney Young, who caught the next flight to Memphis. After the frustrations of the past nine months, King seized on this opportunity to unify and rekindle the movement and focus the nation's attention to the scourge of racism in Mississippi, the most wayward state in the Deep South.[61]

The civil rights leadership and a large media contingent converged on Memphis, and the leaders of the five major civil rights organizations held a summit at the Lorraine Hotel.[62] It did not take long, however, for the internecine bickering to resurface in a sensational fashion under the intense glare of the national spotlight. Instead of bringing the movement together, the Meredith march exposed the growing fissure between the Old Guard, represented by the NAACP's Wilkins and the Urban League's Young, who supported the war and were closely allied with the White House, and the more militant Carmichael and McKissick, who were enamored with black separatism and embittered by the war. While King tried in vain to mediate, Wilkins and Young dropped out when they heard that Carmichael wanted to bar whites and insisted on using the Deacons of Defense, an armed African American organization from Bogalusa, Louisiana, to guard the marchers.[63] Wilkins particularly resented Carmichael's reference to the president as "that cat Johnson" and other insults.[64] King was also suspicious of the participation of the Deacons, but according to Andrew Young, King made a distinction between the Deacons' espousal of "defensive violence" and "retaliatory violence."[65] He implored everyone to recognize the need for interracialism, and he refused to defect when SNCC and CORE protested white involvement in the march. Although whites participated in the Meredith march, according to historian Clayborne Carson, their presence was "less noticeable than at any other major civil rights demonstration in the 1960s."[66]

While Meredith lay in the hospital, recovering from his near-fatal wounds and vowing never to walk through Mississippi unarmed, the march resumed.[67] Within minutes, Mississippi state troopers started bellowing orders at the marchers and shoved SNCC's Cleveland Sellers to the ground. This act was captured by photographers and splashed across the pages of newspapers around the country.[68] According to Sellers, a warm repartee developed between King and SNCC members as they marched through some of the most impoverished hamlets in Mississippi, leaving the inhabitants of the Delta "awestruck by Dr. King's presence."[69] Despite SNCC's longtime resentment of King's top-down leadership style, SNCC marchers grew to appreciate his open-mindedness and his delightful sense of humor.

When the small band of marchers entered the town of Greenwood, Mississippi, on June 16, trouble ensued. Local officials denied SNCC permission to set up its sleeping tent at an African American school, but Carmichael did it anyway. Officials swooped in and arrested him, but he was released six hours later after he posted a $100 bond. Shortly thereafter, Carmichael stood before a crowd of 600 people, including scores of journalists, and said, "This is the 27th time I have been arrested—I ain't going to jail no more. I ain't going to jail no more." *New York Times* columnist Gene Roberts, who was on the ground at Greenwood, reported: "Five times Mr. Carmichael shouted, 'We want black power!' And each time the younger members of the audience shouted back, 'Black Power!' 'Every courthouse in Mississippi ought to be burned down to get rid of the dirt,' Mr. Carmichael added as the audience applauded enthusiastically."[70] Willie Ricks, one of the most outspoken and militant SNCC workers, jumped onto the platform and, to thunderous applause, repeatedly asked, "What do you want?" And the crowd responded, "Black Power." The chants of "Black Power" roused the marchers and the onlookers into a frenzy.[71] The media seized on this outburst and created a national sensation. "More than anything," Sellers later explained, this display of emotion "assured that the Meredith March Against Fear would go down in history as one of the major turning points in the black liberation struggle."[72]

King had flown back to Chicago to deal with a riot in a Puerto Rican neighborhood and thus did not witness the spectacle in Greenwood, but his aides in Mississippi looked on in horror: after all, integration was a cornerstone of King's philosophy. King immediately returned to Mississippi to confer with Carmichael and quell the uproar. A reporter who had covered King for more than two years recalled that he had never seen him so "hard-pressed" and "emotionally and physically shaken."[73] King none-theless continued to preach against violence, including at a rally in Yazoo City.[74] For the rest of the march, chants of "Black Power" reverberated in the muggy Delta air, seeped into the collective national consciousness, and caused trepidation among middle-class white Americans. Although the media sometimes exaggerated King's differences with SNCC, the notion of black separatism was anathema to him. To King, "It was absolutely necessary for the Negro to gain power," but the "Black power" slogan was unfortunate "because it tends to give the impression of black nationalism"; he advocated "the sharing of power with white people."[75] He argued on numerous occasions that since African Americans constituted only 10 per-cent of the population, they could not "by tensions alone induce 90 percent to change a way of life."[76]

The march continued for another ten days before it concluded with Carmichael's speech at a rally of 15,000 in front of the state capitol in Jackson—the largest gathering of African Americans ever in Mississippi. Journalist Paul Good recounted that King's attempt to resurrect his "I Have a Dream" speech from the March on Washington was a "lackluster" effort that turned into a "nightmare." The expulsion of Charles Evers and other NAACP leaders for repudiating the "march manifesto" marred the event's climax.[77] In the end, King's high hopes for uniting the movement were dashed, and it turned into a public relations fiasco.

Roy Wilkins and Whitney Young, already seething over SNCC's and CORE's antiwar stance, blasted Black Power as a racist philosophy.[78] Within hours after Carmichael's first chant in Greenwood, the media had latched on to Black Power and made it the dominant story throughout the summer.[79] Instead of focusing on the war in Vietnam and racism in Mississippi, the media ran dire stories about the imminent collapse of the civil rights movement. King fanned the flames of the media frenzy when he said the civil rights movement was "very close" to a permanent split over the Black Power issue. Reiterating his disapproval of Black Power, he nonetheless claimed the "NAACP wouldn't mind a split because they think they are the only civil rights organization."[80] In the midst of these highly publicized battles within the movement, Whitney Young flew to Vietnam at the behest of President Johnson, becoming the first civil rights leader to go there, and he later reported a "dramatic improvement" in the treatment of African Americans in the military.[81] The resonance of Black Power among young African Americans disquieted King, and virtually all of them hated the Vietnam War. Fearing that he would permanently lose this constituency if he continued to be mute on the war, King began to reconsider his silence.

The internal wrangling over Black Power did not stop King from going forward with his campaign in Chicago. Speaking again in Jackson on August 10, 1966, he called the "spread of the Negro revolution from the sprawling plantations of Mississippi and Alabama to the desolate slums and ghettoes of the North" the most "significant event of the year." Throughout the summer of 1966, troubles over Black Power were heightened by King's frustration over the war. Sensing that the war had turned liberals away from civil rights and toward world peace, King acknowledged, "If you were anticipating the escalation of the war in Vietnam into a nuclear war with China, the voting rights of a few thousand Negroes in Alabama or Mississippi did not seem important."[82] Realizing that the war was sucking the oxygen out of the movement for racial justice, King knew he would have to break his silence on the war.

Nor did the plight of African American slum dwellers in Chicago seem important to a nation and a White House consumed by the war in Southeast Asia. Legendary Chicago columnist Mike Royko cynically quipped, "Chicagoans already knew about slums. Whites were indifferent, and Negroes didn't have to be reminded where they lived."[83] For the SCLC, Chicago represented a radical departure; it was unfamiliar terrain filled with problems that had vexed social workers for years. Racism in Chicago and other northern cities was not embedded in the law, but residential and educational segregation existed because of long-established real estate practices and customs that were sanctioned by powerful political and economic elites.[84] Like the issue of Vietnam, the prospect of tackling de facto segregation in Chicago elicited a host of concerns that deeply divided King's inner circle. Longtime aides Bayard Rustin, Andrew Young, and Hosea Williams strongly advised against it. They argued that the recent voting rights legislation made it crucial to stay in the South, and they warned that the local Democratic machine headed by Chicago mayor Richard Daley was a formidable adversary.[85] Rustin, who had years of experience organizing in the North, was loath to upset the existing power structure and jeopardize his vision of a liberal-labor coalition. He warned King that the patterns of racial discrimination in Chicago were complex and, compared with the SCLC's recent campaigns in Birmingham and Selma, less susceptible to buckling under the media spotlight.[86]

Rustin's protestations notwithstanding, King was determined to launch a campaign in Chicago. His grim observation of the scorched rubble of Watts and his realization that the poverty-ridden slums were breeding a generation susceptible to the appeal of Black Power made him resolute. After all, King argued, the boys and girls growing up hungry in rat-infested flats without heat were also "God's children."[87] Former SNCC member Bernard Lafayette, who had been organizing in Chicago since 1963, reasoned that "Chicago symbolized the things that were happening in the North," and King wanted to see if they "could apply the same organizing techniques and strategies that we had used in the South."[88]

From the outset, King and the SCLC came up against a wall of opposition from Chicago politicians and white citizens.[89] As such, it was a microcosm for the widespread problems of dilapidated housing and patterns of residential, vocational, and educational discrimination that defied easy solutions. Another obstacle was the SCLC's difficulty in devising a coherent, viable plan to combat the troubles plaguing the slums.[90] Unlike Bull Connor in Birmingham and Jim Clark in Selma, who were easily parodied as pot-bellied southern racists, Mayor Daley was a shrewd politician who controlled a powerful machine with African American support, and he was able to preempt King with shallow proposals indicating concern for the poor.[91]

By early summer, the SCLC had changed tactics, holding a series of high-profile demonstrations to demand open housing and targeting the redlining tactics of realtors and financial institutions that reinforced residential segregation. On July 10 King launched his campaign for open housing with a rally that filled only half the seats at Soldiers' Field.[92] Then riots erupted throughout the city that jeopardized King's reputation for nonviolence. In the coming weeks, open-housing demonstrations took place in white neighborhoods near Marquette Park and in the middle-class suburbs of Cicero, Chicago Heights, and Evergreen Park, provoking white violence. Mobs of angry whites screaming "White Power" heckled marchers mercilessly, unfurled racially offensive banners, and threw bottles, rocks, and eggs at the unarmed demonstrators.[93] In a march through Gage Park on August 5, King was struck by a rock, and at least twenty-eight other marchers were injured.[94] King was dumbfounded by this display of northern racial bias: "I've never seen anything like it. I've been in many demonstrations all across the South, but I can say that I have never seen—even in Mississippi and Alabama—mobs as hate-filled as I've seen in Chicago."[95]

Dorothy Tillman, a young SCLC staffer from Alabama, had moved to Chicago the previous year with James Bevel to establish an SCLC office on the West Side. She too was shocked by the virulence of racism in the city: "I'd never seen whites like these in the South. These whites was up in trees like monkeys throwing bricks and bottles and stuff. I mean racism, you could almost cut it, a whole 'nother level of racism and hatred." Andrew Young agreed with Tillman. In the South, he said, they often faced mobs of fifty to a hundred people, but in Chicago, "maybe a couple of hundred demonstrators were surrounded by a mob of ten thousand or more." Young went on to say: "The violence in the South always came from a rabble element. But these were women and children and husbands and wives coming out of their homes becoming a mob—and in some ways it was far more frightening."[96]

Southern-style civil rights demonstrations that had unfolded with such theatrical success in Montgomery, Birmingham, and Selma floundered in Chicago. Whereas the American public increasingly perceived civil rights marchers in the South as noble crusaders, they sympathized with the desire of Chicago's white residents to protect their own neighborhoods.[97] Most observers concluded that Chicago was a defeat for King because his campaign for open housing only hardened the opposition. In addition, the passion that had once suffused the movement had vanished, and many white liberals conflated civil rights demonstrators with angry thugs chanting "Black Power." The day after Johnson's civil rights bill died in the Senate, Chicago congressman Roman Pucinski observed, "Go into Chicago today in any home, any bar, any barbershop, and you will find that people are talking about Martin Luther King and how they are moving in on us and what's going to happen to our neighborhoods."[98] A Gallup poll conducted in September 1966 reported that white resistance to civil rights measures had reached its highest point in years, with 52 percent of all adults believing that the Johnson administration was pushing civil rights too hard.[99] The hatred aimed at King and the SCLC by residents of Chicago's white working-class neighborhoods dramatized the stark reality of the "white backlash" that was gripping the national psyche and turning support for civil rights into a political liability for white liberal politicians like Lyndon Johnson. King's campaign in Chicago was followed by the midterm elections, resulting in a shattering defeat for the Democrats that reduced their majority in the House by forty-seven seats. The emergence of this dreaded white backlash augured a retreat on civil rights.[100]

More than two decades later, King's closest confidant, Ralph Abernathy, called the inability to alter the rigid patterns of racism in Chicago "an embittering experience" for the SCLC and King, and Abernathy was "not sure that Martin ever got over it."[101] However, the difficulties encountered in the northern slums also constituted a "turning point," according to Andrew Young, shifting King's focus to the multifaceted causes of racial injustice.[102] As 1966 drew to a close, King blamed the Vietnam War for draining billions of dollars from the battle against poverty and sacrificing the lives of too many young African American men. Economic justice had always been a focal point of King's vision for civil rights.[103] Now, his sojourn in Chicago and his firsthand experience in the northern slums fortified his commitment to economic justice and to speaking out against the excesses of capitalism. For King, the Vietnam War symbolized the moral depravity of a society that condoned poverty amid unparalleled affluence. Addressing an SCLC planning meeting in Frogmore, South Carolina, on November 14, 1966, he said, "We are living in a sick nation that will brutalize unjustifiably millions of boys and girls, men and women in Vietnam." In a reprise of his Nobel Prize address, he declared that "man's survival is dependent upon his ability to solve the problems of racial injustice, poverty, and war."[104]

For the most part, though, King maintained his self-imposed silence on Vietnam throughout the summer and early fall of 1966. Even prior to the election, the war had dimmed prospects for civil rights legislation and large government expenditures to aid the urban slums.[105] King realized that he now had less to lose if he broke with the White House over Vietnam, but his wife recalled that he still "agonized" over the decision.[106] In December 1966, chastened by Chicago and exasperated by the presence of more than 400,000 American soldiers in Vietnam (approximately 60,000 of whom were African American), King testified before Senator Abraham Ribicoff's Subcommittee on Government Operations. He condemned the nation's misplaced priorities, noting that the government spent billions of dollars on space exploration and the "ill-considered" war in Vietnam "while the antipoverty program is cautiously initiated, zealously supervised, and evaluated for immediate results." The bombs exploding in Vietnam, King testified, "destroy the hopes and possibilities for a decent America," and the raging "chaos of the cities, the persistence of poverty, the degeneration of our national prestige throughout the world are compelling arguments for achieving peace agreements." As for the War on Poverty, King characterized it as "scarcely a skirmish."[107] His despondency over the war was magnified by reports that African American soldiers in Vietnam were dying at higher rates than their white counterparts.[108]

Two days before his Senate testimony, King released a statement that he was taking a two-month sabbatical in Jamaica to write a book that would examine the course of the civil rights movement and suggest new ideas and programs. Tentatively titled "Where Do We Go from Here?" the book would address white backlash, implications of the Black Power slogan, and federal priorities.[109] The question of when King would finally jump aboard the antiwar bandwagon continued to mystify even his closest associates. At the beginning of 1967, King was besieged by a flurry of calls from friends William Sloane Coffin, socialist leader Norman Thomas, and Allard Lowenstein, prodding him to take a public stance against the war. He avoided them all and fled to Jamaica to write his book.[110] Peace activists were heartened by the news that James Bevel was leaving the SCLC to head an antiwar mobilization planned for the spring of 1967.[111] Still, leaders of the antiwar movement looked to King as a savior, believing that he alone could merge the peace and civil rights movements into a powerful political coalition for domestic change.

A Time to Break the Silence

James Bevel, a SNCC pioneer from the Nashville wing of the student movement, had initiated the brilliant "Fill the Jails" strategy in Birmingham in 1963 and directed the Selma campaign for the SCLC.[112] In the fall of 1965 he had moved to Chicago to devise a plan for the anti-slum campaign there. By that time, many of his SNCC comrades had lost faith in the ideal of the "beloved community," endorsed racial separatism, or become casualties of the movement. Bevel, however, had joined King's inner sanctum. Always wearing his trademark black-and-gold yarmulke on his bald pate, the fiery Bevel was becoming obsessed with the conflict in Vietnam.[113] Of course, he was not alone in his anguish over the war. His estranged wife, Diane Nash Bevel, had recently joined a delegation of American women that traveled to North Vietnam to assess the impact of U.S. bombing on innocent Vietnamese civilians.[114] Now alone with his two infant children in a squalid tenement on Chicago's West Side, Bevel was becoming psychologically unhinged. One evening, as he was washing a load of diapers in the basement, he claimed he heard the voice of God. The voice told him that the war in Vietnam could not be stopped by demonstrations alone; a group of prominent figures had to go to Vietnam on a special ship and interject "themselves between the warring armies forcing them to shoot the peace brigade or stop the killing entirely." The next morning, Bevel told Andrew Young that the Lord had instructed him to stop the killing of innocent brothers, sisters, and children in Vietnam.[115]

Shortly thereafter, Bevel related this story to David Dellinger and Fred Halstead, leaders of the Spring Mobilization to End the War in Vietnam (MOBE). Although they suspected that Bevel was mentally unstable, they offered him the position of MOBE leader because of his reputation as a brilliant organizer. Most important, they hoped Bevel would be able to convince King to join the antiwar cause, and Bevel promised that he could do so.[116] They even supplied him with travel funds and babysitting services so that he could go to Atlanta and personally beseech King to participate in MOBE. But by the time Bevel reached Atlanta, King had already left for Jamaica, along with his personal assistant Bernard Lee. Refusing to be deterred the steadfast Bevel followed King to Jamaica.[117]

At the dawn of 1967, there were a number of indicators pointing to King's imminent break with the White House over Vietnam. His measured and occasional thrusts against the war in carefully chosen venues had thus far been ineffective. They only whetted the appetite of the peace movement while angering pro-war stalwarts in the civil rights community, satisfying neither and leaving King personally frustrated at his inability to mold the dialogue. After the disappointment in Chicago, the SCLC was uncertain what the next phase in the civil rights struggle should be.[118] In the meantime, King was losing his luster among large segments of African Americans, particularly the young, who were tuning out his message of nonviolence and becoming increasingly enamored with Black Power.[119] King was also aware that African American public opinion was turning against the war. Indeed, by early 1967, pro-war sentiment among African Americans was plummeting. And although the antiwar movement still lacked cohesion, it was attracting more mainstream, established figures, adding to its respectability and making it less susceptible to charges of being populated by pro-Soviet, unsavory Vietniks.[120] With the coalition of civil rights organizations, students, and intellectuals in disarray under the collective weight of the war, King was beginning to understand that the political risks of opposing the war were dwindling. King had reached a position where he had less to lose and more to gain by following his heart and taking a forceful stand against Vietnam.

On January 14, 1967, during a layover at the Miami airport en route to Jamaica, King experienced a transformative moment, an epiphany of sorts. Browsing through a newspaper rack, King picked up the latest edition of *Ramparts* magazine, a Catholic publication with links to the New Left, which contained an article titled "The Children of Vietnam" by William Pepper, a political scientist and human rights activist who had spent six weeks in Vietnam visiting orphanages. The article was accompanied by twenty-four pages of photographs of Vietnamese babies who had been mutilated by American napalm bombs. In the article's preface, anti-war activist and pediatrician Dr. Benjamin Spock asked how "America, which manufactures and delivers the efficient napalm that causes deep and deforming burns, can deny all responsibility" for the treatment of these children?[121] While King and Lee ate lunch, King opened the magazine and perused the disturbing images of disfigured and maimed children. Years later, Lee vividly recalled King's reaction: "When he came to *Ramparts* magazine he stopped. He froze as he looked at the pictures from Vietnam. He saw a picture of a Vietnamese mother holding her dead baby, a baby killed by our military. I looked up and said, 'Doesn't it taste any good?' and he answered, 'Nothing will ever taste any good for me until I do everything I can to end that war.'"[122] After months of vacillating over the war, these searing photographs pushed King over the edge. He later acknowledged that the gruesome pictures of maimed Vietnamese children had forced him to "come to the conclusion that there is an existential moment when you must decide to speak for yourself; nobody else can speak for you."[123] While writing in relative seclusion in Jamaica, he remained transfixed by the photographs in *Ramparts* and resolved to cast aside political considerations and follow his calling as a minister of the gospel: he would speak out against injustice not only in Selma, Watts, and Chicago, but also in Vietnam.[124]

Only days after their arrival in Jamaica, Lee found a disheveled Bevel on the doorstep of King's secluded villa on the north side of the island. Lee knocked on the door of King's study and announced that Bevel had arrived and wanted to discuss the war. Shocked at Bevel's appearance, King politely ushered him into his office.[125] Bevel told King about his vision in the Chicago basement and warned King that his reputation would be imperiled unless he broke his silence on Vietnam. Breaching decorum with his forthrightness, Bevel demanded to know why King was "teaching non-violence to African Americans in Mississippi, but not to Lyndon Johnson in Vietnam?" Reminding King that his allegiance was to God and God alone, Bevel counseled against being overly political and queried, "Are the Vietnamese not your brothers and sisters?"[126] Bevel also asked for a leave of absence from the SCLC to head MOBE and lobbied for King's participation in the demonstration scheduled for April 15 at the United Nations. Disturbed by Bevel's rambling, King telephoned Andrew Young and told him, "Bevel sounds likes he's off his rocker and needs a psychiatrist."[127] Nonetheless, King listened patiently to Bevel's tirade, promised to give it "serious consideration," granted him leave to head MOBE's rally, and bought him a one-way ticket back to New York City. As King continued to write in solitude, he kept the *Ramparts* photographs nearby.[128]

A few weeks after Bevel's departure, King left Jamaica for Miami and called his key advisers Andrew Young, Stanley Levison, and labor leader Cleveland Robinson. According to the FBI agents who were listening in, King informed them that he wanted to take an active role in the peace movement and had concluded, "We are marking time in the battle of the ghetto with the war in Vietnam." Despite Levison's and Young's vigorous opposition, King vowed that he had no choice but to speak out against the war because America is "morally bankrupt." Nonetheless, the enormity of the move forced King to delay his final decision about participating in Bevel's peace march until March 6.[129]

In the meantime, King accepted an invitation from *Nation* editor Carey McWilliams to address a conference on the Vietnam War in Beverly Hills, California, on February 25, 1967. Appearing with Senators Ernest Gruening, Mark Hatfield, George McGovern, and Eugene McCarthy, all of whom assailed U.S. policy in Vietnam, King devoted his entire speech to the war. Entitled "The Casualties of the War in Vietnam," King's remarks mesmerized the overflow audience of 1,500 at the Beverly Hilton Hotel. In an evocative tone, uttering words he would repeat five weeks later at the Riverside Church in New York City, King proclaimed that "the promises of the Great Society have been shot down on the battlefields of Vietnam." Among the prime casualties of the war, according to King, were the more than 1 million Vietnamese children who had been "incinerated by napalm." King enumerated three primary objections to the war: that U.S. involvement in Vietnam violated the United Nations Charter and the principle of self-determination, that it crippled the antipoverty program, and that it undermined the cherished constitutional right to dissent. In his closing remarks, King distinguished himself from the SNCC and CORE militants who were gravitating to racial separatism and antiwar activism out of disillusionment with America. Instead, King characterized himself as a patriot, and he laid out his vision for a better America: "Let me say finally that I oppose the war in Vietnam because I love America. I speak out against it not in anger but with anxiety and sorrow in my heart, and above all with a passionate desire to see our beloved country stand as the moral example of the world. I speak against this war because I am disappointed with America. There can be no disappointment when there is no great love. . . . We are presently moving down a dead-end road that can lead to national disaster."[130]

The next day, news of the speech was splattered across the front pages of the *New York Times* and the *Los Angeles Times*, but the *Washington Post* ignored it.[131] King's moral strictures against the war harked back to his earlier criticisms, and he was circumspect about his future involvement in antiwar protests. In spite of this, King's broadside against the war penetrated deeper than his previous attacks from the Ebenezer pulpit, and it marked a crucial step in his long struggle with his conscience. King's appearance on the same platform with such outspoken critics demonstrated his willingness to oppose the war and prompted CALCAV to invite him to speak at an antiwar gathering at Riverside Church in New York City on April 4, 1967.[132]

Notwithstanding the Beverly Hills speech, King's chief advisers still fretted over his overtures to the antiwar camp. Levison, in particular, regarded Bevel as emotionally unstable and worried that his recklessness could embarrass King. The day after the speech at the Hilton, Levison complimented King, noting, "Your voice is bigger when you're with four Senators," but he implored King not to get involved with Bevel's peace march.[133] A week later, King's day of reckoning had arrived. His "kitchen cabinet" convened at Harry Wachtel's posh Madison Avenue office to discuss the SCLC's woeful finances (contributions had plummeted 40 percent over the past year) and the final revisions to King's book, which he had completed in Jamaica. But the issue of whether King should participate at the April 15 antiwar rally at the United Nations sidetracked the main agenda. Wiretapped surveillance of the conference indicated that, with the exception of Bevel, "all participants in the meeting" were opposed to King's involvement in the MOBE-sponsored rally.[134] His advisers were worried about King sharing a platform with unelected extremists with communist ties. Andrew Young was uncomfortable with the composition of the mobilization committee and feared they were trying to embarrass King.[135] Levison, tactically conservative, shared Young's reservations. Not surprisingly, Rustin, still holding on to his vision of a broad political coalition, opposed cutting ties with President Johnson. According to Robert L. Greene, a Michigan State University professor who had joined the SCLC staff during the Meredith march, Bevel's emotional plea to King to forsake political expediency had the greatest effect on him. "Bevel had a very uncanny way of making an impact on Martin," Greene told King biographer David Garrow.[136] The emotional discussions lasted for hours but ended with the postponement of a final decision. King was inexorably moving toward the antiwar camp.[137]

FBI reports of King's impending leap to the antiwar movement alarmed a beleaguered Lyndon Johnson. With the war sapping his political vitality, Johnson dreaded a merger between the civil rights and antiwar movements with the charismatic King at the helm.[138] On the day prior to King's address in Beverly Hills, the president informed White House assistant Marvin Watson that he would meet with King on March 13, when the civil rights leader would be in Washington to push for federal funding for the slum-ridden Shaw area.[139] The president was hoping to use his legendary "Johnson treatment" on King to prevent him from straying too far on Vietnam.[140] But King abruptly canceled the meeting, leading a visibly chagrined president to instruct an aide to find out "why Martin Luther King has cancelled two engagements with me."[141] The lack of communication between King and the president—they had not met since preparations for the White House Conference on Civil Rights the previous year—contrasted sharply with their frequent exchanges during the legislative triumphs of 1964 and 1965. Even in their most productive periods, Johnson and King had an ambiguous relationship, but King's mistrust of the president now mingled with a profound bitterness and disappointment over the war. In King's eyes, their longtime association was damaged beyond repair. While Rustin and others in King's inner circle worried about Johnson's reaction to King's position on Vietnam, King no longer cared. He was done with politics and believed the administration was using him for its own short-term political ends.[142]

Fearing the worst, Levison, Rustin, and Wachtel stepped up their insistence that MOBE be purged of radical elements. They worried about the adverse publicity if King shared the stage with the inflammatory Stokely Carmichael. Finally, King informed his anxious aides of his decision: "I'm gonna march. I promised Bevel."[143] On March 16 an ebullient Bevel announced at a news conference that King would lead the antiwar march, observing that his presence "would symbolize the growing awareness in black communities that Vietnam is a racist war."[144] Not to be outdone, Andrew Young issued a statement from SCLC headquarters in Atlanta to reassure uneasy supporters of King's continued commitment to civil rights: "We've just decided to give more attention to the war in Vietnam." In the coming days, King sharpened his rhetoric, declaring, "The war in Vietnam has become the major obstacle to the civil rights movement," and he argued that "programs will suffer less from [my] active opposition to the war than from not opposing it."[145]

Backing up his words with action, on March 25, 1967, King participated in his first antiwar demonstration in Chicago, where he led a crowd of 5,000 down State Street, through throngs of Easter shoppers, to the Chicago Coliseum. Flanked by Dr. Benjamin Spock, King gave his most militant speech against the war, describing it as "a blasphemy against all that America stands for," and he called for an end to the war by "negotiation."[146] Only five days later, at an SCLC convention in Louisville, Kentucky, King insisted that civil disobedience was necessary to arouse the conscience of the nation and end the war: "We are merely marking time in the civil rights movement if we do not take a stand against the war."[147] King's speeches, press interviews, and participation in the Chicago demonstration were merely preliminaries for the major event that would signal his break with the Johnson administration: the April 15 rally at the United Nations.

King's appearance at the UN with radicals such as Stokely Carmichael, CORE's Floyd McKissick, and singer Pete Seeger, who had been blacklisted during the McCarthy era, was sure to be controversial. So, in an effort to mitigate the anticipated damage, his advisers searched for a more august forum where King could articulate his antiwar message.[148] Andrew Young made a few telephone calls and arranged for King to deliver a major address on Vietnam at the Riverside Church in New York City, under the auspices of CALCAV, on the evening of April 4.[149] Following King's speech, distinguished historian Henry Steele Commager, Rabbi Abraham Heschel of the Jewish Theological Seminary, and John C. Bennett, president of the Union Theological Seminary, would participate in a panel discussion on Vietnam. Young was delighted, relieved that these influential theologians would shield King from a communist taint.[150] King enlisted his longtime friend and neighbor Professor Vincent Harding of Spelman College to help him draft the speech.[151] As April 4 approached, King and his advisers were filled with trepidation, keenly aware of the magnitude of the occasion. On the evening of the speech, Levison was so distraught that he returned to his apartment only twenty blocks away and went to bed.[152]

On that cool, clear spring evening, more than 3,000 people, including dozens of religious leaders of all denominations, streamed into the main chapel of the Riverside Church on Manhattan's Upper West Side to hear King speak on the war.[153] John Lewis was one of the thousands who braved the long lines. Over the years, Lewis had heard King speak numerous times, but he was not alone in calling the Riverside speech King's "finest." Its moral clarity reminded Lewis of his own message "delivered on behalf of SNCC a year earlier" after the murder of Sammy Younge Jr.[154] King's Riverside address was undoubtedly one of the most courageous and heartfelt speeches of his life. Even though it was largely a distillation of views he had expressed earlier in his sermons at Ebenezer and in his recent speech in Beverly Hills, King's searing attack on the war, entitled "Beyond Vietnam," sent shock waves through the nation. Friend and foe alike were deeply moved by his eloquence in what was perhaps the most powerful indictment yet of America's policy in Vietnam.

Loud applause and a standing ovation greeted King as he walked up to the dais to begin his remarks. After the cheers subsided, King began by saying, "I come to this magnificent house of worship tonight because my conscience leaves me no other choice." The time had come "when silence is betrayal." He said he was honored to appear before such a distinguished assemblage of religious leaders who have chosen "to move beyond the smooth patriotism to the higher grounds of a firm dissent" predicated on "the mandates of conscience and a reading of history." Over the past few years, he said, as he "moved to break the betrayal of my own silences and speak from the burnings of my own heart," many people questioned the wisdom of his speaking out against the wanton destruction in Vietnam. Taking on these critics, he traced how the path from the Dexter Avenue Baptist Church in Montgomery, where he had begun his pastorate back in May 1954, clearly led "to this sanctuary tonight." As he had done previously, King cited his calling as a minister of the gospel, which gave him the moral legitimacy to speak out on matters outside of civil rights. In the following words, King described his motivation for "bringing Vietnam inside the field of his moral vision":

> There is at the outset a very obvious and almost facile connection between the Vietnam War and the struggle, I, and others have been waging in America. A few years ago, there was a shining moment in that struggle. It seemed as if there was a real promise of hope for the poor—both black and white—through the Poverty Program. There were experiments, hopes, new beginnings. Then came the build-up in Vietnam and I watched the program broken and eviscerated as if it were some idle political plaything of a society gone mad on war, and I knew that America would never invest the necessary funds or energies in rehabilitation of its poor so long

as adventures like Vietnam continued to draw men and skills and money like some demonic sucking tube. I was increasingly compelled to see the war as an enemy of the poor and to attack it as such.

Echoing SNCC's attacks on the war, King pointed out the lunacy of "taking the black men who had been crippled by our society and sending them 8,000 miles away to guarantee liberties which they had not found in Southwest Georgia and East Harlem."[155] As a recipient of the Nobel Prize for Peace in 1964, King reminded the audience that it would be inconsistent for him to preach the gospel of nonviolence when his own government was maiming and mutilating thousands of innocent civilians. For King, issues of world peace and nonviolent protest were indivisible.

Debunking the Cold War narrative that depicted Ho Chi Minh and the Vietcong as mere pawns in the fight against communism, King viewed the history of the Vietnam War through the prism of the long Vietnamese struggle for independence against colonial rule. In spite of Ho's paeans to our Declaration of Independence when the Vietnamese declared their own independence in 1945 "after a combined French and Japanese occupation," we refused to acknowledge them and even "decided to support France in its re-conquest of her former colony." Citing the litany of American military violence against innocent men, women, and children, like that depicted in the *Ramparts* article, King railed that the Vietnamese must see us as "strange liberators":

They watch as we poison their water, as we kill a million acres of their crops. They must weep as the bulldozers roar through their areas preparing to destroy the precious trees. They wander into hospitals with at least 20 casualties from American firepower for every "Vietcong" inflicted injury. So far we may have killed a million of them—mostly children. They wander into the towns and see thousands of children, homeless, without clothes, running in packs on the streets like animals. They see the children degraded by our soldiers as they beg for food. They see the children selling their sisters to our soldiers, soliciting for their mothers.

In a statement that particularly inflamed the Johnson administration, the Jewish community, and the mainstream civil rights establishment, King likened the military's use of its newest weapons to the torture perpetrated by the Germans in the concentration camps of Europe. As a first step in atoning for our sins against the Vietnamese people, King called for a plan to extricate ourselves from this "nightmarish conflict" that included a bombing halt and a unilateral cease-fire.[156]

In his closing remarks, all of King's misgivings about American society poured out with such ferocity that it stunned even his most ardent admirers. After months of restraint, he pulled no punches. To an audience made up largely of clergymen, he extolled the need to educate American youth on the nation's calamitous course in Vietnam and counsel them on conscientious objection as a viable alternative to military service. In chilling words, he called the war in Vietnam "a symptom of a far deeper malady within the American spirit," and he declared that under the cloak of anticommunism, "the United States government was the greatest purveyor of violence in the world today." His pent-up frustration with American capitalism exploded as he called for a "radical revolution of values" and urged a "shift from a 'thing-oriented' society to a 'person-oriented' society." He condemned a society where "profit motives and property rights are considered more important than people." King challenged the American people to rededicate themselves to the struggle for a better world. "The choice is ours, and though we might prefer it otherwise, we *must* choose in this crucial moment of human history."[157] The audience reacted with a second deafening round of applause. After his speech, King and the other panelists held a question-and-answer session. When it was all over, King left the chapel in a jubilant mood, heartened by the audience's appreciation and relieved that he had finally told the world how adamantly he opposed the war.

King's joy was soon dampened by a fusillade of criticism from nearly all quarters, confirming Levison's forebodings. In particular, "Beyond Vietnam" was scorned by members of the African American establishment who adhered to Cold War liberalism and were wary about appearing to be unpatriotic during wartime. The editorial board of the *New York Amsterdam News* urged African Americans to rally around the country and reminded its readers of President Johnson's unparalleled achievements in the area of civil rights.[158] The *Pittsburgh Courier* likewise rebuked King for "tragically preaching the wrong doctrine."[159] World War II veteran and baseball legend Jackie Robinson, whose eldest son Jackie Jr. was fighting in Vietnam, inveighed that King was "utterly on the wrong side of the track in Vietnam," and he could not understand why King placed the blame solely on Americans.[160] The lone African American member of the

Senate, newly elected Edward Brooke (R-Mass.), had just returned from a fact-finding mission in Vietnam and rebuked King's speech for ascribing sole responsibility for the conflict to the United States. Brooke opposed a bombing halt because "the enemy is not disposed to participate in any meaningful negotiations."[161]

In a column that disheartened King and his closest confidants, Bayard Rustin, who had been drifting away from King's inner circle for some time, went public with his opposition to King's antiwar stance. Calling Vietnam "Dr. King's Painful Dilemma," Rustin defended King's right to dissent but argued that the domestic problems confronting African Americans "are so vast and crushing" that blacks have "little energy to focus on international issues."[162] A few weeks later, in his regular column in the *New York Amsterdam News*, Rustin argued that an immediate American withdrawal would impose a totalitarian regime on the Vietnamese people. Rustin, a World War II conscientious objector and lifelong pacifist, enraged antiwar leaders when he accused them of being more anti-American than antiwar.[163] This attack was reminiscent of conservative critiques of the antiwar movement. No African American, however, delivered a more underhanded volley against King than journalist Carl Rowan, a close ally of President Johnson and head of the U.S. Information Agency. Days after King's speech, Rowan telephoned Johnson's press secretary, George Christian, and told him that "everyone in the Civil Rights movement has known that King is getting advice from a communist."[164] In an article published in *Reader's Digest*, Rowan resorted to Red-baiting, accusing King of being an egomaniac who was under the sway of communists.[165]

The African American leadership, seemingly oblivious to the new political realities that rendered additional civil rights legislation improbable, excoriated King because they feared his strident rhetoric would irreparably harm the civil rights movement. Even the venerable Ralph Bunche, a fellow Nobel Peace Prize recipient and the highest-ranking African American in the United Nations Secretariat, made a rare public statement and branded King's proposed merger of the civil rights and peace movements a "serious tactical mistake." He urged King to "either quit the civil rights movement or the anti–Viet[nam] war demonstrations." Similarly, Senator Brooke thought that King was doing "irreparable harm to the civil rights movement" by linking it with the war.[166]

The conservative *Pittsburgh Courier* echoed the opinion that King's antiwar position jeopardized advances in civil rights. In spite of Johnson's stalled civil rights agenda, the *Courier* bemoaned that King's antiwar stance would curtail African Americans' access to the corridors of power.[167] In a move that King expected, on April 10 the NAACP board voted unanimously against his proposal to merge the civil rights and peace movements.[168] At a press conference a few days later at the Biltmore Hotel in Los Angeles, King angrily denied that he advocated a "fusion" of the two movements, and he indicted the NAACP for "pretending that a war does not exist." The war, according to King, "does much more to waken the civil rights movement than my standing against the war."[169] Roy Wilkins charged that King placed "the antiwar effort above all others," and Whitney Young concurred, stating that the issues of peace and civil rights should remain separate.[170] In private, Young was not so decorous and came close to physically assaulting King at a fund-raiser in Great Neck, New York. After Young accused King of abandoning the poor for the antiwar movement, King tartly responded, "Whitney, what you're saying may get you a foundation grant, but it won't get you into the Kingdom of truth."[171]

These attacks from the African American community were disquieting enough, but King was most taken aback by the hostility emanating from the white establishment. *Newsweek*'s Kenneth Crawford branded the Riverside speech shocking for its "demagoguery and reckless distortions of fact."[172] *Life* indicted him for "betraying the cause for which he has worked so long" and suggested that King went "beyond his right to dissent" when he submitted "a proposal that amounts to abject surrender in Vietnam."[173] The *Washington Post* solemnly stated that King had done a "grave injury to those who are his natural allies" in the struggle to end racial discrimination. "Many who have listened to him with respect will never again accord him the same confidence," the *Post* predicted, and it brusquely dismissed his speech as "sheer inventions unsupported by fantasy."[174] Even the *New York Times*, the pillar of the liberal establishment, chastised King for "simplemindedly" fusing two problems that are "distinct and separate."[175] Andrew Young recalled that "Martin was almost reduced to tears by the stridency of the criticism directed against him." The *Washington Post* and *New York Times* editorials "hurt him the most," Young said, "because they challenged his very *right* to take a position."[176] Harry Belafonte agreed that the scathing editorials in the *Post* and the *Times* were so distressing to King because he had previously viewed these newspapers "as responsible instruments of information, but so distorted was their critique of him," he feared that an open debate "would be seriously crippled."[177]

The disparaging editorials provided solace to Lyndon Johnson, who felt personally betrayed by King's address. They substantiated his increasingly paranoid suspicion that young antiwar activists, with their long hair and their draft-card burning, were renegades acting outside the parameters of legitimate dissent. To the White House, King was now the ultimate traitor. White House aide Harry McPherson characterized him as "the crown prince of the Vietniks."[178] The day after King's Riverside speech, White House adviser John Roche, a liberal anticommunist academic, peremptorily dismissed the speech as the mutterings of a "loser" who, in "desperately searching for a constituency," has now "thrown his lot in with the commies."[179] Vice President Hubert Humphrey was more charitable, stating that "King had made a serious misjudgment."[180] In the aftermath of King's address, the White House mobilized its African American allies to support the war and marginalize King as a traitorous radical. Johnson also started paying more attention to the regular reports from J. Edgar Hoover about King's supposed communist activities. On April 19 Hoover sent a particularly inflammatory memo to the White House: "Based on King's recent activities and public utterances, it is clear that he is an instrument in the hands of subversive forces seeking to undermine our nation."[181] King and Johnson would never speak again.

A few laudatory reviews of "Beyond Vietnam" appeared amid the harsh invective. African Americans who had already lodged their opposition to the war were gratified. CORE's Floyd McKissick enthused, "Dr. King has come around and I'm glad to have him with us, no question about that."[182] King's mentor from Morehouse College, Dr. Benjamin E. Mayes, touted his ex-student as "one of the most courageous men alive today" and insisted that King's stand on Vietnam was consistent with Gandhian precepts of nonviolence.[183] Given that King was the most influential African American civil rights leader, the Riverside address encouraged a conversation within black communities on the merits of the war. Antiwar groups were jubilant and hoped it would turn the tide of African American opinion. In fact, it spurred the Black Methodist Board of Missions to oppose the war.[184] The *Detroit Free Press* predicted that the speech would strengthen the antiwar coalition and lead to widespread African American disenchantment with the war.[185] Most notably, Sam Washington of the *Chicago Defender* reported that African Americans in Chicago considered "King a good example to follow," and while opposition to the war was not yet widespread, African Americans were gradually moving "over to King's side" and rejecting the recommendations of the NAACP and the Urban League.[186] The left-leaning *Nation* was predictably delighted at King's

Riverside speech; it targeted pro-war liberals' hypocrisy and lauded King for "exposing the myth that foreign policy has no relation to domestic needs."[187] Rumors began to swirl of King as a possible third-party presidential candidate with Dr. Spock as his running mate. It was heady talk. King never encouraged these rumors, but the Riverside speech provided a well-needed boost to the antiwar movement, which had been experiencing growing pains and was in desperate need of a charismatic leader of King's stature. It also rejuvenated King's standing among young African Americans, who detested the war and had disdained King's silence.

The spate of criticisms notwithstanding, Riverside liberated King and gave him a renewed sense of purpose. Defending his dual role as a civil rights leader and an opponent of the war, King harked back to the SCLC's motto: "To Redeem the Soul of America." This meant, he said, that "we could not limit our vision to certain rights for black people." He reminded audiences at every opportunity that one of the original reasons for forming the SCLC back in 1957 had been to save America from the sins of its racist and violent past.[188] Voicing opposition to the dehumanizing war was in consonance with King's long-standing philosophy, and it somewhat relieved the pain of the personal and media attacks. After months of suppressed guilt over his muted opposition to Vietnam, King felt purged. On April 8 he told Levison that the speech may have been politically unwise, but it was morally necessary. After all, the United States was spending $35 billion a year on the war but less than $2 billion on civil rights.[189] King's sense of personal deliverance did not relieve his chronic exhaustion, and SCLC staff member Dorothy Cotton observed that King fell into a major depression that plagued him until his assassination the following year.[190]

April 15, 1967, was a damp, cold day, but an estimated 100,000 to 125,000 people showed up for MOBE's march in New York City.[191] The controversy surrounding the Riverside speech contributed to the massive turnout. In fact, it was the largest antiwar demonstration since the beginning of the Vietnam War. The *World Journal Tribune*, however, noted "the sparse Negro representation."[192] It was an eclectic throng of marchers, including a group of about seventy draft-card burners and demonstrators carrying signs that read, "No Vietnamese Ever Called Me Nigger." A visibly uncomfortable King led them from Central Park, through Midtown, to the United Nations Plaza. Much to the consternation of King's more cautious aides, Vietcong flags were conspicuous, and King shared the platform with firebrands James Bevel, Stokely Carmichael, and Floyd McKissick. Bevel threatened that unless President Johnson stopped murdering the folks in Vietnam, "we'll close down New York City."[193] Carmichael's speech was interrupted by chants of "Black Power!" King's remarks were largely a reprise of his recent speeches in Beverly Hills and at Riverside Church, and journalist David Halberstam observed that King's presentation was devoid of drama; it seemed as "if he were reading someone else's speech."[194] Regardless of King's lackluster performance, his mere presence was a victory for the antiwar movement. The rally's radical tone clearly discomfited King, and he left the stage immediately. The cultural divide between King's southern-based SCLC and the New Left was evident, presaging difficulties in crafting a coalition between African Americans and the antiwar movement. At the same time, a more relaxed Coretta Scott King shared the podium with Julian Bond and addressed a crowd of approximately 50,000 at Kezar Stadium in San Francisco's Golden Gate Park, a record for that city.[195] The following day, appearing again on CBS's *Face the Nation*, King tried to distance himself from some of the more radical elements at the rally, but he underscored his opposition to the war and called for a massive education campaign against the war in Vietnam.[196]

King's discomfort with some of the more polarizing symbols of the antiwar movement, such as the burning of draft cards and American flags, did not dim his ardor for his new cause. After years of straddling the disparate coalitions in the movement and searching for consensus among the squabbling groups, he had finally gravitated to his natural constituency. King had long spoken out against not only racism but also poverty, economic injustice, and militarism.[197] King's remarks on Vietnam may have sundered his relationship with the moderates, but they burnished his luster with the antiwar militants and the New Left.

Only two weeks after the MOBE rally, King invited Stokely Carmichael and Cleveland Sellers to attend Sunday services at Ebenezer Baptist Church, where King told his congregation that he had chosen "to preach about the war in Vietnam because I agree with Dante that the hottest places in Hell are reserved for those, who in a period of moral crisis, maintained their neutrality."[198] Carmichael was enraptured by King's eloquent sermon and observed that, on his home turf, "Dr. King had an aura, a kind of inner glow."[199] King's closing words—"I do not know and cannot care what others may do. But as for me . . . I'm gonna study war no more"—moved Sellers to tears. At the time, he was being hounded by his draft board in Denmark, South Carolina.[200] The parishioners' response was "just like a shepherd leading his flock, going to give them water on green pastures," Carmichael remembered. The sensational media coverage of their disputes notwithstanding, King's recent antiwar statements had brought the two men closer than most observers realized.[201]

For the next few months, King barnstormed the country, endearing himself to the white New Left and the growing legions of blacks who opposed the war by repeatedly calling for an end to the fighting in Vietnam. Traveling with King in May, journalist David Halberstam noted the civil rights leader's more radical persona and commented that King was becoming closer to the late Malcolm X and moving further away from Roy Wilkins "than anybody could have predicted five years ago." "For years," King told Halberstam, "I labored with the idea of reforming the existing institutions of society, a little change here, and a little change there. Now I feel quite differently. I think you've got to have a reconstruction of the entire society, a revolution of values." Students at the University of California at Berkeley greeted King like a hero and beseeched him to run for president as a third-party candidate. The hubbub surrounding King's every gesture reminded Halberstam of "being with a Presidential campaign."[202] The adulation from the students invigorated King, who was still nursing his wounds from the harsh attacks by the established press.

For a few weeks in the spring of 1967, King thought the antiwar movement might be able to heal the bitterness in America. King's Riverside speech coincided with a number of defections by key figures in the liberal establishment over Johnson's war policies. Only weeks after the MOBE rally, for example, Kennedy associates Arthur Schlesinger Jr. and John Kenneth Galbraith, along with Cold War liberals Joseph Rauh, former University of California president Clark Kerr, former Federal Reserve chairman Marriner S. Eccles, and Victor Reuther of the United Auto Workers, finally broke ranks with the White House and voiced their opposition to the war.[203] The Vietnam War had split the mighty postwar liberal coalition. Just a year before the election, President Johnson looked increasingly vulnerable, and he feared a challenge from his old nemesis Robert Kennedy.

King's long-awaited entry into the antiwar movement coincided with a spike in antiwar sentiment throughout the country. An ever-increasing number of Americans were convinced that military involvement in Vietnam had been a mistake, and the president's approval rate was plummeting. A Gallup poll in July showed that 52 percent of the country disapproved of the president's handling of the war, and only 34 percent thought the United States was making progress in Vietnam.[204] The antiwar movement was becoming more respectable, but the American public was still profoundly divided over the war. Indeed, most still opposed a unilateral withdrawal. On May 19 White House pollster Fred Panzer alerted the president to the results of the latest Harris poll, which indicated that 73 percent of the American people disagreed with King's position on the war, and 60 percent believed it would hurt the civil rights movement. Even though King's stature as the nation's most respected African American leader was convincing many African Americans to oppose the war, the Harris poll found that nearly half of African Americans disagreed with King's anti-war position, and only 25 percent agreed with him; the remaining 28 percent were reserving judgment. Harris speculated that "Dr. King may have within his power a capability of influencing between a third to one half of all Negro voters behind a candidate he might endorse for President in 1968."[205] This obviously alarmed the White House, and the *St. Louis Argus* reported that LBJ had enlisted Louis Martin of the Democratic National Committee to travel the country and remind African American ministers, newspaper publishers, and labor leaders of the president's stellar record on civil rights.[206]

King's public opposition to the war alienated large numbers of ordinary African Americans. Thousands of African American soldiers were stationed in Vietnam, and King's condemnation of U.S. foreign policy rankled them and their families, as well as others. A black man from the South Side of Chicago spoke for many when he called King and peace advocates "a bunch of Communist helpers."[207] These criticisms stung King, and he characterized this time as "a low period in my life."[208] On the whole, however, *Chicago Defender* correspondent Sam Washington reported that after King's Riverside speech, a majority of black Chicagoans favored a withdrawal from Vietnam. Those opposed to the conflict expressed concern over the high percentage of blacks being killed in the war, and they contended that "Negroes' second class position in American society makes Negro youth the most vulnerable to the draft."[209] African Americans were turning against the war in increasing numbers, and black antiwar sentiment outpaced that of whites. Against this backdrop, King was poised to become a major player in the antiwar movement.

The Summer and Fall of 1967: The Fire This Time

Despite widespread and growing opposition to the war, Johnson remained defiant. On August 3, 1967, the president announced that he would give General Westmoreland an additional 55,000 troops, on top of the 470,000 already stationed in Vietnam.[210] King and other antiwar activists were incensed. By the beginning of the summer of 1967, American society seemed to be unraveling. In the Haight-Ashbury district of San Francisco, the hippie movement augured the emergence of a counterculture, which sent tremors through the nation. Meanwhile, the simmering rage in the African American ghettos led to urban uprisings that dwarfed Watts. Former SNCC executive secretary James Forman characterized 1967 as the "High Tide of Black Resistance."[211] On July 11, 1967, Newark, New Jersey, exploded in an orgy of violence, looting, and arson that led to twenty-six deaths.[212] Less than two weeks later, Detroit, Michigan, witnessed the worst civil disorder of the century, resulting in the burning of 2,509 buildings and the loss of forty-three lives; most of the dead were African Americans gunned down by police and National Guardsmen.[213] Instead of addressing the underlying problems of the slums, the president and Congress responded by passing a bill criminalizing the crossing of state lines to incite a riot and making flag desecration a federal crime. Meanwhile, a proposed bill that would have allocated $40 million to eradicate rats in the slums languished in Congress.[214] An enraged King lashed out at this trifling response, arguing that the billions spent in Vietnam should be redirected to rejuvenating the urban slums, and he called for a program to create jobs for everyone, black, and white, in the cities.[215] The urban uprisings reflected the "suicidal debate and delay in Congress," King said.[216]

These urban uprisings in the long, hot summer of 1967 electrified a small group of African American radicals who interpreted this violence as the first phase of a revolution. SNCC's new chairman, H. Rap Brown, articulated this feeling: "If America don't come around, we must burn her down, brother. We are going to burn it down if we don't get our share of it."[217] Speaking in Havana, Cuba, Stokely Carmichael urged African Americans to seek revenge against Dean Rusk, Robert McNamara, and President Johnson for their crimes against the Vietnamese.[218] At about the same time, the Black Panther Party burst on the scene in Oakland, California, preaching self-defense and speaking to the millions of African American youths trapped by hopelessness and poverty. These militants had long ago tuned out King's message of nonviolence. Black Panther cofounder Huey Newton depicted the African American community as a colony within the United States and characterized the police as an "army of occupation," comparing the situation to the U.S. military occupation of Southeast Asia.[219] The Black Panther Party filled the gap left by the collapse of SNCC, but its revolutionary rhetoric appalled the vast majority of white Americans, who were losing patience with the civil rights struggle. King could only watch helplessly as the country teetered on the brink of chaos and Johnson's Great Society lay in ruins. The searing images of urban conflagration confirmed King's oft-stated lament that the war in Vietnam was wreaking havoc with our domestic destinies. Coretta King was concerned about her husband's utter despair after the riots in Newark and Detroit. She had never seen him so depressed. "People expect me to have the answers," King told his wife, "and I don't have any."[220]

On August 17, King vowed that the SCLC "will go all-out to defeat any Presidential candidate, including President Johnson, who does not take a stand against the war in Vietnam."[221] Seeking a new political platform to unite the peace and freedom wings of the movement, King traveled to Chicago over Labor Day weekend to be the keynote speaker at the first convention of the National Conference for a New Politics (NCNP), which had been formed by a coalition of activists to transfer power to the poor and the voiceless.[222] Since 1966, the NCNP had provided financial support to radical political candidates, called for an end to the war in Vietnam, and proposed a full-scale assault against poverty and racism. More than 3,000 people representing a diverse group of approximately 200 organizations gathered at the Palmer House (an ornate hotel) with the goal of building a new political movement that would unseat President Johnson in 1968 and end the war in Vietnam.[223] It was the largest gathering of the American Left since Henry Wallace's Progressive Party convention in Philadelphia in 1948. The NCNP delegates included representatives of peace groups and militant and moderate African American organizations, radical community organizers, and hippies, all in search of a coherent program to challenge the political establishment. The vast majority of the delegates were younger than thirty, and the atmosphere had a youthful exuberance. Many hoped to create a new political party with King as the leader. Some of King's aides urged him not to attend the convention because they feared a repeat of the embarrassing spectacle of MOBE.[224] But King brushed off these concerns, in part because Martin Peretz and his wife Anne Farnsworth, heiress to the Singer fortune, were major SCLC donors and organizers of the conference.[225]

The vision of creating a broad new political movement quickly evaporated. Outside the Palmer House, hordes of young African American men played bongo drums and shouted, "Kill Whitey." On the opening night of the conference, King delivered a perfunctory speech, which was interrupted by insults from African American teenagers, and then hastily departed. From the outset, race dominated the proceedings. Floyd

McKissick argued against a radical third-party presidential effort because it would not help African Americans; he declared, "No longer can the black man be a plank in someone else's platform."[226] The black caucus then presented a militant thirteen-point platform that demanded 50 percent African American representation on all committees, condemned Israel as an "imperialist Zionist" state, and called for white communities to "humanize the savage and beastlike character that runs through America as exemplified by George Lincoln Rockwell and Lyndon Johnson." In an orgy of white guilt that enraged liberal commentators, the convention voted by an overwhelming margin to accept the African Americans' demands.[227] Writing for the *Village Voice*, June Greenlief described the convention as a scene "worthy of Genet or Pirandello, with whites masquerading as either poor or black, blacks posing as revolutionaries or as arrogant whites, conservatives posing as revolutionaries, women feigning to be oppressed, and liberals pretending not to be there at all."[228] Bertram Garskoff, a white member of the Ann Arbor Citizens for Peace, epitomized the glorification of African Americans: "Blacks *were* the movement," he said. "We are just a little tail, on the end of a powerful black panther. And I want to be on that tail—if they'll let me." Many white liberals were aghast at the outpouring of white guilt. Arthur Waskow, one of the founders of the NCNP, was particularly offended by the anti-Zionist resolution and charged, "One thousand liberals are trying to become good radicals, and they think they can do it by castrating themselves." In the end, the NCNP abandoned the idea of challenging President Johnson and decided to focus on local organizing.[229] Fred Halstead sadly concluded that the convention confirmed that mass demonstrations against the war were the only tactic that could unify the movement.[230]

The fiasco at the Palmer House was a particularly sobering experience for King, and it cast doubt on the ability to broaden the coalition for peace and justice. Bevel, Young, and Hosea Williams remained for the duration of the convention, but even the flamboyant Bevel was horrified by the exhibition of revolutionary ardor. In a letter to wealthy SCLC supporter Martin Peretz, Andrew Young observed, "These cats don't seem to know the country has taken a swing to the right."[231] Having spent his life preaching the virtues of interracial harmony, civility, and decency, King cringed at the behavior of the radical Left. The blunt criticism of Israel helped tatter the alliance between African Americans and Jews that had flourished for the past few decades.[232] When ten Jewish organizations asked King to disassociate himself from the NCNP, he responded by disavowing anti-

Semitism as immoral.[233] All in all, Vietnam had hopelessly divided the reigning liberal consensus, and now the radical Left was disintegrating on the shoals of race. King could only yearn for the days when the terms of the struggle against southern racists were so clear.[234]

A few weeks after the disaster in Chicago, the SCLC held a retreat in Warrentown, Virginia, where a despondent King and his staff discussed how to stop the chaos that had engulfed the movement. With the exception of Bevel, most senior members of the SCLC opposed making Vietnam their paramount issue; they did not want to become merely another peace group, nor did they want to stray too far from their roots as a civil rights organization.[235] Marion Wright, a young attorney who directed the NAACP Legal Defense Fund office in Mississippi, mesmerized King with her cogent argument that the antiwar movement had thousands of recruits, but the nation was oblivious to the existence of her indigent clients in Mississippi and elsewhere. She suggested that the SCLC embark on a massive campaign of civil disobedience among the urban and rural poor, reminiscent of the Bonus March of World War I veterans. Wright's idea was the genesis of the Poor People's Campaign.[236]

After his dispiriting experience with the antiwar movement, the idea of fashioning a multiracial coalition of poor people appealed to King as a strategy to rejuvenate the civil rights movement. A frontal assault against poverty struck King as a good way to forestall urban uprisings, which he feared would strengthen the appeal of right-wing candidates.[237] King also believed that the Poor People's Campaign would hasten the U.S. departure from Vietnam because the funds required to alleviate poverty would render financial support of the war unfeasible. As usual, debate raged among SCLC staff about where the movement should go. Hosea Williams and Andrew Young argued that the SCLC should stay in the South.[238] But in December 1967, King announced his intention to bring poor people of all races to Washington, D.C., where they would remain until lawmakers responded to the paradox of poverty in the world's wealthiest country.[239]

King's desire to build a mass movement of the poor did not diminish his antipathy for the war. In his frequent speeches, sermons, and interviews, he continued to lambaste the war in Vietnam. Yet the Poor People's Campaign—his plan to lead a "camp-in" of tens of thousands of impoverished people to showcase the virulence of poverty in America—engrossed him during the final months of his life. King's conspicuous absence from the march on the Pentagon on October 21, 1967, dismayed his allies in the antiwar movement. Demonstrators placing flowers in the barrels of the guns pointed at them became one of the most poignant symbols of the 1960s antiwar movement. Reporters observed the paucity of African American participants among the estimated 100,000 demonstrators who confronted the military. A small contingent of African Americans abandoned the larger demonstration and joined a nearby African American rally across the street from Howard University, prepared to defend themselves only in their own community. John Wilson of SNCC told David Dellinger, "We don't want to play Indian outside the white man's fort."[240] Norman Mailer, who later chronicled the march in *The Armies of the Night*, remarked, "It was like old times on the Left when you took any Negro into the club you could get."[241] In view of King's opposition to the war, it would have been logical for him to take a prominent role in the demonstration. But the disunity within the antiwar movement frustrated him, and he thought the march on the Pentagon was an imprudent public relations stunt.[242]

1968: Death of the Dream

The year 1968 was a pivotal one in twentieth-century history. Insurgencies against the dominant political and economic order erupted in Tokyo, Paris, Prague, and Chicago. In late January the Vietcong and the North Vietnamese army launched the Tet Offensive, whose ferocity stunned the U.S. military and the nation. The Pyrrhic victory by U.S. forces led to a wholesale reappraisal of the war, casting doubt on the veracity of reports that victory was imminent. More than any other event, Tet tipped the scales against Americans' support for the Vietnam War. Avuncular CBS anchorman Walter Cronkite, one of the most trusted men in the country, went to Vietnam to assess the military situation. On February 27, 1968, Cronkite, reporting from Hue, glumly concluded that the war was not winnable. He ended a half-hour special report on Vietnam with this memorable statement: "But it is increasingly clear to this reporter that the only way out then will be to negotiate, not as victors but as an honorable people who lived up to their pledge to defend democracy, and did the best they could."[243]

The Tet Offensive and Cronkite's broadcast dealt a double blow to Lyndon Johnson. Johnson reportedly told an aide, "If I've lost Cronkite, I've lost Middle America."[244] On March 31,1968, Johnson shocked the nation when he announced he would not seek reelection.[245]

In the final months of his life, King was too preoccupied with the Poor People's Campaign and the sanitation workers' strike in Memphis to revel in the president's political misfortunes. With violence in Vietnam continuing apace and the War on Poverty in tatters, he felt no sense of vindication. In a February 23, 1968, speech at Carnegie Hall commemorating the hundredth anniversary of the birth of W. E. B. Du Bois, King praised the great scholar's lifetime of work for the liberation of African Americans. In extolling Du Bois, King paid tribute to his radical heritage and proclaimed, "Dr. Du Bois the man needs to be remembered today when despair was all too prevalent." In King's eyes, Du Bois's turn toward communism did not mitigate his greatness. King acknowledged, "Dr. Du Bois would be in the front movement of the peace movement today."[246] His spirited attacks on the war and American capitalism and his praise of Du Bois were emblematic of King's radicalism. He had always been closer to Du Bois than most of his contemporaries were willing to admit. There was no better illustration of King's kinship with Du Bois than his involvement with the Memphis sanitation workers, perhaps the most downtrodden group of workers in America. Once again, King defied the advice of his aides and diverted his energy from the Poor People's Campaign to help these humble men who wanted to form a union and obtain some dignity.[247]

King was assassinated in Memphis on the evening of April 4, 1968, the one-year anniversary of his Riverside speech. For the second time in five years, the world mourned a charismatic leader gunned down in the prime of life. Luminaries from around the globe eulogized the slain Nobel Peace Prize winner. The *New York Times*, which just a year ago had questioned his judgment, called King's murder "a national disaster that deprived Negroes and Whites alike of a leader of integrity, vision, and restraint."[248]

Hours after King's assassination, Stokely Carmichael appeared on a Washington, D.C., street brandishing a pistol and urged blacks "to go and get your guns."[249] He proclaimed, "When white America killed Dr. King ... she declared war on us. The rebellions that have been occurring around these cities and this country is just light stuff compared to what is about to happen."[250] Meanwhile, the posthumous moderation of King's radicalism began immediately. President Johnson called him an "American martyr."[251] Over the next few days, a wave of violence spread throughout the country. Although forty-six people died in the riots, and the U.S. Army occupied Chicago, Washington, and Baltimore, many were relieved that it was not worse.[252] The rioting contributed to the white backlash and deepened the political isolation of African Americans. Republican Richard M. Nixon would trumpet the slogan of "law and order" all the way to the

White House. A successive generation of conservative politicians would use the law-and-order mantra to gain power and roll back many of the Great Society programs. The era of conservative retrenchment curtailed any hope of additional racial reforms.

Despite official attempts to sever King's radical positions from his persona, on the night of his assassination, one of King's aides rummaged through King's coat pockets and found a handwritten note entitled "The Ten Commandments on Vietnam," refuting the official justifications for the war.[253] Only three weeks later, his widow recited the decalogue at an antiwar rally in New York City's Central Park. It read as follows:

> Thou shalt not believe in a military victory.
> Thou shalt not believe in a political victory.
> Thou shalt not believe they—the Vietnamese—love us.
> Thou shalt not believe that the Saigon Government has the support of the people.
> Thou shalt not believe that the majority of the South Vietnamese look upon the Vietcong as terrorists.
> Thou shalt not believe the figures of killed enemies or killed Americans.
> Thou shalt not believe that the generals know best.
> Thou shalt not believe that the enemy's victory means communism.
> Thou shalt not believe the world supports the United States.
> Thou shalt not kill.[254]

King's painful dilemma over the Vietnam War reflected the divisions it caused in the African American community and in the nation. In Vietnam, news of King's murder shattered the morale of many African American soldiers.[255] Staff Sergeant Don F. Browne's first inclination upon hearing the news was to run out and "punch the first guy he saw. He was hurt and all he wanted to do was run home."[256] In the months after April 4, 1968, African Americans' support for the war declined precipitously. In death, King's impact on African Americans' perception of the war was almost as great as it had been in life. Ironically, it did not take long for Americans to sanitize King and moderate his views to conform to an idealized image, placing him in the narrow framework of civil rights leader. His famous "I Have a Dream" speech became iconic, obscuring his complexity and his outspokenness against what he termed the triple evils of war, poverty, and racism. Two days after his assassination, Coretta, accompanied by

Harry Belafonte, stood outside Ebenezer Baptist Church and encouraged the SCLC to continue her husband's work. "He gave his life for the poor of the world—the garbage workers in Memphis and the peasants of Vietnam," his widow told a throng of teary-eyed reporters.[257]

King's tortuous path to becoming an antiwar activist is instructive in demythologizing him and removing the patriotic patina his critics imposed on him to serve their own political agenda. His good friend and fellow theologian Vincent Harding put it best: "Perhaps the memory of Martin King needs to be broken free from all official attempts to manage, market, and domesticate him. At this moment . . . we need a truly free and inconvenient hero who will enable us to explore new dimensions of our freedom, not simply as a private agenda, but to follow his unmanageable style of seeking and using freedom to serve the needs of the most vulnerable."[258]

Black Muslim leader Malcolm X and world heavyweight boxing champion Muham-mad Ali in New York City, March 1, 1964. (Bettmann/Corbis/AP Images)

(Above) Paul Robeson testifying before the House Un-American Activities Committee on June 12, 1956, where he denounced the committee and accused its members of being the un-Americans. As early as the mid-1950s, Robeson spoke out against American involvement in independence movements in Vietnam and other Third World countries. (Bettmann/Corbis/AP Images) *(Below)* Historian and activist Howard Zinn served as an adviser to SNCC and urged the students to speak out against the Vietnam War in the summer of 1965. (Danny Lyon/Magnum Photos)

(*Above*) Robert Moses, the legendary leader of SNCC who became an early opponent of the Vietnam War. (Danny Lyon/Magnum Photos) (*Below*) Staughton Lynd, David Dellinger, and Robert Moses protesting the Vietnam War on August 6, 1965—the same day President Lyndon Johnson signed the Voting Rights Act. (Staughton Lynd Papers)

James Farmer, the head of CORE, was initially reluctant to oppose the Vietnam War. (Library of Congress)

(Above) Diane Nash and James Bevel were founding members of SNCC who later opposed the war. Nash traveled to Vietnam in the winter of 1967, and Bevel implored Martin Luther King Jr. to oppose the war. (Wisconsin State Historical Society, WHS 91969) *(Below)* Lyndon B. Johnson unveiled the Voting Rights Act in a speech before a joint session of Congress a week after Bloody Sunday and thrilled the civil rights establishment by declaring, "We Shall Overcome." Because of the president's steadfast support of civil rights, many blacks and civil rights leaders were reluctant to oppose the war. (LBJ Library; photo by Yoichi Okamato)

The murder of Navy veteran and SNCC activist Sammy Younge Jr. on January 3, 1966, in Tuskegee prompted SNCC to become the first civil rights organization to oppose the war. (Trenholm Technical State Archives, Gwen Patton, archivist)

President Lyndon B. Johnson and Martin Luther King in the Oval Office on March 18, 1966. They had an uneasy relationship and eventually split over the Vietnam War. (LBJ Library; photo by Yoichi Okamato)

(*Above*) John Lewis (right), leader of SNCC, demanded to know why the U.S. government was willing to send troops to Vietnam but not to protect civil rights workers in the Deep South. (LBJ Library; photo by Yoichi Okamato) (*Below*) Martin Luther King Jr. walking into Riverside Church prior to delivering his address denouncing the Vietnam War. (John C. Goodman)

Martin Luther King Jr. shocked the liberal establishment by speaking out against the Vietnam War at Riverside Church on April 4, 1967. He is flanked by Rabbi Abraham Joshua Heschel (far left), historian Henry Steele Commager (left), and theologian John C. Bennett (right). (John C. Goodman)

Another view of the Riverside speech. (John C. Goodman)

Martin Luther King Jr. answering questions after his Riverside address. (John C. Goodman)

Two African American teenagers in Central Park carrying placards illustrating the growing black opposition to the Vietnam War, April 15, 1967. (John C. Goodman)

Martin Luther King Jr. marching with Dr. Benjamin Spock (left) from Central Park to the United Nations, April 15, 1967. (John C. Goodman)

(Above) Martin Luther King Jr. marching with CALCAV in Arlington National Cemetery, February 6, 1968. (John C. Goodman)

(Left) Martin Luther King addressing a CALCAV meeting at a Presbyterian church in Washington, D.C., on February 6, 1968. (John C. Goodman)

(Above) SNCC leader Stokely Carmichael (second from left) and his lieutenant Cleveland Sellers (far right) outside an armed forces induction center in Atlanta, May 1, 1967. Sellers told reporters he said "No" to the U.S. Army. (Bettmann/Corbis/AP Images) *(Below)* Roy Wilkins, head of the NAACP, was a staunch anticommunist and close ally of President Johnson. He was critical of individual African Americans and civil rights organizations that opposed the Vietnam War. (LBJ Library; photo by Yoichi Okamato)

A. Philip Randolph had pacifist sensibilities, but like his protégé Bayard Rustin, he was opposed to civil rights activists taking a position on the Vietnam War. (LBJ Library; photo by Yoichi Okamato)

(*Above*) Bayard Rustin was a longtime pacifist and theoretician of the civil rights movement. His reluctance to take a stand against the Vietnam War outraged many of his comrades. (LBJ Library; photo by Yoichi Okamato) (*Below*) Whitney Young Jr., head of the National Urban League, meeting with Lyndon B. Johnson. Young and Roy Wilkins were the president's closest allies in the civil rights movement. (Whitney M. Young Jr. Papers, Rare Book and Manuscript Library, Columbia University)

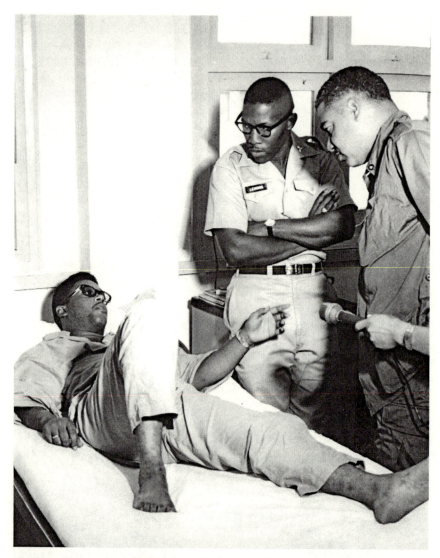

President Johnson dispatched Whitney Young Jr. to Vietnam, where he reported on the high morale among the African American troops in the field. (Whitney M. Young Jr. Papers, Rare Book and Manuscript Library, Columbia University)

7

Moderates and the Vietnam War

All the Way with LBJ

The civil rights movement could gain nothing without President
Johnson's support. . . . The President's support might be diluted if [the]
civil rights movement took strong stands against the Administration's
policy on Vietnam.

—Bayard Rustin, April 1967

Ever since the end of Reconstruction, African Americans had yearned
and struggled for acceptance in mainstream, middle-class American life.
Langston Hughes's "I, Too, Sing America" poignantly encapsulated African Americans' wish to share in the American Dream.[1] By the summer of
1965, in spite of myriad difficulties, African Americans' quest for equal
opportunity no longer seemed to be "A Dream Deferred." While SNCC's,
CORE's, and the SCLC's high-profile direct-action campaigns in the
streets and parks and at the beaches, bus terminals, and lunch counters
of some of the most benighted cities and towns in the Deep South captured the public's imagination and prodded federal action, the strangle-
hold of segregation was ultimately broken by lobbying, litigation, and legislation carried out in the corridors of power. This seemingly vindicated
the NAACP's time-honored strategy of working *with* the federal government to achieve results. The moderate wing of the civil rights movement, headed by Roy Wilkins of the NAACP and Whitney Young Jr. of the
National Urban League (NUL), as well as establishment figures such as
the esteemed A. Philip Randolph, savored their relationship with Lyndon
Johnson and remained wedded to Cold War liberalism. As a consequence,
on the issue of the Vietnam War, they steadfastly argued for a "hands-off"

policy, which widened the fissures in the civil rights movement and alienated its younger antiwar wing.[2]

The "moderate" civil rights leadership eschewed mass demonstrations, preferred to work through existing political channels, and abhorred Black Power and the culture and tactics of the New Left.[3] They were proud of the recent legislative and judicial victories for civil rights and considered their relationship with Johnson a fruitful one. Even in the darkest days of LBJ's tenure, the moderates remained wedded to Cold War liberalism. After all, the NAACP and its moderate allies had survived the ravages of McCarthyism and the Red scare by displaying their liberal anticommunist credentials.[4] So when the war in Vietnam erupted in the mid-1960s, it was not surprising that they perceived SNCC, CORE, and African Americans who opposed the war as irresponsible radicals who were jeopardizing the recent gains in civil rights. The moderates were an older cohort and did not share the younger generation's willingness to critique American institutions and values. Given everything Johnson had done for them in the realm of civil rights, they considered loyalty to the president and support of his Vietnam policy a small price to pay.

Simeon Booker, the peripatetic African American journalist who achieved fame for his coverage of the murder of Emmett Till, went to Vietnam in the fall of 1965 to report on race relations in the military. Reflecting the moderates' pro-military sensibilities, his article, published in *Ebony*, contained unstinting praise for the African American soldier, corroborating African Americans' support of the war. "The untold story in Vietnam," according to Booker, "is that the Negro troops are carrying the brunt of psychological warfare." He went on to say: "By their presence and their actions, they demonstrate to thousands of bewildered Vietnamese that the United States not only means military business but it tries to practice what it preaches on the ideological front. This is a lesson which is finally paying dividends." Praising the military's role in alleviating racism, Booker gushed, the "results of integration are so phenomenal that most frontline reporters comment on the achievement." While conceding that "Vietnam is no racial utopia," he noted that the conflict was devoid of some of the more "obnoxious racial inequities that have characterized America's past wars." An unidentified American soldier echoed Langston Hughes when he told Booker, "Out here, we, too, are Americans."[5] In the early years of the war, African Americans latched on to the image of the good African American soldier and regularly touted his exploits in the jungles of Vietnam.[6] During this critical period, the moderate wing of the civil rights movement emerged as the staunchest defender of U.S. foreign policy in the African American community.

In the mid-1960s, far from the front lines of the civil rights struggle in the South, the president's allies in the civil rights movement failed to realize how much attention the Vietnam War would divert from the civil rights agenda. Their remoteness from the travails of ordinary people also sheltered them from the human cost of the war. SNCC's early opposition to the war was partially rooted in its membership's intimacy with soldiers who had served, sacrificed, and even died in Vietnam. Conversely, the moderate wing of the civil rights movement felt a greater generational and temperamental affinity to the architects of the Vietnam policy. Although the moderates never took an outright hawkish stance on Vietnam, they repeatedly insisted that civil rights and the war were separate and distinct matters. They adhered to the broad contours of liberal anticommunism and disapproved of the confrontational tactics of the younger generation of antiwar activists. As a consequence, they vilified their African American brethren who dared to criticize the president and his conduct of the war in Vietnam.[7] In doing so, they helped justify the FBI's ongoing persecution of Martin Luther King Jr. and other antiwar activists.[8] The moderates' denunciation of SNCC, CORE, and King contributed to the destabilization of the civil rights movement throughout the 1960s.

At their core, these disputes over the war illustrated profound differences in the parties' perceptions of American society, politics, and culture. Whereas the SCLC strove to affirm its motto of "Redeeming the Soul of the Nation," the moderates had no compunction with the dominant American middle-class ethos; their major goal was to eliminate the barriers to African Americans' achievement of the American Dream. These two competing visions exposed the wide chasm between the moderates, wedded to the liberal program of gradual reform and patriotism, and the more radical segment of the civil rights movement, which urged a wholesale restructuring of American values and institutions.

Roy Wilkins, the NAACP, and Liberal Anticommunism

The NAACP was formed in 1909 by a group of white reformers and African American intellectuals as an alternative to Booker T. Washington's policy of accommodation and autocratic style of leadership. Within a few decades, the association became the largest and most prominent civil rights organization in the United States, emphasizing political, economic, and social integration. In its unwavering commitment to combating racism in the 1920s and 1930s, it earned a reputation for radicalism while distancing itself from communism. By the end of World War II, the NAACP had more than 400,000 members in chapters across the nation, and the African American military experience during the war inspired a greater insistence on racial equality. Civil rights had become a mass movement, but the NAACP's meteoric growth spawned a bureaucratic structure that was increasingly removed from the aspirations and goals of its rank and file.[9]

Given the Red scare and the political climate of the late 1940s and early 1950s, the NAACP felt compelled to showcase its anticommunist credentials. In an about-face, the association endorsed Truman's emerging Cold War policies, repudiated its earlier sympathy with anti-imperialism, and espoused an unwillingness to mix civil rights with U.S. foreign policy. In the early 1950s, Roy Wilkins expressed his obeisance to Cold War culture, stating, "The Negro wants change in order that he may be brought in line with the American standard . . . which must be done not only to preserve and strengthen that standard here at home, but to guarantee its potency in the world struggle against dictatorship and Stalinism abroad."[10] In his sympathetic account of the NAACP, historian Manfred Berg acknowledged, "The early Cold War hardly represents a glorious chapter in the NAACP's history. It showed a great deal of opportunism and its rhetoric is replete with devout declarations of loyalty and patriotism."[11] This capitulation to the anticommunist zeitgeist led to some legal victories, most notably the landmark decision in *Brown v. Board of Education*, but it also contributed to the agonizingly slow pace of reform, particularly in the segregated South. The NAACP's embrace of anticommunism narrowed the parameters of reform to a piecemeal struggle for civil rights through litigation. Its embrace of Cold War liberalism presaged its unwillingness to criticize the Vietnam War in the 1960s.[12]

Roy Wilkins had been a leading figure in the NAACP for well over two decades when he became executive secretary in 1955, after the death of Walter White. Raised in the racially tolerant Upper Midwest, Wilkins had a Norman Rockwell–like vision of his childhood in St. Paul, as well as an enduring faith in America and its capacity to rectify the wounds of racism. Abhorring Pan-Africanism, racial separatism, and the tendency to identify with the struggles of the Third World, Wilkins was an ardent anticommunist.[13] Until his retirement in 1977, Wilkins ruled the association with an iron fist, but historian Patricia Sullivan notes that he was also "thin-skinned and could be petty and vindictive."[14] A staunch opponent of

Du Bois, Wilkins left his anticommunist imprimatur on the association.[15] A consummate pragmatist, he conceived the NAACP's goal as fair play between the races, and he spurned the blending of foreign affairs with the struggle for domestic equality for African Americans. He perceived the communists as a legitimate threat to the NAACP and expelled branches that fell under communist control.[16] Years later, he recalled that he "was happy to see them go. God knows, it was hard enough to be black, we certainly didn't need to be Red, too."[17]

Throughout his long tenure at the helm of the association, Wilkins devoted substantial time and energy to rebutting the slew of allegations, usually from segregationists, that communists had infiltrated the NAACP. On March 11, 1957, Wilkins sent a letter to J. W. Reynolds of Boston, wherein he enumerated six reasons why the NAACP was not rife with subversives. The chief reason cited was the association's amicable relationship with the FBI; as proof, Wilkins attached excerpts from J. Edgar Hoover's *Masters of Deceit*, in which the nation's premier communist buster praised the association's extirpation of Reds.[18] In retrospect, Wilkins's staunch anticommunism helped ensure the association's viability during the Red scare and McCarthyism. However, his limited vision enraged the impatient younger generation of civil rights activists who would form SNCC.

His steadfastness in relying on lobbying and litigation, for instance, made Wilkins seem out of touch with new stirrings in the movement, beginning with the Montgomery bus boycott in December 1955. The NAACP did not want to assist the Montgomery Improvement Association because it was involved in too many other matters and thought the Montgomery group was interested only in improving segregation, not eliminating it.[19] In addition, nonviolent direct action was anathema to Wilkins. He explained, "My own view was that the particular form of direct action used in Montgomery was effective only for certain kinds of local problems and could not be applied safely on a national scale."[20] There was also the matter of personal rivalries and egos. From the earliest days, Wilkins was extremely jealous of King's fame and notoriety. Relations between the two men and their respective organizations would always be strained. Clashes over fund-raising and philosophical differences over the legitimacy of nonviolent protests prompted NAACP Defense Fund counsel Thurgood Marshall to brand King an "opportunist" and a "first-rate rabble rouser" as early as 1957.[21] James Farmer recalled Wilkins telling King, "One of these days Martin, some bright young reporter is going to take a good hard look at Montgomery and discover that despite all of the hoopla, your boycott didn't desegregate a single city bus. It was the quiet NAACP-type legal action that did it."[22] Wilkins's bluntness was no match for King's charisma, but he was right.

If King presented a competitive challenge to the NAACP's dominance in the field of civil rights, the formation of SNCC presented an even larger one. Ella Baker, the NAACP's director of branches, abruptly resigned over repeated clashes with the association's hierarchy, and she was influential in steering the students in the direction of an autonomous grassroots organization.[23] Only months after SNCC's founding, the NAACP launched an attack on its "jail without bail" strategy. In June 1960, Thurgood Marshall lectured the students and insisted, "It is an insult to any lawyer for a client to insist on remaining in jail."[24] And it was not just SNCC that raised the ire of the association's leadership. When CORE initiated its Freedom Rides in May 1961, the NAACP staff initially viewed it as a publicity stunt that would incur needless expense.[25]

For its part, SNCC scorned the NAACP and characterized it as a bourgeois debating club. At SNCC's founding meeting in Raleigh, James Lawson lambasted the NAACP for emphasizing "fund-raising and court action rather than developing our greatest resource, a people no longer the victims of racial evil who can in a disciplined manner implement the constitution."[26] Most of the students came from lower-middle-class backgrounds, and they could not identify with the NAACP's elitist orientation. The association's anticommunism was also anathema to the young students, who chafed at the restrictions of Cold War culture and resented the mantra of gradualism. As previously noted, the disputes between them climaxed over the seating of the Mississippi Freedom Democratic Party at the Democratic Convention in Atlantic City. Responding to the delegates' widespread anger over the compromise, Wilkins slammed the MFDP for failing to "recognize victory when it appeared" and derided its "churlish behavior."[27] Wilkins's chief deputy, Gloster Current, similarly castigated SNCC's Mississippi workers as "johnnie-come-latelies" and attacked Robert Moses in particular as an irreverent slacker "who left a very bad impression" on the NAACP's executive board.[28] In almost all respects, the NAACP and SNCC were separated by a generational chasm that would become unbridgeable as the war escalated and the issue of Black Power came to the fore.

Not surprisingly, Wilkins and the NAACP opposed the nascent antiwar movement that emerged in early 1965. Like most Americans, the association's leadership expected a quick victory in Vietnam, and they were preoccupied with the ongoing struggle for voting rights. Wilkins's longtime opposition to the internationalization of the race issue was an important factor. Another element was the warm friendship that developed between Wilkins and President Johnson, which endured until Johnson's death. At first, Wilkins was suspicious of Johnson's civil rights bona fides, but in due course, the two forged the closest bond between any civil rights leader and U.S. president.[29] Johnson's courtship of Wilkins began only days after Kennedy's assassination. LBJ made a conscious effort to reach out to the NAACP leader and impressed Wilkins with his genuine dedication to civil rights. After the meeting, the new president, ever prone to hyperbole, wrote to Wilkins, "Nothing has meant more to me in these hours of sorrow following the death of John F. Kennedy than messages from friends like you."[30] NAACP labor secretary Herbert Hill declared, "I don't think in the entire history of the NAACP the president of the United States had evolved such a close personal relationship with the head of the association."[31] Wilkins ended the NAACP's traditional neutrality in presidential politics by enthusiastically campaigning for Johnson against Senator Barry Goldwater, whose enthusiasm for states' rights made him oblivious to the reasons for African American protest. Only days before King's historic Riverside speech, Secretary of State Dean Rusk presented Wilkins with the Freedom Award, and Johnson read a statement hailing Wilkins as "one of the true leaders, not only of our time, but of all time."[32]

The NAACP's "hands-off" policy with respect to the Vietnam War was not shared by many of its local branches. Even in the early months of the war, many of the rank and file were growing restive with what they regarded as the leadership's outdated reliance on litigation and lobbying. Others resented the association's unbridled support of the White House's Cold War policies. The first challenge to the NAACP's acquiescence to the Johnson administration's Vietnam policy occurred on April 10, 1965, when the executive board of the Flint, Michigan, branch passed a resolution urging "an immediate withdrawal of American forces from Vietnam so that the Vietnamese people may settle their own destiny."[33] This declaration immediately provoked a rebuke from the national office in New York City, which did not condone a local branch adopting its own policy. Assistant executive director John A. Morsell, a close ally of Wilkins, fired off a telegram to the Flint office charging that its resolution lacked "standing in that it does not reflect any official policy position of the NAACP."[34] Shortly thereafter, Gloster Current, another Wilkins loyalist with strong anticommunist views, exaggerated the resolution's impact and stated, "The left-wing in America is having a field day! Its most recent project is to create problems over our country's Vietnam policy."[35] He then admonished the staff that all foreign policy questions should be referred to the national office. Current did not want the branches getting "involved in left-wing shenanigans."[36]

As soon as the controversy over Vietnam surfaced, the NAACP hierarchy distanced itself from any semblance of antiwar dissent in its branches. In a move that rankled many members, the association refused to consider any resolution about the Vietnam War at its annual convention in Denver.[37] Fearing that any involvement with the antiwar movement would sully its respectability and jeopardize its access to the White House, the NAACP took pains to distance itself from the "Vietniks" and other rabble-rousers who dared to protest the war. In late July, it viewed the upcoming rally of "Unrepresented People," also known as the "Mississippi Freedom Drive," with trepidation. To ensure that the public did not associate the NAACP with the demonstration, Wilkins issued another memorandum to the local branches stating that they "have no authority for participating in such a gathering."[38] Wilkins deemed virtually all demonstrations unrespectable—a stance he would maintain throughout Johnson's presidency.

Following SNCC's denunciation of the war on January 6, 1966, the NAACP immediately released a statement condemning this breach with American foreign policy.[39] Wilkins took pains to emphasize that it was "purely and simply, a statement of the position of one organization, SNCC."[40] A few weeks after SNCC's blockbuster statement on Vietnam, Wilkins, Whitney Young, and Clarence Mitchell met with Vice President Hubert Humphrey and expressed concern over the fact that the Johnson administration treated civil rights leaders with a "sort of benevolent neutrality" while "the SNCC outfit engaged in the most outrageous attacks on the President." SNCC's controversial call to resist the draft confirmed the NAACP's long-standing frustration with the students' immaturity and recklessness, which Wilkins branded as "contemptuous of all others, black and white, who did not fit a doctrinaire formula of thinking and acting."[41]

Far removed from the personal hardships experienced by thousands of underprivileged African American men in the South facing white draft boards, the NAACP leadership could not fathom conscientious objection as an alternative to the draft, particularly in the vaunted era of the good African American soldier. In their haste to support the White House, they wittingly abetted the Johnson administration's scheme to isolate SNCC and other African American organizations that were hostile to the Vietnam War. In doing so, the White House preyed on Wilkins's concern that the public would attribute any action by any civil rights organization to the civil rights movement as a whole. Public opinion polls demonstrating that antiwar activity within the civil rights movement was testing the patience of Americans vindicated Wilkins's fears.[42] Having Red-baited individuals suspected of having communist ties in the early 1950s, Wilkins was keenly aware of the danger of appearing soft on communism.[43]

The NAACP's reluctance to take a position on the war did not sit well with many of its members, eroding its financial and grassroots support in the coming years. By the time the war eclipsed civil rights as the paramount issue in America, many longtime members disapproved of the leadership's policy. For instance, days after the NAACP lambasted SNCC's antiwar statement, Henry S. Smith of Colton, California, who had been involved with the NAACP since the Scottsboro cases in the 1930s, wrote to Wilkins demanding the cessation of "any more of your 'freedom propaganda,'" which he saw "as 'hypocritical' in view of [the association's] failure to be interested in the civil rights for people of Vietnam."[44] Wilkins's blunt retort likened the peace advocates to communists, in that their rigid adherence to conformity "tolerates no deviation whatsoever from the handed-down line."[45]

Victor Sidell, another disaffected member from Cambridge, Massachusetts, was so irate about the NAACP's response to SNCC's antiwar statement that he resigned from the association and told Wilkins that, in the future, the "money that would have gone to the NAACP will be contributed to SNCC instead."[46] These rebukes were tame in comparison to that of Henry Wallace of Prospect, Kentucky, whose rage at the association's scurrilous attack on John Lewis's "courageous stand" prompted him to accuse the NAACP of "fast becoming the leading Uncle Tom of the civil rights movement." "You are jumping through President's Johnson's hoop so regularly and humiliatingly that you have become little more than an Administration houseboy," he charged, and then demanded that Wilkins remove his name from the NAACP's membership list.[47]

Despite the shocking number of protests and resignations, the leadership of the NAACP was fortified by letters from supporters like George Field of the Freedom House, who urged them to be vigilant against extremism on the Left.[48] Wilkins wholeheartedly agreed and tried to mitigate the damage inflicted on the civil rights movement by the "connection of a few civil rights workers with the anti-war campaign."[49] As the years passed, expressions of support for the leadership's hands-off policy in Southeast Asia dwindled. Wilkins and the NAACP leadership were swimming against the tide of African American opinion.[50] And in contrast to World War II and the Korean War, in deference to the Johnson administration, the NAACP did not monitor or investigate allegations of racial discrimination in Vietnam.[51]

The erosion of grassroots support did not cause Wilkins to question the NAACP's hands-off policy. SNCC's and CORE's antiwar stance, along with the deteriorating relationship between the president and King, only strengthened the NAACP's bond with the White House. Wilkins became a regular member of Johnson's kitchen cabinet, causing several high-ranking members to grumble that Wilkins's coziness with the White House was becoming a public relations disaster.[52] During a staff meeting in March 1966, Current, typically a Wilkins supporter, charged that Wilkins's proximity with President Johnson had cost the NAACP members.[53] The authoritative Wilkins bristled at Current's charge and called it "gratuitously insulting," causing Current to back off and concede that his comments had been tactless. Yet he refused to backtrack on his belief that Wilkins was too cozy with the administration, suggesting that these concerns pervaded the upper echelons of the NAACP.[54] Wilkins was unfazed by these criticisms and reveled in his role as the president's African American point man on civil rights. The White House returned Wilkins's admiration. For example, adviser Harry McPherson marveled: "If ever a man deserved the Medal of Freedom, it is Roy Wilkins. Time and again last weekend he spoke the word of wisdom, fairness and good sense that turned the tide. In these meetings both whites and Negroes customarily try to out-do one another in civil rights aggressiveness; Roy provides the balance that brings people back to reality."[55] At the White House Conference on Civil Rights, Wilkins and Thurgood Marshall received royal treatment, whereas King was shunned.[56] As for the antiwar movement, LBJ and the NAACP leadership shared a mutual antipathy to those who acted outside the political system. Both also believed that subversives bent on overthrowing the government controlled the antiwar movement. The war's growing unpopularity among African Americans in the final years of the Johnson administration only brought the NAACP leadership and the White House closer.

As the conflicts and rivalries deepened within the civil rights movement in the mid-1960s, and the NAACP hierarchy became increasingly suspicious of the motives of the more militant SNCC and CORE, it also targeted Martin Luther King Jr. After King characterized the hostilities in Southeast Asia as the "gangrene of Vietnam" in the spring of 1966, Current

feared that the "left wing is at work to influence our resolutions," referring to the NAACP's upcoming convention in Los Angeles.[57] Although
there were rumblings of dissent within the association, there was hardly a
left-wing cabal. Nonetheless, Current insisted that the Greenwich Village
branch of the NAACP was "a notorious hotbed of radicalism."[58] A few
weeks after Current's admonition, it proposed a resolution similar to the
one endorsed by the Flint branch the previous year. This time, the Greenwich Village branch called for local branches to consider and debate the
issue of the Vietnam War and its deleterious impact on the civil rights
movement.[59] The resolution was ultimately rejected, and the upper echelons of the NAACP remained unified on the issue of the war, even at
the cost of losing individual members. Instead of perceiving the antiwar
movement as an indigenous campaign rooted in the American tradition of
democracy, the NAACP leadership shared the White House's concern that
King was falling under the spell of communists.

The NAACP's attacks against King's Riverside address evidenced its
solidarity with the White House in demonizing antiwar activists. Ideological differences notwithstanding, the highly personal nature of the attacks
stung King. As the leading civil rights organization in the country, the
NAACP reflected the widespread belief among the liberal establishment
that King was moving outside his area of competence. Speaking a few
days later at Yale University, Wilkins railed, "If I am going to cry about
something, I am going to cry about the murder of Wharlest Jackson in Nat-
chez, Mississippi, rather than about civilians in Vietnam."[60] In the weeks
after King's Riverside address, irate NAACP members inundated branch
offices with so many complaints about the association's stand on Vietnam and its attacks against King that Gertrude Cohen, an employee at the
main office in New York City, sent a memorandum to Current bemoaning that "most of our time is taken up with listening to complaints" about
the Vietnam issue.[61] Martin Kroll of New York City was "appalled" at the
NAACP's criticism of King and excoriated Wilkins's inability "to see no
relationship between the escalation of the Vietnam war and the descalation
[sic] of the war on poverty."[62] The anger among the rank and file was best
summed up by Mrs. M. Franklin, a homemaker from Cleveland, Ohio.
Her terse, handwritten note read: "Dear Mr. Wilkins: You are the one that
is wrong, but I don't think you will admit it. I am glad Dr. King spoke out
and said what so many of us little people believe. I wish you would grow
up while some of our black sons are still living. Please open your eyes and
not only look, but see."[63]

The NAACP leadership viewed the antiwar movement through a Red prism. White House aide Clifford Alexander, Johnson's ranking African American assistant, boasted to the president that there were only about 500 African Americans present at the MOBE rally in New York on April 15, 1967. Gloster Current was one of them. In a memo to Wilkins, Current noted, "The entire performance was reminiscent of the 30s when the commies harangued a crowd of certain well-chosen speakers who threaded in the party line, with the final wrap-up speak[er] giving the unadulterated call to go forth and carry out the line." Current called Carmichael "vulgar," mocked "the skull-cap wearing Bevel" for murdering the King's English, and characterized King's speech as lackluster. He attributed King's uninspiring performance to the NAACP and Wilkins, which had put him on the defensive, not to King's discomfort with the rally's charged atmosphere. Warning the leadership that "this is more serious than meets the eye," he observed, "the extremists will stop at nothing to create havoc and confusion and involve Negroes, perhaps in rioting, to create the impression that Negroes are tired of money being siphoned off for war purposes." Citing the need to mount a public relations offensive to "urge Negroes in the communities to pay no heed to the fools," Current proposed an "off-the-record meeting of the Negro press and key well-chosen leaders to decide how to deal with what seems to be in the offing."[64]

Tensions climaxed later in the summer, when opponents of the NAACP's hands-off policy planned to force a debate on Vietnam at the association's 1967 convention in Boston.[65] A faction of younger militants, known as the Young Turks, threw up a picket line outside the Sheraton-Boston Hotel and carried signs critical of Wilkins.[66] Inside the convention hall, the Young Turks challenged the executive director's support of the Vietnam War. Wilkins easily survived this challenge to his authority, but this did not end the Young Turks' resolve.[67] A few months later, Steven Kidd, from the Youth Division of the NAACP's New York branch, publicly condemned the organization's policy, calling the war "morally unacceptable," branding Wilkins "the most paranoid leader black people have," and charging that Wilkins was willing to step "on anyone in the N.A.A.C.P. who gets more press coverage."[68] The attitudes of the Young Turks reflected a burgeoning militancy that was highly critical of American middle-class mores and, of course, the Vietnam War. In November 1968, three leaders of NAACP branches in the Los Angeles area demanded that Wilkins resign because his policies were eroding the group's membership and its "prestige was up only in the white community."[69] In spite of the Young Turks' vocal attacks, the NAACP remained a predominantly middle-class organization firmly wedded to Cold War liberalism. Its unabashed support of the administration's policies, however, was creating a crisis in legitimacy, particularly among the young, who increasingly viewed the NAACP as a bunch of "Uncle Toms." By the end of the 1960s, the goodwill the association had accumulated over the decades had dwindled precipitously. In 1969, a survey indicated that only about 20 percent of African Americans thought the NAACP was doing an excellent job, compared with 80 percent in 1965.[70] According to a *Newsweek* poll conducted in 1969, over 85 percent of African Americans disagreed with the NAACP and believed that the war had squeezed the campaign against poverty.[71]

Even after LBJ made the shocking announcement on March 31, 1968, that he would not seek reelection, the NAACP leadership remained decidedly opposed to the antiwar movement. Over the objections of the Young Turks and longtime members like Barbara Schaaf of Salem, Oregon—who informed Wilkins that she was "reserving all future contributions to go to SCLC and Fr. Grappi"—Wilkins refused to allow presidential candidate Eugene McCarthy to speak at the NAACP's summer convention in Atlantic City in 1968.[72] Although Senator McCarthy was against the war, he was hardly a paragon of radicalism. However, he had irked Wilkins by challenging LBJ in the New Hampshire primary, and the NAACP threw its support behind Vice President Hubert H. Humphrey. This was the final straw, and the Young Turks staged a highly publicized walkout at the convention.[73] A few months later, eight attorneys from the NAACP's legal department resigned to protest the firing of staff attorney Lewis Steele for writing an article accusing the U.S. Supreme Court of condoning white supremacy.[74] The firing provoked scores of disgruntled members to register their anger. Eugene T. Reed of Amityville, New York, bluntly informed Wilkins, "In view of the indefensible abuse of power by our National Board in the Lewis Steele matter, I now find it almost impossible to get anyone to join or support the NAACP."[75]

The complicated relationship between King and the leadership of the NAACP was evident even after King's assassination. In contrast to the heartfelt eulogies from friends and foes alike, Wilkins's regular column in the *New York Amsterdam News* expressed muted praise for the slain civil rights leader. Wilkins characterized the tragedy as a propitious time for the "black community to move toward the exploration of genuine paths to unity and coordinated action."[76] With the passing of King and the implosion of SNCC and CORE, the NAACP stood virtually alone as it struggled to regain its luster among the African American public. The impetus behind the civil rights movement stalled in the mid-1960s, and Richard Nixon's presidency would mark the end of the NAACP's unprecedented access to the corridors of executive power. Years later, Wilkins lamented that the Nixon administration "did all it could to turn back the clock on the progress we made on Presidents Johnson and Kennedy."[77]

The razor-thin defeat of longtime ally and Vietnam War supporter Hubert Humphrey in 1968 represented a bitter defeat for the NAACP leadership. Wilkins registered his disappointment by turning down Nixon's invitation to appear at the inauguration. Within a matter of months, the Nixon administration's tributes to "law and order" and its pandering to the fears of white southerners caused the civil rights movement to coalesce around its opposition to the new president's policies. The Young Turks now pledged their support and "allegiance to the duly elected officials of the association."[78] At the NAACP's annual convention in Cincinnati in the summer of 1970, Bishop Stephen G. Spottswood, chairman of the NAACP Board of Directors, received repeated ovations when he chastised the Nixon administration for being "anti-Negro" and noted that this was the first time since the 1920s that the White House "has made it a matter of calculated policy to work against the needs and aspirations of the largest minority of its citizens."[79]

Now that Johnson had retired to his ranch in Texas and opposition to the war had penetrated the mainstream, the NAACP leadership was less tethered to the issue of Vietnam. By the late 1960s and early 1970s, polls indicated that the overwhelming majority of African Americans opposed the war. For example, a Harris poll showed that only 9 percent of African Americans supported Nixon's decision to send troops to Cambodia.[80] The days of the NAACP's merciless attacks on antiwar activists were over. Still, the association did not jump on the antiwar bandwagon. It took the revelation of Nixon's secret bombing of Cambodia in June 1970 for the NAACP and the NUL to issue a joint statement demanding an immediate termination of the war.[81] By 1972, Wilkins had changed his tune; he disingenuously claimed that ending U.S. involvement in the war had "long been integral to NAACP policies and programs." But it was too little, too late.[82]

Like its purges of alleged communists in the early years of the Cold War, the NAACP's attacks against King and other African American opponents of the Vietnam War blighted its otherwise noble legacy. Wilkins's close ties to the Johnson administration fortified his fidelity to the "guns and butter" policy. Wilkins and the NAACP leadership were understandably loath to alienate the president in view of LBJ's unprecedented accomplishments in the area of civil rights. Nonetheless, the association's conflation of antiwar dissent with communism indicated a lack of understanding of the war's pernicious impact on African Americans and the civil rights movement. Wilkins's inability to comprehend the intensity of black opposition to the war contributed to LBJ's misreading of the mood of black America.[83] As late as the early 1970s, Wilkins, who had never served in the armed forces, was still exhorting young African Americans to enlist in the military and insisting that "turning down the opportunity of learning to defend your country in uniform is the silliest thing for a black person."[84] Even though the NAACP survived this tempestuous period, its hands-off policy on the Vietnam War and its attacks on those who deviated from it took a toll. It would take years for the breach to heal.

Whitney Young: LBJ's Emissary to Vietnam

Whitney M. Young Jr. served as executive director of the National Urban League from 1961 until his sudden death in 1971. He was twenty years younger than Wilkins and nearly twenty years older than the SNCC and CORE militants, but his policies on Vietnam mirrored those of the NAACP. For his moderation, Young earned the epithet "Uncle Tom," and the younger firebrands disparaged his reluctance to go to jail. "I do not see," Young once claimed, "why I should have to go to jail to prove my leadership."[85] Though not as well known as King, Carmichael, Wilkins, Rustin, or Malcolm X, Young was enormously influential in the 1960s owing to his status as a power broker inside the white establishment. Shortly after the urban uprisings in the summer of 1967, his proposal for a "domestic Marshall Plan" to combat hopelessness in the ghettos landed him on the cover of *Time*, where he was lauded as the most "effective man in America when it comes to drumming up jobs for Negroes."[86] His contributions were significant. In 1967, Young and the NUL created a Veterans Affairs Department, designed to help African American soldiers transition back into the civilian workforce. Young's contemporaries described him as the consummate inside man for his ability to sell the civil rights movement to rich and powerful white Americans who had hitherto been detached from the civil rights struggle. Andrew Young later remarked, "Whitney Young was a man who knew the high art of how to get power from the powerful and share it with the powerless."[87]

Whitney Young's father was the president of Lincoln Institute, a boarding school for African Americans in rural Kentucky, and young Whitney enrolled at Kentucky State Industrial College in Frankfort. Like thousands of young African American men, he enlisted in the segregated armed forces during World War II. His wartime service in Europe was formative, and he displayed an innate talent for mediating disputes between African American soldiers and their white superiors. His exposure to all kinds of people gave him hope that whites could modify their attitudes about race. On his way home from Europe, he wrote to his young wife: "As an American Negro, I don't expect to find any great liberal changes, but at the same time, I don't intend to use that as an excuse to hold me back."[88]

Young returned to civilian life determined to pursue a career in race relations. After obtaining a master's degree from the University of Minnesota's School of Social Work in 1947, he joined the Urban League's St. Paul branch, where he helped persuade department stores to hire African American clerks for the first time. Young's skills as an administrator, fund-raiser, and speaker propelled him to the top of the NUL in 1961 at age thirty-nine. The NUL had been created in 1910 to promote vocational training and employment opportunities for indigent southern migrants, and Young was critical in transforming it into an active participant in the civil rights movement. Despite its traditional aloofness from politics, Young managed to persuade the board to allow the NUL to participate in the March on Washington. Their ideological differences notwithstanding, John Lewis, Bayard Rustin, and Ralph Abernathy all agreed that Young's involvement as a strategist and fund-raiser and his credibility with the white community were critical to the success of the march. Thanks to the indomitable force of Young's personality and leadership, by 1963, the NUL was an integral member of the civil rights coalition.[89]

Like his moderate colleague Roy Wilkins, Young's status as a powerhouse in the civil rights movement was cemented by his closeness with LBJ. Upon first meeting Johnson in 1957, Young found him to be a man of "passion and concern," and he believed that once he was liberated from his role as a senator from Texas, LBJ would "do exactly as he did" on civil rights. LBJ, in turn, felt comfortable with Young's conciliatory approach and his emphasis on behind-the-scenes work rather than street demonstrations.[90] Their mutual ease led to a strong bond that withstood the turbulence of the era. Young's approach, however, led SNCC and other community activists to be highly critical of the NUL's middle-class orientation and propitiation to white elites in return for their financial support.

Prior to the Vietnam crisis, the NUL's overall caution and focus on vocational training caused the militants to brand it the most moderate of the civil rights organizations.

From the beginning of the Americanization of the Vietnam War, antiwar activists disparaged Young's fidelity to Cold War policy. At its convention in Miami in August 1965, the NUL approved a resolution, backed by the national office, that the league would "not divide nor divert its energies and resources by seeking to merge domestic and international issues where armed conflict is involved."[91] Throughout Johnson's presidency, Young was a stalwart defender of the administration's Vietnam policy. For instance, at a news conference during the White House Conference on Civil Rights, he said, "The people are more concerned about the rat tonight and the job tomorrow than they are about Vietnam."[92] When Senator William Fulbright's hearings on the conduct of the war drew praise from the antiwar community, Young reminded African Americans of Fulbright's abysmal record on civil rights and claimed, "Those who criticize LBJ over Vietnam must realize that his domestic program—Medicare, urban aid, anti-poverty programs, aid to education, and countless other far-seeing measures mark the beginning of a new era in American life."[93] During the height of the Black Power controversy a few months later, NBC broadcast a special ninety-minute edition of *Meet the Press* that included James Meredith and leaders of the five major civil rights organizations. Young said:

As far as Vietnam is concerned, the Urban League takes no position on Vietnam. We know this, that we had a race problem in this country before Vietnam; we will have a race problem after it is gone. We know well that the resistance, savage resistance we are running into in Chicago, has nothing to do with Vietnam. We know that unemployment—certainly the lack of employment on the part of some industries, is not related to Vietnam. We think that as an individual, one has a right to take a position. Our concern is that there be no money diverted into Vietnam that ought to go into the poverty programs, and we also are concerned about the 60,000 Negro fellows who are in Vietnam whether we like it or not, and we want to see when they come back that these men, their rights are respected, because one man throwing a rock seems to upset more people in Watts than the hundreds of Negro boys who are dying in Vietnam.[94]

SNCC's and CORE's opposition to the war, along with King's early grumblings, sparked White House aide Clifford Alexander to enlist Young to mitigate the damage.[95] Ever loyal to the president, Young needed no prodding. On July 18, 1966, Young held a press conference and announced that he was undertaking a ten-day tour of South Vietnam, where he would meet with "negro military personnel" and "speak with them on how we can help them upon their return home." He denied that his tour of Vietnam indicated a "value judgment on any aspect of the war," and he reassured African American soldiers that those in the States "care about them, love them, and await the opportunity to serve them upon their return home."[96] During his trip, Young also visited wounded African American men in hospitals and received a warm reception in Saigon from Ambassador Henry Cabot Lodge Jr. African American servicemen treated Young like a celebrity—a far cry from the insults hurled at him by SNCC and CORE militants back home. Young's sanitized tour of South Vietnam reaffirmed his favorable impressions of African American soldiers. Instead of arguing that their overrepresentation in the military was the result of racial discrimination, Young attributed it to high levels of enlistment and reenlistment.[97]

Upon his return, Young penned a series of columns in the *New York Amsterdam News* on the status of the African American soldier in Vietnam.[98] On the whole, Young was pleased with what he saw there. He was heartened by the marked contrast between his own service in the segregated armed forces and the current circumstances in Vietnam. Echoing Booker's *Ebony* article, he extolled the heroism of the African American soldier and lauded General William Westmoreland, a South Carolinian, for his candid acknowledgment of the need for more African American officers. On the downside, Young bewailed the persistence of de facto segregation during off-duty hours.[99] What was missing was any reference to the disproportionate number of African American casualties. In response, CORE's Floyd McKissick noted that although he had not yet visited Vietnam, he had talked to returning African American soldiers, and "they did not voice such high morale."[100] Young's sojourn to Vietnam prompted the establishment of a Veterans Affairs Department under NUL auspices to ease African American GIs' readjustment to civilian life. It turned out to be a successful program and opened offices in nine cities.

Ambassador Henry Cabot Lodge Jr. recommended a meeting between President Johnson and Young to showcase the latter's positive findings, but Young did not require Lodge's intercession. In fact, White House assistant Joseph Califano had already read LBJ the contents of Young's news conference in Saigon, where he had recommended the promotion of more African American officers.[101] On July 26, 1966, Young and the president had a friendly half-hour meeting at the White House, during which LBJ expressed his pleasure at Young's glowing report of the high morale among African American servicemen.[102] Afterward, the president met with the press and endorsed Young's recommendation for more African American officers. The *New York Times* reported that, according to Young, an "unprecedented, unparalleled degree of integration had been achieved among American troops, with Southern soldiers willingly and respectfully taking orders from Negro noncommissioned officers."[103]

Young's trip proved to be a public relations success for the White House and furthered its efforts to isolate African American antiwar dissenters as fringe elements. Not everyone, however, was pleased by Young's role. For instance, Cecil B. Moore of the Philadelphia NAACP accused Young of being a toady to the Johnson administration and claimed that he had been "used to whitewash racial discrimination in Vietnam."[104] A few days after his meeting at the White House, the NUL held its annual convention at the Sheraton Hotel in Philadelphia, where angry African Americans picketed and branded the NUL the "National Convention of Uncles Toms."[105] Young bitterly resented these attacks and defended his trip to Vietnam in a high-profile article in *Harper's*, wherein he reiterated that his purpose had been to facilitate African American soldiers' readjustment to civilian life.[106]

Only thirteen months later, Young returned to Vietnam at the president's behest to help monitor the crucial Southern Vietnamese elections.[107] Days before his departure, Young addressed a convocation of more than 800 civic leaders and remarked, "The greatest freedom that exists for Negroes in this country is the freedom to die in Vietnam."[108] But much had changed in the year since Young's first visit to Vietnam. The nation was experiencing its gravest domestic crisis since the Civil War. Among African Americans, support for the Vietnam War had dropped precipitously, thanks in large part to King's Riverside speech. Young, however, was not swayed by King's eloquence. He led the cavalcade of detractors, condemning the notion that the Vietnam War and civil rights were inextricably linked.[109] As a matter of fact, Young and King nearly came to blows during a fund-raiser in Great Neck, New York.[110] With the ghettos erupting in violence and the Great Society in peril, Young drew closer to the president. As a cherished member of the "black cabinet," Young readily accepted Johnson's invitation to observe the elections in South Vietnam scheduled for September 3, 1967. They were expected to be a crucial indicator of the regime's commitment to democracy. Any hint of fraud would be a severe blow to the administration's quest to cloak its ally in legitimacy.

Young was the only African American monitor in the group of twenty-two bipartisan leaders from government and business that arrived in Saigon on August 30, 1967.[111] With the world's attention focused on the elections, the U.S. government was desperate to demonstrate their legality. South Vietnamese politics was rife with venality and corruption, and opponents of the government charged that scoundrels were running the nation. For example, Nguyen Cao Ky, the vice presidential candidate, had reportedly used the South Vietnamese air force to smuggle opium and gold and had claimed Hitler as his political hero.[112] In preparation for his trip, Young had sifted through reams of unclassified intelligence reports demonstrating that the Vietcong were presumably engaged in a systematic campaign to sabotage the elections. The observers visited polling places, talked to the candidates, and attended the major candidates' preelection news conferences. According to Young's handwritten notes, he was "critical, suspicious, and cynical of the election procedure."[113] It was virtually impossible for Young and the other monitors, who included Senators Edmund Muskie, Bourke Hickenlooper, and George Murphy, to get more than a snapshot of South Vietnamese political life in such a short trip, but Young did the president's bidding and characterized the elections as legitimate. Days before, he had reported from Vietnam, "I didn't get the impression of great pressure by government officials. I've been more concerned about the fairness of the press than the fairness of the election."[114]

Young's many critics charged that his unwavering support of the president vitiated his professed neutrality. The *Pittsburgh Courier* objected to the president's exclusive reliance on Wilkins and Young and accused him of employing the old plantation technique of finding one "safe" Negro and funneling all things through him.[115] In his postelection observations, Young did not disappoint LBJ, stating that he "overcame his skepticism and left terribly impressed." Again, Young painted a rosy portrait of the morale of African American troops and claimed that they were "perplexed by riots that destroy their own neighborhoods and people" and concerned that "Congress seemed to be reacting to a few negro extremists rather than enacting the programs that would help the Negroes who were loyally fighting in South Vietnam and their families."[116]

The delegation's ringing endorsement of the elections brightened the otherwise dour mood of the president, and it bought him time to convince the public that the Saigon government could reconstitute itself as a legitimate ally. *Newsweek*, for one, expressed hope that the South Vietnamese government could gain the support of the people within six months.[117] Meeting with the president and his national security team for a lengthy debriefing session at the White House, several of the monitors believed that the election results—granting power to General Thieu and Air Vice Marshal Nguyen Cao Ky, who allegedly received slightly less than 35 percent of the votes—finally provided an opportunity for peace.[118] Young announced that he was "completely satisfied that it was as free an election as possible to have under the circumstances—so many candidates, such brutal terrorism as they have, inexperienced people, and the high degree of illiteracy."[119] Not everybody in the civil rights community accepted Young's verdict at face value. His position as LBJ's token African American alienated him from many of his allies in the civil rights movement who had long ago severed ties with the White House. King, for one, was troubled by Young's performance. Having immersed himself in the history of the Vietnam conflict, King believed that Young was inexperienced and ignorant about the situation in Southeast Asia.[120] Worse, he thought LBJ had used Young. A member of the National Association of Social Workers agreed and bluntly told Young, "I am ashamed of your support of the USA Vietnam war by participating in that 'white wash' commission and thus contributing to the spurious and illegal election in S. Vietnam. . . . You certainly permitted yourself to be exploited."[121]

By the late 1960s, Young's stance on the Vietnam War, eschewal of nonviolent direct action, and closeness to the political and economic white power structure earned the opprobrium of both white and African American antiwar activists. In the wake of the urban uprisings in Newark and Detroit, legendary white political activist Saul Alinsky derisively compared Young to the "cooperative natives in the Congo" who were used by the colonial rulers "to keep the rest of the natives quiet."[122] Regularly lampooned by his many critics as an "errand boy," "Oreo," and "Uncle Tom," Young continued to support LBJ's Vietnam policy until the president retired to his Texas ranch in January 1969.[123] Whatever his private reservations about the war, Young kept them to himself, realizing that his effectiveness as a civil rights leader was predicated on maintaining his ties to the establishment. Of the approximately $35 million a year the NUL raised in the late 1960s, only about 1 percent came from African Americans. Young was a proud man with a big ego, and the epithets took a toll. He became increasingly angry and lashed out at the impotency of his critics. He retorted that it was easy for the militants to yell "Black Power" and "Kill Whitey," but his tactics produced tangible results for untold numbers of African Americans. What hurt him most was the rift with his daughter Marcia, a student at Bryn Mawr College, who engaged in a hunger strike to demonstrate her opposition to the war.[124] Like so many American families, Young's family split along generational lines over the war, causing the SCLC's Andrew Young to speculate that this intrafamily conflict fueled Whitney's inner turmoil over the war.[125]

Once Johnson left office, Young was free to renounce his support for the Vietnam War. Only five months later, Young confessed to an interviewer, "Dr. King was probably more right than I was, because it is hard to separate the war from the domestic problems in terms of the resources of the country and the manpower and all this."[126] On October 15, 1969, the Vietnam Moratorium Committee staged an antiwar demonstration, and approximately 250,000 people attended various peace rallies in New York City alone. Two days earlier, Young had held a press conference at the NUL's Manhattan headquarters and criticized the Vietnam War as a "moral and spiritual drain" that diverted the nation from "the urban and racial crisis—at the very time that the crisis is at flash point." Echoing King's Riverside speech, Young added, "The agony of Vietnam has twisted America's soul."[127] A few months later, he argued that the economic recession would end if the nation ended the Vietnam War.[128] Young's sudden turnabout pleased a few in the antiwar movement, but most of his critics muttered that it was too little, too late. His apologia on Vietnam did not represent the end of his moderation, and he never became a full-fledged antiwar activist. Nor did it stop the NUL's younger members from complaining that the league was irrelevant to African Americans.[129] Young's conciliatory posture toward President Nixon, whom most African Americans held in contempt, only flamed the passions of Young's many detractors.[130] At the NUL's sixtieth anniversary meeting in the summer of 1970, Young's comment that the Nixon administration "isn't so bad" incensed even his close ally Roy Wilkins.[131] Young's reverence for LBJ's accomplishments in the realm of civil rights was justifiable, but his support for LBJ's foreign policy cost him the respect of many colleagues and added to the strains in the civil rights coalition in the late 1960s.

Whether Young, a skilled mediator, could have healed the rifts in the post-Vietnam era will never be known. On March 11, 1971, the forty-nine-year-old Young drowned in Lagos, Nigeria. The shocking news of the premature death of another civil rights leader generated a flood of tributes. Roy Innis, executive director of CORE, said, "Although we had philosophical and programmatic differences, our points of agreement were numerous."[132] Ironically, Young's body was flown to Riverside Church, where thousands of mourners paid their respects. Amid the overwhelming praise for Young, Stokely Carmichael, speaking before a predominantly African American audience at San Francisco State University, quipped, "Some blacks love the slave master so much that even when they die in Africa they have their body shipped here."[133] Carmichael's impolitic remarks underscored the simmering resentments that stemmed, in large part, from profound disagreements over the Vietnam War. Although Young devoted his life to ameliorating the plight of African Americans—raising millions of dollars and providing employment for thousands of underprivileged youths—his role as LBJ's emissary to South Vietnam cost him the respect of large segments of the African American community. For the thin-skinned Young, the delicate balance between maintaining acceptability within the white power structure and preserving legitimacy among blacks proved too daunting.

The Curious Case of Bayard Rustin

The Vietnam War divided the nation, the Democratic Party, the civil rights movement, the New Deal coalition, and millions of American families. According to his biographer Daniel Levine, the Vietnam War also divided Bayard Rustin.[134] Witty, elegant, urbane, and endowed with a towering intellect, Rustin was a prominent figure in the mid-twentieth-century pacifist movement and in the long civil rights movement. Raised in West Chester, Pennsylvania, by his Quaker grandmother, who became a charter member of the NAACP in 1910, Rustin was exposed to radical pacifism at an early age. As a young man, he moved to New York City and joined the Young Communist League in the years of the Popular Front because it was the only party advocating racial justice, but he left in 1941 because of the Soviet Union's militarism. He then led A. Philip Randolph's youth division of the March on Washington Movement.[135] After Randolph canceled the march, Rustin devoted his energy to pacifism and became active in the Fellowship of Reconciliation (FOR), a Christian nonviolent protest group and the progenitor of CORE.[136]

Rustin did not merely preach pacifism; he lived it. After serving a twenty-eight-month prison term for refusing to serve in the military during World War II, he participated in the FOR-sponsored freedom ride in 1947, which inspired the more famous and successful Freedom Rides of 1961.[137] Although his arrests for homosexual conduct temporarily sidelined him, Rustin resurrected himself in the mid-1950s by becoming a chief adviser to Martin Luther King Jr., providing the charismatic young minister with a tutorial on Gandhian nonviolence in the early days of the Montgomery bus boycott.[138] For the next decade, Rustin was one of King's most trusted lieutenants, and he mentored the young SNCC activists in the early 1960s. Rustin's radical pacifism, his ties to the Old Left, and his homosexuality furnished ammunition for FBI director Hoover's campaign to smear the civil rights movement with a communist brush.[139] Much to the dismay of the hypervigilant Roy Wilkins, who was leery of Rustin's controversial past, Rustin brilliantly orchestrated the 1963 March on Washington, which landed him on the cover of *Life* magazine.[140] After years in the political wilderness, Rustin had become a national celebrity and was seemingly poised to play an instrumental role in the burgeoning antiwar movement.[141]

Rustin was a board member of two of the foremost pacifist organizations in the United States: the War Resisters League and Turn toward Peace. So it came as no surprise that he was involved in some of the first protests against American militarism in the early years of the Vietnam War. Only two days after passage of the Gulf of Tonkin Resolution in August 1964, Rustin, along with Socialist Party leader Norman Thomas and muckraking journalist I. F. Stone, led a rally of 1,000 demonstrators in New York City to commemorate the nineteenth anniversary of the bombing of Hiroshima. The demonstrators were aware of the incipient conflict in Vietnam, and so was Rustin. Addressing the crowd in Washington Square Park, Rustin denounced the government's policy in Vietnam, likening the people in Vietnam to those in nearby Bedford-Stuyvesant and Harlem. He said, "The answer to the problem in Vietnam is that the people will no longer tolerate being without dignity and being poor."[142] Rustin and his fellow editors of *Liberation*, David Dellinger and A. J. Muste, composed and circulated a "Declaration of Conscience" against the Vietnam War.[143]

Nonetheless, around the time Vietnam was first becoming an issue in the peace movement, longtime observers discerned a change in Rustin, who was now in his early fifties. Many close friends commented that Rustin's early critiques of the Vietnam War seemed to be motivated by habit rather than conviction.[144] As early as 1963, a generational clash had erupted, with Rustin, Thomas, Muste, socialist Michael Harrington, and other Old Leftists disagreeing with the New Leftists' inclusion of communist groups in the antiwar movement.[145] Continually Red-baited because of his youthful connections with the Communist Party, Rustin vigorously opposed the nonexclusionary policy of SDS and SNCC, fearing it would destroy the newly resurgent protest movement. This newfound pragmatism baffled many of Rustin's closest allies. Biographer John D'Emilio attributes this transformation to Rustin's status as a homosexual in an age of homophobia. His humiliating arrest for homosexual conduct in 1953 resulted in his ejection from FOR, and it strained his relationship with his mentor, Muste. This marginalization from the movement, according to D'Emilio, ultimately shattered Rustin's acceptance of the New Left's romantic idealization of the Vietcong and other national liberation movements.[146] This theory based on Rustin's sexual orientation raises some interesting questions, but it fails to take into account a variety of other factors, such as his ambition to participate in the powerful political tide sweeping the nation and his gravitation toward coalition politics. By the end of the 1960s, Rustin was a vigorous supporter of the AFL-CIO and the United Federation of Teachers.[147] As a consequence, he became estranged from his former allies in the antiwar and civil rights movements.

Rustin displayed his new pragmatism at the 1963 Easter Peace Walks in New York City. According to Socialist Workers Party leader Fred Halstead, a group of high school students from the Young People's Socialist League showed up at the rally carrying signs protesting the Vietnam War.[148] Dellinger recalled that Rustin, who was chairman of the demonstration, stopped the rally and ordered that the antiwar signs be removed. His pleas were ignored.[149] This incident illustrated Rustin's growing moderation and his reluctance to challenge the Kennedy administration's Cold War policies in the months prior to the March on Washington. And it was not an aberration; Rustin frequently registered the view that SNCC's and SDS's coziness with communists was irresponsible and could jeopardize recent gains. Years later, Rustin told an interviewer that he believed SNCC leaders were emotionally unstable. They "so enjoyed the protests," he said, and "they so enjoyed the attention they got from it." He recalled that they were enraptured by the drama, but they lacked the maturity and political skills to translate their vision into policy.[150]

By 1964, the animus was mutual. The New Left perceived that Rustin was compromising his principles and becoming too friendly with the liberal establishment. As early as the summer of 1963, SNCC resented Rustin's pivotal role in deleting fiery parts of John Lewis's proposed speech at the March on Washington.[151] Relations between Rustin and SNCC were further compromised when he lobbied for the MFDP to accept the two-delegate compromise at the 1964 Democratic Convention in Atlantic City.[152] Robert Moses alleged that Rustin "flip-flopped" and sided "with Humphrey and the Administration."[153] To add insult to injury, Rustin had joined the moderate wing of the civil rights movement in urging a moratorium on demonstrations until after the election.[154] While SNCC sulked over the betrayal at Atlantic City, Rustin viewed LBJ's landslide victory as a historic opportunity and promptly called on African Americans to take advantage of the Democratic Party's electoral gains. Along with Harrington, Rustin believed that a political realignment was imminent, providing an auspicious climate for unprecedented reforms. By this point, however, SNCC was in no mood to exult and had retreated from politics. By the end of 1964, Rustin and the militants in both the civil rights and the antiwar movements were locking horns over tactics and ideology.[155] The Johnson administration's escalation of the Vietnam War would aggravate this rift.

The crux of Rustin's ideological differences with the New Left and many of his comrades in the Old Left was his realization that the civil rights movement had reached a crossroads: it needed to move beyond protest and into politics. Only weeks after LBJ's landslide victory (which temporarily eased concerns of a white backlash), Rustin began writing what would become his most famous essay: "From Protest to Politics: The Future of the Civil Rights Movement." It appeared in the February 1965 edition of *Commentary*, an intellectual magazine dominated by Jewish liberals. Rustin's major premise was that nonviolent direct action, which had been instrumental in recent civil rights victories, was becoming obsolete now that segregation was in its death throes. Although desegregation in public accommodations was a historic achievement, Rustin argued that it only "affected institutions which are relatively peripheral both to the American socioeconomic order and to the fundamental conditions of life of the Negro people." The "decline of Jim Crow" was a substantial achievement, but a new strategy was required to tackle the rapidly deteriorating economic conditions in the urban ghettos. His proposed remedy was for African Americans to transform their street activism into a political movement and fashion a progressive coalition with liberals, Jews, and labor under the umbrella of the Democratic Party. Rustin was buoyed by Johnson's victory, which he believed ushered in a new era of politics where "economic interests are more fundamental than prejudice."[156]

Rustin's prescription for wielding political power was largely a response to the stirrings of Black Power and the popularity of his occasional debating foe Malcolm X. Racial separatism was anathema to Rustin, a consummate integrationist, and he argued that African Americans were in a critical period and "need[ed] allies." The future of the African American freedom struggle, Rustin claimed, "depends on whether the contradictions of this society can be resolved in a coalition of progressive forces which becomes the effective political majority in the United States." For this coalition to function effectively, "compromise was imperative," and the civil rights movement had to expand its vision. What was needed, Rustin argued, was not the angry rhetoric of Malcolm X or a separatist posture but a massive infusion of government largesse, in the amount of $100 billion to eliminate slums, improve schools, and provide jobs. In perhaps his most memorable phrase, Rustin criticized the civil rights movement for its "strong moralistic strain," which "would remind us that power corrupts, forgetting the absence of power also corrupts."[157]

"From Protest to Politics" appeared the same month LBJ initiated Operation Rolling Thunder, which escalated the Vietnam War and doomed the long-term prospects for Rustin's liberal coalition. Even if the Vietnam War had not subsumed all other political issues, Rustin was unrealistic about the prospects for an interracial coalition within the established power structure of the Democratic Party. In the mid-1960s, African Americans were outsiders knocking at the doors of power. There was a big difference between letting African Americans eat a hamburger at a public establishment in the South and actually sharing political power with them. Stokely Carmichael angered liberals and middle-class whites with his fiery rhetoric, but he was an astute observer of contemporary political trends when he remarked: "There is in fact no group at present in which to form a coalition in which blacks will not be absorbed and betrayed."[158]

Rustin also misread the significance of Johnson's landside victory over right-wing senator Barry Goldwater. Johnson's win was largely attributable to nostalgia for Kennedy and the portrayal of Goldwater as unacceptably conservative. Rustin, however, interpreted the 1964 election results as indicating the subsidence of white backlash, leading him to conclude that economic interests were now more important than racial prejudice. A normally keen observer of politics (he had even advised King against going to Chicago), Rustin misread the results. Johnson's victory and the passage of civil rights legislation belied the persistence of a backlash that had existed for decades, especially at the local level in cities such as Detroit, and then accelerated after Watts.[159] By the midterm elections of 1966, Catholics and other working-class white ethnics who had been mainstays of the New

Deal coalition began to defect from the Democratic Party, a trend compounded by urban uprisings and deindustrialization, which resulted in the
rise of the Reagan Democrats by the late 1970s.[160]

Rustin's faith in labor unions as agents of racial change was also
unduly optimistic. Traditionally, a large segment of organized labor had
been tinged with racism. Most notably, George Meany and his AFL predecessors were not friendly to the civil rights movement.[161] By the early
1960s, the progressive wing of the labor movement (such as the packing-
house workers) had strong ties to the New Left, including SNCC and SDS;
likewise, under the leadership of Walter Reuther, the United Auto Workers
was closely allied with the civil rights movement. Still, too many working-
class whites clung to their whiteness as a badge of distinction.[162] The Vietnam War, Black Power, and the emergence of the counterculture frayed the
vestiges of goodwill between the labor movement and the activist wing of
the civil rights movement.[163] Organized labor's privileging of whiteness
precluded the creation of a cohesive working class that transcended differences in race and ethnicity. Perhaps Rustin's embrace of organized labor
and the AFL-CIO was a result of Meany's decision to mete out funds for
the creation of the A. Philip Randolph Institute, which Rustin headed for
nearly a decade.

Rustin's confidence in the beneficence of the Jewish community was
similarly overblown. His fruitful association with progressive Jews during
his years as an antiwar and civil rights activist led him to believe that the
liberal Jewish community would continue to fight for African Americans
in the post–Jim Crow era. However, many Jews opposed the preferential
treatment and the billions of dollars in federal funds necessary to alleviate race-based economic injustice. Within a few years, the African American–Jewish alliance would be strained over the militants' embrace of
anti-Zionism as well as Jewish opposition to affirmative action and other
government programs.[164]

Noticeably absent from Rustin's *Commentary* piece was any mention
of Vietnam. Of course, at the time, Johnson was still deliberating whether
to escalate the war, so the resulting quagmire was not yet discernible. Nevertheless, its exclusion was predictive of Rustin's newfound pragmatism
based on his unwillingness to alienate the president, whose leadership in
shepherding civil rights legislation through Congress and implementing
the Great Society ratified Rustin's view of the efficacy of coalition politics. In this respect, he was taking a more moderate position and moving
closer to Roy Wilkins and Whitney Young. Implicit in Rustin's prescrip-

tions for African American political empowerment was the notion that the U.S. economy would continue to grow at a spectacular pace, enabling the progressive coalition to deliver the $100 billion needed "to overhaul our schools, clear the slums, and really abolish poverty."[165] The billions of dollars expended in Vietnam would slow the pace of economic growth and the Great Society. But because of his faith in coalition politics, Rustin, like Wilkins and Young, refused to speak out against the administration's war in Vietnam.

From the moment of its publication, "From Protest to Politics" provoked criticism from Rustin's erstwhile allies in the peace movement. Writing in *Liberation*, Mississippi Freedom School director and antiwar activist Staughton Lynd blasted Rustin for advocating a "coalition with the marines."[166] Just prior to the April 17, 1965, March on Washington to End the War in Vietnam, Rustin signed a statement that was critical of allowing communists to participate in the march. Already angry at Rustin, Lynd circulated an open letter to him that stated in part:

I was distressed that you took part in Red-baiting the march. . . . What I think it means is that you do not believe in an independent peace movement. You believe in a peace movement dependent on the Johnson administration. . . . We can oppose this horrible war only as house radicals, only as court jesters. And you, who should be leading us in civil disobedience, have gone along.

Why Bayard? You must know in your heart that your position betrays your essential moralism over the years. The lesson of your apostasy on Vietnam appears to be that the gains for American Negroes you advise them to seek through coalition within the Democratic party come not only at a price. . . . The price is to make our brothers in Vietnam a burnt offering on the altar of political expediency.[167]

In a direct swipe at Rustin, David Dellinger chimed in and called the antiwar demonstration "even more inspiring than the 1963 March on Washington."[168]

Many African American activists were angry at Rustin's apostasy on the peace issue. SNCC workers, who had dedicated their lives to nurturing grassroots organizations to empower people in the Deep South, decried Rustin's coalition tack as elitist and self-serving. After the "sellout" in Atlantic City, the Young Turks in SNCC and CORE were done compromising their core principles for political expediency. In fact, they had been repulsed by their brief foray into the political process. SNCC's Joyce Ladner observed that Atlantic City spelled "the end of innocence."[169] The Vietnam War only confirmed their view that violence and racism were endemic in American society and its institutions. When King called for a cease-fire in Vietnam in August 1965, Rustin hoped the controversy would die down. He stated, "I think Negro people are so overwhelmed and so deeply involved in the obtaining of freedom here that there is no likelihood of getting involved as a movement in the Vietnam crisis."[170] Upon hearing that SNCC was plotting to disrupt the White House Conference on Civil Rights scheduled for June 1, 1966, Rustin went so far as to notify White House authorities.[171] These actions rendered him a pariah among his onetime comrades. Ironically, the man who had gone to prison for his pacifist principles in the early 1940s, when pacifism was the province of a fringe minority, was missing in action when antimilitarism crested in the 1960s and early 1970s.

In spite of the vocal and highly personal criticisms from many of his longtime comrades in the peace and freedom movements, Rustin continued to distance himself from the antiwar movement. Given his abiding commitment to pacifism, this stance confounded his contemporaries. His aide Rachelle Horowitz recalled Rustin telling her, "I'm in the black movement now. I'm not a peacenik."[172] Another plausible explanation for his position was the mutual tension between Rustin and the New Left. The New Leftists' disdain at Rustin's elitism was matched by his aversion to what he perceived as their juvenile tactics and overblown rhetoric. Rustin also looked askance at the Black Power and feared that its adherents' anger would only hasten the dreaded backlash.[173] Since Rustin had been forced to operate in the shadows because of his homosexuality and youthful affiliations with the Left, his old colleagues in the New Left surmised that he had been seduced by power and was constrained by his dependence on the AFL-CIO.[174]

His disquiet with the anti-American tone of the New Left and his relationship with the AFL-CIO are perhaps the most plausible explanations for Rustin's break with the peace movement. After receiving a grant from the AFL-CIO, one of the staunchest supporters of the Vietnam War, Rustin formed the A. Philip Randolph Institute in the spring of 1965, where he remained safely ensconced for the rest of the decade. He resigned from the War Resisters League and stopped writing for *Liberation.* In October 1966, Rustin proposed the "Freedom Budget," a $185 billion plan designed to eliminate poverty within ten years that neither endorsed nor condemned current military spending policies.[175] Under his Freedom Budget, every citizen would be guaranteed a job, an annual income, and health insurance. It was the ultimate expression of "guns and butter" economics. Influential economists disparaged it as Pollyannaish, given the billions of dollars devoted to Vietnam. Columbia University economist Seymour Melman argued that the high level of military spending "prevented serious repair of American poverty and city decay."[176] Rustin nonetheless persisted in his contention that "guns and butter" were not mutually exclusive and argued that "it would be most unfortunate if we made the Freedom Budget dependent upon the debate about military spending."[177] He submitted his proposal to the White House, but his plea for billions of dollars fell on deaf ears.[178] The Republican comeback during the 1966 midterm elections doomed Rustin's vision of coalition politics. Perhaps more important, the Vietnam War deflated Rustin's ambitious agenda for a domestic Marshall Plan.

Rustin's equivocations on the interrelationship between the civil rights movement and the antiwar movement revealed a divided mind. All along, Rustin claimed to be uncomfortable with the civil rights movement injecting itself into the antiwar movement, and although he was not sympathetic to the war, he brooded that a precipitate withdrawal from Vietnam would impose a totalitarian regime on South Vietnam.[179] During the height of the Vietnam controversy in 1967, he urged African Americans "to ally themselves individually with the peace struggle without committing the civil rights movement" to the antiwar movement.[180] Similarly, in his criticisms of King's stance on Vietnam, Rustin acknowledged that the "war is a tragedy," but he also contended that the problems facing African Americans were so vast and crushing that King performed a disservice by focusing on international issues.[181] Yet Rustin's professed pacifism was also punctuated by a curious deference to governmental prerogatives. For instance, in 1968, the former conscientious objector opposed a unilateral withdrawal from Vietnam and stated, "Many groups in the peace movement fail to provide a step-by-step method by which the U.S. can get out and still have any national pride."[182] As late as 1985, he told an interviewer he had believed in finding "a third force in Vietnam that could actually win because I really felt, and I think it's been proven, that the domino theory works."[183] Such paeans to national pride and the oft-discredited domino theory signified a radical departure from Rustin's youthful pacifism and from his key allies in the peace and freedom movements. Although Rustin's radical background precluded a personal relationship with the president, he believed a break with the Johnson administration would be inimical to the best interests of the civil rights movement.

Furthermore, Rustin's apostasy strained his relationship with King and others in the SCLC. As King became more outspoken against the war and American capitalism, Rustin, his onetime mentor, became more aligned with the moderate wing of the civil rights movement. He grew increasingly fond of Roy Wilkins, who had vehemently opposed Rustin's leadership of the March on Washington.[184] At the end of his life, Rustin called the NAACP leader the "most politically astute and urbane civil rights leader."[185] His commitment to the Freedom Budget remained unshakeable, and as late as March 1968, Rustin told a radio interviewer that he still believed "the nation could afford to finance both the Vietnam War and the war on poverty."[186] Soon after King's Riverside speech, Rustin disputed King's contention that the conflict in Vietnam was a "racist war," but Vietnam was not the only source of their disagreement.[187] Rustin's fidelity to coalition politics led him to oppose taking the civil rights movement to Chicago and the Poor People's Campaign. For his part, King had grown disillusioned with liberalism and coalition politics. In spite of their disagreements, King still sought Rustin's counsel, to the dismay of some members of King's inner circle, who were less forgiving and felt betrayed when Rustin joined the chorus criticizing King's Riverside speech. Harry Wachtel called Rustin's views on the Vietnam War "nauseating," and Stanley Levison urged King "to rethink the business of treating Bayard as one of your advisors."[188] In the end, King and Rustin became increasingly estranged, in large part because of their differences on the Vietnam War.[189]

Nixon's election marked the death knell of Rustin's dream of a great liberal coalition enacting reforms to benefit African Americans. British historian and journalist Godfrey Hodgson summed it up best: Rustin "found himself in the tragic posture, for a lifelong pacifist, of justifying the war in the name of a radical coalition that never materialized."[190] Ironically, in Rustin's quest to find a comfortable perch in the establishment, he lost his true home in both the pacifist movement and the protest wing of the civil rights movement. A month after Nixon's ascension to power, the *New York Times Magazine* ran a feature story on Rustin, fittingly titled "A Strategist without a Movement." His old FOR comrade James Farmer expressed the views of many civil rights activists when he said, "Rustin's commitment is to labor, not to the black man."[191]

In this unfavorable political milieu, Rustin remained active in the labor movement, particularly with the United Federation of Teachers and his A.

Philip Randolph Institute. Meanwhile, he continued to rail against black separatism.[192] In his final years, he shifted his focus to international affairs, particularly human rights in South Africa and Haiti. Rustin renounced pacifism as "politically irrelevant" and further angered many of his old friends by his intense support for Israel, even calling for the United States to arm Israel for its defense.[193] By the end of his life, he had become an elder statesman of the radical movement and had mended some of the frayed relationships stemming from his stance on Vietnam, but not all. In his 1993 memoir, David Dellinger insisted that Rustin was on the CIA's payroll.[194] At the end of the day, the emotions unleashed by Rustin's stance on Vietnam marred cherished friendships and cast a pall on an otherwise stellar career. His renunciation of pacifism notwithstanding, Rustin, like the NAACP, survived and continued the fight for civil rights and economic justice.

Roy Wilkins, Whitney Young Jr., and Bayard Rustin were three of the most influential civil rights leaders who adhered to the "hands-off" policy on the Vietnam War throughout LBJ's tenure. Of course, they were not alone. A. Philip Randolph, who had opposed Du Bois's call for African Americans to "close ranks" during World War I and had called for civil disobedience during the early mobilization against fascism in 1941, also opposed the civil rights movement's involvement in the antiwar movement. Well into his seventies by the time the Vietnam controversy racked the nation and the civil rights coalition, Randolph, a mentor to Rustin and a staunch anticommunist, also made the pragmatic decision not to break with the Johnson administration over foreign policy and adhered to his protégé's call for coalition politics.[195] Randolph's long-standing antipathy to the Communist Party, rooted in its volte-face on fascism, was one factor in his unwillingness to denounce the president's Vietnam policies.[196] Randolph's public justification was similar to that of the other moderates—namely, he argued that fighting two battles at the same time was not feasible.[197] In the twilight of Randolph's career, Rustin "had become a kind of alter ego to the aged leader." As a consequence, Randolph followed Rustin in not speaking out against the war, but Randolph's criticisms of his fellow civil rights activists were more muted.[198] Like Rustin, Randolph was never close to LBJ, but he extolled the president's record on civil rights.[199] In the end, Randolph decided that the hands-off policy was in the best interests of the African American freedom struggle.

The vitriol with which the moderate wing of the civil rights move-

ment attacked fellow members who deviated from the Johnson administration's policy on the Vietnam War aggravated the fissures in the civil
rights coalition at a critical time. For Whitney Young Jr., Roy Wilkins,
and the NAACP hierarchy, the intensely personal attacks on King, SNCC,
and others who took an antiwar position underscored the strength of their
attachment to Cold War liberalism and their fidelity to Lyndon Johnson,
even though the momentum for civil rights had been stalled. The civil
rights coalition, always unwieldy, was fractured by the war.

The bitterness over the Vietnam War, of course, extended beyond the
civil rights movement to virtually every corner of American society and
was instrumental in the unraveling of the postwar liberal consensus. For
African Americans, the wrecking of the New Deal coalition on the shoals
of the Vietnam War was particularly tragic, for it ushered in a period of
conservative hegemony that was inimical to their aspirations. Ironically,
their hostility to Richard Nixon helped repair the rifts in the civil rights
coalition. Much of the animus that had previously been directed at one
another over Vietnam was now directed at Nixon and his attempts to roll
back civil rights advances. Most dramatic was Nixon's two unsuccessful
Supreme Court nominations: Clement Haynsworth and G. Harrold Car-
swell, both southerners with segregationist sympathies. Nixon's southern strategy and his appeals to the silent majority liberated the NAACP
and other moderates to protest Nixon's extension of the war to Cambodia.[200] The editorial pages of four major African American publications
went from generally supporting LBJ's Vietnam policy to opposing the war
shortly after Nixon became president.[201] With the disintegration of SNCC
and the SCLC following King's assassination, the NAACP's newfound,
albeit dilatory, antiwar attitude enabled it to regain much of the support
from ordinary African Americans and civil rights leaders. Since the Vietnam War, African American political leaders and civil rights organizations
have been the most vocal opponents of U.S. militarism and aggression
abroad. And by the end of the 1990s, Julian Bond, whose antiwar views
had so angered Wilkins, had assumed the helm of the NAACP, where he
served until 2010.

The moderates' adherence to a hands-off policy on Vietnam was rooted
in their political pragmatism and loyalty to President Johnson. Furthermore, many moderates were still haunted by the specter of the Red scare
and McCarthyism, which testified to the enduring legacy of the Cold War
zeitgeist well into the late 1960s. As political tacticians, their approaches
contrasted with King's moving jeremiads against the violence, racism, and

poverty endemic in American society and modern capitalism. In contrast to King, SNCC, CORE, and other opponents of U.S. foreign policy, the moderates displayed a lack of courage. In spite of their years of dedication to social justice, it was not one of their finest moments.[202]

Conclusion

By the time U.S. troops finally withdrew from Vietnam in January 1973, all the civil rights organizations had expressed their opposition to the war—some sooner than others, and for differing rationales. However, it was Lyndon Johnson's departure from the White House that marked the end of the civil rights movement's support for the war.[1]

Johnson's successor, Richard M. Nixon, referred to African Americans as "niggers," "jigaboos," and "jungle bunnies," and he crafted a "southern strategy" to entice white southerners into the Republican Party.[2] Prior to the 1968 election, Nixon confided to a supporter, "If I am president, I am not going to owe anything to the black community."[3] The Nixon administration opposed busing, nominated two southern conservatives to the Supreme Court, and requested a delay in school desegregation. On top of that, the president asked the FBI to target the Black Panther Party, which, by the end of 1968, had emerged as the leading black organization in the nation.[4] Not surprisingly, African Americans vigorously opposed Nixon's civil rights agenda, and their opposition extended to his policies on Vietnam. Only 9 percent of African Americans supported the invasion of Cambodia in the spring of 1970.[5] In his landslide reelection victory over George McGovern in 1972, Nixon lost only Massachusetts and the District of Columbia, but he won only 12 percent of the African American vote.[6] Even the usually measured Roy Wilkins accused Nixon of "turn[ing] the clock back on everything" and claimed the president was on the side of the "enemies of little black children."[7] A Gallup poll conducted in August 1972 showed that 77 percent of nonwhites thought the United States should withdraw all troops from Vietnam by the end of the year.[8] When President Nixon signed the Paris Peace Accords on January 27, 1973, officially ending U.S. participation in the Vietnam War, Daphne Busby, a black college student from Brooklyn, captured the sentiments of many African Americans when she said: "Perhaps we can now use the billions of dollars used in the Vietnam War to improve life here at home instead of destroying lives elsewhere."[9]

Only a few days prior to the signing of the Paris Peace Accords, Lyndon B. Johnson died of a heart attack at age sixty-four. A broken man, Johnson was haunted by the war until the very end. Scorned by liberals, intellectuals, and southerners, he lived his last years in lonely exile at his Texas ranch. But African Americans and the mainstream civil rights organizations remained loyal. In his last public appearance at his new presidential library, he told a gathering of civil rights veterans, "Of all the records that are housed in this library," it is the "record of this work that holds the most meaning for me."[10] At his funeral several weeks later, on a cold day in the hill country near Austin, Ralph Ellison said that LBJ would "have to settle for being recognized as the greatest American President for the poor and for the Negroes, but that, as I see it, is a very great honor indeed."[11] One mourner estimated that 60 percent of the attendees at Johnson's memorial service were African American.[12] In a cruel twist of fate, news of the signing of the Paris Peace Accords diverted attention from Johnson's funeral.

Nixon's presidency marked the end of the postwar liberal consensus. Although the momentum for civil rights advances had slowed in the final years of Johnson's presidency, Nixon's hostile rhetoric toward African Americans, his references to "law and order," and his deference to white southerners and Sun Belt suburbanites brought the impetus for racial reform to a standstill. Nixon failed to reverse the triumphs of the civil rights revolution, but he ensured that the symbolic power of the presidency was no longer used to make racism an unacceptable feature of the American creed.[13] Nixon's domestic policies enraged the entire spectrum of the civil rights coalition and liberated them to reject his policies in Vietnam and Cambodia. The de-escalation of the Cold War following Nixon's election also facilitated greater African American opposition to the war. Once the great Red-baiter himself had gone to China and the Soviet Union, the fear of speaking out against U.S. Cold War policy dissipated.

King's Riverside speech was the civil rights movement's most dramatic expression of the injustices of the Vietnam War. While the shared animosity toward Nixon helped heal much of the internecine strife over the Vietnam War, King's assassination left a profound void. The civil rights movement was further weakened by the ongoing radicalization and splintering of the black Left. By the early 1970s, the Congressional Black Caucus (CBC) stepped into the breach. Formed in early 1969, it included only a handful of the growing number of African American members of Congress, but it emerged as a vocal opponent of the Nixon administration's war policies.[14] On March 25, 1971, the CBC met with the president and handed him a list of sixty demands, including withdrawal from Vietnam by the end of the year.[15] One of its members, Congressman Ronald Dellums, even chaired unofficial hearings where he urged Congress to investigate allegations that American soldiers had committed atrocities in Vietnam.[16] The CBC's opposition did not faze Nixon, but it symbolized a new era in the civil rights movement and in African Americans' repudiation of hawkish military policies. Since the Vietnam War, African Americans have been vocal opponents of military ventures abroad. The dissonant, often personal debates over American foreign policy within the civil rights community were not replicated in the post-Vietnam era. In fact, African Americans closed ranks and remained unified in their opposition to the war in the final years of Nixon's presidency. In the ensuing decades, the African American political establishment has been opposed to U.S. military intervention in Central America and the Middle East.[17] For instance, on October 10, 2002, only four out of thirty-six members of the CBC voted for the joint resolution authorizing the Iraq War.[18]

The iconic images of panic-stricken Vietnamese trying to get seats on the last helicopters leaving the American embassy in Saigon encapsulated America's humiliation in Vietnam. In the immediate aftermath of the war, Americans yearned to forget its divisiveness, turmoil, and pain.[19] The term *Vietnam fatigue* entered the public lexicon, leading to collective amnesia about the suffering and pain of Vietnam veterans. Tens of thousands of African American veterans struggled to rebuild their lives. Forest Farley Jr., a former marine who worked at a Florida veterans' center, claimed that although "endemic disillusionment" affected both white and black veterans, it was substantially greater among African Americans. Farley noted that, for African American veterans, the racial problems of the 1960s "were still going on when they came back." Many of them felt they had two strikes against them—being black and being a Vietnam veteran.[20] In 1981, the House Committee on Veterans Affairs published a survey demonstrating that whereas 75 percent of white soldiers and marines claimed their combat experience had been positive, only 20 percent of African Americans shared this sentiment.[21]

The Vietnam Veterans Memorial in Washington, D.C., was completed in 1984, more than a decade after America's withdrawal from the war.[22] Since then, it has become one of the most visited sites in the nation's capital. The names of the dead are inscribed on the wall in chronological order. Grieving visitors leave notes and mementos, and a trip to the wall has been a cathartic experience for millions of Americans. For a brief moment after the wall's commemoration, the nation set aside its differences and united to honor the 58,000 men, including approximately 7,200 African Americans, who made the ultimate sacrifice. Not far from the wall stands Frederick Hart's bronze statue portraying three American servicemen dressed in Vietnam-era uniforms and identifiable as Caucasian, African American, and Hispanic. Since the war, the military has implemented a number of reforms that rectified much of the institutionalized racism in the armed forces.[23] The elevation of Vietnam veteran Colin Powell to chairman of the Joint Chiefs of Staff was a testament to African Americans' ability to flourish in the military after the Vietnam War. For thousands of African Americans who fought in Southeast Asia, however, that vindication was too little, too late.

This study has shown that one enduring legacy of the Vietnam War was that it led to the collapse of the Great Society and the postwar liberal consensus. For African Americans, the emotional debates over the war aggravated fissures within the civil rights movement along generational and ideological lines. Indeed, the Vietnam War punctured the hopes shared by African Americans and liberals in 1965, which were best expressed by President Johnson in his Howard University commencement address: "It is not enough to just open the gates of opportunity. All of our citizens must have the ability to walk through those gates."[24] By 1966, the war had siphoned the moral fervor from the civil rights struggle, exacerbated schisms within the civil rights coalition, and cost the lives of thousands of young African American men. By the beginning of 1968, the vaunted New Deal coalition lay in shambles. The Watergate scandal further delegitimized the federal government as a beneficent force in American life, dooming the Great Society and the vision of further rectifying the historical legacy of racial discrimination. This had tragic repercussions for African Americans. By the late 1970s, African Americans were disheartened by the unrealized expectations of the civil rights movement and pessimistic about the intentions of the majority of whites.[25] Other factors, such as crime and the economic impact of deindustrialization and stagflation, contributed to the dour mood of African Americans, but the Vietnam War changed the political climate, to the detriment of African American aspirations.

By the 1980s, Ronald Reagan and the conservatives rose to power, opposing further civil rights legislation and vowing to cut programs for the poor. Launching his fall campaign at the Neshoba County Fair near Philadelphia, Mississippi (only a few miles from where Schwerner, Chaney, and Goodman were murdered in 1964), Reagan touted "states' rights," decried "welfare queens," and invoked other racial code words.[26] Reagan's election marked a seismic change in American politics and signified the triumph of conservatism. While the hegemony of the Republican Party and conservatism in presidential politics was not directly caused by the Vietnam War, the fractious debates over the war weakened the civil rights movement and liberalism, thereby expediting the triumph of conservatism.

George Kennan, architect of the U.S. containment policy, bemoaned that the Vietnam War was "the most disastrous of all America's undertakings in the whole 200 years of its history."[27] It unleashed the greatest wave of protest since the Civil War, which swamped the civil rights movement. For African Americans, the war had a tragic subtext. It divided African Americans and the civil rights movement more than any other issue in the twentieth century. It left painful scars, which burned with a unique intensity. Decades later, many of these scars have not healed. With this study, the corrosive impact of the Vietnam War on the civil rights coalition has been exposed.

Acknowledgments

Historians research and write in relative isolation, but this book could not have been completed without the support and assistance of family, friends, librarians, institutions, and numerous historians who offered valuable advice and critical feedback. I am thrilled to acknowledge the numerous debts incurred during the eight years I worked on this project. It was indeed a collective effort. And for me, it was a labor of love.

The Department of History at the University of California at Berkeley, where this project originated as a doctoral dissertation, has been pivotal to my intellectual development since my undergraduate years back in the early 1980s. I remember being mesmerized by the brilliance, passion, and dynamism of my professors, who brought history to life. Sadly, many of these individuals are now deceased, but their legacy infused my spirit as I labored on this project. Although I took a detour and went to law school and worked as an attorney for years, my undergraduate professors remained role models. In particular, I would like to thank one of them, the late Kenneth M. Stampp, for encouraging me to go back to graduate school later in life.

Leon F. Litwack, my mentor and dissertation adviser, has been exceptionally supportive of this project since he first suggested I write a seminar paper on African Americans and the Vietnam War during my first year in graduate school. A Pulitzer Prize winner, a spellbinding lecturer, and an overall mensch, Leon has been an inspiration to generations of students and historians. This book could not have been written without his unflagging encouragement and support. He diligently read the chapters I gave him, provided critical feedback, and pointed me in new directions. And long after I completed the dissertation, he was always available when I sought his advice on academic or personal matters. He is a gentleman and a scholar, and working with him has been an honor. I cannot thank him enough.

A host of other faculty members at Berkeley also read complete drafts at various stages. I am grateful to Richard Candida-Smith, Charles Henry, and Waldo E. Martin Jr., who made excellent suggestions on how to revise my dissertation for publication. At Berkeley, I was privileged to be part of a community of historians and scholars who inspired me to pursue scholarly excellence. I thank Robin L. Einhorn, Paula Fass, Diane Clemens, Margaret L. Anderson, Kerwin Klein, Mark Billiant, and Anthony Adamwaithe for their encouragement and support. Sadly, James H. Kettner, Reginald Zelnik, Susanna Barrows, and Lawrence Levine all passed away during my tenure as a graduate student or prior to the publication of this book. They were instrumental to my development as a scholar, and I owe them a debt of gratitude. Along with way, I benefited from the friendship and advice of a number of fellow graduate students: Theodore Varno, Dylan Esson, Mary Murrell, Kevin Adams, and J. Branden Little. I am also grateful to the University of California's History Department for providing me with a Dean's Normative Fellowship during the 2005–2006 academic year and a Dissertation Writing Fellowship in 2007–2008.

Writing my dissertation and revising it for publication took me to archives and libraries throughout the country. At Berkeley, I would like to thank Phyllis Bischof for getting me started on my research. At the Lyndon B. Johnson Presidential Library in Austin, Texas, Sarah Haldeman and the archivists there were always helpful and courteous and made my stay in Texas a pleasure (despite the sweltering humidity). I would also like to thank the staffs at the Library of Congress in Washington, D.C.; the Martin Luther King Jr. Center in Atlanta, Georgia; the Schomburg Center for Research in Black Culture in New York City; the Rare Books and Manuscript Library at Columbia University; the Taminent Library and Robert F. Wagner Labor Archives at New York University; and the Swarthmore College Peace Collection.

Several other scholars read chapters or drafts of my entire manuscript at critical stages. I would like to thank Gerald Horne, Marilyn Young, Ellen Schrecker, Robert Cohen, Robbie Lieberman, Todd Gitlin, Staughton Lynd, Peter Levy, Steven Lawson, and the late Michael Nash for their time.

I was very fortunate to have a number of close friends and family who provided invaluable assistance and emotional support during the long process of writing this book. I would like to thank my cousins Gary Lucks, Lisa Gibson, and Dylan Lucks for their gracious hospitality whenever I traveled back to Berkeley. In the Bay Area, Taeko Jenkins, the late Mike Jenkins, James Taylor, Kirk Crist, Megan Nicely, and Phillip Neumark offered their warm friendship and support. Other lifelong friends such as Kaete Salomon, Linda Randall, Andy Alcock, Robert Craig, and Wilfred and Martha Herrera and their sons Richard, Charles, Willy, and Lewis merit mention for their enduring support.

In New York City, I was fortunate to make a number of good friends. Special thanks to Nancy Payne, who proofread the manuscript and pointed out how to make it more accessible to nonhistorians. I would also like to acknowledge Elizabeth Gaffney, Wendy Liles, Patty McGuigan, and my nephews Bryan, Joshua, and Zachary Meisel for making my years in New York City enjoyable and rewarding and for encouraging me to finish the book. The members and staff of the Paragraph Workspace for Writers provided a pleasant environment to put the finishing touches on the manuscript. I would also like to thank my students at Yeshiva University and the John Jay College of Criminal Justice.

John Goodwin took photographs of Martin Luther King Jr. during the last year of his life. I would like to thank him for sending me copies of King's Riverside address and for allowing me to use the photographs.

I could not have been luckier to meet Stephen Wrinn of the University Press of Kentucky at the OAH meeting in Milwaukee. Steve's enthusiasm for this project has continued unabated. Steve, Allison Webster, and the rest of the staff at the University Press of Kentucky displayed a unique commitment and dedication to excellence. A special thanks to Linda Lotz for a great copyediting job executed with patience and skill. They all made this manuscript better and saved me from a number of errors. Of course, any errors that remain are my responsibility.

My family has been my guiding star throughout my life. Though not officially a member of my family, Christopher Canzone has been a good friend since high school and provided me with a safe haven in Southern California. I consider him and his children my family. I would also like to thank Tracy Gage for her love and support. My cousins Laurence Lux, Sandra Glass, Gordon Lucks, and Lisa Mendel Lucks have always graced me with their humor and warmth. My aunt Mimi Habush and uncle Bob Habush of Milwaukee, Wisconsin, are role models of success mixed with kindness, compassion, and generosity. My sister-in-law Gail Kiefer Lucks and her three grown children have been a source of support and laughter for decades. Special thanks to my sister Deborah Meisel and her husband Lee for their love and generous support over the years. I could not have completed this endeavor without them.

My mother, Sheila Lucks, has always been my biggest supporter and inspiration. Her love and devotion have sustained our family throughout the years. Sadly, my father, Herbert Lucks, and my brother, David Lucks,

MD, are no longer alive. At an early age, my father instilled in me a love of history and ideas. He died in 2006, but his spirit continues to move me. During the final stages of production of this book, my brother David died suddenly, tragically, and much too soon. He was a pioneer in the medical profession, and his spirit, compassion, and humanity touched everybody he met. It is to my mother and the memory of my father and brother that I dedicate this book.

Notes

Abbreviations

CUOHC	Columbia University Oral History Collection
LBJL	Lyndon Baines Johnson Presidential Library, Austin, TX
LOC	Library of Congress
MLK	Martin Luther King Jr.
MLKC	Martin Luther King Jr. Center for Nonviolent Social Change, Atlanta, GA
WHCF	White House Central Files
WSHS	Wisconsin State Historical Society, Madison

Introduction

The epigraphs are from Langston Hughes, *The Backlash Blues* (Detroit: 1967), and Muhammad Ali, *The Greatest: My Own Story* (New York: 1975), 123.

1. George H. Gallup, *The Gallup Poll: Public Opinion 1935–1971*, vol. 3 (New York: 1972), 1934, 1973, 1974.

2. Simon Hall's monograph on the antiwar and civil rights movements' failure to forge a cohesive coalition is a welcome addition to the historiography and raises a host of interesting questions. My study complements Hall's and adds a Cold War context and a focus on the clashing egos and personalities among the civil rights leadership. I incorporated Hall's notion of a "moderate" wing of the civil rights movement in analyzing the NAACP's "hands-off" policy with respect to the Vietnam War. See Simon Hall, *Peace and Freedom: The Civil Rights and Antiwar Movements in the 1960s* (Philadelphia: 2005). See also Simon Hall, "The Response of the Moderate Wing of the Civil Rights Movement to the Vietnam War," *Historical Journal* 46, no. 3 (September 2003): 669–701; Manfred Berg, "Guns, Butter, and Civil Rights: The National Association for the Advancement of Colored People and the Vietnam War, 1964–1968," in *Aspects of War in American History*, ed. David K. Adams and Cornelis A. Van Minnen (Keele, UK: 1997), 213–38; Lawrence Allen Eldridge, *Chronicles of a Two-Front War: Civil Rights and Vietnam in the African American Press* (Columbia, MO: 2009); Rhodri Jeffreys-Jones, *Peace Now! American Society and the Ending of the Vietnam War* (New Haven, CT: 1999); Steven F. Lawson, "Mixing Moderation with Militancy," in *Civil Rights Crossroads: Nation, Community, and the Black Freedom*

Struggle (Lexington, KY: 2003), 75–91; Benjamin T. Harrison, "Impact of the Vietnam War on the Civil Rights Movement in the Midsixties," *Studies in Conflict and Terrorism* 19, no. 3 (1996): 261–78; Peter Levy, "Blacks and the Vietnam War," in *The Legacy: Vietnam War in the Historical Imagination*, ed. D. Michael Shafer (Boston: 1990), 209–32.

3. On African Americans in Vietnam, see Clyde Taylor, ed., *Vietnam and Black America: An Anthology of Protest and Resistance* (Garden City, NY: 1973); Wallace Terry, *Bloods: An Oral History of the Vietnam War by Black Veterans* (New York: 1984); Richard R. Moser, *The New Winter Soldiers: GI and Veteran Dissent during the Vietnam Era* (New Brunswick, NJ: 1996), esp. chap. 3; James Westheider, *Fighting on Two Fronts: African Americans and the Vietnam War* (New York: 1997); Herman Graham III, *The Brothers' Vietnam War: Black Power, Manhood, and the Military Experience* (Gainesville, FL: 2003); Yvonne Latty and Ron Tarver, *We Were There: Voices of African American Veterans from World War II to the War in Iraq* (New York: 2004); John Darrel Sherwood, *Black Sailor, White Navy: Racial Unrest in the Fleet during the Vietnam Era* (New York: 2007); Natalie Kimbrough, *Equality of Discrimination? African Americans in the U.S. Military during the Vietnam War* (New York: 2006); James E. Westheider, *The African American Experience in Vietnam: Brothers in Arms* (New York: 2008); Kimberley Phillips, *War! What Is It Good For?* (Chapel Hill, NC: 2012).

4. For interesting articles on King and Vietnam, see Herbert Shapiro, "The Vietnam War and the American Civil Rights Movement," *Journal of Ethnic Studies* 16 (Winter 1989): 117–41; Adam Fairclough, "Martin Luther King and the War in Vietnam," *Phylon* 45, no. 1 (March 1984): 19–39; Henry Darby and Margaret N. Rowley, "King on Vietnam and Beyond," *Phylon* 47, no. 1 (March 1986): 43–50. See also Clayborne Carson, "King Scholarship and Iconoclastic Myths," *Reviews in American History* 16, no. 1 (March 1988): 130–36; Thomas J. Noer, "Martin Luther King, Jr., and the Cold War," *Peace and Change* 22, no. 2 (April 1997): 111–31.

5. Van Gosse and other historians have noted that SNCC and CORE were part of the New Left. See Van Gosse, "A Movement of Movements: The Definition of Periodization of the New Left," in *A Companion for Post-1945 America*, ed. Jean Christophe Agnew and Roy Rosenzweig (Malden, MA: 2002), 294.

6. Clayborne Carson, *In Struggle: SNCC and the Black Awakening of the 1960s* (Cambridge, MA: 1981), 188; SNCC news release, January 6, 1966, SNCC Papers, box 52, folder 6, MLKC.

7. "Move to Draft Rights Leader," *Baltimore Afro-American*, January 22, 1966, 13.

8. "SNCC Leader's Statement Is Deplorable, Misleading," *Atlanta Daily World*, January 7, 1966.

9. Jeff Woods, *Black Struggle, Red Scare: Segregation and Anti-Communism in the South, 1948–1968* (Baton Rouge, LA: 2004).

10. See Kenneth O'Reilly, *Racial Matters: The FBI's Secret File on Black America* (New York: 1989); David Garrow, *The FBI and Martin Luther King, Jr.* (New York: 1981).

11. There has been a spate of scholarship emphasizing the relationship between civil rights and American foreign policy during the Cold War. See Mary L. Dudziak, *Cold War Civil Rights: Race and the Image of American Democracy* (Princeton, NJ: 2000); Thomas Borstelmann, *The Cold War and the Color Line: American Race Relations in a Global Arena* (Cambridge, MA: 2001); Jonathan Skrentny, *The Minority Rights Revolution* (Cambridge, MA: 2002); Jonathan Rosenberg, *How Far the Promised Land? World Affairs and the American Civil Rights Movement from the First World War to Vietnam* (Princeton, NJ: 2006). The past few decades have also witnessed a number of pioneering works on the intersection of race, anticolonialism, and American foreign policy during the early years of the Cold War. See Penny Von Eschen, *Race against Empire: Black Americans and Anti-Colonialism* (Ithaca, NY: 1997); Brenda Gayle Plummer, *Rising Wind: Black Americans and U.S. Foreign Affairs* (Chapel Hill, NC: 1996); Carol Anderson, *Eyes off the Prize: African Americans, the United Nations, and the Struggle for Civil Rights, 1944–1955* (Cambridge: 2003); Timothy B. Tyson, *Radio Free Dixie: Robert F. Williams and the Roots of Black Power* (Chapel Hill, NC: 1999); James H. Meriwether, *Proudly We Can Be Africans: Black Americans and Africa, 1935–1961* (Chapel Hill, NC: 2002); Glenda Gilmore, *Defying Dixie: The Radical Roots of Civil Rights, 1919–1950* (New York: 2008); Robbie Lieberman and Clarence Lang, eds., *Anti-Communism and the African American Freedom Movement: "Another Side of the Story"* (New York: 2009).

12. Among the chief historical works relating to Lyndon B. Johnson and the civil rights movements are Taylor Branch, *At the Edge of Canaan: America in the King Years 1965–1968* (New York: 2006); Nick Kotz, *Judgment Days: Lyndon Baines Johnson, Martin Luther King, Jr., and the Laws that Changed America* (New York: 2005); Lawson, "Mixing Moderation with Militancy," 71–94; Robert Dallek, *Flawed Giant: Lyndon Johnson and His Times 1961–1973* (New York: 1998).

13. Roy Wilkins Oral History, April 1, 1969, LBJL.

14. Clarence Mitchell Oral History, April 30, 1969, LBJL.

15. Whitney Young Jr. quoted in James Forman, *The Making of Black Revolutionaries* (New York: 1972), 339–40.

16. Bernard C. Nalty, *Strength for the Fight: A History of Black Americans in the Military* (New York: 1986).

17. Hattie Dodson quoted in "The War in Vietnam: Where Do You Stand?" *New York Amsterdam News*, January 15, 1966, 40.

18. Christian G. Appy, *Working Class War: American Combat Soldiers and Vietnam* (Chapel Hill, NC: 1993).

19. Martin Luther King Jr., "A Time to Break Silence," *Freedomways* 7, no. 2 (Spring 1967): 103.

20. Ali quoted in Phillips, *War!* 209.

21. See Mike Marqusee, *Redemption Song: Muhammad Ali and the Spirit of the Sixties* (New York: 1999).

22. "Clay Remains Classified 1-A: Board Rejects Exemption Plea," *New York Times*, January 13, 1967, 50.

23. Robert Lipsyte, "Clay Refused Oath, Stripped of Boxing Crown," *New York Times*, April 29, 1967, 1.

24. Martin Waldron, "Clay Guilty in Draft Case; Gets Five Years in Prison," *New York Times*, June 21, 1967, 1.

25. See M. J. Heale, "The Sixties as History: A Review of the Political Historiography," *Reviews in American History* 33 (March 2005): 133–52. For other notable examples of the declension narrative, see Allen Matusow, *The Unraveling of America: A History of Liberalism in the 1960s* (New York: 1984); Todd Gitlin, *The Sixties: Years of Hope, Days of Rage* (New York: 1987); David Burner, *Making Peace with the 60s* (Princeton, NJ: 1996); Maurice Isserman and Michael Kazin, *America Divided: The Civil War of the 1960s* (New York: 2000); Winifred Breines, "Whose New Left?" *Journal of American History* 75, no. 2 (September 1988): 528–45.

26. For an alternative view that focuses on the connections between the different movements over time, see Van Gosse, *Rethinking the New Left: An Interpretive History* (New York: 2005).

1. The Cold War and the Long Civil Rights Movement

The epigraph is from Martin Duberman, *Paul Robeson* (New York: 1989), 344.

1. Ellen Schrecker, *Many Are the Crimes: McCarthyism in America* (Boston: 1998).

2. See Nikhil Pal Singh, *Black Is a Country: Race and the Unfinished Struggle for Democracy* (Cambridge, MA: 2004). For an analysis of the suppression of African American activists, artists, and intellectuals who spoke out against the Cold War in the late 1940s and early 1950s, see Robbie Lieberman, "'Another Side of the Story': African American Intellectuals Speak out for Peace and Freedom during the Early Cold War Years," in Lieberman and Lang, *Anti-Communism and the African American Freedom Movement*, 17–49.

3. Paul Robeson, "Ho Chi Minh Is the Toussaint L'Ouverture of Indo-China," *Freedom*, March 1954, reprinted in Esther Cooper Jackson, ed., *Freedomways Reader: Prophets in Their Own Country* (Boulder, CO: 2000), 147–49.

4. Robbie Lieberman, *The Strangest Dream: Communism, Anti-Communism, and the U.S. Peace Movement* (Syracuse, NY: 2000).

5. Michael S. Sherry, *In the Shadow of War: The United States since the 1930s* (New Haven, CT: 1995).

6. Dudziak, *Cold War Civil Rights*, 12. See also Mary L. Dudziak, "Desegregation as a Cold War Imperative," *Stanford Law Review* 41 (November 1988):

61–120. For other views on the relationship between the Cold War and the civil rights movement, see Charles W. Cheng, "The Cold War: Its Impact on the Black Liberation Struggle within the United States," *Freedomways* 13, no. 3 (1973): 281–93; Plummer, *Rising Wind*; Von Eschen, *Race against Empire*; Michael Krenn, ed., *The African American Voice in U.S. Foreign Policy* (New York: 1999); Robin D. G. Kelly, *Freedom Dreams: The Black Radical Imagination* (Boston: 2002); Anderson, *Eyes off the Prize*; Rosenberg, *How Far the Promised Land?* Brenda Gayle Plummer, ed., *Window on Freedom: Race, Civil Rights and Foreign Affairs, 1945–1988* (Chapel Hill, NC: 2003); Kevin Gaines, *African Americans in Ghana: Black Expatriates and the Civil Rights Era* (Chapel Hill, NC: 2006); Brenda Gayle Plummer, *In Search of Power: African Americans in the Era of Decolonization, 1956–1974* (Cambridge: 2013).

7. This issue has been addressed by Lieberman, Von Eschen, Plummer, and Singh. See also Gerald Horne, *Communist Front: The Civil Rights Congress, 1946–1956* (Rutherford, NJ: 1988).

8. See Robbie Lieberman, "Peace and Civil Rights Don't Mix, They Say: Anticommunism and the Dividing of U.S. Social Movements, 1947–1967," in *Peace Movements in Western Europe, Japan and the USA during the Cold War*, ed. Benjamin Ziemann (Essen, Germany: 2007), 91–107.

9. For early protests against the propensity to deify King, see "A Roundtable: Martin Luther King, Jr.," *Journal of American History* 74 (September 1987): 436–81. See also Singh, *Black Is a Country*, 1–8.

10. For accounts of the standard narrative of a short civil rights movement, see Carl M. Brauer, *John F. Kennedy and the Second Reconstruction* (New York: 1977); Carson, *In Struggle*; Matusow, *Unraveling of America*; Aldon Morris, *Origins of the Civil Rights Movement: Black Communities Organizing for Change* (New York: 1986).

11. In her valedictory address before the Organization of American Historians in March 2004, Hall provided a trenchant view on this subject. See Jacqueline Dowd Hall, "The Long Civil Rights Movement and the Political Uses of the Past," *Journal of American History* 91 (2005): 1233–336. See also Charles W. Eagles, "Toward New Histories of the Civil Rights Era," *Journal of Southern History* 66, no. 4 (November 2000): 815–48; Adam Fairclough, "Historians and the Civil Rights Movement," *Journal of American Studies* 24 (1990): 387–98; Steven F. Lawson, "Freedom Then, Freedom Now: The Historiography of the Civil Rights Movement," *American Historical Review* 96, no. 2 (1991): 456–71. For recent views criticizing aspects of the long civil rights movement, see Steven F. Lawson, "Long Origins of the Short Civil Rights Movement," in *Freedom Rights: New Perspectives on the Civil Rights Movement*, ed. Danielle McGuire and John Dittmer (Lexington, KY: 2011); Sundiata Keita Cha-Jua and Clarence Lang, "The 'Long Civil Rights Movement' as Vampire: Temporal and Spatial Fallacies on Recent Black Freedom Studies," *Journal of African American History*

92 (2007): 265–88; Eric Arnesen, "Reconsidering the Long Movement," *Historically Speaking* 10, no. 2 (April 2009): 31–34. For an early analysis of the need to situate the civil rights struggle in a longer historical narrative that began in the more radical milieu of the 1930s, see Robert Korstad and Nelson Lichtenstein, "Opportunities Found and Lost: Labor, Radicals, and the Early Civil Rights Movement," *Journal of American History* 75, no. 3 (1988): 786–811. For additional studies of the long civil rights movement, see Timothy Tyson, "Robert F. Williams, Black Power and the Roots of the Black Freedom Struggle," *Journal of American History* 85, no. 2 (September 1998): 540–70; Tyson, *Radio Free Dixie*; Kevin Gaines, "The Historiography of the Struggle for Black Equality since 1945," in *A Companion for Post-1945 America*, ed. Jean Christophe Agnew and Roy Rosenzweig (Malden, MA: 2002), 211–34; Jeanne Theoharis, "Black Freedom Studies: Re-Imagining and Redefining the Fundamentals," *History Compass* 4, no. 2 (March 2006): 348–67; Robert Korstad, *Civil Rights Unionism: Tobacco Workers and the Struggle for Democracy in the Mid-20th Century South* (Chapel Hill, NC: 2003); Robert O. Self, *American Babylon: Race and the Struggle for Postwar Oakland* (Princeton, NJ: 2003); Martha Biondi, *To Stand and Fight: The Struggle for Civil Rights in Postwar New York City* (Cambridge, MA: 2003); Singh, *Black Is a Country*; Gilmore, *Defying Dixie*; Thomas J. Sugrue, *Sweet Land of Liberty: The Forgotten Struggle for Civil Rights in the North* (New York: 2008); Phillips, *War!*

12. Quoted in Jeff Woods, "The Cold War and the Struggle for Civil Rights," *OAH Magazine of History* 24 (October 2010): 13.

13. Von Eschen, *Race against Empire*; Plummer, *Rising Wind*; Anderson, *Eyes off the Prize*; Gilmore, *Defying Dixie*; Lieberman and Lang, *Anti-Communism and the African American Freedom Movement*.

14. Woods, *Black Struggle, Red Scare*.

15. Dudziak, *Cold War Civil Rights*; Borstelmann, *Cold War and the Color Line*; Rosenberg, *How Far the Promised Land?*

16. Manfred Berg, *The Ticket to Freedom: The NACCP and the Struggle for Black Political Integration* (Tallahassee, FL: 2005); Manfred Berg, "Black Civil Rights and Liberal Anticommunism: The NAACP in the Early Cold War," *Journal of American History* 94 (June 2007): 75–96.

17. Adam Fairclough, *Race and Democracy: The Civil Rights Struggle in Louisiana, 1915–1972* (Athens, GA: 1995), 146.

18. Walter White, *A Rising Wind* (New York: 1945), 155.

19. Phillips, *War!* 158–61.

20. For an illuminating discussion of White's reversal, see Kenneth R. Janken, *White: The Autobiography of Mr. White, Mr. NAACP* (New York: 2003), esp. 297–323.

21. See Von Eschen, *Race against Empire*.

22. Singh, *Black Is a Country*, 48. On African Americans and World War I, see

Andriane Lentz-Smith, *Freedom Struggles: African Americans and World War I* (Cambridge, MA: 2009).

23. For an interesting examination of the impact of Gandhi's nonviolence on the African American community from the 1920s to 1947, see Sudarshan Kapur, *Raising up a Prophet: The African-American Encounter with Gandhi* (Boston: 1992).

24. "Will a Gandhi Arise?" *Chicago Defender*, November 5, 1932.

25. Robin D. G. Kelly, *Race Rebels: Culture, Politics, and the Black Working Class* (New York: 1994), 128–33.

26. Gilmore, *Defying Dixie*, 183.

27. Judith Stein, *The World of Marcus Garvey: Race and Class in Modern Society* (Baton Rouge, LA: 1986).

28. Roi Ottley, *A New World a-Coming: Inside Black America* (New York: 1968), 109–12.

29. John Hope Franklin and Alfred A. Moss Jr., *From Slavery to Freedom: A History of Negro Americans*, 7th ed. (New York: 1994), 456.

30. W. E. B. Du Bois, "Inter-racial Implications of the Ethiopian Crisis: A Negro View," *Foreign Affairs*, October 1935, 82–92. On the pivotal importance of Ethiopia, see William R. Scott, *Sons of Sheba: African Americans and the Italo-Ethiopia War 1935–1941* (Bloomington, IN: 1993); James H. Meriwether, *Proudly We Can Be Africans: Black Americans and Africa, 1935–1961* (Chapel Hill, NC: 2002); Joseph Harris, *African-American Reactions to War in Ethiopia, 1936–1941* (Baton Rouge, LA: 1994); Andrew Bunie, *Robert L. Vann of the* Pittsburgh Courier: *Politics and Black Journalism* (Pittsburgh, PA: 1974); J. A. Rogers, *The Real Facts about Ethiopia* (Baltimore, MD: 1982).

31. William R. Scott, "Black Nationalism and the Italo-Ethiopian Conflict, 1934–1936," *Journal of Negro History* 63, no. 2 (April 1978): 118–36.

32. Singh, *Black Is a Country*, 69. On the impact of the black press, see Bill V. Mullen, *Popular Fronts: Chicago and African-American Cultural Politics* (Urbana, IL: 1999), 44–75; Von Eschen, *Race against Empire*, 8.

33. On the number of African American papers, see Sugrue, *Sweet Land of Liberty*, 47.

34. Robin D. G. Kelly, "'This Ain't Ethiopia, But It'll Do': African Americans and the Spanish Civil War," in *Race Rebels*, 123–24.

35. Paul Robeson, *Here I Stand* (Boston: 1988), 53.

36. For an analysis of this anticolonial consciousness, see Von Eschen, *Race against Empire*, 7–21. For the Council on African Affairs, see Hollis R. Lynch, *Black American Radicals and the Liberation of Africa: The Council on African Affairs* (Ithaca, NY: 1977).

37. On Ella Baker, see Barbara Ransby, *Ella Baker and the Black Freedom Movement: A Radical Democratic Vision* (Chapel Hill, NC: 2003), 100.

38. Daniel W. Aldridge III, "A War for the Colored Races: Anti-intervention-

ism and the African American Intelligentsia," *Diplomatic History* 28, no. 3 (June 2004): 321–53.

39. "National Defense and Negroes," *Crisis*, February 1939, 49.

40. George Padmore, "A Negro Looks at British Imperialism," *Crisis*, December 1938, 396–97.

41. On the NAACP resolution, see Rosenberg, *How Far the Promised Land?* 141.

42. For a recent discussion of the tensions within the African American community over the Double V campaign and the segregated military, see Phillips, *War!* 20–63.

43. Manning Marable, *Malcolm X: A Life of Reinvention* (New York: 2011), 59–60.

44. Carey M. McWilliams, *Brothers Under the Skin* (Boston: 1942), 26, 28, 42.

45. See, for example, L. D. Reddick, "Africa: Test of the Atlantic Charter," *Crisis*, July 1943, 202–3; "Race Equality at the Peace," *Crisis*, October 1944, 312; Ernest E. Johnson, "A Voice at the Peace Table," *Crisis*, November 1944, 345–46.

46. George Schuyler, "The Caucasian Problem," in *What the Negro Wants*, ed. Rayford W. Logan (Chapel Hill, NC: 1944), 282.

47. For the *Negro Digest* polls, see Plummer, *Rising Wind*, 87.

48. See Richard Dalfiume, "The Forgotten Years of the Negro Revolution," *Journal of American History* 55, no. 1 (June 1968): 90–106.

49. White, *Rising Wind*, 154.

50. Ho quoted in Stanley Karnow, *Vietnam: A History* (New York: 1983), 147.

51. Ottley, *New World a-Coming*, 344.

52. Roosevelt quoted in Fredrik Logevall, *Embers of War: The Fall of an Empire and the Making of America's War in Vietnam* (New York: 2012), 46.

53. Ibid., 11.

54. William J. Duiker, *Ho Chi Minh: A Life* (New York: 2000), 50–51.

55. FDR quoted in Frank Costigliola, *Roosevelt's Lost Alliances: How Personal Politics Helped Start the Cold War* (Princeton, NJ: 2011), 200.

56. Dixee Bartholomew-Feis, *The OSS and Ho Chi Minh: Unexpected Allies in the War against Japan* (Lawrence, KS: 2006), 3.

57. William Roger Louis, *Imperialism at Bay: The United States and the Decolonization of the British Empire 1941–1945* (New York: 1978).

58. On Roosevelt's opposition to French colonialism in Indochina, see Gary Hess, "Franklin Roosevelt and Indochina," *Journal of American History* 59, no. 2 (September 1972): 353–68; Walter LaFeber, "Roosevelt, Churchill, and Indochina, 1942–1945," *American Historical Review* 80, no. 5 (December 1975): 1277–95.

59. For estimates of the NAACP membership see, Patricia Sullivan, *Lift Every Voice: The NAACP and the Making of the Civil Rights Movement* (New York: 2009), 288; Berg, "Black Civil Rights and Liberal Anticommunism," 75.

60. James L. Roark, "American Black Leaders: The Response of Colonialism and the Cold War," *African Historical Studies* 4, no. 2 (1971): 253–70.

61. W. E. B. Du Bois, *Color and Democracy: Colonies and Peace* (New York: 1945).

62. Robert L. Harris Jr., "Racial Equality and the United Nations Charter," in *New Directions in Civil Rights Studies*, ed. Armstead L. Robinson and Patricia Sullivan (Charlottesville, VA: 1991), 133.

63. "NAACP Sets Equality as Parley Goal," *Pittsburgh Courier*, April 28, 1945, 1; "Smaller Nations Demand Race Equality at Conference," *Pittsburgh Courier*, May 5, 1945, 1.

64. "Storm Signals at the Golden Gate," *Chicago Defender*, May 10, 1945, 10.

65. "Smaller Nations Demand Race Equality at Conference," 1.

66. Anderson, *Eyes off the Prize.*

67. Eden quoted in Costigliola, *Roosevelt's Lost Alliances*, 2.

68. Roosevelt's commitment to decolonization should not be underestimated. See Robert Dallek, *Franklin D. Roosevelt and American Foreign Policy, 1932–1945* (New York: 1979); Townsend Hoopes and Douglass Brinkley, *FDR and the Creation of the UN* (New Haven, CT: 1997).

69. Walter White, *A Man Called White: The Autobiography of Walter White* (New York: 1948), 295. On the attempts of Du Bois and White to influence U.S. policy at the San Francisco conference, see Plummer, *Rising Wind*, 131–48; Anderson, *Eyes off the Prize*, 40–45.

70. Robert L. Beisner, *Dean Acheson: A Life in the Cold War* (New York: 2006), 51–52; James Chace, *Acheson: The Secretary of State Who Created the American World* (New York: 1998), 106–8; Michael Krenn, *Black Diplomacy: African Americans and the State Department, 1945–1969* (New York: 1999), 12.

71. Plummer, *Rising Wind*, 131, 176.

72. Anderson, *Eyes off the Prize*, 48.

73. Dean Acheson, *Present at the Creation: My Years in the State Department* (New York: 1969), 7, 111.

74. Dr. Rayford Logan, "The 'Little Man' Just Isn't Here," *Pittsburgh Courier*, May 5, 1945, 1; "Farewell to Frisco," *Pittsburgh Courier*, June 9, 1945, 1; "U.S. Knifes Colonial Freedom," *Chicago Defender*, May 26, 1945, 1.

75. "International Scene Is Analyzed by Editor Lochard," *Chicago Defender*, May 19, 1945, 1, 2.

76. "Dr. Logan Calls New Charter 'Tragic Joke,'" *Pittsburgh Courier*, June 16, 1945, 1.

77. "San Francisco," *Crisis*, June 1945, 161.

78. Quoted in Marilyn Young, *The Vietnam Wars* (New York: 1992), 2; Singh, *Black Is a Country*, 158.

79. Quoted in Kenneth R. Janken, "From Colonial Liberation to Cold War Liberalism: Walter White, the NAACP, and Foreign Affairs, 1941–1955," *Journal of Ethnic and Racial Studies* 21, no. 6 (November 1998): 1079.

80. Biondi, *To Stand and Fight*, 138.

81. Mark Solomon, "Black Critics of Colonialism and the Cold War," in *Cold War Critics: Alternatives to American Foreign Policy in the Truman Years*, ed. Thomas G. Paterson (Chicago: 1971), 205–21.

82. See Joy Gleason Carew, *Blacks, Reds, and Russians: Sojourners in Search of the Soviet Promise* (Princeton, NJ: 2010).

83. Rayford Logan, *The Negro and the Post-War World: A Primer* (Washington, DC: 1945), 77.

84. Du Bois quoted in David Levering Lewis, *W. E. B. Du Bois and the Fight for Equality and the American Century: 1919–1963* (New York: 2000), 517.

85. "What Churchill Wants," *Chicago Defender*, March 16, 1946, 15.

86. "Invitation to Imperialism," *Pittsburgh Courier*, March 16, 1946, 5.

87. S. Chandrasekhar, "Imperialism Returns to Asia," *Crisis*, March 1946, 79–80, 91–92; "Democracy Defined at Moscow," *Crisis*, April 1947, 4.

88. See Melvyn Leffler, *A Preponderance of Power: National Security, the Truman Administration and the Cold War* (Palo Alto, CA: 1992).

89. Richard M. Fried, *Nightmare in Red: The McCarthy Era in Perspective* (New York: 1990), 67–96.

90. Woods, *Black Struggle, Red Scare*, 27–29.

91. Arthur Schlesinger Jr., "The U.S. Communist Party," *Life*, July 29, 1946, 84–96.

92. "Defender Publisher Aids in Forming Liberal Group," *Chicago Defender*, April 5, 1947, 1.

93. Von Eschen, *Race against Empire*, 118.

94. George Streator, "U.N. Gets Charges of Wide Bias in the U.S.," *New York Times*, October 23, 1947, 9.

95. On White's transformation, see Janken, "From Colonial Liberation to Cold War Liberalism," 1074–91.

96. David Henry Anthony III, *Max Yergan: Race Man, Internationalist, Cold Warrior* (New York: 2006).

97. Rayford Logan, *The African Mandates in World Politics* (Washington, DC: 1948), v–viii.

98. Von Eschen, *Race against Empire*, 107.

99. Alonzo L. Hamby, *Man of the People: A Life of Harry S. Truman* (New York: 1995), 640–41.

100. See Clarence Lang, "Freedom Train Derailed," in Lieberman and Lang, *Anti-Communism and the African American Freedom Movement*, 163.

101. For a positive view of Truman's civil rights agenda, see Michael R. Gardner, *Harry Truman and Civil Rights* (Carbondale, IL: 2002). For an array of views on the legacy of Truman's foreign policy, see Raymond H. Geselbracht, ed., *The Civil Rights Legacy of Harry Truman* (Kirksville, MO: 2007).

102. Quoted in Sullivan, *Lift Every Voice*, 330.

103. "Mr. Roosevelt and Mr. Truman," *Pittsburgh Courier*, July 12, 1947, 6.

104. On the NAACP and the Truman administration, see Berg, *Ticket to Freedom*, 123–40; Sullivan, *Lift Every Voice*, 342–66.

105. Quoted in Phillips, *War!* 111.

106. William Berman's analysis compliments Truman for publicly embracing the cause of civil rights but also notes his caution, the complexity of his views, and the political considerations underlying his rhetoric. See William C. Berman, *The Politics of Civil Rights in the Truman Administration* (Columbus, OH: 1971), 238–40.

107. Thomas Borstelmann, "Jim Crow's Coming Out: Race Relations and American Foreign Policy during the Truman Years," *Presidential Studies Quarterly* 29, no. 3 (September 1999): 549–69.

108. Barton J. Bernstein, "The Ambiguous Legacy: Civil Rights," in *Politics and Policies of the Truman Administration*, ed. Barton J. Bernstein (Chicago: 1970), 269–314.

109. "Candidate Wallace," *Crisis*, February 1948, 41.

110. W. E. B. Du Bois, "The Winds of Time, Candidates," *Chicago Defender*, January 3, 1948.

111. Richard J. Walton, *Henry Wallace, Harry Truman and the Cold War* (New York: 1976); Curtis D. MacDougall, *Gideon's Army* (New York: 1965). On the Wallace campaign, see Thomas W. Devine, *Henry Wallace's 1948 Presidential Campaign and the Future of Postwar Liberalism* (Chapel Hill, NC: 2013).

112. For an account of the violence surrounding Wallace's campaign in the South, see Patricia Sullivan, *Days of Hope: Race and Democracy in the New Deal Era* (Chapel Hill, NC: 1996), 260–73.

113. Lieberman, *Strangest Dream*, 32–56.

114. Paula F. Pfeffer, *A. Philip Randolph, Pioneer of the Civil Rights Movement* (Baton Rouge, LA: 1990), 128.

115. See Janken, *White*, 315–17; Berg, *Ticket to Freedom*, 129–37; Sullivan, *Lift Every Voice*, 369–76.

116. For election results, see John C. Culver and John Hyde, *American Dreamer: The Life and Times of Henry A. Wallace* (New York: 2000), 511; Plummer, *Rising Wind*, 189.

117. Reminiscences of Roy Wilkins, 1960, 93, CUOHC. On Wilkins's antipathy to communists, see Roy Wilkins with Tom Matthews, *Standing Fast: The Autobiography of Roy Wilkins* (New York: 1982), 209–11.

118. Steven M. Gillon, *Politics and Vision: The ADA and American Liberalism, 1947–1985* (New York: 1987), 47–50.

119. Fried, *Nightmare in Red*, 120–43.

120. See Lieberman and Lang, *Anti-Communism and the African American Freedom Movement*.

121. Anderson, *Eyes off the Prize*, 196.

122. Berg, "Black Civil Rights and Liberal Anticommunism," 88; "White Pays Tribute to Harry Moore," *New York Times*, December 30, 1951.

123. Berg, "Black Civil Rights and Liberal Anticommunism," 95; Berg, *Ticket to Freedom*, 138.

124. Horne, *Communist Front*, 29; Sullivan, *Lift Every Voice*, 374.

125. On the NAACP resolution, see Berg, *Ticket to Freedom*, 132.

126. Wilkins quoted in Biondi, *To Stand and Fight*, 167. See also "NAACP Delegates Battle to Clean out 'Reds' from Ranks: Clean House Big Order at Convention," *Pittsburgh Courier*, June 24, 1950, 1; James Q. Emory, "NAACP Adopts Strong Anti-Red Resolution," *Atlanta Daily World*, June 24, 1950, 1.

127. Wilkins with Mathews, *Standing Fast*, 209, 211.

128. Marjorie McKenzie, "Pursuit of Democracy," *Pittsburgh Courier*, January 28, 1950; Sullivan, *Lift Every Voice*, 375.

129. Woods, *Black Struggle, Red Scare*. On McCarthyism's impact on CORE, see August Meier and Elliott Rudwick, *CORE: A Study in the Civil Rights Movement, 1942–1968* (New York: 1973), 61–69.

130. Dudziak, *Cold War Civil Rights*, 13.

131. Gerald Horne, *Black & Red: W. E. B. Du Bois and the Afro-American Response to the Cold War 1944–1963* (Albany, NY: 1986).

132. *Chicago Defender* quoted in Manning Marable, *W. E. B. Du Bois: Black Radical Democrat* (New York: 1986), 184.

133. W. E. B. Du Bois, *The Autobiography of W. E. B. Du Bois: A Soliloquy of Viewing My Life from the Last Decade of Its First Century*, ed. Henry Louis Gates (Oxford: 2007), 294–95.

134. Duberman, *Robeson*, 388; "Truman Assailed on Move in Korea," *New York Times*, June 29, 1950.

135. On the timidity of the African American press with respect to the Robeson passport issue, see Barbara J. Beeching, "Paul Robeson and the Black Press: The 1950 Passport Controversy," *Journal of African American History* 87 (Summer 2002): 339–54.

136. Walter White, "The Strange Case of Paul Robeson," *Ebony*, February 1951, 78–84. Later that same year, *Crisis* published a similarly critical article on Robeson; see Robert Alan, "Paul Robeson—The Lost Shepherd," *Crisis*, November 1951, 569–73.

137. Duberman, *Robeson*, 534.

138. "NAACP's Challenge to Robeson's Statement," April 29, 1949, NAACP Papers, group II, box A511, LOC; Robeson, *Here I Stand*, 41; Duberman, *Robeson*, 342–44.

139. Duberman, *Robeson*, 540.

140. For an extensive discussion of other African American victims of McCarthyism, see Horne, *Communist Front*.

141. On Charlotta Bass, see Rodger Streitmatter, *Raising Her Voice: African American Journalists Who Changed History* (Lexington, KY: 1994), 95–106.

142. "U.S. Accused in UN of Negro Genocide," *New York Times*, December 18, 1951; "US Seizes Passport of W. L. Patterson, *New York Times*, January 24, 1952, 8; Horne, *Communist Front*, 155–81; Dudziak, *Cold War Civil Rights*, 63–66; Anderson, *Eyes off the Prize*, 180–209.

143. Erik McDuffie, "The Long March of Young Southern Black Women," in Lieberman and Lang, *Anti-Communism and the African American Freedom Movement*, 89.

144. Biondi, *To Stand and Fight*, 176–77; C. P. Trussell, "Dashiell Hammett Silent at Inquiry," *New York Times*, March 27, 1953.

145. Dorothy Hunton, *Alphaeus Hunton: The Unsung Valiant* (New York: 1986); Von Eschen, *Race against Empire*, 137; Russell Porter, "Dashiell Hammett and Hunton Jailed in Red Bail Inquiry; On Way to Prison," *New York Times*, July 10, 1951, 1.

146. Phillips, *War!* 119.

147. On African American soldiers in Korea, see Nalty, *Strength for Fight*; Phillips, *War!* 116–65.

148. Phillips, *War!* 131–36.

149. Juan Williams, *Thurgood Marshall: American Revolutionary* (New York: 1998), 168–71.

150. Thurgood Marshall, "Summary Justice—The Negro GI in Korea," *Crisis*, May 1951, 297–304, 350–55; Plummer, *Rising Wind*, 205.

151. Quoted in Phillips, *War!* 152.

152. Von Eschen, *Race against Empire*, 146.

153. A. Philip Randolph, "Attack on Korea Discussed," *New York Times*, July 1, 1950.

154. For an analysis of Randolph and the Communist Party, see Eric Arnesen, "'No Graver Danger': Black Anti-Communism, the Communist Party, and the Race Issue," *Labor: Studies in Working Class History of the Americas* 3, no. 4 (Winter 2006): 13–52.

155. Williams quoted in Plummer, *Rising Wind*, 206.

156. On Lawson's influence over SNCC leaders in the early 1960s, see David Halberstam, *The Children* (New York: 1998), 11.

157. Carson, *In Struggle*, 46.

158. Kelly, *Freedom Dreams*, 63.

159. Lieberman, *Strangest Dream*, 114–34.

160. Sullivan, *Lift Every Voice*, 384–428.

161. Dudziak, *Cold War Civil Rights*, 99.

162. Walter A. Jackson, "White Liberal Intellectuals, Civil Rights and Gradualism," in *The Making of Martin Luther King and the Civil Rights Movement*, ed. Brian Ward and Tony Badger (London: 1996), 96–114.

163. Gillon, *Politics and Vision*, 97–98.

164. Dudziak, *Cold War Civil Rights*, 118–26.

165. Eisenhower quoted in Robert Weisbrot, *Freedom Bound: A History of America's Civil Rights Movement* (New York: 1990), 12.

166. For the definitive treatment of Eisenhower's civil rights record, including his manifold shortcomings on the issue, see Robert Frederick Burk, *The Eisenhower Administration and Black Civil Rights* (Knoxville, TN: 1984).

167. Fanon Che Wilkins, "The Making of Black Internationalists: SNCC and Africa before the Launching of Black Power, 1960–1965," *Journal of African American History* 92, no. 4 (September 2007): 468–91.

2. African Americans and the Long Cold War Thaw, 1954–1965

The epigraph is a quote from Jack Newfield, "The Question of SNCC," *Nation*, July 19, 1965, 41.

1. See David L. Anderson, *Trapped by Success: The Eisenhower Administration and Vietnam, 1953–1961* (New York: 1991).

2. Charles DeBenedetti, *An American Ordeal: The Antiwar Movement of the Vietnam Era* (Syracuse, NY: 1990).

3. Phillip S. Foner, ed., *Paul Robeson Speaks* (New York: 1978), 403.

4. David Dellinger, *From Yale to Jail: The Life Story of a Moral Dissenter* (New York: 1993), 149–50.

5. On Lorraine Hansberry's commitment to peace, see Robbie Lieberman, "'Measure Them Right': Lorraine Hansberry and the Struggle for Peace," *Science and Society* 75, no. 2 (April 2011): 206–35. See also Bayard Rustin, "Montgomery Diary," *Liberation*, February 1956, 7–10.

6. Albert S. Bigelow, "Why I Am Sailing into the Pacific Bomb-Test Area," *Liberation*, February 1958, 4–6; Albert Bigelow, *The Voyage of the* Golden Rule: *An Experiment with Truth* (Garden City, NY: 1959); DeBenedetti, *American Ordeal*, 35.

7. On Rustin's life, see John D'Emilio, *Lost Prophet: The Life and Times of Bayard Rustin* (Chicago: 2003); Daniel Levine, *Bayard Rustin and the Civil Rights Movement* (New Brunswick, NJ: 2000).

8. On the WRL, see Scott H. Bennett, *Radical Pacifism: The War Resisters League and Gandhian Nonviolence in America, 1915–1963* (Syracuse, NY: 2003).

9. On the revival of the peace movement after 1957, see Lawrence S. Wittner, *Rebels against War: The American Peace Movement, 1941–1960* (New York: 1969), 240–75.

10. David Dellinger, "Are Pacifists Willing to Be Negroes?" *Liberation*, September 1959, 3.

11. John Lewis with Michael D'Orso, *Walking with the Wind: A Memoir of the Movement* (New York: 1998), 57.

12. On the Montgomery bus boycott, see Martin Luther King Jr., *Stride toward Freedom: The Montgomery Story* (New York: 1958); Taylor Branch, *Parting the*

Waters: America in the King Years 1954–1963 (New York: 1988); David Garrow, *Bearing the Cross: Martin Luther King, Jr., and the Southern Leadership Conference* (New York: 1986), 11–82.

13. Reminiscences of Anne Braden, December 7, 1978, 40–41, CUOHC.

14. See Woods, *Black Struggle, Red Scare.*

15. Thomas F. Jackson, *From Civil Rights to Human Rights: Martin Luther King, Jr., and the Struggle for Economic Justice* (Philadelphia: 2006), 75.

16. Tillman Durdin, "Premiers to Plan Africa-Asia Talks," *New York Times,* December 23, 1954.

17. For scholarly treatments of Bandung and African Americans, see Cary Fraser, "An American Dilemma: Race and Realpolitik in the American Response to the Bandung Conference, 1955," in Plummer, *Window on Freedom,* 115–40; Plummer, *Rising Wind,* 246–56; Von Eschen, *Race against Empire,* 168–73.

18. Tillman Durdin, "Red China Invited to Talks of Asian-African Powers," *New York Times,* December 30, 1954, 1.

19. Von Eschen, *Race against Empire,* 173. See Louis Lautier, "Asian-African Conference Is Acclaimed by Du Bois, Robeson," *Baltimore Afro-American,* April 30, 1955, 8.

20. Richard Wright, *The Color Curtain: A Report on the Bandung Conference* (Cleveland, OH: 1956), 202.

21. Powell quoted in Singh, *Black Is a Country,* 178. On Powell in Bandung, see Borstlemann, *Cold War and the Color Line,* 98.

22. On William Worthy, see Phillips, *War!* 155–56, 164–65; Peniel E. Joseph, *Waiting 'til the Midnight Hour: A Narrative of Black Power in America* (New York: 2006), 45–50.

23. William Worthy, "Our Disgrace in Indo-China," *Crisis,* February 1954, 77–84.

24. Joseph, *Waiting 'til the Midnight Hour,* 46.

25. "News Men in China Penalized by U.S.; Passport of 3 Who Ignored Travel Ban to Be Revoked," *New York Times,* December 29, 1956, 1.

26. Robbie Lieberman, "Another Side of the Story," in Lieberman and Lang, *Anti-Communism and the African American Freedom Movement,* 17.

27. *Kent v. Dulles,* 357 U.S. 116 (1958).

28. See Gaines, *African Americans in Ghana*; Thomas F. Brady, "Ghana Head Asks U.S. 'Cooperation,'" *New York Times,* March 6, 1957, 1.

29. On the black press's coverage of Ghana, see Meriwether, *Proudly We Can Be Africans,* 157–65.

30. "Dominion of Ghana," *Chicago Defender,* March 6, 1957, 9.

31. Thomas Brady, "Nixon Is in Accra for Ghana Fete," *New York Times,* March 4, 1957, 1.

32. On King in Ghana, see Gaines, *African Americans in Ghana,* 89; Jackson, *From Civil Rights to Human Rights,* 81–83; Branch, *Parting the Waters,* 214–16; Garrow, *Bearing the Cross,* 90–91.

33. C. Wright Mills, "Letter to the New Left," *New Left Review*, September–October 1960.

34. Gosse, *Rethinking the New Left*, 63–64.

35. On the Greensboro sit-in, see William Chafe, *Civilities and Civil Rights: Greensboro, North Carolina, and the Struggle for Black Freedom* (New York: 1980).

36. For more on the Shaw University conference, see Carson, *In Struggle*, 19–25.

37. Ella J. Baker, "Bigger than a Hamburger," *Southern Patriot* 18, no. 5 (May 1960): 4. On Baker's influence, see Ransby, *Ella Baker*.

38. Ransby, *Ella Baker*, 231–37.

39. "Non-violence Speaks to the Movement," photocopies SNCC Papers, reel 1, frame 001; Ella Baker interview with Anne Romaine, February 1967, 5, Anne Romaine Papers, WSHS.

40. Howard Zinn, *SNCC: The New Abolitionists* (Boston: 1965), 45.

41. For Lawson's pacifist background, see Wesley C. Hogan, *Many Minds, One Heart: SNCC's Dream for a New America* (Chapel Hill, NC: 2007), 13–17.

42. On James Lawson and the Nashville student movement, see Halberstam, *The Children*, 90–234.

43. James M. Lawson, "From a Lunch-Counter Stool," reprinted in August Meier, Elliott Rudwick, and Frances L. Broderick, eds., *Black Protest and Thought in the Twentieth Century*, 2nd ed. (Indianapolis: 1971), 308–15.

44. Maurice Isserman, *If I Had a Hammer: The Death of the Old Left and the Birth of the New Left* (New York: 1987).

45. For a view of the New Left, see Douglass Rossinow, *The Politics of Authenticity: Liberalism, Christianity, and the New Left in America* (New York: 1998).

46. Forman, *Making of Black Revolutionaries*, 383.

47. Casey Hayden, "Fields of Blue," in *Deep in Our Hearts: Nine White Women in the Civil Rights Movement*, ed. Constance Curry (Athens, GA: 2000), 348.

48. On the quest for "authenticity," see Rossinow, *Politics of Authenticity*.

49. Tom Hayden, *Reunion: A Memoir* (New York: 1988), 35.

50. Ibid., 39.

51. Ibid., 40.

52. Hogan, *Many Minds, One Heart*, 9.

53. On the formation of the SDS and its early years, see James Miller, *"Democracy Is in the Streets": From Port Huron to the Siege of Chicago* (New York: 1987); Kirkpatrick Sale, *SDS* (New York: 1973), 20–70.

54. Miller, *"Democracy Is in the Streets,"* 59.

55. "2 Beaten in Mississippi; White Youths Attacked by Man Near School," *New York Times*, October 12, 1962. For Hayden's recollection of his harrowing experience in McComb, Mississippi, see Cheryl Greenberg, ed., *Circle of Trust: Remembering SNCC* (New Brunswick, NJ: 1998), 71–73.

56. Hayden, *Reunion*, 73.

57. Tom Hayden's letter to his SDS friends from the Albany, Georgia, jail, SDS Papers, box 1, folder 3, WSHS.

58. Hayden, *Reunion*, 86–90.

59. "The Port Huron Statement," in *The New Left: A Documentary History*, ed. Teodori Massimo (New York: 1969), 163–72.

60. Nick Bryant, *The Bystander: John F. Kennedy and the Struggle for Black Equality* (New York: 2006), 283.

61. Branch, *Parting the Waters*, 587.

62. Harris Wofford, *Of Kennedys and Kings: Making Sense of the Sixties* (Pittsburgh: 1980), 124; Dudziak, *Cold War Civil Rights*, 168.

63. Carson, *In Struggle*, 70–71; Bryant, *Bystander*, 284–85.

64. Arsenault, *Freedom Riders*, 164.

65. Wofford, *Of Kennedys and Kings*, 125.

66. Robert Kennedy quoted in Victor S. Navasky, *Kennedy Justice* (New York: 1971), 97. See also Lewis, *Walking with the Wind*, 178.

67. Taylor Branch, *Pillar of Fire: America in the King Years 1963–1965* (New York: 1998), 143.

68. Bryant, *Bystander*, 13.

69. Branch, *Parting the Waters*, 809–13.

70. On the Birmingham campaign, see Glenn. T. Eskew, *But for Birmingham: The Local and National Campaigns in the Civil Rights Struggle* (Chapel Hill, NC: 1997); Diane McWhorter, *Carry Me Home: Birmingham, Alabama, and the Climactic Battle for the Civil Rights Revolution* (New York: 2001).

71. Lewis, *Walking with the Wind*, 225–29.

72. Plummer, *Rising Wind*, 257–97.

73. "Castro's Army to Be Fully Integrated Force," *Atlanta Daily World*, January 15, 1959, 1; "Cuban Army Is 'Completely Integrated,'" *Baltimore Afro-American*, January 24, 1959, 17.

74. Simeon Booker, "Negro Heroes of the Cuban Revolt," *Ebony*, April 1959, 51–52.

75. Tyson, *Radio Free Dixie*, 222.

76. Peniel E. Joseph, ed., *Rethinking the Civil Rights–Black Power Era* (New York: 2006), 13.

77. Van Gosse, *Where the Boys Are: Cuba, Cold War America, and the Making of the New Left* (New York: 1993), 1.

78. On the creation of the FPCC, see Tyson, *Radio Free Dixie*, 223–24; Gosse, *Where the Boys Are*, 138–45.

79. "Negroes Offered Tour of Cuba," *New York Times*, October 11, 1960; Joseph, *Waiting 'til the Midnight Hour*, 29–34.

80. Tyson, *Radio Free Dixie*, 227.

81. Amiri Baraka, *The Autobiography of LeRoi Jones* (New York: 1984), 163.

82. John Henrik Clarke, "Journey to the Sierra Madre (in Cuba)," *Freedomways* (Spring 1961): 32–35.

83. For Castro in New York, see Tyson, *Radio Free Dixie*, 232–34; Plummer *Rising Wind*, 289–91; Joseph, *Waiting 'til the Midnight Hour*, 35–38: Marable, *Malcolm X*, 172–73; Gosse, *Where the Boys Are*, 149–52.

84. Hicks quoted in Plummer, *Rising Wind*, 290.

85. Max Frankel, "Cuban in Harlem; Balks at East Side Bill," *New York Times*, September 20, 1960, 1; Wayne Phillips, "Castro Is Seeking Negroes' Support," *New York Times*, September 21, 1960, 17.

86. Malcolm X quoted in Joseph, *Waiting 'til the Midnight Hour*, 36.

87. Plummer, *Rising Wind*, 293.

88. "Castro Stay in Harlem Denounced by Powell," *New York Times*, September 26, 1960; "Adam Powell Raps Castro's Stay in Harlem," *Chicago Defender*, September 26, 1960.

89. Tyson, *Radio Free Dixie*, 163.

90. William Worthy, "Castro: Man of Power," *Baltimore Afro-American*, January 7, 1961, 1.

91. "Reporter Must Answer to Passport Indictment," *New York Times*, May 22, 1962.

92. On Worthy's arrest and conviction for returning from Cuba without a passport, see Plummer, *Rising Wind*, 306; Joseph, *Waiting 'til the Midnight Hour*, 47–50; Gosse, *Where the Boys Are*, 152.

93. Will Lisner, "Pro-Castro Group Disbanding; Oswald Episode the Fatal Blow," *New York Times*, December 28, 1963, 44.

94. Marian Mollin, *Radical Pacifism in Modern America: Egalitarianism and Protest* (Philadelphia: 2006).

95. Ibid., 128.

96. Barbara Deming, "Southern Peace Walk: Two Issues or One," *Liberation*, July–August 1962, 5.

97. On the history of the conflict between the French and the Vietminh, see Logevall, *Embers of War.*

98. Kennedy quoted in Robert Dallek, *An Unfinished Life: John F. Kennedy, 1917–1963* (New York: 2003), 166–67.

99. Ibid., 167.

100. For the period between 1961 and 1965, see David Halberstam, *The Best and the Brightest* (New York: 1972); Fredrik Logevall, *Choosing War: The Lost Chance for Peace and the Escalation of War in Vietnam* (Berkeley, CA: 1999); David Kaiser, *American Tragedy: Kennedy, Johnson, and the Origins of the Vietnam War* (Cambridge, MA: 2000); Gordon Goldstein, *Lessons in Disaster: McGeorge Bundy and the Path to War in Vietnam* (New York: 2008).

101. Karnow, *Vietnam*, 272.

102. Logevall, *Embers of War*, 705.

103. Homer Bigart, "A 'Very Real War' in Vietnam—And the Deep U.S. Commitment," *New York Times*, February 25, 1962, E3.

104. Logevall, *Choosing War*, 41.

105. Dallek, *Unfinished Life*, 679. See, for example, David Halberstam "Vietnamese Reds Gain in Key Area," *New York Times*, August 15, 1963, 1; David Halberstam, "Set-back in Vietnam: Failure of U.S. to Mold Effective Policy Is Blow to American Prestige," *New York Times*, September 8, 1963, E4.

106. David Halberstam, "The Buddhist Crisis in Vietnam," *New York Times*, September 11, 1963, 14.

107. Dallek, *Unfinished Life*, 680–82.

108. Kaiser, *American Tragedy*, 279.

109. See Judy Tzu-Chun Wu, "An African-Vietnamese American: Robert S. Browne, the Anti-War Movement, and the Personal/Political Dimensions of Black Internationalism," *Journal of African American History* 92, no. 4 (Autumn 2007): 491–515.

110. Letters to the editor of the *New York Times*, August 22, 1962, October 22, 1962, November 8, 1963, March 23, 1964, Papers of Robert S. Browne, box 20, folder 1, Manuscripts, Archives, and Rare Books Division, Schomburg Center for Black Culture, New York Public Library; Robert S. Browne, "The Freedom Movement and the War in Vietnam," *Freedomways* (Fall 1965): 467–80.

111. Len Holt, *The Summer that Didn't End: The Story of the Mississippi Civil Rights Project of 1964* (New York: 1965); Sally Belfage, *Freedom Summer* (Charlottesville, VA: 1965); Seth Cagin and Philip Dray, *We Are Not Afraid: The Story of Goodman, Schwerner, and Chaney, and the Civil Rights Campaign for Mississippi* (New York: 1988); Doug McAdam, *Freedom Summer* (New York: 1988); Charles Payne, *I've Got the Light of Freedom: The Organizing Tradition and Mississippi Politics* (Berkeley, CA: 1995); John Dittmer, *Local People: The Struggle for Civil Rights in Mississippi* (Urbana, IL: 1995); Bruce Watson, *Freedom Summer: The Savage Season of 1964 that Made Mississippi Burn and Made America a Democracy* (New York: 2010).

112. For an account of the collision between Freedom Summer and Vietnam, see Hall, *Peace and Freedom*, 13–38.

113. Eric Burner, *And Gently He Shall Lead Them: Robert Parris Moses and Civil Rights in Mississippi* (New York: 1995).

114. Dittmer, *Local People*, 103–38.

115. Bernard Grofman, Lisa Handley, and Richard G. Niemi, *Minority Representation and the Quest for Voting Equality* (New York: 1992), 1, 23–24.

116. Forman, *Making of Black Revolutionaries*, 292.

117. Anne Moody, *Coming of Age in Mississippi* (New York: 1968). Coles quoted in O'Reilly, *Racial Matters*, 75–76.

118. For two excellent biographies of Allard Lowenstein, see William Chafe, *Never Stop Running: Allard Lowenstein and the Struggle to Save American Lib-*

eralism (New York: 1998); David Harris, *Dreams Die Hard: Three Men's Journey through the Sixties* (New York: 1982).

119. Chafe, *Never Stop Running*, 181.

120. John Herbers, "Mississippi 'Vote' Cast by Negroes," *New York Times*, August 26, 1963, 18.

121. John Herbers, "50 Yale Men Aid Mississippi Negro," *New York Times*, October 30, 1963, 24; campaign materials, October 10, 1963, photocopies of SNCC Papers, reel 41, frames 0457–58; John Herbers, "Vote Drive Planned to Register 80,000 Negroes in Mississippi," *New York Times*, November 7, 1963, 30; Joseph A. Sinsheimer, "The Freedom Vote of 1963: New Strategies of Racial Protest in Mississippi," *Journal of Southern History* 55, no. 2 (May 1989): 217–44.

122. "A New Politics in Mississippi," *Southern Patriot* 21, no. 9 (November 1963): 1.

123. Carson, *In Struggle*, 98–103.

124. Forman, *Making of Black Revolutionaries*, 356; Ransby, *Ella Baker*, 341.

125. See the interview of Hollis Watkins in Henry Hampton and Steven Fraser, eds., *Voices of Freedom: An Oral History of the Civil Rights Movement from the 1950s through the 1980s* (New York: 1990), 182–83.

126. Lawrence Guyot, interview in Howell Raines, *My Soul Is Rested: Movement Days in the Deep South Remembered* (New York: 1977), 287–88.

127. Dittmer, *Local People*, 219.

128. On Moses's instrumental role, see Burner, *And Gently He Shall Lead Them*, 128–32; Dittmer, *Local People*, 210–15.

129. Branch, *Pillar of Fire*, 366–72.

130. Letter from Hoover to Jenkins, July 13, 1964, WHCF, HU2 ST 24, box 26, LBJL.

131. Belfrage, *Freedom Summer*, 180–81.

132. Gallup, *Gallup Poll*, 3:1882.

133. Belfrage, *Freedom Summer*, xii–xiv.

134. Stokely Carmichael with Ekwueme Michael Thelwell, *Ready for Revolution: The Life and Struggles of Stokely Carmichael (Kwame Ture)* (New York: 2003), 359.

135. Howard Zinn, *Vietnam: The Logic of Withdrawal* (Boston: 1967), 27; Howard Zinn, *You Can't Be Neutral on a Moving Train: A Personal History of Our Time* (Boston: 1994), 103–4.

136. Quoted in Hall, *Peace and Freedom*, 13. See also Branch, *Pillar of Fire*, 437.

137. Pat Watters, *Down to Now: Reflections on the Southern Civil Rights Movement* (New York: 1971), 309.

138. McAdam, *Freedom Summer*, 172.

139. On the McGhee shooting, see "Rights Worker Shot in Miss.," *New York Times*, August 16, 1964, 55.

140. McAdam, *Freedom Summer*, 172.

141. Claude Sitton, "Mississippi Freedom Party Bids for Democratic Convention Role," *New York Times*, July 21, 1964, 19.

142. Dittmer, *Local People*, 272; "Mississippi Demos Face Party Challenge," *Student Voice*, May 19, 1964, 147; "Over 800 Meet at MFDP Convention," *Student Voice*, August 12, 1964, 1, 4; Carson, *In Struggle*, 123.

143. See Robert Cohen, *Freedom's Orator: Mario Savio and the Radical Legacy of the 1960s* (New York: 2009).

144. Lewis, *Walking with the Wind*, 277.

145. Victoria Gray quoted in Hampton and Fraser, *Voices of Freedom*, 197.

146. "Mississippi's Delegates," *New York Times*, August 19, 1964, 19.

147. See Garrow, *The FBI and Martin Luther King*, 118–19; O'Reilly, *Racial Matters*, 189–90; Dittmer, *Local People*, 292; Branch, *Pillar of Fire*, 458.

148. Branch, *Pillar of Fire*, 461.

149. Mary McGory, "Freedom: A Grueling Task," *Washington Star*, August 23, 1964.

150. Dittmer, *Local People*, 302; Carson, *In Struggle*, 126.

151. On Reuther's role, see Kevin Boyle, *The UAW and the Heyday of American Liberalism: 1944–1968* (Ithaca: NY: 1994), 194–95.

152. Andrew Young, *An Easy Burden: The Civil Rights Movement and the Transformation of America* (New York: 1996), 310.

153. On King in Atlantic City, see Lewis, *Walking with the Wind*, 281.

154. Wilkins quoted in Chana Kai Lee, *For Freedom's Sake: The Life of Fannie Lou Hamer* (Urbana, IL: 1999), 100.

155. Forman, *Making of Black Revolutionaries*, 396–406.

156. Joseph Rauh corroborates this point. See Hampton and Fraser, *Voices of Freedom*, 201–2.

157. Dittmer, *Local People*, 297; Branch, *Pillar of Fire*, 470.

158. Reminiscences of Edwin King, October 30, 1988, 108, CUOHC.

159. Theodore White contributed to the erroneous idea that Moses had accepted the compromise. Theodore White, *The Making of the President, 1964* (New York: 1965), 280.

160. Forman, *Making of Black Revolutionaries*, 395–96.

161. Cleveland Sellers, *The River of No Return: The Autobiography of a Black Militant and the Life and Death of SNCC* (Jackson, MS: 1973), 111.

162. Moses quoted in Boyle, *UAW*, 196.

163. Lewis, *Walking with the Wind*, 291, 293.

164. Reminiscences of Edwin King, March 10, 1988, 122, CUOHC.

165. On Belafonte and Lewis in Africa, see Hampton and Fraser, *Voices of Freedom*, 204, 206; Forman, *Making of Black Revolutionaries*, 408–11.

166. Harry Belafonte with Michael Shnayerson, *My Song: A Memoir* (New York: 2011), 115–20.

167. Ibid., 291–98.

168. On meeting Malcolm X, see Marable, *Malcolm X*, 372; Gaines, *African Americans in Ghana*, 201; Lewis, *Walking with the Wind*, 287–88; Carson, *In Struggle*, 135–36; George Breitman, ed., *Malcolm X Speaks: Selective Speeches and Statements* (New York: 1994), 136–46.

169. On Waveland, see Carson, *In Struggle*, 145–49; Hogan, *Many Minds, One Heart*, 197–218; Lewis, *Walking with the Wind*, 298–300.

170. Logevall, *Choosing War*, 78.

171. DeBenedetti, *American Ordeal*, 81–92.

172. Ronald Steel, *Walter Lippmann and the American Century* (New York: 1980), 549.

173. Richard Flacks, "New Crisis in Vietnam," February 29, 1964, SDS Papers, box 8, folder 4, WSHS.

174. Carson, *In Struggle*, 183.

175. Simon Hall attributes this heightened awareness to the organizing tradition in the Deep South. Hall, *Peace and Freedom*, 13–38.

176. On the University of Michigan poll, see Foster Hailey, "Many in U.S. Held Hazy about Asia," *New York Times*, December 15, 1964, 9.

177. "Key Negro Groups Call on Members to Curb Protests," *New York Times*, July 30, 1964, 1, 12. Support for President Johnson ran so strong that the moratorium was endorsed by most African Americans, and the African American press unanimously supported him. See "No Demonstrations against Democrats," *Pittsburgh Courier*, August 29, 1964, 10.

178. In the aftermath of the election, the African American press had difficulty restraining its exuberance. See "It's up to You, Now," *New York Amsterdam News*, October 31, 1964, 8; "The People Speak," *New York Amsterdam News*, November 7, 1964, 16. In its November 14, 1964, edition, the *Pittsburgh Courier* ran the following front-page headline: "Election Showed Nation Is Growing Up."

179. Logevall, *Choosing War*, 256; Dallek, *Flawed Giant*, 184.

180. LBJ quoted in Brian VanDeMark, *Into the Quagmire: Lyndon Johnson and the Escalation of the Vietnam War* (New York: 1995), 19.

181. Ibid., 67–68.

182. On Johnson's portrayal of himself as the peace candidate, see Lloyd C. Gardner, *Pay Any Price: Lyndon Johnson and the Wars for Vietnam* (Chicago: 1995), 129–50; Dallek, *Flawed Giant*, 240. On Johnson's belief that his mandate was limited, see "Deep Background," *Time*, December 25, 1964.

183. Gitlin, *The Sixties*, 179.

184. Robert Moses, speech at *National Guardian* dinner, November 24, 1964, MFDP Papers, box 23, folder 3, MLKC.

185. Branch, *Pillar of Fire*, 589; Carson, *In Struggle*, 156–57.

186. Jack Newfield, "The Question of SNCC," *Nation*, July 19, 1965, 41.

187. Whitney Young, "Reasons for Optimism," *New York Amsterdam News*, January 16, 1965, 8.

188. On Moses's reaction to the Greensboro sit-ins, see Zinn, *SNCC*, 17; Jack Newfield, "The Invisible Man Learns His Name," *Village Voice*, December 3, 1964, 3, 23.

189. Belfrage, *Freedom Summer*, 11.

190. Mary King, *Freedom Song: A Personal Story of the Civil Rights Movement of the 1960s* (New York: 1987), 493.

191. Hayden, *Rebel*, 118.

192. Marable, *Malcolm X*, 399–404; Malcolm X, "To Mississippi Youth," in Breitman, *Malcolm X Speaks*, 144.

193. Sale, *SDS*, 171–72; Burner, *And Gently He Shall Lead Them*, 214.

3. Vietnam and Civil Rights

The epigraphs are from the following: Lyon quoted in Greenberg, *Circle of Trust*, 209; Randolph quoted in Hall, *Peace and Freedom*, 89.

1. Carroll Kilpatrick, "Voting Rights Bill Signed by Johnson," *Washington Post*, August 7, 1965, A1; E. W. Kenworthy, "Capitol Is Serene," *New York Times*, August 7, 1965, 1, 8.

2. Polls indicated that African Americans possessed a palpable sense of optimism. See "The Negro in America—1965—Louis Harris Finds Hopes Surging and Goals Intact," *Newsweek*, February 15, 1965, 24–28.

3. Andrew E. Hunt, *David Dellinger: The Life and Times of a Nonviolent Revolutionary* (New York: 2006), 75–78; Dellinger, *From Yale to Jail*, 120.

4. Staughton Lynd, "Coalition Politics or Non-Violent Revolution?" *Liberation*, May 1965, 18–21; letter from Lynd to Rustin, April 19, 1965, photocopies of Papers of Bayard Rustin, reel 21, frame 0346 (accessed at the Doe Library, University of California–Berkeley).

5. Branch, *At the Edge of Canaan*, 276; Dellinger, *From Yale to Jail*, 220.

6. D'Emilio, *Lost Prophet*, 117–20.

7. Parris quoted in A. J. Muste, "Assembly of Unrepresented People: The Weekend that Was," *Liberation*, September 1965, 29.

8. See "Assembly of Unrepresented People," *Southern Patriot*, June 1965, 1; "White House Picketed by Peace Group," *Washington Post*, August 7, 1965, A1, 14; *Life*, August 13, 1965, 31. In a famous article in the liberal magazine *Commentary*, Rustin explained his controversial view that the civil rights movement had to move beyond the advocacy of civil rights and put forth an agenda to refashion the political economy, as well as his worry that antiwar activity would thwart this aim. Bayard Rustin, "From Protest to Politics," *Commentary*, February 1965, 25–31.

9. A Gallup poll conducted on April 16, 1965, found that 52 percent of the respondents listed civil rights as the most important problem facing the country, compared with 39 percent who cited foreign affairs. By the fall of 1965, 37 percent listed Vietnam as the most important problem, and only 17 percent listed civil rights. Gallup, *Gallup Poll*, 3:1934, 1973, 1974.

10. Dallek, *Flawed Giant*, 84–90.

11. Ibid., 99.

12. For a journalistic account highlighting the impact of domestic political considerations on Johnson's decision, especially the baneful legacy of McCarthyism, see Halberstam, *The Best and the Brightest*.

13. Dallek, *Flawed Giant*, 91.

14. Karnow, *Vietnam*, 411. For an examination of Johnson's wrenching personal dilemma, see Dallek, *Flawed Giant*, 240–62. On Johnson's decision for war, see Logevall, *Choosing War*, 333–74; Larry Berman, *Planning a Tragedy: The Americanization of the War in Vietnam* (New York: 1982); Kaiser, *American Tragedy*, 289.

15. Doris Kearns, *Lyndon Johnson and the American Dream* (New York: 1976), 251–52.

16. Logevall, *Choosing War*, 374.

17. Kennan quoted in Walter L. Hixson, *George F. Kennan: Cold War Iconoclast* (New York: 1989), 236.

18. On Johnson's determination to conceal the scope of the United States' deepening involvement, see H. R. McMaster, *Dereliction of Duty: Lyndon Johnson, Robert McNamara, the Joint Chiefs of Staff, and the Lies that Led to Vietnam* (New York: 1997).

19. Halberstam quoted in Stephen B. Oates, *Let the Trumpet Sound: The Life of Martin Luther King Jr.* (New York: 1982), 364.

20. "Why a Happy New Year," *Baltimore Afro-American*, January 9, 1965, 5; Frederick V. Seabrook, "Here Is My Salute to the New Year," letter to the editor, *Baltimore Afro-American*, January 16, 1965, 4; "We Are Overcoming," *New York Amsterdam News*, March 20, 1965, 1, 10.

21. Eldridge, *Chronicles of a Two-Front War*, 8.

22. "Doesn't Make Sense," *Pittsburgh Courier*, January 2, 1965, 10.

23. P. L. Prattis, "What Do We Want to Save?" *Pittsburgh Courier*, January 16, 1965, 10.

24. "Tell Us the Facts," *Chicago Defender*, February 27–March 5, 1965, 8; "African Criticism," *Chicago Defender*, February 20–26, 1965, 6.

25. "No Immediate End to War in South Vietnam," *Pittsburgh Courier*, May 15, 1965, 11.

26. Carson, *In Struggle*, 183.

27. Forman, *Making of Black Revolutionaries*, 445.

28. Letter from AJ Muste and David Dellinger to John Lewis, January 16, 1965, and letter from Clark Kissinger to John Lewis, February 28, 1965, SNCC Papers, box 2, folder 8, MLKC.

29. Lewis, *Walking with the Wind*, 343.

30. "The Power to Protect," *New Republic*, March 20, 1965, 5–6.

31. Carson, *In Struggle*, 183; Hall, *Peace and Freedom*, 22–48.

32. DeBenedetti, *American Ordeal*, 108; Gitlin, *The Sixties*, 180; Sale, *SDS*, 173–76.

33. Carson, *In Struggle*, 176–80; Hall, *Peace and Freedom*, 25–26; Hogan, *Many Minds, One Heart*, 95–140; Rossinow, *Politics of Authenticity*. For a contrary, albeit flawed, argument that SDS failed to fundamentally reorient American values of racism and sexism, see David Barber, *A Hard Rain Fell: SDS and Why It Failed* (Jackson, MS: 2008).

34. Carl Ogelsby, "Democracy is Nothing if Not Dangerous," SDS Papers, microfilm edition, reel 38, no. 265, WSHS.

35. Sale, *SDS*, 170–72.

36. Letter from Paul Booth to John Clayden, March 4, 1965, SDS Papers, box 9, folder 5, WSHS.

37. "Professors Hold Vietnam Protest," *New York Times*, March 25, 1965, 9. On the teach-ins, see Nancy L. Zaroulis and Gerald Sullivan, *Who Spoke Up? American Protest against the War in Vietnam* (Garden City, NY: 1984), 37–38; DeBenedetti, *American Ordeal*, 107–8.

38. Garvy quoted in Hogan, *Many Minds, One Heart*, 252.

39. The SDS Papers are rife with references to civil rights in the years prior to 1965. After the upsurge in American military activity in Vietnam in late 1964, writings on the freedom struggle ceased, reflecting a single-minded focus on the war. See, for example, Paul Booth, "Working Papers, Summer Projects: 1965," SDS Papers, box 9, folder 7, WSHS, which contains no references to civil rights.

40. Sue Thrasher, "Circle of Trust," in Curry, *Deep in Our Hearts*, 239.

41. King, *Freedom Song*, 515.

42. Sale, *SDS*, 102; Miller, *"Democracy Is in the Streets,"* 190–93.

43. Forman, *Making of Black Revolutionaries*, 451–52; Hall, *Peace and Freedom*, 48–72.

44. On Parris's embrace of the antiwar movement, see Burner, *And Gently He Shall Lead Them*, 200–214.

45. Andrew B. Lewis, *Shadows of Youth: The Remarkable Journey of the Civil Rights Generation* (New York: 2009), 242.

46. Sellers, *River of No Return*, 83.

47. Quoted in Carson, *In Struggle*, 184.

48. E-mail from Staughton Lynd to the author, May, 8, 2013.

49. Lewis, *Shadows of Youth*, 186–88, 240–46.

50. Robert Moses, speech at *National Guardian* dinner, November 24, 1964, MFDP Papers, box 23, folder 3, MLKC.

51. For Rustin's view, see D'Emilio, *Lost Prophet*, 407–16; Levine, *Bayard Rustin*, 171–76; Bayard Rustin, *Down the Line: The Collected Writings of Bayard Rustin* (Chicago: 1971), 111–22.

52. See Hall, *Peace and Freedom*, 13–38.

53. "A Talk with Bob Parris," *Southern Patriot*, October 1965, 3.

54. Ibid.

55. Malcolm X quoted in Branch, *Pillar of Fire*, 585; Marable, *Malcolm X*, 412.

56. Gitlin, *The Sixties*, 6.

57. "A Call to All Students to March on Washington Saturday, April 17, 1965 to End the War in Vietnam," *Liberation*, March 1965, 45. See also the advertisement for the march in the *Nation*, March 22, 1965, 302.

58. "White House Picketed on Viet Policy," *Washington Post*, February 21, 1965, A26.

59. Fred Powledge, "The Student Left: Spurring Reform," *New York Times*, March 15, 1965, 1, 26.

60. Fred Halstead, *Out Now! A Participant's Account of the American Movement against the War in Vietnam* (New York: 1978), 35.

61. On the importance of the April 17 march, see Tom Wells, *The War Within: America's Battle over Vietnam* (Berkeley, CA: 1994), 13–18, 25.

62. "Rebels with a Cause," *New Republic*, May 1, 1965, 5–6.

63. For a discussion of SDS's views on nonexclusion, see "SDS March on Washington," *Studies on the Left* 5, no. 2 (Spring 1965): 61–69; "The New Peace Movement," *Studies on the Left* 5, no. 4 (Fall 1965): 8–12.

64. See Zaroulis and Sullivan, *Who Spoke Up?* 38–42; DeBenedetti, *American Ordeal*, 111–12; Sale, *SDS*, 181.

65. On the dispute between Muste and Rustin, see Jack Newfield, "The Octogenarian & the Student Left," *Village Voice*, May 6, 1965, 3, 16.

66. Carson, *In Struggle*, 173–74.

67. Woods, *Black Struggle, Red Scare.*

68. Rowland Evans and Robert Novak, "Danger from the Left," *Washington Post*, March 18, 1965, A25.

69. Rowland Evans and Robert Novak, "A Longer Look at SNCC," *Washington Post*, April 9, 1965, A25. See also Rowland Evans and Robert Novak, "Pacifist, Rights Militants Marching Together," undated clipping in Howard Zinn Papers, box 3, folder 5, WSHS.

70. "Waving the Red Flag," *Newsweek*, April 12, 1965, 30–31.

71. Quoted in Rowland Evans and Robert Novak, "Inside Report . . . The Moses Rally," *Washington Post*, July 27, 1965, A13.

72. Quoted in Paul Good, "SNCC Head Denies Control by Reds," *Washington Post*, March 28, 1965, A7.

73. Andrew Kopkind, "New Radicals in Dixie: Those 'Subversive' Civil Rights Leaders," *New Republic*, April 10, 1965, 13–16.

74. On the view that the march was a success, see DeBenedetti, *American Ordeal*, 112; Zaroulis and Sullivan, *Who Spoke Up?* 38.

75. Sue Cronk, "10,000 to Protest War in Viet-Nam with Rally, Parade," *Washington Post*, April 17, 1965, A4; "15,000 White House Pickets Denounce Vietnam

War," *New York Times*, April 18, 1965, 1, 3: Halstead, *Out Now!* 40; "Viet-Nam Protest Is Staged by 16,000," *Washington Post*, April 18, 1965, A1, A18.

76. Jack Newfield, *A Prophetic Minority* (New York: 1966), 27.

77. Gitlin, *The Sixties*, 128.

78. The text of Potter's speech was reprinted in *National Guardian*, April 24, 1965, 4. Martin Luther King Jr. invoked Potter's speech when he famously declared in his Riverside speech that the Vietnam War was "a symptom of a deeper malaise within the American spirit." King, "Beyond Vietnam," in Taylor, *Vietnam and Black America*, 92.

79. Todd Gitlin, *The Whole World Is Watching: Mass Media in the Making and Unmaking of the New Left* (Berkeley, CA: 1980), 56–57, 65.

80. Featherstone quoted in *Washington Post*, April 18, 1965, A18.

81. Brown quoted in Hall, *Peace and Freedom*, 25.

82. William A. Price, "A Joining of Forces," *National Guardian*, April 24, 1965, 1, 6.

83. Jack Newfield, "The Student Left: Revolt without Dogma," *Nation*, May 10, 1965, 491–95.

84. DeBenedetti, *American Ordeal*, 120.

85. James Farmer, *Lay Bare the Heart: An Autobiography of the Civil Rights Movement* (New York: 1985), 298.

86. On Farmer's views of his relationship with LBJ, see James Farmer Oral History, July 20, 1971, LBJL.

87. Raymond Arsenault, *Freedom Riders: 1961 and the Struggle for Racial Justice* (New York: 2006), 29–33.

88. Face the Nation *1965: The Collected Transcripts*, vol. 8 (New York: 1972), 106; Meier and Rudwick, *CORE*, 62–68.

89. King quoted in Garrow, *Bearing the Cross*, 394.

90. "Dr. King Declares U.S. Must Negotiate in Asia," *New York Times*, July 3, 1965, 6.

91. "Senator Rips King on Viet Statement," *Baltimore Afro-American*, September 18, 1965, 20.

92. "Civil Rights: One War at a Time," *Newsweek*, July 19, 1965, 24.

93. *The Johnson Presidential Press Conferences* (New York: 1978), 1:349.

94. Carl Mirra, *The Admirable Radical: Staughton Lynd and Cold War Dissent* (Kent, OH: 2010).

95. Hayden, *Reunion*, 159–80; Staughton Lynd and Tom Hayden, *The Other Side* (New York: 1966); Tom Hayden, "A Visit to Hanoi," *Liberation* 11, no. 3 (May–June 1966): 23, 25.

96. Arsenault, *Freedom Riders*, 23–24.

97. "Resolutions for the Resolution Committee of the National Convention of CORE," CORE Papers, box 29, folder 12, MLKC.

98. Farmer Oral History, 9.

99. Nick Kotz and Mary Lynn Kotz, *A Passion for Equality: George Wiley and the Movement* (New York: 1977), 153.

100. On CORE's 1965 convention, see "CORE Head Raps Equal Job Law," *Baltimore Afro-American*, July 10, 1965, 1–2; "Civil Rights: One War at a Time," *Newsweek*, July 19, 1965, 24–25; "Is Vietnam to Become a 'Civil Rights' Issue," *U.S. News and World Report*, July 19, 1965, 12; "CORE Retreats on Vietnam," *National Guardian*, July 10, 1965; Farmer, *Lay Bare the Heart*, 300; Gene Roberts, "CORE in a Switch to Push Politics," *New York Times*, July 5, 1965, clipping in DNC Research Series I, box 38, LBJL.

101. "Capital March Stresses Vietnam Instead of Rights," *New York Times*, August 11, 1965, 3.

102. Jack Newfield, "Some Things Unite Them, Some Things Divide Them," *Village Voice*, August 19, 1965, 3, 16–17. See also Anne Braden, "Issue of Peace Confronts Freedom Movement," *Southern Patriot*, September 1965, 4.

103. Zaroulis and Sullivan, *Who Spoke Up?* 47. On the importance of the Kewadin conference, see Wells, *The War Within*, 45–48; Sale, *SDS*, 203–17; Gitlin, *The Sixties*, 189–92.

104. Booth quoted in Miller, *"Democracy Is in the Streets,"* 235–36.

105. For a definitive treatment of the Watts uprising, see Gerald Horne, *The Fire This Time: The Watts Uprising and the 1960s* (Charlottesville, VA: 1995).

106. James Baldwin, *The Fire Next Time* (New York: 1963).

107. On Baldwin's importance, see Carol Polsgrove, *Divided Minds: Intellectuals and the Civil Rights Movement* (New York: 2001), 155–72.

108. Sugrue, *Sweet Land of Liberty*, 416.

109. Branch, *Pillar of Fire*, 418; Joseph, *Waiting 'til the Midnight Hour*, 110–12.

110. Thomas Sugrue, *Origins of the Urban Crisis* (Princeton, NJ: 1996).

111. Milton Viorst, *Fire in the Streets: America in the 1960s* (New York: 1979), 309.

112. Joseph A. Califano Jr., *Triumph and Tragedy of Lyndon Johnson* (New York: 1991), 59–64.

113. Dallek, *Flawed Giant*, 222–25.

114. "MLK Statement at SCLC Convention in Birmingham, AL," August 12, 1965, MLK Papers, box 9, MLKC.

115. Bayard Rustin, "The Watts 'Manifesto' and the McCone Report," in Rustin, *Down the Line*, 142.

116. Levine, *Bayard Rustin*, 185.

117. Laura Pulido, *Black, Brown, Yellow, and Left: Radical Activism in Los Angeles* (Berkeley, CA: 2006), 70.

118. Quoted in Joshua Bloom and Waldo E. Martin Jr., *Black against Empire: The History and Politics of the Black Panther Party* (Berkeley, CA: 2013), 29.

119. Sellers, *River of No Return*, 147, 151–54. On the Lowndes County project, see Hassan Kwame Jeffries, *Bloody Lowndes: Civil Rights and Black Power*

in Alabama's Black Belt (New York: 2009); Carson, *In Struggle*, 164–66; Carmichael, *Ready for Revolution*, 460–68.

120. See Appy, *Working Class War.*

121. Hall, *Peace and Freedom*, 28–30; "McComb Soldier's Death in Vietnam Sparks Protest," July 28, 1965, MFDP Papers, box 21, MLKC.

122. Lewis, *Walking with the Wind*, 354.

123. "MFDP and Vietnam," Zinn Papers, box 3, folder 5, WSHS.

124. Ibid.

125. Ruthie Reed, "On Vietnam—Why and Because," MFDP newsletter, November 5, 1965, clipping in MFDP Papers, box, 21, folder 1, MLKC.

126. See "Private Faces Trial for Refusing Food," *New York Times*, ca. August 1965, newspaper clipping in Zinn Papers, box 3, folder 5, WSHS; "Mississippi Freedom Party Raps Military Draft for Vietnam," *Baltimore Afro-American*, August 7, 1965, 2. SNCC created the MFDP in 1964 as an instrument to register African Americans to vote, and even though it was an autonomous organization, it retained its affiliation with SNCC.

127. Evers quoted in Lewis, *Shadows of Youth*, 241.

128. Roy Reed, "U.S. Study Asked on Draft Evasion," *New York Times*, August 3, 1965.

129. Ibid.

130. Carson, *In Struggle*, 185; Dittmer, *Local People*, 351.

131. Quoted in Roy Reed, "Freedom Party Head Disavows Plea to Negroes to Dodge Draft," *New York Times*, August 4, 1965.

132. Reminiscences of Edwin King, October 30, 1988, 137–38, CUOHC; Dittmer, *Local People*, 350.

133. Carson, *In Struggle*, 187.

134. On Zinn's life, see Martin Duberman, *Howard Zinn: A Life on the Left* (New York: 2012).

135. Howard Zinn, "Should Civil Rights Workers Take a Stand on Vietnam?" *Student Voice*, August 30, 1965, 3.

136. Duberman, *Howard Zinn*, 115–20.

137. Julian Bond interview in James Finn, *Protest, Pacifism and Politics: Some Passionate Views on War and Non-Violence* (New York: 1967), 304–5.

138. Richards quoted in Carson, *In Struggle*, 187.

139. Hall, *Peace and Freedom*, 45–46.

140. Mitchell Zimmerman, "SNCC Should Not Take a Stand on Vietnam," Zinn Papers, box 3, folder 5, WSHS.

141. "November 19, 1965, Gallop Poll," WHCF, box 71 HU6 10/28/65–12/20/65, LBJL.

142. Hall, *Peace and Freedom*, 45–46.

143. Carson, *In Struggle*, 187.

144. Louis Harris, "We Have to Finish the Job," *Newsweek*, September 26,

1965, 27. By early December, the number of Americans who responded that it was necessary to support any measures to prevent a communist takeover in Vietnam jumped to 71 percent. "Vietnam: Still on the Escalator," *Newsweek*, December 13, 1965, 27.

145. On the mainstream media's gross distortion of the antiwar movement, see Melvin Small, *Covering Dissent: The Media and the Anti-War Movement* (New Brunswick, NJ: 1994), 2.

146. DeBenedetti, *American Ordeal*, 122–42.

147. I. F. Stone, "What Should the Peace Movement Do?" *Liberation*, August 1965, 27–28.

148. "They March, Doubting They Will Overcome," *New Republic*, October 30, 1965, 9.

149. DeBenedetti, *American Ordeal*, 126.

150. Michael S. Foley, *Confronting the War Machine: Draft Resistance during the Vietnam War* (Chapel Hill, NC: 2003), 29.

151. Austin C. Wehrwein, "U.S. Investigates Anti-Draft Groups," *New York Times*, October 18, 1965, 1, 8; "Why the Protests?" *New Republic*, October 30, 1965.

152. DeBenedetti, *American Ordeal*, 129–30; Thomas Buckley, "Man, 22, Immolates Himself at Antiwar Protest at U.N.," *New York Times*, November 10, 1965, 1.

153. James Reston, "Washington: The Stupidity of Intelligence," *New York Times*, October 17, 1965, 10E.

154. "Demonstrators Try to Stop Troop Train on Coast," *New York Times*, August 7, 1965, 3; "The Demonstrators: Why? How Many?" *Newsweek*, November 1, 1965, 31.

155. See, for example, "And Now the Vietnik," *Time*, October 22, 1965, 25.

156. Linda Charlton, "Peace, Rights Groups Go Their Own Ways," *Newsday*, October 22, 1965, 98.

157. See, for example, Simeon Booker, "Negroes in Vietnam: 'We, Too, Are Americans,'" *Ebony*, November 1965, 89–98.

158. Michael Harrington, "Does the Peace Movement Need Communists?" *Village Voice*, November 11, 1965; Thomas Powers, *The War at Home: Vietnam and the American People* (New York: 1973), 89.

159. "March on Washington for Peace," n.d., SNCC Papers, box 59, folder 1, MLKC.

160. Sanford Gottlieb to Clark Kissinger, August 31, 1965, SDS Papers, box 31, WSHS; SANE's telegram to Ho Chi Minh cited in *New York Times*, October 29, 1965, 3.

161. Dellinger, *From Yale to Jail*, 20; DeBenedetti, *American Ordeal*, 131.

162. Hall, *Peace and Freedom*, 35; Zaroulis and Sullivan, *Who Spoke Up?* 63–66.

163. Letter from Bayard Rustin to Dana Greeley, September 1, 1965, photocopies of Rustin Papers, reel 6, frame 0260.

164. James Farmer, "Imperfect Nation," *New York Amsterdam News*, October 30, 1965, 17.

165. James Farmer, "The CORE of It!" *New York Amsterdam News*, November 27, 1965, 15.

166. Farmer, *Lay Bare the Heart*, 300–302.

167. Estimates of the total number of marchers varied from the *Chicago Tribune*'s laughably low tally of 12,000 to SANE coordinator Sanford Gottlieb's count of 40,000 to 50,000. See "Thousands Walk in Capital to Protest War in Vietnam," *New York Times*, November 28, 1965, 1; "Throng of 20,000 Marchers in Protest of the Vietnam War," *Washington Post*, November 28, 1965, A1, A5.

168. Quoted in John Herbers, "Typical Marcher: Middle-Class Adult," *New York Times*, November 28, 1965, 87.

169. Ibid.

170. Andrew Kopkind, "Radicals on the March, but Where to, and by What Route?" *New Republic*, December 11, 1965, 15.

171. See, for example, Robert G. Sherrill, "Patriotism of Protest, the Consensus Marchers . . . ," *Nation*, December 13, 1965, 463.

172. For a view of the frenzied convention from a member of the YSA, see Halstead, *Out Now!* 105–20.

173. Quoted in Renata Adler, "The Price of Peace Is Confusion," *New Yorker*, December 11, 1965.

174. Lauter quoted in Greenberg, *Circle of Trust*, 83.

175. "Watts Report," Zinn Papers, box 3, folder 5, WSHS.

176. Sellers, *River of No Return*, 149.

177. Memo to SNCC staff, December 6, 1965, SNCC Papers, box 52, folder 4, MLKC.

178. Lewis, *Walking with the Wind*, 371; memo from John Lewis to SNCC staff, December 7, 1965, SNCC Papers, box 52, folder 4, MLKC.

179. For interesting discussions of the importance of 1965, see James T. Patterson, *The Eve of Destruction: How 1965 Transformed America* (New York: 2012); G. Calvin MacKenzie and Robert Weisbrot, *The Liberal Hour: Washington and the Politics of Change in the 1960s* (New York: 2008).

180. "The Truth about Negro Progress in U.S.," *U.S. News and World Report*, December 13, 1965, 68.

181. "A Bright Outlook," *Chicago Defender*, January 1–7, 1966, 10.

182. Statement on 1966 by John Lewis, chairman of SNCC, December 30, 1965, SNCC Papers, box 52, folder 4, MLKC.

4. The Vietnam War and Black Power

The epigraphs are from the following: Lawrence quoted in Staughton Lynd, "A Radical Speaks in Defense of SNCC," *New York Times Magazine*, September 10, 1967, 271; "SNCC's Statement on the War in Vietnam," January 6, 1966, SNCC Papers, box 52, folder 4, MLKC.

1. Lewis, *Walking with the Wind*, 346–47.

2. "Student Slain in Alabama for Using Washroom," *New York Amsterdam News*, January 8, 1966, 1, 43.

3. James Forman, *Sammy Younge, Jr.: The First Black College Student to Die in the Black Liberation Movement* (New York: 1968).

4. For a history of Tuskegee, see Robert J. Norrell, *Reaping the Whirlwind: The Civil Rights Movement in Tuskegee* (Chapel Hill, NC: 1985), 445; Louis Harlan, *Booker T. Washington: The Making of a Black Leader, 1856–1901* (New York: 1972), 109–33.

5. On the biracial nature of Tuskegee's local government, see Anne Braden, "Hope in Tuskegee: A Deep South First," *Southern Patriot* 22, no. 10 (December 1964): 1–2.

6. Arnold S. Kaufman, "Murder in Tuskegee: Day of Wrath in the Model Town," *Nation*, January 31, 1966, 118–25; Jeffrey A. Turner, *Sitting in and Speaking Out: Student Movements in the American South, 1960–1970* (Athens, GA: 2010), 174–75.

7. "The Trial . . . ," *Southern Courier*, December 17–18, 1966, 1; Norrell, *Reaping the Whirlwind*, 192–93.

8. Quoted in Forman, *Sammy Younge*, 138.

9. "Civil Rights: End of the Façade," *Time*, January 14, 1966, 29.

10. Carmichael, *Ready for Revolution*, 447.

11. Cleveland Sellers interview, May 10, 1989, University of North Carolina, Greensboro.

12. Forman, *Sammy Younge*, 138, 194. See also Norrell, *Reaping the Whirlwind*.

13. Lewis, *Walking with the Wind*, 374.

14. Forman, *Sammy Younge*, 25.

15. "SNCC's Statement on the War in Vietnam," January 6, 1966, SNCC Papers, box 52, folder 4, MLKC.

16. "Move to Draft Rights Leader," *Baltimore Afro-American*, January 22, 1966, 13.

17. "Editorial," *Atlanta Journal*, January 7, 1966.

18. "NAACP Disassociates Itself from Attack on Vietnam Policy," *New York Times*, January 9, 1966, 4; "War Critics Opposed by NAACP," *Washington Post*, January 9, 1966, A4.

19. "Leader's Statement Is Deplorable, Misleading," *Atlanta World*, January 7, 1966.

20. "The War in Vietnam: Where Do You Stand?" *New York Amsterdam News*, January 15, 1966, 1, 40.

21. Ibid.

22. Branch, *At the Edge of Canaan*, 408.

23. SNCC memo from Clifford L. Alexander Jr. to LBJ, January 6, 1966, WHCF, box 25, LBJL.

24. LBJ note to Alexander, January 7, 1966, WHCF, box 25, LBJL.

25. SNCC memo from Alexander to LBJ.

26. "King Opens New Rights Drive," *Washington Post*, January 8, 1966, A6.

27. Telegram from Roy Wilkins to LBJ, January 13, 1966, NAACP Papers, group IV, box A37, LOC.

28. John Neary, *Julian Bond: Black Rebel* (New York: 1971), 64; Lewis, *Shadows of Youth*, 257–60.

29. Roger M. Williams, *The Bonds: An American Family* (New York: 1971), 221–23; Neary, *Julian Bond*, 92–97.

30. "Defiance of Draft Call Urged by SNCC Leader," *Atlanta Constitution*, January 7, 1966, 1.

31. "Rep-elect Bond Facing an Ouster Fight after Urging Draft Dodging," *Atlanta Constitution*, January 8, 1966, 1.

32. Geer quoted in Neary, *Julian Bond*, 108.

33. See M. J. Heale, *McCarthy's Americans: Red Scare Politics in State and Nation, 1935–1965* (Athens, GA: 1998), 270–71.

34. For a discussion on the legal significance of the Bond case, see Tomiko Brown-Nagin, *Courage to Dissent: Atlanta and the Long History of the Civil Rights Movement* (New York: 2011).

35. "The South: One Word Too Many," *Time*, January 21, 1966, 20.

36. Press conference: Junius Griffin reads Dr. King's statement, John Lewis reads statement of Georgia legislature on SNCC and statement of SNCC supporting Julian Bond, January 8, 1966, SNCC Papers, box 52, folder 4, MLKC.

37. Garrow, *Bearing the Cross*, 458.

38. "The South: One Word Too Many," 20.

39. "Harm to All," *Atlanta World*, January 12, 1966.

40. "Bond Issue Puts in Focus Civil Rights vs. Vietnam," *Pittsburgh Courier*, February 5, 1966, 8.

41. Letter from Zinn to the *Atlanta Constitution*, January 7, 1966, clipping in SNCC Papers, box 52, folder 4, MLKC.

42. Neary, *Julian Bond*, 109–10.

43. Statement by Julian Bond, January 10, 1966, SNCC Papers, box 52, folder 4, MLKC.

44. Neary, *Julian Bond*, 108.

45. Roy Reed, "Georgia House Bars War Critic, a Negro," *New York Times*, January 11, 1966, 1, 8.

46. Neary, *Julian Bond*, 109–10; "Georgia: Two-Time Loser," *Newsweek*, January 24, 1966, 24–25.

47. James Forman's statement in support of Bond, January 11, 1966, SNCC Papers, box 52, folder 4, MLKC.

48. See Woods, *Black Struggle, Red Scare.*

49. "Mr. Bond of Georgia," *New York Times*, January 12, 1966, 20.

50. Branch, *At the Edge of Canaan*, 413; Neary, *Julian Bond*, 125.

51. Lillian Smith, "Old Dream, New Killers," *Atlanta Constitution*, January 15, 1966, 11; Roy Reed "Rights Group Heavily Criticized for Attacking United States Foreign Policy," *New York Times*, January 16, 1966.

52. Letter from 24 U.S. representatives, January 11, 1966, SNCC Papers, box 52, folder 4, MLKC.

53. Poll cited in Brown-Nagin, *Courage to Dissent*, 263.

54. Interview with John Lewis, n.d., Julian Bond Papers, box 1, folder 3, MLKC.

55. Neary, *Julian Bond*, 125–27.

56. Brown-Nagin, *Courage to Dissent*, 294; "Bond Seeking Draft Exemption in Conscientious Objector Role," *New York Times*, January 22, 1966, 12.

57. Lewis, *Walking with the Wind*, 378; Sam Pope Brewer, "Bond Hailed at UN Luncheon Given by Africans of 15 Nations," *New York Times*, January 22, 1966, 12.

58. Jacob Sherman, "Ousted Ga. Legislator Impressive Sunday on 'Meet the Press,'" *Philadelphia Tribune*, February 1, 1966, 5.

59. On the legal strategy and history of *Bond v. Floyd*, see Brown-Nagin, *Courage to Dissent*, 290–300.

60. Carson, *In Struggle*, 190; Garrow, *Bearing the Cross*, 458–62; Branch, *At the Edge of Canaan*, 412–13.

61. *Bond v. Floyd*, 385 US 166 (1966); Brown-Nagin, *Courage to Dissent*, 294–97.

62. Cartoon on Vietnam, WHCF, Office Files of Harry McPherson, box 29, LBJL.

63. Quoted in Brown-Nagin, *Courage to Dissent*, 296.

64. Interview of Julian Bond by Gwen Gillon, July 6, 1967, tape 497, WSHS.

65. Bob Zellner with Constance Curry, *The Wrong Side of Murder Creek: A White Southerner in the Freedom Movement* (Montgomery, AL: 2008), 287–95.

66. See Peniel E. Joseph, "The Black Power Movement: A State of the Field," *Journal of American History* 96, no. 3 (December 2009): 751–76.

67. Nell Irvin Painter, "Elitism and Black Nationalism," in *Black Leaders of the Nineteenth Century*, ed. Leon Litwack and August Meier (Urbana, IL: 1988), 149–71.

68. Sugrue, *Sweet Land of Liberty*, 14–16; Kelly, *Freedom Dreams*, 23–29; Lawrence Levine, "Marcus Garvey and the Politics of Revitalization," in *Black Leaders of the Twentieth Century*, ed. John Hope Franklin and August Meier (Urbana, IL: 1982), 105–38.

69. Marable, *Malcolm X*, 86.

70. Joseph, *Waiting 'til the Midnight Hour*, 11.

71. Sugrue, *Sweet Land of Liberty*, 315.

72. Ibid.

73. Ibid., 315–26.

74. On RAM, see Kelly, *Freedom Dreams*, 73–91.

75. Bloom and Martin, *Black against Empire*, 33.

76. Sugrue, *Sweet Land of Liberty*, 336.

77. William Brink and Louis Harris, *The Negro Revolution in America: What Negroes Want, Why and How They Are Fighting, Whom They Support, What Whites Think of Them and Their Demands* (New York: 1963), 118–22.

78. Carson, *In Struggle*, 162–66.

79. Carmichael, *Ready for Revolution*, 547.

80. Reminiscences of James Farmer, February 2, 1979, 217, CUOHC.

81. Quoted in Gene Roberts, "Fund Lag Plagues Rights Movement," *New York Times*, January 10, 1966, 1, 11.

82. Berg, *Ticket to Freedom*, 241; "CORE Broke Again," *New York Amsterdam News*, August 21, 1965, 1, 3.

83. Gene Roberts, "Student Groups Lack Money and Help but Not Projects," *New York Times*, December 10, 1965, 37.

84. On the SCLC's fund-raising woes, see Adam Fairclough, *To Redeem the Soul of America: The Southern Christian Leadership Conference and Martin Luther King, Jr.* (Athens, GA: 1987), 255–66, 287.

85. Louis Harris, "The Backlash Issue," *Newsweek*, July 13, 1964, 24–26.

86. Sellers, *River of No Return*, 187.

87. Lewis, *Walking with the Wind*, 364–65.

88. Kelly, *Freedom Dreams*, 69.

89. "John Robert Lewis Is Tired," Penny Patch memo to Jim, Nancy, Jimmy, et al., December 11, 1965, SNCC Papers, box 2, folder 1, MLKC.

90. Brown-Nagin, *Courage to Dissent*, 266–72; Carson, *In Struggle*, 191.

91. Fred Powledge, "Changes in CORE Accent Problems," *New York Times*, January 5, 1966, 13.

92. "Farmer Opposed to Taking Stand on Viet," *Baltimore Afro-American*, February 19, 1966, 14.

93. Edward McHale, "McKissick, New Chief of CORE Tells His Views," *Chicago Defender*, January 15–21, 1966; "Recommendation on Statement—War on Poverty or War in Vietnam," January 1, 1966, CORE Papers, box 29, folder 17, MLKC.

94. "Position on the Congress of Racial Equality on the War in Vietnam," n.d., CORE Papers, box 42, folder 6, MLKC; Meier and Rudwick, *CORE*, 415.

95. Hall, *Peace and Freedom*, 67.

96. "CORE Convention: Rights Group to Stress Militant Stand," *Chicago Defender*, July 2, 1966, 2.

97. "Key Leaders in Baltimore for CORE Meeting," *Baltimore Afro-American*, July 9, 1966, 10.

98. "Position on the Congress of Racial Equality on the War in Vietnam."

99. Jeffries, *Bloody Lowndes.*

100. Carmichael, *Ready for Revolution*, 95, 101, 104–5.

101. On Carmichael at Parchman, see Arsenault, *Freedom Riders*, 362–63; Zinn, *SNCC*, 40.

102. Lewis, *Walking with the Wind*, 171; Carmichael, *Ready for Revolution*, 204.

103. See Peniel E. Joseph, *Dark Days, Bright Nights: From Black Power to Barack Obama* (New York: 2010), 107–10.

104. Sellers, *River of No Return*, 155.

105. Carson, *In Struggle*, 200.

106. "Excerpts from Paper on Which 'Black Power' Philosophy Is Based," *New York Times*, August 5, 1966, 10.

107. Lewis, *Walking with the Wind*, 381–82.

108. Carmichael, *Ready for Revolution*, 476–83.

109. Gene Roberts, "Militants Take over Student Coordinating Group," *New York Times*, May 17, 1966, 22; Jack Nelson, "SNCC Dumps 2 Top Leaders, Names 'Black Panther' Chairman," *Los Angeles Times*, May 17, 1966, A1, A4.

110. Long quoted in Carson, *In Struggle*, 203.

111. Gene Roberts, "New Leaders and New Course for 'Snick,'" *New York Times*, May 22, 1966, 4B.

112. Forman, *Making of Black Revolutionaries*, 447–56; "Civil Rights: Thinking Big," *Time*, May 27, 1966, 22. See also Branch, *At the Edge of Canaan*, 464–66.

113. Joseph, *Dark Days, Bright Nights*, 107–10.

114. "Civil Rights: The New Racism," *Time*, July 1, 1966, 11.

115. See Simon Hall, "The NAACP, Black Power, and the African American Freedom Struggle, 1966–1969," *Historian* 69, no. 1 (Spring 2007): 49–82.

116. Roy Wilkins's keynote address at 57th annual NAACP convention, July 5, 1966, NAACP Papers, group IV, box A3, LOC.

117. Young quoted in "Civil Rights: The New Racism."

118. M. S. Handler, "Whitney Young Urges Attempt Be Made to Reach Ghetto 'Unreachables,'" *New York Times*, August 1, 1966, 14.

119. Transcript of *Face the Nation*, June 19, 1966, photocopies of SNCC Papers, reel 58, frame 1155 (accessed at the Cecil H. Green Library, Stanford University).

120. Edith Evans Asbury, "Protests Today to Mark Hiroshima Anniversary," *New York Times*, August 6, 1966, 4; telegram from King, Randolph, Wilkins, and Young to SNCC, August 6, 1966, photocopies of SNCC Papers, reel 23, frame 0084; Carmichael's response to telegram, ibid., frame 0114.

121. "Dr. King Declares Rights Movement Is 'Close' to a Split," *New York Times*, July 9, 1966, 1, 8.

122. Roy Reed, "Rights Unit Quits Parley in Capital," *New York Times*, May 24, 1966, 28; Jack Nelson, "White House Bid Spurned by SNCC," *Washington Post*, May 24, 1966, A1, A24.

123. "SNCC Statement on the White House Conference," May 23, 1966, NAACP Papers, group IV, box A92, LOC; Cynthia Griggs Fleming, *Soon We Will Not Cry: The Liberation of Ruby Doris Smith Robinson* (New York: 1998), 177–78.

124. Transcript of *Face the Nation*, May 29, 1966, MLK Papers, box 10, MLKC.

125. Robert Baker, "CORE Head Alleges Conference Called by LBJ Is Rigged," *Washington Post*, June 1, 1966, A1, A24.

126. William Ransberry and John Carmody, "Leaders at Odds: Efforts Fail to Block Rights Talks," *Washington Post*, June 2, 1966, A1, A4.

127. Kevin L. Yuill, "The 1966 White House Conference on Civil Rights and the End of the American Creed," *Historical Journal* 41, no. 1 (March 1998): 259–82.

128. Lewis, *Walking with the Wind*, 383.

129. "Lewis Quits SNCC; Shuns Black Power," *New York Times*, July 1, 1966, 1; "Ex-Chairman Quits 'Black Power' SNCC," *Washington Post*, July 1, 1966, clipping in DNC Series 1, box 37, LBJL.

130. Paul Good, "Odyssey of a Man and a Movement," *New York Times Magazine*, June 25, 1967, 23–29.

131. Carson, *In Struggle*, 229–36.

132. Lewis, *Shadows of Youth*, 205–6.

133. "Mrs. Bevel Hanoi-Bound, Gregory Still Waiting," *Chicago Defender*, December 20, 1966, 6.

134. "Mrs. Bevel Links Viet, Civil War," *Chicago Defender*, December 28, 1966, 4.

135. Diane Nash Bevel, "Journey to North Vietnam," *Freedomways* 6, no. 2 (Spring 1967): 118–28.

136. Mary Hershberger, *Traveling to Vietnam: American Peace Activists and the War* (Syracuse, NY: 1998), 76–78.

137. Betty Washington, "Diane Bevel Calls U.S. 'Aggressor,'" *Chicago Defender*, January 23, 1967, 4.

138. Lewis, *Shadows of Youth*, 214, 246–47.

139. Dallek, *Flawed Giant*, 324–26.

140. Ibid., 323.

141. John Herbers, "GOP Will Press Racial Disorders as Election Issues," *New York Times*, October 4, 1966, 1.

142. Quoted in Gary May, *Bending toward Justice: The Voting Rights Act and the Transformation of American Democracy* (New York: 2013), 192.

143. "Nixon and the GOP Comeback," *Newsweek*, October 10, 1966, 30–33.

144. Matthew Dallek, *The Right Moment: Ronald Reagan's First Victory and the Decisive Turning Point in American Politics* (New York: 2000); Michelle Reeves, "'Obey the Rule or Get Out': Ronald Reagan's Gubernatorial Campaign and the Trouble in Berkeley," *Southern California Quarterly* 92, no. 3 (Fall 2010): 275–305.

145. Mark J. Brilliant, *The Color of America Has Changed: How Racial Diversity Shaped Civil Rights* (New York: 2010), 222.

146. See Matusow, *Unraveling of America.*

147. Greenberg, *Circle of Trust*, 11–12.

148. Danny Lyon, *Memories of the Southern Civil Rights Movement* (Chapel Hill, NC: 1992), 175–77.

149. Carson, *In Struggle*, 240.

150. Forman, *Making of Black Revolutionaries*, 476–78.

151. For a critical assessment of the "Peg Leg" meeting, see Andrew Kopkind, "The Future of 'Black Power': A Movement in Search of a Program," *New Republic*, January 7, 1967, 16–18.

152. Fleming, *Soon We Will Not Cry*, 179–80; Carmichael, *Ready for Revolution*, 567, 570–71; Carson, *In Struggle*, 236–41.

153. "Director of CORE Criticizes Non-Violence as a Dying Policy," *Los Angeles Times*, July 3, 1966, 1; "CORE Rejects Technique of Non-Violence," *Washington Post*, July 5, 1966, A1.

154. Sugrue, *Sweet Land of Liberty*, 281–85.

155. "CORE Will Insisted on 'Black Power': Delegation Also Opposed War in Vietnam—Offers Aid to Draft Resisters," *New York Times*, July 5, 1966, 1, 22.

156. Linn Allen, "We'll Meet Violence with Violence—CORE," *Baltimore Afro-American*, July 9, 1966, 1–2,

157. John J. Goldman, "Administration Called Racist by McKissick," *Los Angeles Times*, July 8, 1966, 5.

158. Meier and Rudwick, *CORE*, 414–15; Hall, *Peace and Freedom*, 67.

159. "Lillian Smith Leaves CORE," *Baltimore Afro-American*, July 16, 1966, 13.

160. Meier and Rudwick, *CORE*, 425.

161. On African Americans soldiers and the Vietnam War, see Westheider, *Fighting on Two Fronts.*

162. Phillips, *War!* 190.

163. Terry, *Bloods*, 228.

164. Lawrence M. Baskir and William Strauss, *Chance and Circumstance: The War, the Draft, and the Vietnam Generation* (New York: 1978), 125.

165. Simeon Booker, "Negroes in Vietnam: 'We, Too, Are Americans,'" *Ebony*, November 1965, 92.

166. On the "good soldier" stereotype, see Westheider, *Fighting on Two Fronts*, 9–11.

167. Westmoreland quoted in Thomas A. Johnson, "The Negro in Vietnam: Strides toward Partnership Contrast with Lag at Home," *New York Times*, April 29, 1968, 16.

168. For a general discussion of Project 100,000, see Lisa Hsaio, "Project 100,000," *Vietnam Generation* 1, no. 2 (Spring 1989): 14–37.

169. Lee Rainwater and William Yancey, *The Moynihan Report and the Politics of Controversy* (Cambridge, MA: 1967), 42.

170. Memo from Moynihan to McPherson, July 16, 1965, WHCF, Office Files of Harry McPherson, box 21, LBJL.

171. Albert B. Fitt Oral History, October 25, 1968, LBJL.

172. Homer Bigart, "McNamara Plans to 'Salvage' 40,000 Rejected in Draft," *New York Times*, August 24, 1966, 1, 18.

173. Benjamin Welles, "Negroes Expected to Make up 30% of Draft 'Salvage,'" *New York Times*, August 25, 1966, 1 6.

174. McKissick and Carmichael quoted in "Rights Leaders Deplore Plan to 'Salvage' Military Rejects," *New York Times*, August 26, 1966, 3.

175. Whitney Young Jr., "To Be Equal," *Baltimore Afro-American*, February 19, 1966, 1.

176. "Valor Praised by Pentagon, Negroes Dying Faster than Whites in Vietnam," *New York Amsterdam News*, March 19, 1966, 1; "Negro Deaths Exceed Whites' in Vietnam," *Pittsburgh Courier*, May 28, 1966; Jack Raymond, "Negro Death Ratio in Vietnam Exceeds Whites," *New York Times*, March 10, 1966, 4; Ted Sell, "Ratio of Negroes Killed in Vietnam Tops White," *Los Angeles Times*, March 10, 1966, 16.

177. "What Changes Are Needed in the Draft," *Pittsburgh Courier*, July 23, 1966, 8.

178. On the paucity of African Americans on draft boards in the Deep South, see Appy, *Working Class War*, 6. "All White Boards in MS Hit by NAACP," *Pittsburgh Courier*, July 17, 1966, 3. See also Paul T. Murray, "Blacks and the Draft: A History of Institutional Racism," *Journal of Black Studies* 2, no. 1 (September 1971): 57–76; Paul T. Murray, "Local Draft Board Composition and Institutional Racism," *Social Problems* 19, no. 1 (Summer 1971): 129–37.

179. "GI Refused Home Rites Gets Burial," *Pittsburgh Courier*, June 11, 1966, 1.

180. See Phillips, *War!* 226–27.

181. Moser, *New Winter Soldiers*, 71.

182. Edwards quoted in Terry, *Bloods*, 4, 12.

183. Jack Olsen, *Last Man Standing: The Tragedy and Triumph of Geronimo Pratt* (New York: 2000), 24–26.

184. Seale quoted in Thomas A. Jackson, "The Negro in Vietnam," *New York Times*, April 29, 1968, 16. See also Curtis J. Austin, *Up against the Wall: Violence in the Making and Unmaking of the Black Panther Party* (Fayetteville, AR: 2006).

185. DeBenedetti, *American Ordeal*, 158; Hall, *Peace and Freedom*, 59–60.

186. Barber, *Hard Rain Fell*, 23–25.

187. McKissick quoted in Phillips, *War!* 254.

188. Hall, *Peace and Freedom*, 61.

189. Stokely Carmichael, *Stokely Speaks: From Black Power to Pan-Afri-*

canism (Chicago: 1971), 45, 53; Julius Duscha, "Crowd Laps up Carmichael's Insults," *Washington Post*, October 31, 1966, A8.

190. Carmichael, *Stokely Speaks*, 53.

191. Susan Goodman, "No Longer Lily White: Changing the Complexion of the Peace Movement," *Village Voice*, September 8, 1966, 2, 23.

192. Hall, *Peace and Freedom*, 61; *New Left Notes*, June 24, 1966, 2.

193. Carmichael quoted in *National Guardian*, April 22, 1967, 2.

194. James Peck, "Black Power: Two Views," *Liberation*, October 1966, 31–32. See also James Peck, *Freedom Ride* (New York: 1962); Arsenault, *Freedom Riders*, 94–99.

195. Branch, *At the Edge of Canaan*, 492.

196. David Dellinger, "The Fort Hood Three," *Liberation*, August 1966, 3–5.

197. Bayard Rustin, "'Black Power' and Coalition Politics," *Commentary*, September 1966, 35–41.

198. "Statement of Pfc. James Johnson," *Liberation*, August 1966, 4.

199. Hunt, *David Dellinger*, 156–57; Wells, *War Within*, 115.

200. Adam Mack, "No 'Illusion of Separation': James L. Bevel, the Civil Rights Movement, and the Vietnam War," *Peace and Change* 28, no. 1 (January 2003): 108–33.

201. In his memoirs, Dellinger overplays his role in King's turn against the war. See Dellinger, *From Yale to Jail*, 259–62, 275–79.

202. King quoted in Garrow, *Bearing the Cross*, 485.

203. Young, *Easy Burden*, 425.

204. On Johnson's blaming African Americans for the election defeat, see Branch, *At the Edge of Canaan*, 548.

205. "Dr. King Will Write Book during Leave," *New York Times*, December 14, 1966, 42.

5. Dr. King's Painful Dilemma

The epigraph is from Martin Luther King FBI Files, part I, reel 8, frame 00281, and part II, reel 5, frames 000203–10, September 15, 1965.

1. David Garrow, *Protest at Selma: Martin Luther King, Jr., and the Voting Rights Act of 1965* (New Haven, CT: 1978), 31.

2. Young, *Easy Burden*, 433.

3. "Mass Arrests Fail to Halt Selma Drive," *Pittsburgh Courier*, February 13, 1965, 1, 4.

4. Young, *Easy Burden*, 347.

5. Ralph David Abernathy, *And the Walls Came Tumbling Down* (New York: 1989), 321.

6. Forman quoted in Lewis, *Walking with the Wind*, 335.

7. Andrew Young's telephone call to the White House, relaying the contents of a note King had written from the Dallas County jail, failed to elicit action from

the Johnson administration. Memo from LW to LBJ: Message from Dr. Martin Luther King, Jr., February 3, 1965, WHCF, HU2/ST1, box 24, LBJL.

8. Carroll Kilpatrick, "Ten Demonstrators Ejected from White House at Sit-ins," *Washington Post*, March 12, 1965, A1, A9.

9. Dallek, *Flawed Giant*, 215.

10. Lady Bird Johnson cited in Michael Beschloss, *Reaching for Glory: Lyndon Johnson's Secret White House Tapes, 1964–1965* (New York: 2001), 227–28.

11. Lewis, *Walking with the Wind*, 339–40.

12. Copy of the speech reprinted in *New York Amsterdam News*, May 1, 1965, 10.

13. Tom Wicker, "President in TV Talk Pledges that 'We Shall Overcome,'" *New York Times*, March 16, 1965, 1, 31; Garrow, *Bearing the Cross*, 408–9. Roy Wilkins was sitting in the audience and confessed, at "that moment, I loved LBJ." Wilkins, *Standing Fast*, 307, 311.

14. "We Are Overcoming," *New York Amsterdam News*, March 20, 1965, 1, 10.

15. Telegram from MLK to LBJ, March 16, 1965, WHCF, Name File MLK, box 144, LBJL.

16. *Houston Post* quoted in Editors News Service, "President's Address Draws Strong Support from Morning Newspapers and Columnists," March 17, 1965, clippings in Office Files of Bill Moyers, box 6, LBJL.

17. Forman quoted in Lewis, *Walking with the Wind*, 340.

18. Gallup, *Gallup Poll*, 1944.

19. Commencement address at Howard University: "To Fulfill These Rights," June 4, 1965, in *Public Papers of the Presidents: Lyndon B. Johnson* (Washington, DC: 1966), 2:635–40.

20. Telegram from MLK to LBJ, June 7, 1965, WHCF, Name File MLK, box 144, LBJL.

21. On King and Johnson's complicated relationship, see Kotz, *Judgment Days*.

22. McPherson quoted in Hampton and Fraser, *Voices of Freedom*, 338.

23. Louis Martin Oral History, June 12, 1986, 54, LBJL.

24. Carl T. Rowan, *Breaking Barriers: A Memoir* (New York: 1991), 258.

25. Noer, "Martin Luther King, Jr., and the Cold War."

26. For the tendency to encase King in legend, see Clayborne Carson, "Martin Luther King, Jr.: Charismatic Leadership in a Mass Struggle," *Journal of American History* 74, no. 2 (September 1987): 448–54.

27. Vincent Harding, *Martin Luther King: An Inconvenient Hero* (New York: 1996).

28. On Niebuhr's influence on King, see Branch, *Parting the Waters*, 81–87. On King's recollections of Crozer and his evolving notions of pacifism, see King, *Stride toward Freedom*, 95–100.

29. Reinhold Niebuhr, *Moral Man and Immoral Society: A Study in Ethics and Politics* (New York: 1932), 242.

30. King quoted in Jackson, *From Civil Rights to Human Rights*, 43.

31. King quoted in Christopher Lasch, *The True and Only Heaven: Progress and Its Critics* (New York: 1991), 389.

32. David Garrow, "Martin Luther King Jr., and the Spirit of Leadership," *Journal of American History* 74, no. 2 (September 1987): 438–47.

33. Garrow, *Bearing the Cross*, 59–60; Raines, *My Soul Is Rested*, 53.

34. Rustin quoted in Branch, *Parting the Waters*, 179.

35. Young, *Easy Burden*, 120.

36. King quoted in Michael Kazin, *American Dreamers: How the Left Changed a Nation* (New York: 2011), 210.

37. On King's internationalism, see James Cone, "Martin Luther King, Jr. and the Third World," *Journal of American History* 74, no. 2 (September 1987): 455–67.

38. On King in Ghana, see Gaines, *African Americans in Ghana*, 5.

39. Garrow, *Bearing the Cross*, 91.

40. Jackson, *From Civil Rights to Human Rights*, 82.

41. Clayborne Carson, "Rethinking African-American Political Thought in the Post-Revolutionary Era," in *The Making of Martin Luther King and the Civil Rights Movement*, ed. Brian Ward and Tony Badger (London: 1996), 115.

42. King quoted in Oates, *Let the Trumpet Sound*, 167.

43. Plummer, *Rising Wind*, 305.

44. King quoted in Garrow, *Bearing the Cross*, 104.

45. Ibid., 224.

46. John D. Pomfret, "President Promises Dr. King Vote Move," *New York Times*, February 10, 1965, 1, 18; *Time*, February 19, 1965, 23.

47. Paul Schuette, "King Preaches on Non-violence at Police-Guarded Howard Hall," *Washington Post*, March 3, 1965, D2.

48. Charles Fager, *Selma 1965: The March that Changed the South* (New York: 1974), 85.

49. Roy Reed, "Alabama Victim Called Martyr," *New York Times*, March 4, 1965, 23; Andrew Kopkind, "Ain't Gonna Let Nobody Turn Me Around," *New Republic*, March 20, 1965, 7–9.

50. Richard Gid Powers, *Secrecy and Power: The Life of J. Edgar Hoover* (New York: 1987); O'Reilly, *Racial Matters*.

51. Hoover quoted in Kotz, *Judgment Days*, 77.

52. Garrow, *The FBI and Martin Luther King*.

53. O'Reilly, *Racial Matters*, 126.

54. William C. Sullivan with Bill Brown, *The Bureau: My Thirty Years in Hoover's FBI* (New York: 1979), 139.

55. Ben A. Franklin, "Hoover Assails Warren Findings: Says FBI Was Crit-

icized Unfairly on Oswald Check—Calls Dr. King a Liar," *New York Times*, November 19, 1964, 1, 28; "Department of Justice: Off Hoover's Chest," *Newsweek*, November 30, 1964, 29–30.

56. Kotz, *Judgment Days*, 278; memo from J. E. Hoover to Marvin Watson, March 5, 1965, Office Files of Mildred Stegall, box 32, LBJL.

57. Eric Goldman, *The Tragedy of Lyndon Johnson* (New York: 1968), 312.

58. Garrow, *Bearing the Cross*, 422.

59. Branch, *At the Edge of Canaan*, 216.

60. Warren Berry, "King's New Tack: End the Viet War," *New York Herald Tribune*, April 23, 1965, 1, 6.

61. UPI dispatch, "Dr. King Declares U.S. Must Negotiate in Asia," July 3, 1965, 6; "Dr. King Calls Vietnam Negotiation Essential," *Los Angeles Times*, July 3, 1965.

62. Garrow, *Bearing the Cross*, 430; Branch, *At the Edge of Canaan*, 263.

63. Memo from JEH to MW, July 7, 1965, Office Files of Stegall, box 32, LBJL.

64. Richard Goodwin, *Remembering America: A Voice from the Sixties* (New York: 1988), 394.

65. Ibid., 402.

66. Moyers quoted in Wofford, *Of Kennedys and Kings*, 221.

67. Wicker quoted in Patterson, *Eve of Destruction*, 165.

68. LBJ phone call with MLK, July 7, 1965, 8:05 pm, PNO 3, cit. #8313, audiotape WH6507.02, LBJL.

69. Carroll Kirkpatrick, "Voting Rights Bill Signed by Johnson," *Washington Post*, August 7, 1965, A5.

70. Harding's comments were made at a panel at Riverside Church commemorating the fortieth anniversary of King's death, April 1, 2008.

71. Branch, *At the Edge of Canaan*, 286.

72. Young, *Easy Burden*, 376.

73. See "The President's News Conference of July 28, 1965," *Public Papers of the Presidents: LBJ*, 2:794–803.

74. Bevel quoted in Branch, *At the Edge of Canaan*, 286.

75. Statement of Martin Luther King Jr. at the SCLC convention in Birmingham, Alabama, August 12, 1965, MLK Papers, box 10, MLKC.

76. Homer Bigart, "Dr. King to Send Appeal to Hanoi," *New York Times*, August 13, 1965, 1, 2.

77. Letter from Stewart Meacham of AFSC to MLK, August 13, 1965, MLK Papers, box 2, folder 33, MLKC.

78. "King, Not SCLC to See Viet Nam Peace Negotiations," *Baltimore Afro-American*, August 21, 1965, 1–2; The Martin Luther King Jr. FBI Files, ed. David J. Garrow (Bethesda, MD: 1984), part I, reel 8, frame 00031, August 17, 1965.

79. Branch, *At the Edge of Canaan*, 289.

80. Martin Luther King Jr. FBI Files (King-Levison File), part II, reel 5, frames 000129–32, August 13, 1965.

81. Garrow, *Bearing the Cross*, 439.

82. See Horne, *Fire This Time*, 182–84, 288–89.

83. Drew Pearson, "Brown, Who Tried to Help Negro, One of the Worst Hurt by the Riots," *Los Angeles Times*, August 20, 1965, A6.

84. Young, *Easy Burden*, 380.

85. King quoted in Michael Honey, *Going down Jericho Road: The Memphis Strike, Martin Luther King's Last Campaign* (New York: 2007), 83.

86. Califano, *Triumph and Tragedy*, 59.

87. Roger Wilkins, *A Man's Life: An Autobiography* (New York: 1982), 162.

88. Matusow, *Unraveling of America*, 196.

89. Horne, *Fire This Time*, 282.

90. Lawrence E. Davies, "California Issue for '66 Emerges," *New York Times*, August 17, 1965, 1, 17.

91. John Herbers, "Johnson Rebukes Rioters as Destroyers of Rights," *New York Times*, August 21, 1965, 1, 8; Robert E. Thompson, "Johnson Compares LA Rioters to Klan Riders," *Los Angeles Times*, August 21, 1965, 1, 6.

92. See Kotz, *Judgment Days*, 345–46.

93. LBJ telephone call with MLK, August 20, 1965, 5:10 pm, PNO 12, cit. #8578, WH6508.07, LBJL.

94. Branch, *At the Edge of Canaan*, 305–9.

95. "Weaver Raps King on Vietnam," *Baltimore Afro-American*, August 28, 1965, 1–2; "Viet Policy Criticisms by Rights Leaders Hit," *Los Angeles Times*, August 20, 1965, 11.

96. "Dr. King, Other Nobel Winners Sign War Appeal," *Baltimore Afro-American*, August 28, 1965, 12.

97. Transcript of *Face the Nation*, August 29, 1965, MLK Papers, box 9, MLKC.

98. Louis Harris, "Support Solidifying for Johnson Course in Viet-Nam Crisis," *Washington Post*, September 12, 1965, A2.

99. On King's preparation for the Goldberg meeting, see Branch, *At the Edge of Canaan*, 324; Garrow, *Bearing the Cross*, 443–45.

100. Young, *Easy Burden*, 431.

101. Branch, *At the Edge of Canaan*, 326.

102. Andrew Young Oral History, June 18, 1970, 15, LBJL.

103. Statement of MLK and Ambassador Goldberg on the Vietnam War, September 10, 1965, MLK Papers, box 9, MLKC.

104. Kathleen Teltsch, "Dr. King Urges U.S. to Press for Seat for Peking in the U.N." *New York Times*, September 11, 1965, 9; "Dr. King Wants Red China in U.N.," *Washington Post*, September 11, 1965, A7.

105. Statement of MLK and Goldberg on the Vietnam War.

106. "Dodd Scores King for View on China," *New York Times*, September 12, 1965, 12.

107. "Senator Dodd Raps Dr. King's Stand on Foreign Policy," *Chicago Defender*, September 11–17, 1965, 1.

108. Thurmond quoted in Teltsch, "Dr. King Urges U.S. to Press for Seat for Peking."

109. *Washington Evening Star* editorial quoted in Kotz, *Judgment Days*, 352.

110. "Keep Rights, Viet Issues Apart: Young," *Chicago Defender*, October 23–29, 1965, 1. On the close personal relationship between Young and LBJ, see Nancy J. Weiss, *Whitney M. Young, Jr., and the Struggle for Civil Rights* (Princeton, NJ: 1989), 157; Dennis Dickerson, *Militant Mediator, Whitney Young, Jr.* (Lexington, KY: 1998), 247.

111. Memo from Hoover to Watson, September 15, 1965, Office Files of Stegall, box 32, LBJL.

112. Martin Luther King FBI Files, part I, reel 8, frame 00281, September 12, 1965; ibid., part II, reel 5, frames 000203–10, September 12, 1965; ibid., frame 000213, September 13, 1965.

113. Memo from Hoover to Watson, September 15, 1965.

114. Memo from Watson to LBJ, September 15, 1965, Office Files of Stegall, box 32, LBJL.

115. See Kotz, *Judgment Days*, 353.

116. Coretta Scott King, *My Life with Martin Luther King* (London: 1969), 291.

117. Martin Luther King FBI Files, part I, reel 8, frame 00324, September 15, 1965.

118. Memo from Hoover to Watson, September 16, 1965, Office Files of Stegall, box 32, LBJL.

119. Memo from Watson to LBJ, September 17, 1965, ibid.

120. "Letters to the Editor of the *Times*," *New York Times* (International Edition), September 28, 1965, 4.

121. "The Right to Dissent," *Chicago Defender*, October 2–8, 1965, 10.

122. "Sheer Arrogance," *Baltimore Afro-American*, September 25, 1965, 4.

123. Martin Luther King FBI Files, part I, reel 8, frames 00498–99, September 28, 1965.

124. Ibid., part II, reel 5, frame 000249, September 28, 1965.

125. Memo from Hoover to Watson, September 30, 1965, Office Files of Stegall, box 32, LBJL; Michael Friedly and David Gallen, eds., *Martin Luther King, Jr. and the FBI File* (New York: 1993), 438.

126. Spock quoted in King, *My Life*, 293.

127. Letter from Rabbi Gendler to MLK, October 1, 1965, MLK Papers, box 25, folder 17, MLKC.

128. Malcolm Nash, "Churchmen Weigh Dr. King's Viet Move," *New York Amsterdam News*, October 2, 1965, 14.

129. Quoted in Jackson, *From Human Rights to Civil Rights*, 314.

130. William Brink and Louis Harris, *Black and White: A Story of U.S. Racial Attitudes Today* (New York: 1967), 274.

131. Statement of Dr. Martin Luther King Jr., October 5, 1965, MLK Papers, box 9, MLKC.

132. Address to SCLC Retreat, Frogmore, SC, n.d. [May 1967], box 13, MLKC.

133. Tom Wicker, "Johnson Is Beset by Tax Issue: Cost of War and Domestic Programs Strain Budget," *New York Times*, December 20, 1965, 1, 39.

134. Gordon Hanock, "King off Base with Viet Policy," *Chicago Defender*, December 15, 1965, 15.

135. "Mrs. King Sees War-Rights Link," *Baltimore Afro-American*, December 11, 1965, 14.

136. Letter from Hoover to Watson, October 12, 1965, Office Files of Stegall, box 32, LBJL.

137. "King Says 'Ugly' Views Dim Viet Peace Hopes," *New York Herald Tribune*, December 6, 1965, 16; MLK address, December 5, 1965, MLK Papers, box 9, MLKC.

138. "Dr. King Sees Move against Pacifists," *New York Times*, December 6, 1965, 73.

139. Silberman quoted in Patterson, *Eve of Destruction*, 225.

140. Martin Luther King Jr., "Peace: God's Man's Business," *Chicago Defender*, January 1–7, 1966, 10.

6. The Second Coming of Martin Luther King Jr.

The epigraphs are from "Interview with Martin Luther King, Jr.," *New York Times*, April 2, 1967, 76; Harvard Sitkoff, *The Struggle for Black Equality: 1954–1992* (New York: 1993), 185.

1. In early 1966, the African American press reported on the war's adverse impact on the Great Society. See, for example, Arnold B. Sawislak, "Vietnam War Expected to Cut Poverty Funds," *Chicago Defender*, January 6, 1966, 5.

2. Ronald Steel, "A Visit to Washington," *New York Review of Books*, October 6, 1966, 5–6.

3. Roy Reed, "Georgia Legislature Convenes Today amid Controversy over Seating of Negro," *New York Times*, January 10, 1966, 10.

4. Gene Roberts, "Fund Lag Plagues Rights Movement," *New York Times*, January 10, 1966, 1, 11.

5. Garrow, *Bearing the Cross*, 458–59; Branch, *At the Edge of Canaan*, 411.

6. On Carmichael's fondness for King, see Carmichael, *Ready for Revolution*, 511–15.

7. Sellers, *River of No Return*, 168–69.

8. See "NAACP Disassociates Itself from Attack on Vietnam Policy," *New York Times*, January 9, 1966, 4.

9. Garrow, *Bearing the Cross*, 458.

10. Press statement regarding refusal to seat Representative Julian Bond, January 12, 1966, MLK Papers, box 10, MLKC.

11. "Why Quotas on Our Defense of Our County?" *Baltimore Afro-American*, October 8, 1966, 5.

12. "Ministers Quit Rights Group," *New York Times*, January 15, 1966, 28.

13. Roy Reed, "1,000 Stage March on Georgia Capitol; Back Ousted Negro," *New York Times*, January 15, 1966, 1, 28.

14. Address at state capitol, January 14, 1966, MLK Papers, box 10, MLKC; Reed, "1,000 Stage March."

15. Al Kuetner, "Bond Supporters Scuffle with State Troopers in Atlanta Protest," *Boston Globe*, January 15, 1966, 8; "King Leads Rally for Bond: Blasts Legislature for 'Punishment' for Anti-War Views," *Washington Post*, January 15, 1966, A2.

16. "Sermon on Non-Conformity: Julian Bond," January 16, 1966, MLK Papers, box 10, MLKC.

17. "Perspective: The State of the Union: More of Great Society," *Los Angeles Times*, January 16, 1966, F4.

18. Dallek, *Flawed Giant*, 299–302.

19. Goodwin, *Remembering America*, 423.

20. On LBJ's anxiety before the State of the Union address, see Randall Woods, *LBJ: Architect of Ambition* (New York: 2006), 685–86.

21. "Text of the State of the Union Address," *New York Times*, January 13, 1966, 14.

22. On the inner circle's reservations about the viability of the "guns and butter" program, see Dallek, *Flawed Giant*, 302. See also Irving Bernstein, *Guns or Butter: The Presidency of Lyndon Johnson* (New York: 1996).

23. Goodwin, *Remembering America*, 424.

24. Telegram from MLK to LBJ, January 12, 1966, WHCF, Name File MLK, box 144, LBJL. The *Baltimore Afro-American* disagreed that the State of the Union speech augured well for the Great Society; it believed the Vietnam War would inevitably force cutbacks in funding for many of the poverty programs. "Poverty and the War in Vietnam," *Baltimore Afro-American*, January 15, 1966, 15.

25. "Dr. King Will Occupy Chicago Slum Flat in New Rights Drive," *Chicago Defender*, January 8–14, 1966, 1.

26. Austin Werheim, "Dr. King Occupies a Flat in Slums," *New York Times*, January 27, 1966, 1.

27. "Bombing Pause Ended by LBJ," *Washington Post*, February 1, 1966, A1, A9.

28. See Randall Bennett Woods, *Fulbright: A Biography* (Cambridge: 1995).

29. "From Containment to Isolation," *Time*, February 18, 1966; Murray

Marder, "Kennan's Testimony: A Profound Challenge," *Washington Post*, February 11, 1966; "Scholarly Diplomat," *New York Times*, February 11, 1966.

30. Bryce Nelson, "Fulbright Sees Active Role in Vietnam," *Washington Post*, February 8, 1966, A10; Whitney Young Jr., "Liberals and Civil Rights," *New York Amsterdam News*, March 26, 1966, 12.

31. King quoted in Garrow, *Bearing the Cross*, 461.

32. Vincent Harding: "Vietnam: History, Judgment and Redemption," *Christianity and Crisis*, October 18, 1965, 215–17; Roger I. Shinn, "Pathways of Miscalculation," *Christianity and Crisis*, January 10, 1966, 289–90.

33. John C. Bennett, "From Supporter of War in 1940 to Critic in 1966," *Christianity and Crisis*, February 26, 1966, 13.

34. Reinhold Niebuhr and Ursula Niebuhr, "The Peace Offensive," *Christianity and Crisis*, January 24, 1966, 301–2.

35. See Michael Friedlander, *Lift up Your Voice Like a Trumpet: White Clergy and the Civil Rights and Antiwar Movements* (Chapel Hill, NC: 1998).

36. Letter to fellow clergy from Coffin, January 24, 1966, Papers of CALCAV, box 1, series 1, Swarthmore College Peace Collection, Swarthmore, PA.

37. See Mitchell K. Hall, *Because of Their Faith: CALCAV and Religious Opposition to the Vietnam War* (New York: 1990).

38. See Warren Goldstein, *William Sloane Coffin, Jr.: A Holy Impatience* (New Haven, CT: 2004).

39. Wells, *War Within*, 75.

40. Fager would later write a history of the Selma campaign. See Fager, *Selma 1965*.

41. Charles Fager, "Dilemma for Dr. King," *Christian Century*, March 16, 1966, 331–32.

42. Martin Luther King Jr., "Our Jewish Brother," *Chicago Defender*, March 5–11, 1966, 10.

43. Quoted in Jackson, *From Civil Rights to Human Rights*, 315.

44. Louis Harris, "The Harris Survey: Anti-Viet Stand Hurts Civil Rights Movement," *Washington Post*, April 11, 1966, A2.

45. "Dr. King in Stockholm," *New York Times*, April 1, 1966, 14; "Dr. King, Belafonte Are Swedish Heroes," *Chicago Defender*, April 4, 1966, 4.

46. Quoted in Branch, *At the Edge of Canaan*, 457.

47. Garrow, *Bearing the Cross*, 469–70.

48. Roy Reed, "Dr. King's Group Scores Ky Junta: Calls on Johnson to Weigh a Vietnam Withdrawal," *New York Times*, April 14, 1966, 1, 6; "Dr. King's Group Asks U.S. to Study Viet Pullout," *Washington Post*, April 14, 1966, A8.

49. "Statement on the War: Chicago," April 22, 1966, MLK Papers, box 10, MLKC.

50. See Branch, *At the Edge of Canaan*, 458.

51. "Is Integration Irrelevant?" *New Republic*, June 4, 1966, 4.

52. Nicolas von Hoffman, "King Terms SNCC Ideas 'Unrealistic,'" *Washington Post*, May 30, 1966, A1, A8.

53. Transcript of *Face the Nation*, May 29, 1966, MLK Papers, box 10, MLKC.

54. "Negro G.I. Is Buried at Andersonville," *New York Times*, May 31, 1966, 24.

55. Branch, *At the Edge of Canaan*, 470–72.

56. Rowland Evans and Robert Novak, "The Rights Conference—Better than Nothing," *Boston Globe*, June 7, 1966, 13.

57. See Young, *Easy Burden*, 412–13.

58. Robert G. Sherrill, "Bubble of Unreality," *Nation*, June 20, 1966, 736–38.

59. "The March Meredith Began," *Newsweek*, June 20, 1966, 27–30; Roy Reed, "Meredith Begins Mississippi Walk to Combat Fear," *New York Times*, June 6, 1966, 1, 27; Roy Reed, "Meredith Is Shot in Back on Walk into Mississippi," *New York Times*, June 7, 1966.

60. Garrow, *Bearing the Cross*, 475.

61. See Paul Good, "The Meredith March," *New South* (Summer 1966): 2–16.

62. Hampton and Fraser, *Voices of Freedom*, 285; Joseph, *Waiting 'til the Midnight Hour*, 132–38.

63. Gene Roberts, "Whites' Role Splits Leaders of March," *New York Times*, June 12, 1966, 1, 82; Martin Luther King Jr. *Where Do We Go from Here: Chaos or Community?* (Boston: 1968), 28.

64. Wilkins, *Standing Fast*, 315–16.

65. Young quoted in Hampton and Fraser, *Voices of Freedom*, 287.

66. Carson, *In Struggle*, 208.

67. Roy Reed, "Meredith Regrets He Was Not Armed," *New York Times*, June 8, 1966, 1, 26.

68. Gene Roberts, "Troopers Shove Group Resuming Meredith March," *New York Times*, June 8, 1966, 1, 26.

69. Sellers, *River of No Return*, 164–66.

70. Gene Roberts, "Mississippi Cuts Police Protection for Marchers," *New York Times*, June 17, 1966, 1, 33.

71. Joseph, *Waiting 'til the Midnight Hour*, 142.

72. Sellers, *River of No Return*, 167.

73. Quoted in Garrow, *Bearing the Cross*, 487–88.

74. MLK rally speech at Yazoo City, Mississippi, June 21, 1966, MLK Papers, box 10, MLKC.

75. King quoted in *Time*, July 1, 1966, 11.

76. King, *Where Do We Go from Here*, 51.

77. Gene Roberts, "Meredith Hailed at Rally at Mississippi Capitol," *New York Times*, June 27, 1966, 1, 29; "Mississippi Rights March Reaches Capitol; Discord Threatens Efforts of Major Groups," *Wall Street Journal*, June 27, 1966, clipping in Office Files of Frederick Panzer, box 330, LBJL; Good, "Meredith March."

78. Wilkins, *Standing Fast*, 315–16.

79. See Joseph, *Waiting 'til the Midnight Hour*, 146.

80. Gene Roberts, "Dr. King Declares Civil Rights Movement Is 'Close' to a Split," *New York Times*, July 9, 1966, 1, 9.

81. On Young in Vietnam, see Weiss, *Whitney M. Young*, 161.

82. "President's Annual Report to the SCLC," August 10, 1966, MLK Papers, box 11, MLKC.

83. Mike Royko, *Boss: Richard J. Daley of Chicago* (New York: 1971), 146.

84. For the most comprehensive study of the SCLC campaign in Chicago, see James R. Ralph Jr., *Martin Luther King, Chicago, and the Civil Rights Movement* (Cambridge, MA: 1993).

85. Young, *Easy Burden*, 381–84.

86. See D'Emilio, *Lost Prophet*, 454.

87. Martin Luther King, "Why We Are in Chicago," *New York Amsterdam News*, February 5 and March 12, 1966.

88. Lafayette quoted in Hampton and Fraser, *Voices of Freedom*, 299.

89. Young, *Easy Burden*, 406.

90. Gene Roberts, "Dr. King Stirs Chicago but Still Lacks a Program," *New York Times*, March 24, 1966, 33.

91. See Royko, *Boss*, 146–54.

92. "Thousands Go to Soldiers' Field Rights Rally," *Chicago Tribune*, July 11, 1966, 1.

93. Ralph, *King, Chicago, and the Civil Rights Movement*, 109–10.

94. Gene Roberts, "Whites in Chicago Mob Negro March," *New York Times*, August 8, 1966, 1, 55; "600 Police Halt Hecklers," *Chicago Tribune*, August 8, 1966, 1–2.

95. King quoted in Weisbrot, *Freedom Bound*, 183.

96. Tillman and Young quoted in Hampton and Fraser, *Voices of Freedom*, 312–13.

97. For a sampling of adverse reactions to the Chicago campaign, see Ralph, *King, Chicago, and the Civil Rights Movement*, 188–90.

98. Quoted in Matusow, *Unraveling of America*, 214.

99. "Backlash Is Found at a 4-Year Peak," *New York Times*, September 30, 1966, 39.

100. Fairclough, *To Redeem the Soul*, 279–301; John Herbers, "Rights Backers Fear a Backlash," *New York Times*, September 21, 1966, 1, 33.

101. Abernathy, *And the Walls*, 362.

102. Young, *Easy Burden*, 421.

103. On King's commitment to economic justice, see Jackson, *From Civil Rights to Human Rights*.

104. Speech to Frogmore planning meeting, November 14, 1966, MLK Papers, box 11, MLKC.

105. David C. Carter, *The Music Went out of the Movement: Civil Rights and the Johnson Administration* (Chapel Hill, NC: 2009).

106. Hampton and Fraser, *Voices of Freedom*, 335.

107. U.S. Senate Committee on Government Operations, Subcommittee on Executive Reorganization, *Federal Role in Urban Affairs* (Washington, DC: 1967), 2970; Robert B. Semple Jr., "Dr. King Scores Poverty Budget," *New York Times*, December 16, 1966, 33; Garrow, *Bearing the Cross*, 539.

108. "Valor Praised by Pentagon, Negroes Dying Faster than Whites in Vietnam," *New York Amsterdam News*, March 19, 1966, 1; "Negro Deaths Exceed Whites' in Vietnam," *Pittsburgh Courier*, May 28, 1966, 8; "Pct. of Negroes in Vietnam Could Rise," *Pittsburgh Courier*, September 3, 1966, 1, 4.

109. "Dr. King Will Write Book during Leave," *New York Times*, December 14, 1966, 42.

110. Branch, *At the Edge of Canaan*, 575.

111. "An Aid to Dr. King Appointed to Head New Antiwar Group," *New York Times*, January 28, 1967.

112. On the Nashville contingent of SNCC, see Halberstam, *The Children*.

113. Mack, "No 'Illusion of Separation,'" 108–33.

114. Diane Nash Bevel, "Journey to North Vietnam," *Freedomways* 6, no. 2 (Spring 1967): 118–28.

115. Young, *Easy Burden*, 425.

116. See David Halberstam, "The Second Coming of Martin Luther King," *Harper's Magazine*, August 1967, 39–51; Halstead, *Out Now!* 262–63.

117. Dellinger, *From Yale to Jail*, 261; Wells, *War Within*, 116.

118. Fairclough, *To Redeem the Soul*, 323.

119. Robert E. Baker, "Rights Coalition—Fractious, Fragmented," *Washington Post*, January 16, 1967, A1, A3.

120. DeBenedetti, *American Ordeal*, 171; Wells, *War Within*, 123.

121. "The Children of Vietnam," *Ramparts*, January 1967, 44–69.

122. Lee quoted in Garrow, *Bearing the Cross*, 543. See also Hampton and Fraser, *Voices of Freedom*, 342–43.

123. Martin Luther King Jr., "Beyond Vietnam," in Taylor, *Vietnam and Black America*, 79–98.

124. Oates, *Let the Trumpet Sound*, 413.

125. Halberstam, *The Children*, 537–38.

126. Bevel quoted in Branch, *At the Edge of Canaan*, 576.

127. King quoted in Fairclough, *To Redeem the Soul*, 335.

128. Young, *Easy Burden*, 425–26.

129. Friedly and Gallen, *Martin Luther King*, 553; Martin Luther King FBI Files, part II, reel 6, frame 000746, February 18, 1967.

130. Transcript of King's speech "The Casualties of the War in Vietnam," February 25, 1967, photocopies of SCLC Papers, reel 4, frame 0025 (accessed at the Doe Library, University of California–Berkeley).

131. Gladwin Hill, "Dr. King Advocates Quitting Vietnam," *New York Times*,

February 26, 1967, 1, 10; Richard Bergholz, "Conferees Assail Johnson's Policy on the Vietnam War," *Los Angeles Times*, February 26, 1967, 1–2.

132. Friedlander, *Lift up Your Voice*, 182.

133. Martin Luther King FBI Files, part II, reel 6, frame 000797, February 27, 1967.

134. Ibid., frame 000818, March 6, 1967.

135. Young, *Easy Burden*, 427.

136. Garrow, *Bearing the Cross*, 546.

137. On the March 6 meeting, see Branch, *At the Edge of Canaan*, 584.

138. "War Issue Saps LBJ's Strength," *Washington Post*, March 12, 1967, A6.

139. John Carmody, "Dr. King Pushes Shaw-Area Renewal," *Washington Post*, March 13, 1967, A1, A8.

140. Memo from MW to LBJ, February 24, 1967, WHCF, Name File MLK, box 144, LBJL.

141. Ibid., March 13 and 23, 1967.

142. Andrew Young Oral History, June 18, 1970, 17, LBJL.

143. Branch, *At the Edge of Canaan*, 586.

144. Douglas Robinson, "Dr. King to Play Leading Role in War Protest Here," *New York Times*, March 17, 1967, 4.

145. "Dr. King to Press Antiwar Stand," *New York Times*, March 24, 1967, 1, 7.

146. "Dr. King Leads Chicago Peace Rally," *New York Times*, March 26, 1967, 44; Ronald Berquist, "King Assails Viet Policy as Barbaric," *Washington Post*, March 26, 1967, A1, A10; statement of Martin Luther King, Chicago, March 24, 1967, MLK Papers, box 12, MLKC.

147. Quoted in Zaroulis and Sullivan, *Who Spoke Up?* 108.

148. "Dr. King to Weigh Civil Disobedience if War Intensifies," *New York Times*, April 2, 1967, 2.

149. Hampton and Fraser, *Voices of Freedom*, 343.

150. Young, *Easy Burden*, 428.

151. Hampton and Fraser, *Voices of Freedom*, 344.

152. See Branch, *At the Edge of Canaan*, 591.

153. Douglas Robinson, "Dr. King Proposes a Boycott of the War," *New York Times*, April 5, 1967, 1, 2.

154. Lewis, *Walking with the Wind*, 377.

155. King, "Beyond Vietnam," 79–82.

156. Ibid., 84–91.

157. Ibid., 93, 97.

158. "Where We Stand: An Editorial," *New York Amsterdam News*, April 15, 1967, 9.

159. "Dr. King's Tragic Doctrine," *Pittsburgh Courier*, April 15, 1967, 1.

160. Jackie Robinson, "An Open Letter to Dr. Martin L. King," *Chicago Defender*, May 13–19, 1967, 12; Jackie Robinson, "What I Think of Dr. Martin

Luther King," *New York Amsterdam News*, July 1, 1967, 17; Jackie Robinson, "Vote for LBJ on Issue of Vietnam," *Pittsburgh Courier*, October 28, 1967, 15.

161. "Brooke on Vietnam: U.S. Is Committed to Fight," *Pittsburgh Courier*, April 8, 1967; "Vocal Senator Brooke," *Pittsburgh Courier*, April 22, 1967; Edward Brooke, *Bridging the Divide: My Life* (New Brunswick, NJ: 2007), 164.

162. Bayard Rustin, "Dr. King's Painful Dilemma," *New York Amsterdam News*, April 22, 1967, 16.

163. Bayard Rustin, "Vietnam: Where I Stand," *New York Amsterdam News*, May 20, 1967, 16.

164. Memo from George Christian to LBJ, April 8, 1967, WHCF, Name File MLK, box 144, LBJL.

165. Carl Rowan, "Martin Luther King's Tragic Decision," *Reader's Digest*, September 1967, 37–42.

166. "Bunche Disputes King on Peace," *New York Times*, April 13, 1967, 1, 32; "Senator Brooke Puts Down MLK," May 22, 1967, MLK Papers, box 14, MLKC; "War-Rights Link Brings about Break," *New York Amsterdam News*, April 22, 1967, 1, 30.

167. "Dr. King's Inherent Rights," *Pittsburgh Courier*, May 27, 1967, 6.

168. "N.A.A.C.P. Decries Stand of Dr. King on Vietnam," *New York Times*, April 11, 1967, 1, 11.

169. Transcript of MLK press conference on NAACP stand, April 12, 1967, MLK Papers, box 12, MLKC.

170. "Urban League Head Hits King's Stand on War," *Washington Post*, April 6, 1967, A6.

171. Young, *Easy Burden*, 431. See also Weiss, *Whitney M. Young*, 151.

172. Kenneth Crawford, "King and the Soldiers," *Newsweek*, April 17, 1967, 46.

173. "Dr. King's Disservice to His Cause," *Life*, April 21, 1967, 4.

174. "A Tragedy," *Washington Post*, April 6, 1967, A20.

175. "Dr. King's Error," *New York Times*, April 7, 1967, 20.

176. Young, *Easy Burden*, 433.

177. Belafonte quoted in Hampton and Fraser, *Voices of Freedom*, 345–46.

178. Memo from Harry McPherson to LBJ, April 4, 1967, Office Files, McPherson, box 14, LBJL.

179. John P. Roche to LBJ, April 5, 1967, WHCF, box 56, LBJL.

180. Humphrey quoted in DeBenedetti, *American Ordeal*, 173.

181. Memo from Hoover to Watson, April 19, 1967, Office Files of Mildred Stegall, box 32, LBJL.

182. McKissick quoted in Oates, *Let the Trumpet Sound*, 423.

183. Dr. Benjamin E. Mayes, "Dr. King Is Sincere," *Pittsburgh Courier*, May 20, 1967, 6.

184. "Methodist Journal Lauds King's Anti-War Stand," *Chicago Defender*, May 13–19, 1967, 3.

185. "As We See It," *Detroit Free Press*, April 6, 1967.

186. Sam Washington, "Negro Opinion on Viet Is Shifting: Majority Favor Pull-out," *Chicago Defender*, April 22–28, 1967.

187. "With but One Voice," *Nation*, April 24, 1967, 515–16.

188. "MLK on His Role as Civil Rights Leader and His Opposition to Vietnam," April 5, 1967, MLK Papers, box 12, MLKC.

189. Martin Luther King FBI File, part II, reel 7, frame 000030, April 8, 1967.

190. Cotton cited in Garrow, *Bearing the Cross*, 602.

191. Douglass Robinson, "100,000 Rally at U.N. against Vietnam War," *New York Times*, April 16, 1967, 1–2.

192. "Negroes and the War," *World Journal Tribune*, April 18, 1967.

193. Paul Good, "On the March Again: New York," *Nation*, May 1, 1967, 550–52.

194. Halberstam, "Second Coming," 39.

195. Paul Hoffman, "50,000 at San Francisco Peace Rally," *New York Times*, April 16, 1967, 3.

196. "Speech to UN Rally Regarding Vietnam," April 15, 1967, MLK Papers, box 12, MLKC; transcript of *Face the Nation*," April 16, 1967, ibid.

197. Jackson, *From Civil Rights to Human Rights*.

198. "Why I Am Opposed to War in Vietnam," Ebenezer Church sermon, April 30, 1967, MLK Papers, box 12, MLKC.

199. Carmichael, *Ready for Revolution*, 518–19.

200. Sellers, *River of No Return*, 190–91; Gene Roberts, "Rights Leader Refuses to Be Inducted into Army," *New York Times*, May 2, 1965, 7; "SNCC Leader Refuses Oath," *Pittsburgh Courier*, May 13, 1967, 1, 11.

201. Carmichael quoted in Hampton and Fraser, *Voices of Freedom*, 348.

202. Halberstam, "Second Coming," 47– 48.

203. On the liberals' break with the war, see Wells, *War Within*, 135–38.

204. Dallek, *Flawed Giant*, 474.

205. Memo from Fred Panzer to LBJ, May 19, 1967, WHCF, Name File MLK, box 144, LBJL.

206. Eldridge, *Chronicles of a Two-Front War*, 112.

207. Quoted in Washington, "Negro Opinion on Viet Is Shifting," 1–2.

208. Martin Luther King Jr., *The Autobiography of Martin Luther King*, ed. Clayborne Carson (New York: 1998), 342.

209. Washington, "Negro Opinion on Viet Is Shifting," 1–2.

210. "The President's News Conference on the Tax Message," August 3, 1967, *Public Papers of the Presidents: LBJ*, 3:744.

211. James Forman, *High Tide of Black Resistance and Other Political & Literary Writings* (Seattle: 1998), 131.

212. See Kevin Mumford, *Newark: A History of Race, Rights, and Riots in America* (New York: 2007).

213. The most complete history of the 1967 Detroit uprising is Sidney Fine, *Violence in the Model City: The Cavanaugh Administration, Race Relations and the Detroit Riot of 1967* (Ann Arbor, MI: 1989).

214. Dallek, *Flawed Giant*, 415; Howard Schmeck Jr., "Rat Damage Is Put at a Billion a Year," *New York Times*, July 29, 1967, 9.

215. Telegram from MLK to LBJ, July 25, 1967, WHCF, Name File MLK, box 144, LBJL.

216. Quoted in Jackson, *From Civil Rights to Human Rights*, 334.

217. Quoted in Carson, *In Struggle*, 255.

218. "Carmichael Ask for Revolution in U.S." *New York Times*, August 18, 1967, 17.

219. Bloom and Martin, *Black against Empire*, 61, 67.

220. Garrow, *Bearing the Cross*, 571.

221. Jack Nelson, "SCLC to Seek Defeat of Pro-War Candidates," *Los Angeles Times*, August 18, 1967, 8.

222. On the NCNP convention, see Simon Hall, "On the Trail of the Panther: Black Power and the 1967 Convention of the National Conference for New Politics," *Journal of American Studies* 37, no. 1 (April 2003): 59–78.

223. Warren Weaver Jr., "Radicals Convene to Plan '68 Drive," *New York Times*, September 1, 1967, 15.

224. Branch, *At the Edge of Canaan*, 637.

225. On the background of the NCNP, see Hall, *Peace and Freedom*, 63–65; Zaroulis and Sullivan, *Who Spoke Up?* 128–29; DeBenedetti, *American Ordeal*, 191–92.

226. Warren Weaver Jr., "Whites and Negroes Split at New Politics Parley," *New York Times*, September 2, 1967, 10.

227. Warren Weaver Jr., "New-Politics Group Gives Equal Votes to Negro Minority," *New York Times*, September 4, 1967, 1, 15.

228. June Greenlief, "Static on the Left: Politics of Masquerade," *Village Voice*, October 12, 1967.

229. Renata Adler, "Letter from the Palmer House," *New Yorker*, September 23, 1967; Richard Blumenthal, "New Politics at Chicago," *Nation*, September 25, 1967; Walter Goodman, "Yessir Boss, Said the White Radicals," *New York Times*, September 24, 1967, 257.

230. Halstead, *Out Now!* 320.

231. Quoted in Fairclough, "King and the War in Vietnam," 35.

232. See Cheryl Greenberg, *Troubling Waters: Black-Jewish Relations in the American Century* (Princeton, NJ: 2006), chap. 6.

233. "Anti-Semitism Held Immoral by Dr. King," *New York Times*, October 11, 1967, 59.

234. See Hall, *Peace and Freedom*, 111–20; Branch, *At the Edge of Canaan*, 638–40.

235. Fairclough, *To Redeem the Soul*, 358–59.

236. On Wright's persuasiveness, see Young, *Easy Burden*, 437–38.

237. Paul Hathaway, "King Warns New Rioting Risks Right-Wing Backlash," *Washington Star*, February 8, 1968.

238. On SCLC divisions over the Poor People's Campaign, see Andrew Young quoted in Hampton and Fraser, *Voices of Freedom*, 455.

239. Walter Rugaber, "Dr. King Planning to Disrupt Capital in Drive for Jobs," *New York Times*, December 4, 1967, 1, 32.

240. Wilson quoted in Zaroulis and Sullivan, *Who Spoke Up?* 137.

241. Norman Mailer, *The Armies of the Night: History as a Novel, the Novel as History* (New York: 1968), 109.

242. Joseph Loftus, "Guards Repulse War Protesters at the Pentagon," *New York Times*, October 22, 1967, 1, 58; Halstead, *Out Now!* 333.

243. Quoted in Zaroulis and Sullivan, *Who Spoke Up?* 151–52.

244. Dallek, *Flawed Giant*, 506.

245. See Horace Busby, *The Thirty-First of March: An Inside Portrait of Lyndon Johnson's Final Days in Office* (New York: 2005).

246. Martin Luther King Jr., "Honoring Dr. Du Bois," *Freedomways* 7, no. 2 (Spring 1968): 104–11.

247. On King's final weeks, see Honey, *Going down Jericho Road.*

248. "The Need of All Humanity," *New York Times*, April 5, 1968, 4.

249. "Looting in Washington," *New York Times*, April 5, 1968.

250. Honey, *Going down Jericho Road*, 444.

251. "President's Plea: On TV, He Deplores 'Brutal' Murder of Negro Leader," *New York Times*, April 5, 1968, 1

252. "Rampage and Restraint," *Time*, April 19, 1968, 46. For a detailed study, see Clay Risen, *A Nation on Fire: America in the Wake of the King Assassination* (New York: 2009).

253. Honey, *Going down Jericho Road*, 450.

254. "Mrs. King Reads War Decalogue," *New York Times*, April 28, 1968, 73.

255. Westheider, *Fighting on Two Fronts*, 98.

256. Terry, *Bloods*, 167.

257. King, *My Life*, 327.

258. Harding, *Martin Luther King*, x.

7. Moderates and the Vietnam War

The epigraph is quoted in Martin Arnold, "Rights Leaders Hold Unity Talks; Map Efforts to Ease Tension in Cleveland," *New York Times*, June 15, 1967, 31.

1. Langston Hughes, *The Dream Keeper* (New York: 1946), 76.

2. Hall, *Peace and Freedom*, 80–104.

3. Hall, "Response of the Moderate Wing"; Berg, "Guns, Butter, and Civil Rights."

4. Berg, *Ticket to Freedom*, 116–39.

5. Simeon Booker, "Negroes in Vietnam: 'We, Too, Are Americans,'" *Ebony*, November 1965, 89–98.

6. On the image of the "good soldier," see Westheider, *Fighting on Two Fronts*, 8–17.

7. On NAACP policy during the Vietnam years, see Berg, "Guns, Butter, and Civil Rights," 213–38.

8. See O'Reilly, *Racial Matters.*

9. Sullivan, *Lift Every Voice.*

10. Quoted in Dudziak, *Cold War Civil Rights*, 29.

11. Berg, *Ticket to Freedom*, 110, 138.

12. See Anderson, *Eyes off the Prize.*

13. Ibid., 161.

14. Sullivan, *Lift Every Voice*, 374.

15. Ibid., 373–75.

16. Anderson, *Eyes off the Prize*, 167.

17. Wilkins, *Standing Fast*, 210.

18. Letter from Wilkins to Reynolds, March 11, 1957, NAACP Papers, group 3, box A76, LOC; excerpts from Hoover, *Masters of Deceit*, clipping in ibid.

19. Garrow, *Bearing the Cross*, 52; Wilkins, *Standing Fast*, 228.

20. Wilkins, *Standing Fast*, 237.

21. Branch, *Parting the Waters*, 217.

22. Farmer, *Lay Bare the Heart*, 216.

23. Ransby, *Ella Baker*, 241–47.

24. Quoted in memo from James Farmer to Wilkins regarding the meeting with Ella Baker and company, June 10, 1960, NAACP Papers, group 3, box A212, LOC.

25. Memo from Herbert Wright to Wilkins and Current, May 3, 1961, NAACP Papers, group 3, box A201, LOC.

26. Quoted in Carson, *In Struggle*, 23.

27. Roy Wilkins, "Lost Victory in Atlantic City," *New York Amsterdam News*, September 5, 1964, 18.

28. Quoted in Branch, *Pillar of Fire*, 496.

29. Roy Wilkins Oral History, April 1, 1969, 1, LBJL.

30. Letter from LBJ to Wilkins, November 30, 1963, WHCF, Name File Roy Wilkins, box 312, LBJL.

31. Quoted in Hall, *Peace and Freedom*, 91.

32. "Freedom House Award," March 29, 1967, Roy Wilkins Papers, box 25, LOC; Edward C. Burks, "Roy Wilkins Receives Freedom Award of 1967," *New York Times*, March 30, 1967, 50.

33. "Executive Board Resolution on Vietnam," April 10, 1965, NAACP Papers, group 3, box A328, LOC.

34. Telegram from Morsell to Flint Branch, April 14, 1965, ibid. On the close relationship between Morsell and Wilkins, see Gilbert Jonas, *Freedom's Sword: The NAACP and the Struggle against Racism in America, 1909–1969* (New York: 2004), 344.

35. Memo from Current to Staff, April 14, 1965, NAACP Papers, group 3, box A328, LOC. See also Hall, *Peace and Freedom*, 94–95; Berg, "Guns, Butter, and Civil Rights," 215.

36. Memo from Current to Staff, April 22, 1965, NAACP Papers, group 3, box A328, LOC.

37. Ibid.

38. Memo from Wilkins, July 30, 1965, NAACP Papers, group 3, box A328, LOC.

39. "NAACP Disassociates Itself from Attack on Vietnam Policy," *New York Times*, January 9, 1966, 4.

40. "SNCC's Foreign Policy," January 16, 1966, Roy Wilkins Papers, box 39, folder newspaper column clippings, LOC.

41. Memo from Humphrey to Califano, January 22, 1966, WHCF, Name File, box 630, LBJL.

42. Louis Harris, "The Harris Survey: Anti-Viet Stand Hurts Civil Rights Movement," *Washington Post*, April 11, 1966, A2.

43. On Wilkins's Red-baiting, see Anderson, *Eyes off the Prize*, 166–209.

44. Letter from Henry S. Smith to Wilkins, January 15, 1966, NAACP Papers, group 4, box A88, LOC.

45. Letter from Wilkins to Smith, January 25, 1966, ibid.

46. Letter from Victor M. Sidell to Wilkins, March 5, 1966, photocopies of NAACP Papers, part 28, reel 7, frame 185 (accessed at the Doe Library, University of California–Berkeley).

47. Letter from Henry Wallace to Wilkins, January 17, 1966, ibid., reel 11, frame 0743.

48. Memo from George Field to Board of NAACP, November 5, 1965, NAACP Papers, group 3, box A328, LOC.

49. Roy Wilkins, "Civil Rights Being Hurt," *New York Amsterdam News*, December 12, 1965, 16.

50. Berg, *Ticket to Freedom*, 241.

51. Ibid., 225.

52. Hall, *Peace and Freedom*, 93–94.

53. Memo to Staff from Wilkins, March 3, 1966, Roy Wilkins Papers, box 7, LOC.

54. Memo from Current to Wilkins, March 3, 1966, ibid.

55. Memo from McPherson to LBJ, May 12, 1966, Office Files of Harry McPherson, box 22, LBJL.

56. Carter, *Music Went out of the Movement*, 91–92.

57. Memo from Current to Staff, April 14, 1966, NAACP Papers, group 4, box A88, LOC.

58. Ibid. See also Berg, "Guns, Butter, and Civil Rights," 221.

59. "Greenwich Village Chelsea Branch's Resolution," April 27, 1966, NAACP Papers, group 4, box A88, LOC.

60. Wilkins statement about King, photocopies of NAACP Papers, part 28, series B, reel 11, frame 526.

61. Memo from Cohen to Current, May 8, 1967, ibid.

62. Letter from Kroll to Wilkins, April 11, 1967, NAACP Papers, group 4, box A88, LOC.

63. Letter from Franklin to Wilkins, April 21, 1967, photocopies of NAACP Papers, part 28, series B, reel 13, frame 0818.

64. Memo from Clifford Alexander to LBJ, April 28, 1967, WHCF, Name File MLK, box 144, LBJL; memo from Current to Wilkins, April 16, 1967, photocopies of NAACP Papers, part 28, series B, reel 14, frames 0053–56.

65. M. S. Handler, "Wilkins Foes Ask More Militancy," *New York Times*, July 13, 1967, 25.

66. "Critics of Wilkins Set up Picket Line at N.A.A.C.P. Talk," *New York Times*, July 14, 1967, 30.

67. George Collins, "NAACP 'Old Guard' Holds Reins on Balance of Power," *Baltimore Afro-American*, July 22, 1967, 8.

68. Earl Caldwell, "N.A.A.C.P. Division Decries the War," *New York Times*, September 11, 1967, 15.

69. "Wilkins Is Urged to Resign by 3 N.A.A.C.P. Leaders," *New York Times*, November 12, 1968, 35.

70. Survey cited in Berg, *Ticket to Freedom*, 241.

71. "Angry—But They Still Have a Dream," *Newsweek*, June 30, 1969, 20.

72. Letter from Barbara Schaaf to Roy Wilkins, June 26, 1968, NAACP Papers, group 4, box A37, LOC; Thomas A. Johnson, "Wilkins Assails McCarthy Visit to Atlantic City as 'Intruding,'" *New York Times*, June 28, 1968, 23.

73. Thomas A. Johnson, "N.A.A.C.P. Youths Quit Convention," *New York Times*, June 29, 1968, 29.

74. Thomas A. Johnson, "N.A.A.C.P. Is Facing Showdown on Ouster," *New York Times*, November 24, 1968, 81; "Quit-in at the N.A.A.C.P.," *Time*, November 8, 1968, 57.

75. Letter from Eugene T. Reed to Wilkins, November 1, 1968, NAACP Papers, group 4, box A11, LOC.

76. Roy Wilkins, "The Late Dr. King . . . and Human Dignity," *New York Amsterdam News*, April 13, 1968, 20.

77. Wilkins, *Standing Fast*, 333.

78. Martin Arnold, "NAACP Decides It Has a New Enemy," *New York Times*, July 5, 1970, 91.

79. Thomas A. Johnson, "N.A.A.C.P. Young Turks Now Salute Wilkins," *New York Times*, July 5, 1969, 23.

80. Louis Harris and associates, *The Harris Survey Yearbook of Popular Opinion: 1970* (New York: 1971), 110–21.

81. On the joint NUL-NAACP demand to end the war, see DeBenedetti, *American Ordeal*, 286.

82. Wilkins quoted in Berg, "Guns, Butter, and Civil Rights," 228.

83. Clifford Alexander Oral History, November 1, 1971, 15, LBJL.

84. Wilkins quoted in Jack Foner, *Blacks and the Military in American History: A New Perspective* (New York: 1974), 259.

85. Quoted in Weisbrot, *Freedom Bound*, 166.

86. "Urban League's Whitney Young," *Time*, August 11, 1967.

87. Quoted in Aaron Taylor, "Whitney Young Tribute Held at Spelman," *Atlanta Constitution*, March 18, 1971, 2.

88. Weiss, *Whitney M. Young*, 34. On Young's childhood, see Dickerson, *Militant Mediator*, 24–34.

89. Weiss, *Whitney M. Young*, 99–106.

90. Whitney Young Oral History, June 18, 1969, 1, 9, LBJL.

91. Fred Powledge, "Young of the Urban League Says Negroes Seek Lasting Changes," *New York Times*, August 3, 1965, 16.

92. Quoted in John Herbers, "Rights Conference Averts Showdown on War Policy," *New York Times*, June 3, 1966, 21.

93. Whitney Young, "Liberals and Civil Rights," *New York Amsterdam News*, March 26, 1966, 12.

94. Transcript of NBC News *Meet the Press*, August 21, 1966, 20, McCabe Library, Swarthmore College.

95. Memo from CA to LBJ, January 7, 1966, WHCF, Name File MLK, box 144, LBJL.

96. Statement to the press by Whitney Young, July 18, 1966, Whitney Young Jr. Papers, box 209, Rare Book and Manuscript Library, Columbia University.

97. "Whitney Young Tours Vietnam," *New York Times*, July 22, 1966, 4; "Army Opportunities Lure Negroes into Military, Young Says," *Chicago Defender*, June 10, 1967, 14. See also Weiss, *Whitney M. Young*, 160–61.

98. "Whitney Young, Report from Vietnam," *New York Amsterdam News*, July 30, 1966, 1, 2; "Whitney Young, Report from Vietnam," *New York Amsterdam News*, August 27, 1966, 14.

99. "Young Says Negro Morale Is High, but Is It?" *Pittsburgh Courier*, August 6, 1966, 3.

100. McKissick quoted in ibid.

101. Memo from Joe Califano to LBJ, July 25, 1966, Name File Whitney Young Jr., box, 41, LBJL.

102. See Dickerson, *Militant Mediator*, 272–74; Weiss, *Whitney M. Young*, 161.

103. John Finney, "President Backs Negro Promotion," *New York Times*, July 27, 1966, 24.

104. Quoted in Hall, *Peace and Freedom*, 103.

105. M. S. Handler, "Whitney Young Urges Attempt Be Made to Reach Ghetto 'Unreachables,'" *New York Times*, August 1, 1966, 14.

106. See Whitney M. Young Jr., "When the Negroes in Vietnam Come Home," *Harper's*, June 1967, 63–69.

107. Robert H. Phelps, "20 Observers Going to Vietnam to Watch Voting," *New York Times*, August 24, 1967, 1.

108. "Young Cites Freedom to 'Die in Vietnam,'" *New York Times*, August 26, 1967.

109. "Urban League Head Hits King's Stand on the War," *Washington Post*, April 6, 1967, 6.

110. See David Halberstam, "The Second Coming of Martin Luther King," *Harper's Magazine*, August 1967, 49; Young, *Easy Burden*, 43; Weiss, *Whitney M. Young*, 151.

111. "22 U.S. Observers Arrive in Saigon," *Washington Post*, August 31, 1967, A16.

112. "Premier Ky in Saigon Denies that He Called Hitler His Hero," *New York Times*, July 16, 1965, 3.

113. "Background Papers: VC Plans for Sept. 3, Elections," Papers of Whitney M. Young, box 8, Columbia University.

114. Thomas A. Buckley, "Some U.S. Observers Praise Voting Preparations," *New York Times*, September 2, 1967, 6.

115. "The White House Myopia," *Pittsburgh Courier*, September 2, 1967, 17.

116. Max Frankel, "Observers Tell Johnson South Vietnam's Election Was Fair," *New York Times*, September 7, 1967, 3.

117. "The Test of Time," *Newsweek*, September 11, 1967, 31.

118. R. W. Apple Jr., "Thieu's Power at Polls: Dispute over Rigging Fails to Take His Built-in Advantage into Account," *New York Times*, September 6, 1967, 2; William Tuohy, "Assembly Pledges Investigation of Election Charges: Voting Inquiry," *Los Angeles Times*, September 11, 1967, 1.

119. Carroll Kirkpatrick, "Election Observers Make Favorable Report to Johnson," *Washington Post*, September 7, 1967, A30.

120. See Young, *Easy Burden*, 431.

121. Quoted in Weiss, *Whitney M. Young*, 163.

122. Quoted in "Races," *Time*, August 11, 1967, 13.

123. Tom Buckley, "Whitney Young: Black Leader or 'Oreo Cookie'?" *New York Times Magazine*, September 20, 1970, 275.

124. Weiss, *Whitney M. Young*, 168.

125. Young, *Easy Burden*, 431.

126. Whitney Young Oral History, June 18, 1969, 12, LBJL.

127. Thomas A. Johnson, "Whitney Young, Ending Silence Condemns War," *New York Times*, October 14, 1969, 24; Whitey Young Jr., "To Be Equal: Moratorium Day Message Was Loud and Clear: Let's Get Out," *Baltimore Afro-American*, October 25, 1969, 4.

128. Whitney Young Jr., "To Be Equal: The Economic Recession Could Be Ended by Quitting Vietnam," *Baltimore Afro-American*, August 1, 1970, 4.

129. "Young Blacks Criticize League," *Washington Post*, July 31, 1969, C3.

130. Carroll Kirkpatrick, "Negro Leader Conciliatory on Nixon," *Washington Post*, November 16, 1968, A1.

131. Weiss, *Whitney M. Young*, 210–11.

132. "Tributes Are Paid to Whitney Young," *New York Times*, March 12, 1971, 41.

133. Quoted in Weiss, *Whitney M. Young*, 222.

134. Levine, *Bayard Rustin*, 194.

135. Reminiscences of Bayard Rustin, February 1985, 64, CUOHC.

136. See Jervis Anderson, *Bayard Rustin: Troubles I've Seen* (New York: 1997); Levine, *Bayard Rustin*; D'Emilio, *Lost Prophet*.

137. See Arsenault, *Freedom Riders*, 12–55; Derek Catsam, *Freedom's Main Line: The Journey of Reconciliation and the Freedom Rides* (Lexington, KY: 2008), 13–46.

138. Raines, *My Soul Is Rested*, 55–56.

139. See O'Reilly, *Racial Matters*.

140. On Wilkins's opposition to Rustin heading the March on Washington, see Branch, *Parting the Waters*, 846–47. Rustin and A. Philip Randolph appeared on the cover of the September 6, 1963, edition of *Life* magazine.

141. See "On the March," *Newsweek*, September 2, 1963, 18, including the photo captioned "Out of the Shadows."

142. "1,000 Here Mark Hiroshima Bomb," *New York Times*, August 7, 1964, 3.

143. D'Emilio, *Lost Prophet*, 408; Zaroulis and Sullivan, *Who Spoke Up?* 20.

144. Levine, *Bayard Rustin*, 128–29.

145. Hall, *Peace and Freedom*, 83.

146. John D'Emilio, "Homophobia and the Trajectory of Postwar American Radicalism: The Career of Bayard Rustin," *Radical History Review* 62 (Spring 1995): 80–103.

147. Daniel Perlstein, "The Dead End of Despair, Bayard Rustin, the 1968 New York School Crisis, and the Struggle for Racial Justice," *African Americans in New York Life and History* 31 (Summer 2007): 89–120.

148. Halstead, *Out Now!* 20–21.

149. David Dellinger Oral History, December 10, 1982, 3, LBJL.

150. Reminiscences of Bayard Rustin, April 3, 1985, 169–70, CUOHC.

151. Carson, *In Struggle*, 93. For Lewis's view of Rustin's editing of his speech, see Lewis, *Walking with the Wind*, 220.

152. See Forman, *Making of Black Revolutionaries*, 389; Sellers, *River of No Return*, 109.

153. Levine, *Bayard Rustin*, 169.

154. See Farmer, *Lay Bare the Heart*, 299; R. W. Apple Jr., "Negro Leaders Split over Call to Curtail Drive," *New York Times*, July 31, 1964, 1, 11.

155. Jack Anderson, "What Next for Negroes?" *Washington Post*, November 15, 1964, E7.

156. Bayard Rustin, "From Protest to Politics: The Future of the Civil Rights Movement," *Commentary*, February 1965, 25–31.

157. Ibid.

158. Carmichael, *Stokely Speaks*, 25.

159. See Sugrue, *Origins of the Urban Crisis*.

160. For a trilogy of local studies on the white backlash which contend it was not monolithic or solely motivated by racial animus, see Jonathan Reider, *Canarsie: The Jews and Italians of Brooklyn against Liberalism* (Cambridge, MA: 1985); Ronald P. Formisano, *Boston against Busing: Race, Class, and Ethnicity in the 1960s and 1970s* (Chapel Hill, NC: 1991); Kenneth Durr, *Behind the Backlash: White Working-Class Politics in Baltimore, 1940–1980* (Chapel Hill, NC: 2003).

161. For racism in organized labor, see Paul Buhle, *Taking Care of American Business: Samuel Gompers, George Meany, Lane Kirkland and the Tragedy of American Labor* (New York: 1999).

162. See Peter B. Levy, *The New Left, Labor, in the 1960s* (Urbana, IL: 1994); David Roediger, *The Wages of Whiteness: Race and the Making of the American Working Class* (New York: 1991).

163. Levy, *New Left, Labor.*

164. See Murray Friedman, *What Went Wrong? The Creation and Collapse of the Black-Jewish Alliance* (New York: 1994).

165. Rustin, "From Protest to Politics," 59–65.

166. Staughton Lynd, "Coalition Politics or Non-Violent Revolution?" *Liberation*, June 1965, 18–21.

167. Letter from Lynd to Rustin, April 19, 1965, photocopies of Papers of Bayard Rustin, reel 21, frame 0346.

168. David Dellinger, "The March on Washington and Its Critics," *Liberation*, May 1965, 6–7, 31.

169. Quoted in Dittmer, *Local People*, 302.

170. Quoted in Fred Powledge, "Vietnam Issue Divides Leaders of Rights Groups," *New York Times*, August 29, 1965, E4.

171. Memo from James Booker to Clifford Alexander, Edward Sylvester Jr., and Louis Martin, May 3, 1966, Office Files of Harry McPherson, box 22, LBJL.

172. Quoted in D'Emilio, *Lost Prophet*, 446.

173. "Rustin Calls Black Power a Negative Negro Concept," *New York Times*, October 16, 1966.

174. D'Emilio, *Lost Prophet*, 444–45.

175. "$185 Billion on Freedom Drive Is Launched: Budget Called Urgent," *New York Amsterdam News*, October 29, 1966, 1; "185 Billion Freedom Fund Urged," *Baltimore Afro-American*, November 5, 1966, 1.

176. Letter from Seymour Melman to Benjamin Spock, Norman Thomas, and Rustin, November 1, 1966, photocopies of Papers of Bayard Rustin, reel 13, frame 0556.

177. Letter from Rustin to Irving Howe, November 11, 1966, ibid., frame 0189.

178. Memo from Rustin to LBJ, July 31, 1967, Name File Bayard Rustin, box 347, LBJL.

179. Bayard Rustin, "Vietnam: Where I Stand," *New York Amsterdam News*, May 20, 1967, 16.

180. Bayard Rustin, "Guns, Bread and Butter," in Rustin, *Down the Line*, 168.

181. Bayard Rustin, "Dr. King's Painful Dilemma," *New York Amsterdam News*, April 22, 1967, 14.

182. Quoted in Finn, *Protest, Pacifism and Politics*, 330.

183. Reminiscences of Bayard Rustin, February 1985, 96, CUOHC.

184. Levine, *Bayard Rustin*, 134; Branch, *Parting the Waters*, 846.

185. Reminiscences of Bayard Rustin, May 8, 1985, 212, CUOHC.

186. "Rights Leader Issues Stern Warning Here," *Chicago Defender*, March 19, 1968, 3.

187. Rustin, "Dr. King's Painful Dilemma," 16; "Rights Leader Hits Dr. King's Viet Tactics," *Chicago Tribune*, April 15, 1967, 8.

188. Wachtel and Levison quoted in Fairclough, *To Redeem the Soul*, 339.

189. Levine, *Bayard Rustin*, 203.

190. Godfrey Hodgson, *America in Our Time: From World War II to Nixon— What Happened and Why* (New York: 1976), 284.

191. Quoted in Thomas R. Brooks, "A Strategist without a Movement," *New York Times Magazine*, February 16, 1969, 24.

192. Levine, *Bayard Rustin*, 216–17.

193. Quoted in D'Emilio, *Lost Prophet*, 479.

194. Dellinger, *From Yale to Jail*, 219–20.

195. Pfeffer, *A. Philip Randolph*, 278–79.

196. See Arnesen, "No Graver Danger" 15.

197. Hall, *Peace and Freedom*, 88–90.

198. Pfeffer, *A. Philip Randolph*, 281.

199. A. Philip Randolph Oral History, October 29, 1969, LBJL.

200. Berg, *Ticket to Freedom*, 246–48.

201. Eldridge, *Chronicles of a Two-Front War*, 162.

202. Manfred Berg, a sympathetic chronicler of the NAACP, castigates it for its hypocrisy and opportunism. See Berg, "Guns, Butter and Civil Rights," 231.

Conclusion

1. Hall, *Peace and Freedom*, 187.

2. Borstelmann, *Cold War and the Color Line*, 226.

3. Quoted in Hugh Davis Graham, *The Civil Rights Era: Origins and Development of National Policy, 1960–1972* (New York: 1990), 304.

4. Bloom and Martin, *Black against Empire*, 202, 210; O'Reilly, *Racial Matters*, 298.

5. Harris and associates, *Harris Survey Yearbook of Public Opinion, 1970*, 110–21.

6. Ollie L. Johnson III and Karin L. Stanford, eds., *Black Political Organizations in the Post–Civil Rights Era* (New Brunswick, NJ: 2002), 205.

7. C. Gerald Fraser, "Wilkins Puts Nixon with Foes of Blacks," *New York Times*, May 25, 1972.

8. *The Gallup Opinion Index* (Princeton, NJ: 1972), 20.

9. "Peace in Vietnam Hailed in Harlem: War Took Heavy Toll on Blacks," *New York Amsterdam News*, January 27, 1973, A1.

10. Quoted in Dallek, *Flawed Giant*, 621.

11. Quoted in David L. Chappell, "Civil Rights: Grass Roots, High Politics, or Both?" *Reviews in American History* 32, no. 4 (Fall 2004): 566.

12. Dallek, *Flawed Giant*, 623.

13. Hugh Graham Davis, "Richard Nixon and Civil Rights: Explaining an Enigma," *Presidential Studies Quarterly* 26, no. 1 (Winter 1996): 93–106.

14. Ethel Payne, "Caucus Blasts Nixon's War: Demands He Explain," *Chicago Defender*, May 11, 1972, 2; "Caucus Hits War Escalation: Initiates Impeachment Drive," *Baltimore Afro-American*, May 20, 1972, 6.

15. Robert C. Maynard, "Hill's Blacks Offer Nixon 60 Plans," *Washington Post*, March 26, 1971, A1.

16. William Greider, "Atrocity Hearings Ended by Dellums," *Washington Post*, April 30, 1971, A3.

17. Peter Levy, "Blacks and the Vietnam War," in Shafer, *The Legacy*, 238–39.

18. Shin Chiba and Thomas J. Schoenbaum, eds., *Peace Movements and Pacifism after September 11* (Northampton, MA: 2008), 212.

19. Robert D. Schulzinger, *A Time for Peace: The Legacy of the Vietnam War* (New York: 2006).

20. Quoted in Myra McPherson, *Long Time Passing: Vietnam and the Haunted Generation* (New York: 1984), 571.

21. U.S. House of Representatives, Committee on Veterans Affairs, *Legacies of Vietnam: Comparative Adjustment of Veterans and Their Peers: A Study Prepared for the Veterans' Administration, March 9, 1981* (Washington, DC: 1981), 358.

22. Patrick Hagopian, *The Vietnam War in American Memory: Veterans, Memory, and the Politics of Healing* (Amherst, MA: 2009).

23. Nalty, *Strength for the Fight*, 326–32.

24. See Ira Katznelson, *When Affirmative Action Was White* (New York: 2005), 7; commencement address at Howard University: "To Fulfill These Rights," June 4, 1965, *Public Papers of the Presidents: LBJ*, 3:635–40.

25. Jennifer Hochschild, *Facing up to the American Dream: Race, Class, and the Soul of the Nation* (Princeton, NJ: 1995), 94–98.

26. Joseph Crespino, *In Search of Another Country: Mississippi and the Conservative Counterrevolution* (Princeton, NJ: 2007), 1; Douglas Kneeland, "Reagan Campaigns at Mississippi Fair," *New York Times*, August 4, 1980, A11.

27. Quoted in Hixson, *George F. Kennan*, 236.

Bibliography

Archives and Manuscript Collections

Columbia University, New York, New York

Oral Histories: Anne Braden, Edwin King, Bayard Rustin, Roy Wilkins
Papers of Whitney M. Young Jr., Butler Library, Rare Book and Manuscript Division

Lyndon Baines Johnson Presidential Library, Austin, Texas

Manuscript Collections
Confidential Name File
Office Files of Harry McPherson
Office Files of Bill Moyers
Office Files of Mildred Stegall
Office Files of Lee White
To Fulfill These Rights
White House Central Files (WHCF)
    Confidential Files
    Gen Pl—St. 24
    Name File

Oral Histories
Clifford Alexander
David Dellinger
James Farmer
Albert Fitt
Clarence Mitchell
A. Philip Randolph
Roy Wilkins
Andrew Young Jr.
Whitney Young Jr.

Recordings of Telephone Conversations—White House Series

LBJ and Martin Luther King Jr., July 7, 1965. Tape WH6507.02 [citation #8313]
LBJ and Martin Luther King Jr., August 20, 1965. Tape WH6508.07 [citation #8578]

Martin Luther King Jr. Center for Nonviolent Social Change, Atlanta, Georgia

Julian Bond Papers
Congress of Racial Equality Papers
Martin Luther King Jr. Papers
Martin Luther King Jr. Papers Series III: Speeches, Sermons, Articles, Statements
Mississippi Freedom Democratic Party Papers
Southern Christian Leadership Conference Papers
Student Nonviolent Coordinating Committee Papers

Library of Congress, Manuscript Division, Washington, D.C.

National Association for the Advancement of Colored People Records
Roy Wilkins Papers

Schomburg Center for Research in Black Culture, New York Public Library

Robert S. Browne Papers

State Historical Society of Wisconsin, Madison

Staughton Lynd Papers
Students for Democratic Society Records, 1958–1970
Howard Zinn Papers

Swarthmore College, McCabe Library—Swarthmore College Peace Collection, Swarthmore, Pennsylvania

Clergy and Laymen Concerned about Vietnam Papers
National Mobilization Committee to End the War in Vietnam Records

Face the Nation *Collected Transcripts*

The Johnson Presidential Press Conferences

Meet the Press *Collected Transcripts*

Microfilms

The Martin Luther King Jr. FBI Files, ed. David J. Garrow. Bethesda, MD: University Publications of America Microfilms, 1984.
The Bayard Rustin Papers. Introduction by John H. Bracey and August Meier. Guide compiled by Nanette Dobroasky. Frederick, MD: University Publications of America Microfilms, 1988.
The Southern Christian Leadership Conference. Part 1. Records of the President's Office. Bethesda, MD: University Publications of America Microfilms, 1995.

The Student Non-Violent Coordinating Committee Papers, 1959–1972. Micro-
filming Corporation of America, 1982.

Books and Articles

Abernathy, Ralph David. *And the Walls Came Tumbling Down.* New York: Harper,
1989.

Acheson, Dean. *Present at the Creation: My Years in the State Department.* New
York: W. W. Norton, 1969.

Aldridge, Daniel W., III. "A War for the Colored Races: Anti-interventionism
and the African American Intelligentsia." *Diplomatic History* 28, no. 3 (June
2004): 321–53.

Ali, Muhammad. *The Greatest: My Own Story.* New York: Hart-Davis MacGib-
bon, 1975.

Anderson, Carol. *Eyes off the Prize: African Americans, the United Nations, and
the Struggle for Civil Rights, 1944–1955.* Cambridge: Cambridge University
Press, 2003.

Anderson, David L. *Trapped by Success: The Eisenhower Administration and
Vietnam, 1953–1961.* New York: Oxford University Press, 1991.

Anderson, Jervis. *A. Philip Randolph: A Biographical Portrait.* New York: Har-
vest Books, 1972.

———. *Bayard Rustin: Troubles I've Seen.* New York: HarperCollins, 1997.

Anderson, Terry H. *The Movement and the Sixties: Protest in America from
Greensboro to Wounded Knee.* New York: Oxford University Press, 1995.

Anthony, David Henry, III. *Max Yergan: Race Man, Internationalist, Cold Warrior.* New York: NYU Press, 2006.

Appy, Christian G. *Working Class War: American Combat Soldiers and Vietnam.*
Chapel Hill: University of North Carolina Press, 1993.

Arnesen, Eric. "'No Graver Danger': Black Anti-Communism, the Communist
Party, and the Race Issue." *Labor: Studies in Working Class History of the
Americas* 3, no. 4 (Winter 2006): 13–52.

———. "Reconsidering the Long Movement." *Historically Speaking* 10, no. 2
(April 2009): 31–34.

Arsenault, Raymond. *Freedom Riders: 1961 and the Struggle for Racial Justice.*
New York: Oxford University Press, 2006.

Austin, Curtis J. *Up against the Wall: Violence in the Making and Unmaking of
the Black Panther Party.* Fayetteville: University of Arkansas Press, 2006.

Baldwin, James. *The Fire Next Time.* New York: Dell, 1963.

Baraka, Amiri. *The Autobiography of LeRoi Jones.* New York: Freundlich Books, 1984.

Barber, David. *A Hard Rain Fell: SDS and Why It Failed.* Jackson: University of
Mississippi Press, 2008.

Bartholomew-Feis, Dixee. *The OSS and Ho Chi Minh: Unexpected Allies in the
War against Japan.* Lawrence: University Press of Kansas, 2006.

Baskir, Lawrence M., and William Strauss. *Chance and Circumstance: The War, the Draft, and the Vietnam Generation.* New York: Random House, 1978.

Beeching, Barbara J. "Paul Robeson and the Black Press: The 1950 Passport Controversy." *Journal of African American History* 87 (Summer 2002): 339–54.

Beisner, Robert L. *Dean Acheson: A Life in the Cold War.* New York: Oxford University Press, 2006.

Belafonte, Harry, with Michael Shnayerson. *My Song: A Memoir.* New York: Knopf, 2011.

Belfage, Sally. *Freedom Summer.* Charlottesville: University of Virginia Press, 1965.

Bennett, Scott H. *Radical Pacifism: The War Resisters League and Gandhian Nonviolence in America, 1915–1963.* Syracuse, NY: Syracuse University Press, 2003.

Berg, Manfred. "Black Civil Rights and Liberal Anticommunism: The NAACP and the Early Cold War." *Journal of American History* 94 (June 2007): 75–96.

———. "Guns, Butter, and Civil Rights: The National Association for the Advancement of Colored People and the Vietnam War, 1964–1968." In *Aspects of War in American History*, ed. David K. Adams and Cornelis A. Van Minnen, 213–38. Keele, UK: European Papers in American History, 1997.

———. *The Ticket to Freedom: The NAACP and the Struggle for Black Integration.* Tallahassee: University of Florida Press, 2005.

Berman, Larry. *Planning a Tragedy: The Americanization of the War in Vietnam.* New York: W. W. Norton, 1982.

Berman, William C. *The Politics of Civil Rights in the Truman Administration.* Columbus: Ohio State University Press, 1971.

Bernstein, Barton J., ed. *Politics and Policies of the Truman Administration.* Chicago: Franklin Watts, 1970.

Bernstein, Irving. *Guns or Butter: The Presidency of Lyndon Johnson.* New York: Oxford University Press, 1996.

Beschloss, Michael. *Reaching for Glory: Lyndon Johnson's Secret White House Tapes, 1964–1965.* New York: Simon and Schuster, 2001.

Bigelow, Albert. *The Voyage of the* Golden Rule: *An Experiment with Truth.* Garden City, NY: Doubleday, 1959.

Biondi, Martha. *To Stand and Fight: The Struggle for Civil Rights in Postwar New York City.* Cambridge, MA: Harvard University Press, 2003.

Bloom, Joshua, and Waldo E. Martin Jr. *Black against Empire: The History and Politics of the Black Panther Party.* Berkeley: University of California Press, 2013.

Borstelmann, Thomas. *The Cold War and the Color Line: American Race Relations in a Global Arena.* Cambridge, MA: Harvard University Press, 2001.

———. "Jim Crow's Coming Out: Race Relations and American Foreign Policy during the Truman Years." *Presidential Studies Quarterly* 29, no. 3 (September 1999): 549–69.

Boyle, Kevin. *The UAW and the Heyday of American Liberalism: 1944–1968.* Ithaca, NY: Cornell University Press, 1994.

Branch, Taylor. *At the Edge of Canaan: America in the King Years 1965–1968.* New York: Simon and Schuster, 2006.

———. *Parting the Waters: America in the King Years 1954–1963.* New York: Simon and Schuster, 1988.

———. *Pillar of Fire: America in the King Years 1963–1965.* New York: Simon and Schuster, 1998.

Brauer, Carl M. *John F. Kennedy and the Second Reconstruction.* New York: Columbia University Press, 1977.

Breines, Winifred. "Whose New Left?" *Journal of American History* 75, no. 2 (September 1988): 528–45.

Breitman, George, ed. *Malcolm X Speaks: Selective Speeches and Statements.* New York: Random House, 1994.

Brilliant, Mark J. *The Color of America Has Changed: How Racial Diversity Shaped Civil Rights.* New York: Oxford University Press, 2010.

Brink, William, and Louis Harris. *Black and White: A Story of U.S. Racial Attitudes Today.* New York: Simon and Schuster, 1967.

———. *The Negro Revolution in America: What Negroes Want, Why and How They Are Fighting, Whom They Support, What Whites Think of Them and Their Demands.* New York: Simon and Schuster, 1963.

Brooke, Edward. *Bridging the Divide: My Life.* New Brunswick, NJ: Rutgers University Press, 2007.

Brown-Nagin, Tomiko. *Courage to Dissent: Atlanta and the Long History of the Civil Rights Movement.* New York: Oxford University Press, 2011.

Bryant, Nick. *The Bystander: John F. Kennedy and the Struggle for Black Equality.* New York: Basic Books, 2006.

Buhle, Paul. *Taking Care of American Business: Samuel Gompers, George Meany, Lane Kirkland and the Tragedy of American Labor.* New York: Monthly Review Press, 1999.

Bunie, Andrew. *Robert L. Vann of the* Pittsburgh Courier: *Politics and Black Journalism.* Pittsburgh: University of Pittsburgh Press, 1974.

Burk, Robert Frederick. *The Eisenhower Administration and Black Civil Rights.* Knoxville: University of Tennessee Press, 1984.

Burner, David. *Making Peace with the 60s.* Princeton, NJ: Princeton University Press, 1996.

Burner, Eric. *And Gently He Shall Lead Them: Robert Parris Moses and Civil Rights in Mississippi.* New York: New York University Press, 1995.

Busby, Horace. *The Thirty-First of March: An Inside Portrait of Lyndon Johnson's Final Days in Office.* New York: Farrar, Straus and Giroux, 2005.

Cagin, Seth, and Philip Dray. *We Are Not Afraid: The Story of Goodman, Schwerner, and Chaney, and the Civil Rights Campaign for Mississippi*. New York: Nation Books, 1988.

Califano, Joseph A., Jr. *Triumph and Tragedy of Lyndon Johnson*. New York: Simon and Schuster, 1991.

Carew, Joy Gleason. *Blacks, Reds, and Russians: Sojourners in Search of the Soviet Promise*. Princeton, NJ: Princeton University Press, 2010.

Carmichael, Stokely. *Stokely Speaks: From Black Power to Pan-Africanism*. Chicago: Chicago Review Press, 1971.

Carmichael, Stokely, with Ekwueme Michael Thelwell. *Ready for Revolution: The Life and Struggles of Stokely Carmichael (Kwame Ture)*. New York: Scribner, 2003.

Carson, Clayborne. *In Struggle: SNCC and the Black Awakening of the 1960s*. Cambridge, MA: Harvard University Press, 1981.

———. "King Scholarship and Iconoclastic Myths." *Reviews in American History* 16, no. 1 (March 1988): 130–36.

———. "Martin Luther King, Jr.: Charismatic Leadership in a Mass Struggle." *Journal of American History* 74, no. 2 (September 1987): 448–54.

Carter, David C. *The Music Went out of the Movement: Civil Rights and the Johnson Administration*. Chapel Hill: University of North Carolina Press, 2009.

Catsam, Derek. *Freedom's Main Line: The Journey of Reconciliation and the Freedom Rides*. Lexington: University Press of Kentucky, 2008.

Chace, James. *Acheson: The Secretary of State Who Created the American World*. New York: Simon and Schuster, 1998.

Chafe, William. *Civilities and Civil Rights: Greensboro, North Carolina, and the Struggle for Black Freedom*. New York: Oxford University Press, 1980.

———. *Never Stop Running: Allard Lowenstein and the Struggle to Save American Liberalism*. New York: Basic Books, 1998.

Cha-Jua, Sundiata Keita, and Clarence Lang. "The 'Long Civil Rights Movement' as Vampire: Temporal and Spatial Fallacies on Recent Black Freedom Studies." *Journal of African American History* 92 (2007): 265–88.

Chappell, David L. "Civil Rights: Grass Roots, High Politics, or Both?" *Reviews in American History* 32, no. 4 (Fall 2004): 566–72.

Cheng, Charles W. "The Cold War: Its Impact on the Black Liberation Struggle within the United States." *Freedomways: A Quarterly Review of the Freedom Movement* 13, no. 3 (1973): 281–93.

Chiba, Shin, and Thomas J. Schoenbaum, eds. *Peace Movements and Pacifism after September 11*. Northampton, MA: Edward Elgar, 2008.

Cohen, Robert. *Freedom's Orator: Mario Savio and the Radical Legacy of the 1960s*. New York: Oxford University Press, 2009.

Cone, James. "Martin Luther King, Jr. and the Third World." *Journal of American History* 74, no. 2 (September 1987): 455–67.

Costigliola, Frank. *Roosevelt's Lost Alliances: How Personal Politics Helped Start the Cold War.* Princeton, NJ: Princeton University Press, 2011.

Crespino, Joseph. *In Search of Another Country: Mississippi and the Conservative Counterrevolution.* Princeton, NJ: Princeton University Press, 2007.

Culver, John C., and John Hyde. *American Dreamer: The Life and Times of Henry A. Wallace.* New York: W. W. Norton, 2000.

Curry, Constance, ed. *Deep in Our Hearts: Nine White Women in the Civil Rights Movement.* Athens: University of Georgia Press, 2000.

Dalfiume, Richard. "The Forgotten Years of the Negro Revolution." *Journal of American History* 55, no. 1 (June 1968): 90–106.

Dallek, Matthew. *The Right Moment: Ronald Reagan's First Victory and the Decisive Turning Point in American Politics.* New York: Free Press, 2000.

Dallek, Robert. *Flawed Giant: Lyndon Johnson and His Times 1961–1973.* New York: Oxford University Press, 1998.

———. *Franklin D. Roosevelt and American Foreign Policy, 1932–1945.* New York: Oxford University Press, 1979.

———. *An Unfinished Life: John F. Kennedy, 1917–1963.* New York: Little Brown, 2003.

Darby, Henry, and Margaret N. Rowley. "King on Vietnam and Beyond." *Phylon* 47, no. 1 (March 1986): 43–50.

DeBenedetti, Charles. *An American Ordeal: The Antiwar Movement of the Vietnam Era.* Syracuse, NY: Syracuse University Press, 1990.

Dellinger, David. *From Yale to Jail: The Life Story of a Moral Dissenter.* New York: Pantheon, 1993.

D'Emilio, John. "Homophobia and the Trajectory of Postwar American Radicalism: The Career of Bayard Rustin." *Radical History Review* 62 (Spring 1995): 80–103.

———. *Lost Prophet: The Life and Times of Bayard Rustin.* Chicago: University of Chicago Press, 2003.

Devine, Thomas W. *Henry Wallace's 1948 Presidential Campaign and the Future of Postwar Liberalism.* Chapel Hill: University of North Carolina Press, 2013.

Dickerson, Dennis. *Militant Mediator: Whitney Young, Jr.* Lexington: University Press of Kentucky, 1998.

Dittmer, John. *Local People: The Struggle for Civil Rights in Mississippi.* Urbana: University of Illinois Press, 1995.

Duberman, Martin. *Howard Zinn: A Life on the Left.* New York: New Press, 2012.

———. *Paul Robeson.* New York: Knopf, 1989.

Du Bois, W. E. B. *The Autobiography of W. E. B. Du Bois: A Soliloquy of Viewing My Life from the Last Decade of Its First Century.* Edited by Henry Louis Gates. Oxford: Oxford University Press, 2007.

———. *Color and Democracy: Colonies and Peace.* New York: Harcourt Brace, 1945.

————. "Inter-racial Implications of the Ethiopian Crisis: A Negro View." *Foreign Affairs*, October 1935, 82–92.

Dudziak, Mary L. *Cold War Civil Rights: Race and the Image of American Democracy.* Princeton, NJ: Princeton University Press, 2000.

————. "Desegregation as a Cold War Imperative." *Stanford Law Review* 41 (November 1988): 61–120.

Duiker, William J. *Ho Chi Minh: A Life.* New York: Hyperion, 2000.

Durr, Kenneth. *Behind the Backlash: White Working-Class Politics in Baltimore, 1940–1980.* Chapel Hill: University of North Carolina Press, 2003.

Eagles, Charles W. "Toward New Histories of the Civil Rights Era." *Journal of Southern History* 66, no. 4 (November 2000): 815–48.

————, ed. *The Civil Rights Movement in America.* Jackson: University Press of Mississippi, 1986.

Eldridge, Lawrence Allen. *Chronicles of a Two-Front War: Civil Rights and Vietnam in the African American Press.* Columbia: University of Missouri Press, 2009.

Eskew, Glenn T. *But for Birmingham: The Local and National Campaigns in the Civil Rights Struggle.* Chapel Hill: University of North Carolina Press, 1997.

Face the Nation 1965: The Collected Transcripts. Vol. 8. New York: Holt Information Systems, 1972.

Fager, Charles. *Selma 1965: The March that Changed the South.* New York: Scribner, 1974.

Fairclough, Adam. "Historians and the Civil Rights Movement." *Journal of American Studies* 24 (1990): 387–98.

————. "Martin Luther King and the War in Vietnam." *Phylon* 45, no. 1 (March 1984): 19–39.

————. *Race and Democracy: The Civil Rights Struggle in Louisiana, 1915–1972.* Athens: University of Georgia Press, 1995.

————. *To Redeem the Soul of America: The Southern Christian Leadership Conference and Martin Luther King, Jr.* Athens: University of Georgia Press, 1987.

Fanon, Frantz. *Wretched of the Earth.* New York: Grove Press, 1963.

Farmer, James. *Lay Bare the Heart: An Autobiography of the Civil Rights Movement.* New York: Plume, 1985.

Fine, Sidney. *Violence in the Model City: The Cavanaugh Administration, Race Relations and the Detroit Riot of 1967.* Ann Arbor: University of Michigan Press, 1989.

Finn, James. *Protest, Pacifism and Politics: Some Passionate Views on War and Non-Violence.* New York: Random House, 1967.

Fleming, Cynthia Griggs. *Soon We Will Not Cry: The Liberation of Ruby Doris Smith Robinson.* New York: Rowman and Littlefield, 1998.

Foley, Michael S. *Confronting the War Machine: Draft Resistance during the Vietnam War.* Chapel Hill: University of North Carolina Press, 2003.

Foner, Jack. *Blacks and the Military in American History: A New Perspective.* New York: Praeger, 1974.

Foner, Phillip S., ed. *Paul Robeson Speaks.* New York: Brunel Mazel, 1978.

Forman, James. *High Tide of Black Resistance and Other Political & Literary Writings.* Seattle: Open Hand, 1998.

———. *The Making of Black Revolutionaries.* New York: Macmillan, 1972.

———. *Sammy Younge, Jr.: The First Black College Student to Die in the Black Liberation Movement.* New York: Open Hand, 1968.

Formisano, Ronald P. *Boston against Busing: Race, Class, and Ethnicity in the 1960s and 1970s.* Chapel Hill: University of North Carolina Press, 1991.

Franklin, John Hope, and August Meier, eds. *Black Leaders of the Twentieth Century.* Urbana: University of Illinois Press, 1982.

Franklin, John Hope, and Alfred A. Moss Jr. *From Slavery to Freedom: A History of Negro Americans,* 7th ed. New York: Knopf, 1994.

Fried, Richard M. *Nightmare in Red: The McCarthy Era in Perspective.* New York: Oxford University Press, 1990.

Friedlander, Michael. *Lift up Your Voice Like a Trumpet: White Clergy and the Civil Rights and Antiwar Movements.* Chapel Hill: University of North Carolina Press, 1998.

Friedly, Michael, and David Gallen, eds. *Martin Luther King, Jr. and the FBI File.* New York: Carroll and Graf, 1993.

Friedman, Murray. *What Went Wrong? The Creation and Collapse of the Black-Jewish Alliance.* New York: Simon and Schuster, 1994.

Gaines, Kevin. *African Americans in Ghana: Black Expatriates and the Civil Rights Era.* Chapel Hill: University of North Carolina Press, 2006.

———. "The Historiography of the Struggle for Black Equality since 1945." In *A Companion for Post-1945 America,* ed. Jean Christophe Agnew and Roy Rosenzwieg, 211–34. Malden, MA: Blackwell, 2002.

Gallup, George H. *The Gallup Poll: Public Opinion 1935–1971.* Vol. 3. New York: Random House, 1972.

The Gallup Opinion Index. Princeton, NJ: Gallup International, August 1972.

Gardner, Lloyd C. *Pay Any Price: Lyndon Johnson and the Wars for Vietnam.* Chicago: Ivan R. Dee, 1995.

Gardner, Michael R. *Harry Truman and Civil Rights.* Carbondale: Southern Illinois Press, 2002.

Garfinkle, Adam. *Telltale Hearts: Origins and Impact of the Vietnam Antiwar Movement.* New York: St. Martin's Griffin, 1997.

Garrow, David. *Bearing the Cross: Martin Luther King, Jr., and the Southern Leadership Conference.* New York: Vintage, 1986.

———. *The FBI and Martin Luther King, Jr.: From Solo to Memphis.* New York: W. W. Norton, 1981.

———. "Martin Luther King Jr., and the Spirit of Leadership." *Journal of American History* 74, no. 2 (September 1987): 438–47.

———. "Picking up the Books: The New Historiography of the Black Panther Party." *Reviews in American History* 35, no. 4 (2007): 650–70.

———. *Protest at Selma: Martin Luther King, Jr., and the Voting Rights Act of 1965.* New Haven, CT: Yale University Press, 1978.

Geselbracht, Raymond H., ed. *The Civil Rights Legacy of Harry Truman.* Kirksville, MO: Truman State University Press, 2007.

Gillon, Steven M. *Politics and Vision: The ADA and American Liberalism, 1947–1985.* New York: Oxford University Press, 1987.

Gilmore, Glenda. *Defying Dixie: The Radical Roots of Civil Rights, 1919–1950.* New York: W. W. Norton, 2008.

Gitlin, Todd. *The Sixties: Years of Hope, Days of Rage.* New York: Bantam Books, 1987.

———. *The Whole World Is Watching: Mass Media in the Making and Unmaking of the New Left.* Berkeley: University of California Press, 1980.

Goldberg, Robert Alan. *Barry Goldwater.* New Haven, CT: Yale University Press, 1995.

Goldman, Eric. *The Tragedy of Lyndon Johnson.* New York: Knopf, 1968.

Goldstein, Gordon. *Lessons in Disaster: McGeorge Bundy and the Path to War in Vietnam.* New York: Times Books, 2008.

Goldstein, Warren. *William Sloane Coffin, Jr.: A Holy Impatience.* New Haven, CT: Yale University Press, 2004.

Goodwin, Richard. *Remembering America: A Voice from the Sixties.* New York: Little Brown, 1988.

Gosse, Van. "A Movement of Movements: The Definition of Periodization of the New Left." In *A Companion for Post-1945 America,* ed. Jean Christophe Agnew and Roy Rosenzweig. Malden, MA: Blackwell, 2002.

———. *Rethinking the New Left: An Interpretive History.* New York: Palgrave Macmillan, 2005.

———. *Where the Boys Are: Cuba, Cold War America, and the Making of the New Left.* New York: Verso, 1993.

Graham, Herman, III. *The Brothers' Vietnam War: Black Power, Manhood, and the Military Experience.* Gainesville: University of Florida Press, 2003.

Graham, Hugh Davis. *The Civil Rights Era: Origins and Development of National Policy, 1960–1972.* New York: Oxford University Press, 1990.

———. "Richard Nixon and Civil Rights: Explaining an Enigma." *Presidential Studies Quarterly* 26, no. 1 (Winter 1996): 93–106.

Greenberg, Cheryl. *Troubling Waters: Black-Jewish Relations in the American Century.* Princeton, NJ: Princeton University Press, 2006.

———, ed. *Circle of Trust: Remembering SNCC.* New Brunswick, NJ: Rutgers University Press, 1998.

Grofman, Bernard, Lisa Handley, and Richard G. Niemi. *Minority Representation and the Quest for Voting Equality.* New York: Cambridge University Press, 1992.

Hagopian, Patrick. *The Vietnam War in American Memory: Veterans, Memory, and the Politics of Healing.* Amherst: University of Massachusetts Press, 2009.

Halberstam, David. *The Best and the Brightest.* New York: Random House, 1972.

———. *The Children.* New York: Ballantine, 1998.

Hall, Jacqueline Dowd. "The Long Civil Rights Movement and the Political Uses of the Past." *Journal of American History* 91 (2005): 1233–336.

Hall, Mitchell K. *Because of Their Faith: CALCAV and Religious Opposition to the Vietnam War.* New York: Columbia University Press, 1990.

Hall, Simon. "The NAACP, Black Power, and the African American Freedom Struggle, 1966–1969." *Historian* 69, no. 1 (Spring 2007): 49–82.

———. "On the Trail of the Panther: Black Power and the 1967 Convention of the National Conference for New Politics." *Journal of American Studies* 37, no. 1 (April 2003): 59–78.

———. *Peace and Freedom: The Civil Rights and Antiwar Movements in the 1960s.* Philadelphia: University of Pennsylvania Press, 2005.

———. "The Response of the Moderate Wing of the Civil Rights Movement to the Vietnam War." *Historical Journal* 46, no. 3 (September 2003): 669–701.

Halstead, Fred. *Out Now! A Participant's Account of the American Movement against the War in Vietnam.* New York: Monad Press, 1978.

Hamby, Alonzo L. *Man of the People: A Life of Harry S. Truman.* New York: Oxford University Press, 1995.

Hampton, Henry, and Steven Fraser, eds. *Voices of Freedom: An Oral History of the Civil Rights Movement from the 1950s through the 1980s.* New York: Bantam, 1990.

Harding, Vincent. *Martin Luther King: An Inconvenient Hero.* New York: Orbis Books, 1996.

Harlan, Louis. *Booker T. Washington: The Making of a Black Leader, 1856–1901.* New York: Oxford University Press, 1972.

Harris, David. *Dreams Die Hard: Three Men's Journey through the Sixties.* New York: St. Martin's Press, 1982.

Harris, Joseph. *African-American Reactions to War in Ethiopia, 1936–1941.* Baton Rouge: Louisiana State University Press, 1994.

Harris, Louis, and Associates. *The Harris Survey Yearbook of Public Opinion, 1970.* New York: Louis Harris and Associates, 1971.

Harrison, Benjamin T. "Impact of the Vietnam War on the Civil Rights Movement in the Midsixties." *Studies in Conflict and Terrorism* 19, no. 3 (1996): 261–78.

Hayden, Tom. *Reunion: A Memoir.* New York: Random House, 1988.

Heale, M. J. *McCarthy's Americans: Red Scare Politics in State and Nation, 1935–1965.* Athens: University of Georgia Press, 1998.

———. "The Sixties as History: A Review of the Political Historiography." *Reviews in American History* 33 (March 2005): 133–52.

Hershberger, Mary. *Traveling to Vietnam: American Peace Activists and the War.* Syracuse, NY: Syracuse University Press, 1998.

Hess, Gary. "Franklin Roosevelt and Indochina." *Journal of American History* 59, no. 2 (September 1972): 353–68.

Hixson, Walter L. *George F. Kennan: Cold War Iconoclast.* New York: Columbia University Press, 1989.

Hochschild, Jennifer. *Facing up to the American Dream: Race, Class, and the Soul of the Nation.* Princeton, NJ: Princeton University Press, 1995.

Hodgson, Godfrey. *America in Our Time: From World War II to Nixon—What Happened and Why.* New York: Macmillan, 1976.

Hogan, Wesley C. *Many Minds, One Heart: SNCC's Dream for a New America.* Chapel Hill: University of North Carolina Press, 2007.

Holt, Len. *The Summer that Didn't End: The Story of the Mississippi Civil Rights Project of 1964.* New York: Morrow, 1965.

Honey, Michael. *Going down Jericho Road: The Memphis Strike, Martin Luther King's Last Campaign.* New York: W. W. Norton, 2007.

Hoopes, Townsend, and Douglass Brinkley. *FDR and the Creation of the UN.* New Haven, CT: Yale University Press, 1997.

Horne, Gerald. *Black & Red: W. E. B. Du Bois and the Afro-American Response to the Cold War 1944–1963.* Albany, NY: Albany State University Press, 1986.

———. *Communist Front: The Civil Rights Congress, 1946–1956.* Rutherford, NJ: Fairleigh Dickinson Press, 1988.

———. *The Fire This Time: The Watts Uprising and the 1960s.* Charlottesville: University of Virginia Press, 1995.

Hsaio, Lisa. "Project 100,000." *Vietnam Generation* 1, no. 2 (Spring 1989): 14–37.

Hughes, Langston. *The Backlash Blues.* Detroit: Broadside Press, 1967.

———. *The Dream Keeper.* New York: Knopf, 1946.

Hunt, Andrew E. *David Dellinger: The Life and Times of a Nonviolent Revolutionary.* New York: New York University Press, 2006.

Hunton, Dorothy. *Alphaeus Hunton: The Unsung Valiant.* New York: Dorothy Hunton, 1986.

Isserman, Maurice. *If I Had a Hammer: The Death of the Old Left and the Birth of the New Left.* New York: Basic Books, 1987.

Isserman, Maurice, and Michael Kazin. *America Divided: The Civil War of the 1960s.* New York: Oxford University Press, 2000.

Jackson, Esther Cooper, ed. *Freedomways Reader: Prophets in Their Own Country.* Boulder, CO: Westview Press, 2000.

Jackson, Thomas F. *From Civil Rights to Human Rights: Martin Luther King, Jr., and the Struggle for Economic Justice.* Philadelphia: University of Pennsylvania Press, 2006.

Janken, Kenneth R. "From Colonial Liberation to Cold War Liberalism: Walter White, the NAACP, and Foreign Affairs, 1941–1955." *Journal of Ethnic and Racial Studies* 21, no. 6 (November 1998): 1074–91.

———. *White: The Autobiography of Mr. White, Mr. NAACP.* New York: New Press, 2003.

Jeffreys-Jones, Rhodri. *Peace Now! American Society and the Ending of the Vietnam War.* New Haven, CT: Yale University Press, 1999.

Jeffries, Hassan Kwame. *Bloody Lowndes: Civil Rights and Black Power in Alabama's Black Belt.* New York: New York University Press, 2009.

Johnson, Ollie L., III, and Karin L. Stanford, eds. *Black Political Organizations in the Post–Civil Rights Era.* New Brunswick, NJ: Rutgers University Press, 2002.

The Johnson Presidential Press Conferences. New York: E. M. Coleman Enterprises, 1978.

Jonas, Gilbert. *Freedom's Sword: The NAACP and the Struggle against Racism in America, 1909–1969.* New York: Routledge, 2004.

Joseph, Peniel E. "The Black Power Movement: A State of the Field." *Journal of American History* 96, no. 3 (December 2009): 751–76.

———. *Dark Days, Bright Nights: From Black Power to Barack Obama.* New York: Basic Books, 2010.

———. *Waiting 'til the Midnight Hour: A Narrative of Black Power in America.* New York: Henry Holt, 2006.

———, ed. *Rethinking the Civil Rights–Black Power Era.* New York: Routledge, 2006.

Kaiser, David. *American Tragedy: Kennedy, Johnson, and the Origins of the Vietnam War.* Cambridge, MA: Harvard University Press, 2000.

Kapur, Sudarshan. *Raising up a Prophet: The African-American Encounter with Gandhi.* Boston: Beacon Press, 1992.

Karnow, Stanley. *Vietnam: A History.* New York: Penguin, 1983.

Katznelson, Ira. *When Affirmative Action Was White.* New York: W. W. Norton, 2005.

Kazin, Michael. *American Dreamers: How the Left Changed a Nation.* New York: Knopf, 2011.

Kearns, Doris. *Lyndon Johnson and the American Dream.* New York: Harper and Row, 1976.

Kelly, Robin D. G. *Freedom Dreams: The Black Radical Imagination.* Boston: Beacon Press, 2002.

———. *Race Rebels: Culture, Politics, and the Black Working Class.* New York: Free Press, 1994.

Kimbrough, Natalie. *Equality of Discrimination? African Americans in the U.S. Military during the Vietnam War.* New York: University Press of America, 2006.

King, Coretta Scott. *My Life with Martin Luther King.* London: Hodder and Stoughton, 1969.

King, Martin Luther, Jr. *The Autobiography of Martin Luther King.* Edited by Clayborne Carson. New York: Warner Books, 1998.

———. *Stride toward Freedom: The Montgomery Story.* New York: Harper and Brothers, 1958.

———. "A Time to Break Silence." *Freedomways* 7, no. 2 (Spring 1967): 103–17.

———. *Where Do We Go from Here: Chaos or Community?* Boston: Beacon Press, 1968.

King, Mary. *Freedom Song: A Personal Story of the Civil Rights Movement of the 1960s.* New York: William Morrow, 1987.

Korstad, Robert. *Civil Rights Unionism: Tobacco Workers and the Struggle for Democracy in the Mid-20th Century South.* Chapel Hill: University of North Carolina Press, 2003.

Korstad, Robert, and Nelson Lichtenstein. "Opportunities Found and Lost: Labor, Radicals, and the Early Civil Rights Movement." *Journal of American History* 75, no. 3 (1988): 786–811.

Kotz, Nick. *Judgment Days: Lyndon Baines Johnson, Martin Luther King, Jr., and the Laws that Changed America.* New York: Houghton Mifflin, 2005.

Kotz, Nick, and Mary Lynn Kotz. *A Passion for Equality: George Wiley and the Movement.* New York: W. W. Norton, 1977.

Krenn, Michael. *Black Diplomacy: African Americans and the State Department, 1945–1969.* New York: M. E. Sharpe, 1999.

———, ed. *The African American Voice in U.S. Foreign Policy.* New York: Garland, 1999.

LaFeber, Walter. "Roosevelt, Churchill, and Indochina: 1942–1945." *American Historical Review* 80, no. 5 (December 1975): 1277–95.

Lasch, Christopher. *The True and Only Heaven: Progress and Its Critics.* New York: W. W. Norton, 1991.

Latty, Yvonne, and Ron Tarver. *We Were There: Voices of African American Veterans from World War II to the War in Iraq.* New York: Amistad, 2004.

Lawson, Steven F. *Civil Rights Crossroads: Nation, Community and the Black Freedom Struggle.* Lexington: University Press of Kentucky, 2003.

———. "Freedom Then, Freedom Now: The Historiography of the Civil Rights Movement." *American Historical Review* 96, no. 2 (1991): 456–71.

Lawson, Steven, and Charles Payne. *Debating the Civil Rights Movement, 1945–1968.* New York: Rowman and Littlefield, 1998.

Lee, Chana Kai. *For Freedom's Sake: The Life of Fannie Lou Hamer.* Urbana: University of Illinois Press, 1999.

Leffler, Melvyn. *A Preponderance of Power: National Security, the Truman Administration and the Cold War.* Palo Alto, CA: Stanford University Press, 1992.

Lentz-Smith, Andriane. *Freedom Struggles: African Americans and World War I.* Cambridge, MA: Harvard University Press, 2009.

Levine, Daniel. *Bayard Rustin and the Civil Rights Movement.* New Brunswick, NJ: Rutgers University Press, 2000.

Levy, Peter B. *The New Left, Labor, in the 1960s.* Urbana: University of Illinois Press, 1994.

Lewis, Andrew B. *Shadows of Youth: The Remarkable Journey of the Civil Rights Generation.* New York: Hill and Wang, 2009.

Lewis, David Levering. *W. E. B. Du Bois and the Fight for Equality and the American Century: 1919–1963.* New York: Henry Holt, 2000.

Lewis, John, with Michael D'Orso. *Walking with the Wind: A Memoir of the Movement.* New York: Simon and Schuster, 1998.

Lieberman, Robbie. "'Measure Them Right': Lorraine Hansberry and the Struggle for Peace." *Science and Society* 75, no. 2 (April 2011): 206–35.

———. *The Strangest Dream: Communism, Anti-Communism, and the U.S. Peace Movement.* Syracuse, NY: Syracuse University Press, 2000.

Lieberman, Robbie, and Clarence Lang, eds. *Anti-Communism and the African American Freedom Movement: "Another Side of the Story."* New York: Palgrave Macmillan, 2009.

Litwack, Leon, and August Meier, eds. *Black Leaders of the Nineteenth Century.* Urbana: University of Illinois Press, 1988.

Logan, Rayford. *The African Mandates in World Politics.* Washington, DC: Public Affairs Press, 1948.

———. *The Negro and the Post-War World: A Primer.* Washington, DC: Minorities Publishers, 1945.

———, ed. *What the Negro Wants.* Chapel Hill: University of North Carolina Press, 1944.

Logevall, Fredrik. *Choosing War: The Lost Chance for Peace and the Escalation of War in Vietnam.* Berkeley: University of California Press, 1999.

———. *Embers of War: The Fall of an Empire and the Making of America's War in Vietnam.* New York: Random House, 2012.

Louis, William Roger. *Imperialism at Bay: The United States and the Decolonization of the British Empire 1941–1945.* New York: Oxford University Press, 1978.

Lynch, Hollis R. *Black American Radicals and the Liberation of Africa: The Council on African Affairs.* Ithaca, NY: Cornell University Press, 1977.

Lynd, Staughton, and Tom Hayden. *The Other Side.* New York: New American Library, 1966.

Lyon, Danny. *Memories of the Southern Civil Rights Movement.* Chapel Hill: University of North Carolina Press, 1992.

MacDougall, Curtis D. *Gideon's Army.* New York: Marzani and Munsell, 1965.

Mack, Adam. "No 'Illusion of Separation': James L. Bevel, the Civil Rights

Movement, and the Vietnam War." *Peace and Change* 28, no. 1 (January 2003): 108–33.

MacKenzie, G. Calvin, and Robert Weisbrot. *The Liberal Hour: Washington and the Politics of Change in the 1960s.* New York: Penguin Press, 2008.

Mailer, Norman. *The Armies of the Night: History as a Novel, the Novel as History.* New York: Dutton, 1968.

Marable, Manning. *Malcolm X: A Life of Reinvention.* New York: Penguin, 2011.

———. *W. E. B. Du Bois: Black Radical Democrat.* New York: Twayne, 1986.

Marqusee, Mike. *Redemption Song: Muhammad Ali and the Spirit of the Sixties.* New York: Verso, 1999.

Massimo, Teodori, ed. *The New Left: A Documentary History.* New York: Bobbs-Merrill, 1969.

Matusow, Allen. *The Unraveling of America: A History of Liberalism in the 1960s.* New York: Harper and Row, 1984.

May, Gary. *Bending toward Justice: The Voting Rights Act and the Transformation of American Democracy.* New York: Basic Books, 2013.

McAdam, Doug. *Freedom Summer.* New York: Oxford University Press, 1988.

McGuire, Danielle L., and John Dittmer, eds. *Freedom Rights: New Perspectives on the Civil Rights Movement.* Lexington: University Press of Kentucky, 2011.

McMaster, H. R. *Dereliction of Duty: Lyndon Johnson, Robert McNamara, the Joint Chiefs of Staff, and the Lies that Led to Vietnam.* New York: Harper Perennial, 1997.

McPherson, Myra. *Long Time Passing: Vietnam and the Haunted Generation.* New York: Doubleday, 1984.

McWhorter, Diane. *Carry Me Home: Birmingham, Alabama, and the Climactic Battle for the Civil Rights Revolution.* New York: Simon and Schuster, 2001.

McWilliams, Carey M. *Brothers under the Skin.* Boston: Little Brown, 1942.

Meier, August, and Elliott Rudwick. *CORE: A Study in the Civil Rights Movement, 1942–1968.* New York: Oxford University Press, 1973.

Meier, August, Elliott Rudwick, and Frances L. Broderick, eds. *Black Protest and Thought in the Twentieth Century.* 2nd ed. Indianapolis: Indiana University Press, 1971.

Meriwether, James H. *Proudly We Can Be Africans: Black Americans and Africa, 1935–1961.* Chapel Hill: University of North Carolina Press, 2002.

Miller, James. *"Democracy Is in the Streets": From Port Huron to the Siege of Chicago.* New York: Simon and Schuster, 1987.

Mirra, Carl. *The Admirable Radical: Staughton Lynd and Cold War Dissent.* Kent, OH: Kent State University Press, 2010.

Mollin, Marian. *Radical Pacifism in Modern America: Egalitarianism and Protest.* Philadelphia: University of Pennsylvania Press, 2006.

Moody, Anne. *Coming of Age in Mississippi.* New York: Delta, 1968.

Morris, Aldon. *Origins of the Civil Rights Movement: Black Communities Organizing for Change.* New York: Free Press, 1986.

Moser, Richard R. *The New Winter Soldiers: GI and Veteran Dissent during the Vietnam Era.* New Brunswick, NJ: Rutgers University Press, 1996.

Mullen, Bill V. *Popular Fronts: Chicago and African-American Cultural Politics.* Urbana: University of Illinois Press, 1999.

Mumford, Kevin. *Newark: A History of Race, Rights, and Riots in America.* New York: New York University Press, 2007.

Murray, Paul T. "Blacks and the Draft: A History of Institutional Racism." *Journal of Black Studies* 2, no. 1 (September 1971): 57–76.

———. "Local Draft Board Composition and Institutional Racism." *Social Problems* 19, no. 1 (Summer 1971): 129–37.

Nalty, Bernard C. *Strength for the Fight: A History of Black Americans in the Military.* New York: Free Press, 1986.

Navasky, Victor S. *Kennedy Justice.* New York: Scribner, 1971.

Neary, John. *Julian Bond: Black Rebel.* New York: William Morrow, 1971.

Newfield, Jack. *A Prophetic Minority.* New York: Dutton, 1966.

Niebuhr, Reinhold. *Moral Man and Immoral Society: A Study in Ethics and Politics.* New York: Charles Scribner's Sons, 1932.

Noer, Thomas J. "Martin Luther King, Jr., and the Cold War." *Peace and Change* 22, no. 2 (April 1997): 111–31.

Norrell, Robert J. *Reaping the Whirlwind: The Civil Rights Movement in Tuskegee.* Chapel Hill: University of North Carolina Press, 1985.

Oates, Stephen B. *Let the Trumpet Sound: The Life of Martin Luther King Jr.* New York: Harper Perennial, 1982.

Olsen, Jack. *Last Man Standing: The Tragedy and Triumph of Geronimo Pratt.* New York: Doubleday, 2000.

O'Reilly, Kenneth. *Racial Matters: The FBI's Secret File on Black America.* New York: Free Press, 1989.

Ottley, Roi. *A New World a-Coming: Inside Black America.* New York: Arno Press, 1968.

Paterson, Thomas G., ed. *Cold War Critics: Alternatives to American Foreign Policy in the Truman Years.* Chicago: Quadrangle Books, 1971.

Patterson, James T. *The Eve of Destruction: How 1965 Transformed America.* New York: Basic Books, 2012.

Payne, Charles. *I've Got the Light of Freedom: The Organizing Tradition and Mississippi Politics.* Berkeley: University of California Press, 1995.

Peck, James. *Freedom Ride.* New York: Grove Press, 1962.

Perlstein, Daniel. "The Dead End of Despair, Bayard Rustin, the 1968 New York School Crisis, and the Struggle for Racial Justice." *African Americans in New York Life and History* 31 (Summer 2007): 89–120.

Pfeffer, Paula F. *A. Philip Randolph, Pioneer of the Civil Rights Movement.* Baton Rouge: Louisiana State University Press, 1990.

Phillips, Kimberley. *War! What Is It Good For?* Chapel Hill: University of North Carolina Press, 2012.

Plummer, Brenda Gayle. *In Search of Power: African Americans in the Era of Decolonization, 1956–1974.* Cambridge: Cambridge University Press, 2013.

———. *Rising Wind: Black Americans and U.S. Foreign Affairs.* Chapel Hill: University of North Carolina Press, 1996.

———, ed. *Window on Freedom: Race, Civil Rights and Foreign Affairs, 1945–1988.* Chapel Hill: University of North Carolina Press, 2003.

Polsgrove, Carol. *Divided Minds: Intellectuals and the Civil Rights Movement.* New York: W. W. Norton, 2001.

Powers, Richard Gid. *Secrecy and Power: The Life of J. Edgar Hoover.* New York: Free Press, 1987.

Powers, Thomas. *The War at Home: Vietnam and the American People.* New York: Grossman, 1973.

Public Papers of the Presidents: Lyndon B. Johnson, 1965. Washington, DC: Government Printing Office, 1966.

Pulido, Laura. *Black, Brown, Yellow, and Left: Radical Activism in Los Angeles.* Berkeley: University of California Press, 2006.

Raines, Howell. *My Soul Is Rested: Movement Days in the Deep South Remembered.* New York: G. P. Putnam's Sons, 1977.

Rainwater, Lee, and William Yancey. *The Moynihan Report and the Politics of Controversy.* Cambridge, MA: MIT Press, 1967.

Ralph, James R., Jr. *Martin Luther King, Chicago, and the Civil Rights Movement.* Cambridge, MA: Harvard University Press, 1993.

Ransby, Barbara. *Ella Baker and the Black Freedom Movement: A Radical Democratic Vision.* Chapel Hill: University North Carolina Press, 2003.

Reeves, Michelle. "'Obey the Rule or Get Out': Ronald Reagan's Gubernatorial Campaign and the Trouble in Berkeley." *Southern California Quarterly* 92, no. 3 (Fall 2010): 275–305.

Reider, Jonathan. *Canarsie: The Jews and Italians of Brooklyn against Liberalism.* Cambridge, MA: Harvard University Press, 1985.

Risen, Clay. *A Nation on Fire: America in the Wake of the King Assassination.* New York: Wiley, 2009.

Roark, James L. "American Black Leaders: The Response of Colonialism and the Cold War." *African Historical Studies* 4, no. 2 (1971): 253–70.

Robeson, Paul. *Here I Stand.* Boston: Beacon Press, 1988.

Robinson, Armstead L., and Patricia Sullivan, eds. *New Directions in Civil Rights Studies.* Charlottesville: University of Virginia Press, 1991.

Roediger, David. *The Wages of Whiteness: Race and the Making of the American Working Class.* New York: Verso, 1991.

Rogers, J. A. *The Real Facts about Ethiopia.* Baltimore: Black Classic Press, 1982.

Rosenberg, Jonathan. *How Far the Promised Land? World Affairs and the Ameri-*

can Civil Rights Movement from the First World War to Vietnam. Princeton, NJ: Princeton University Press, 2006.

Rossinow, Douglass. *The Politics of Authenticity: Liberalism, Christianity, and the New Left in America.* New York: Columbia University Press, 1998.

"A Roundtable: Martin Luther King, Jr." *Journal of American History* 74 (September 1987): 436–81.

Rowan, Carl T. *Breaking Barriers: A Memoir.* New York: Little Brown, 1991.

Royko, Mike. *Boss: Richard J. Daley of Chicago.* New York: Dutton, 1971.

Rustin, Bayard. *Down the Line: The Collected Writings of Bayard Rustin.* Chicago: Quadrangle Books, 1971.

Sale, Kirkpatrick. *SDS.* New York: Random House, 1973.

Schrecker, Ellen. *Many Are the Crimes: McCarthyism in America.* Boston: Harvard University Press, 1998.

Schulzinger, Robert D. *A Time for Peace: The Legacy of the Vietnam War.* New York: Oxford University Press, 2006.

Scott, William R. "Black Nationalism and the Italo-Ethiopian Conflict, 1934–1936." *Journal of Negro History* 63, no. 2 (April 1978): 118–36.

———. *Sons of Sheba: African Americans and the Italo-Ethiopia War 1935–1941.* Bloomington: Indiana University Press, 1993.

Self, Robert O. *American Babylon: Race and the Struggle for Postwar Oakland.* Princeton, NJ: Princeton University Press, 2003.

Sellers, Cleveland. *The River of No Return: The Autobiography of a Black Militant and the Life and Death of SNCC.* Jackson: University Press of Mississippi, 1973.

Shafer, D. Michael, ed. *The Legacy: Vietnam War in the Historical Imagination.* Boston: Beacon Press, 1990.

Shapiro, Herbert. "The Vietnam War and the American Civil Rights Movement." *Journal of Ethnic Studies* 16 (Winter 1989): 117–41.

Sherry, Michael S. *In the Shadow of War: The United States since the 1930s.* New Haven, CT: Yale University Press, 1995.

Sherwood, John Darrel. *Black Sailor, White Navy: Racial Unrest in the Fleet during the Vietnam Era.* New York: New York University Press, 2007.

Singh, Nikhil Pal. *Black Is a Country: Race and the Unfinished Struggle for Democracy.* Cambridge, MA: Harvard University Press, 2004.

Sinsheimer, Joseph A. "The Freedom Vote of 1963: New Strategies of Racial Protest in Mississippi." *Journal of Southern History* 55, no. 2 (May 1989): 217–44.

Sitkoff, Harvard. *The Struggle for Black Equality: 1954–1992.* New York: Hill and Wang, 1993.

Skrenty, Jonathan. *The Minority Rights Revolution.* Cambridge, MA: Harvard University Press, 2002.

Small, Melvin. *Covering Dissent: The Media and the Anti-War Movement.* New Brunswick, NJ: Rutgers University Press, 1994.

Steel, Ronald. *Walter Lippmann and the American Century.* New York: Transaction Publishers, 1980.

Stein, Judith. *The World of Marcus Garvey: Race and Class in Modern Society.* Baton Rouge: Louisiana State University Press, 1986.

Streitmatter, Rodger. *Raising Her Voice: African American Journalists Who Changed History.* Lexington: University Press of Kentucky, 1994.

Sugrue, Thomas. *Origins of the Urban Crisis.* Princeton, NJ: Princeton University Press, 1996.

———. *Sweet Land of Liberty: The Forgotten Struggle for Civil Rights in the North.* New York: Random House, 2008.

Sullivan, Patricia. *Days of Hope: Race and Democracy in the New Deal Era.* Chapel Hill: University of North Carolina Press, 1996.

———. *Lift Every Voice: The NAACP and the Making of the Civil Rights Movement.* New York: New Press, 2009.

Sullivan, William C., with Bill Brown. *The Bureau: My Thirty Years in Hoover's FBI.* New York: W. W. Norton, 1979.

Taylor, Clyde, ed. *Vietnam and Black America: An Anthology of Protest and Resistance.* Garden City, NY: Anchor/Doubleday, 1973.

Terry, Wallace. *Bloods: An Oral History of the Vietnam War by Black Veterans.* New York: Random House, 1984.

Theoharis, Jeanne. "Black Freedom Studies: Re-Imagining and Redefining the Fundamentals." *History Compass* 4, no. 2 (March 2006): 348–67.

Turner, Jeffrey A. *Sitting in and Speaking Out: Student Movements in the American South, 1960–1970.* Athens: University of Georgia Press, 2010.

Tyson, Timothy B. *Radio Free Dixie: Robert F. Williams and the Roots of Black Power.* Chapel Hill: University of North Carolina Press, 1999.

———. "Robert F. Williams, Black Power and the Roots of the Black Freedom Struggle." *Journal of American History* 85, no. 2 (September 1998): 540–70.

U.S. House of Representatives, Committee on Veterans Affairs. *Legacies of Vietnam: Comparative Adjustment of Veterans and Their Peers: A Study Prepared for the Veterans' Administration, March 9, 1981.* Washington, DC: Government Printing Office, 1981.

U.S. Senate Committee on Government Operations, Subcommittee on Executive Reorganization. *Federal Role in Urban Affairs.* Washington, DC: Government Printing Office, 1967.

VanDeMark, Brian. *Into the Quagmire: Lyndon Johnson and the Escalation of the Vietnam War.* New York: Oxford University Press, 1995.

Viorst, Milton. *Fire in the Streets: America in the 1960s.* New York: Simon and Schuster, 1979.

Von Eschen, Penny. *Race against Empire: Black Americans and Anti-Colonialism.* Ithaca, NY: Cornell University Press, 1997.

Walton, Richard J. *Henry Wallace, Harry Truman and the Cold War.* New York: Viking, 1976.

Ward, Brian, and Tony Badger, eds. *The Making of Martin Luther King and the Civil Rights Movement.* London: Macmillan, 1996.

Watson, Bruce. *Freedom Summer: The Savage Season of 1964 that Made Mississippi Burn and Made America a Democracy.* New York: Penguin, 2010.

Watters, Pat. *Down to Now: Reflections on the Southern Civil Rights Movement.* New York: Pantheon Books, 1971.

Weisbrot, Robert. *Freedom Bound: A History of America's Civil Rights Movement.* New York: Plume, 1990.

Weiss, Nancy J. *Whitney M. Young, Jr., and the Struggle for Civil Rights.* Princeton, NJ: Princeton University Press, 1989.

Wells, Tom. *The War Within: America's Battle over Vietnam.* Berkeley: University of California Press, 1994.

Westheider, James E. *The African American Experience in Vietnam: Brothers in Arms.* New York: Rowman and Littlefield, 2008.

———. *Fighting on Two Fronts: African Americans and the Vietnam War.* New York: New York University Press, 1997.

White, Theodore. *The Making of the President, 1964.* New York: HarperCollins, 1965.

White, Walter. *A Man Called White: The Autobiography of Walter White.* New York: Viking Press, 1948.

———. *A Rising Wind.* New York: Praeger, 1945.

Wilkins, Fanon Che. "The Making of Black Internationalists: SNCC and Africa before the Launching of Black Power, 1960–1965." *Journal of African American History* 92, no. 4 (September 2007): 468–91.

Wilkins, Roger. *A Man's Life: An Autobiography.* New York: Simon and Schuster, 1982.

Wilkins, Roy, with Tom Matthews. *Standing Fast: The Autobiography of Roy Wilkins.* New York: Da Capo Press, 1982.

Williams, Juan. *Thurgood Marshall: American Revolutionary.* New York: Random House, 1998.

Williams, Roger M. *The Bonds: An American Family.* New York: Atheneum, 1971.

Wittner, Lawrence S. *Rebels against War: The American Peace Movement, 1941–1960.* New York: Columbia University Press, 1969.

Wofford, Harris. *Of Kennedys and Kings: Making Sense of the Sixties.* Pittsburgh: University of Pittsburgh Press, 1980.

Woods, Jeff. *Black Struggle, Red Scare: Segregation and Anti-Communism in the South, 1948–1968.* Baton Rouge: Louisiana State University Press, 2004.

———. "The Cold War and the Struggle for Civil Rights." *OAH Magazine of History* 24 (October 2010): 13–17.

Woods, Randall Bennett. *Fulbright: A Biography.* Cambridge: Cambridge University Press, 1995.

———. *LBJ: Architect of Ambition.* New York: Free Press, 2006.

Wright, Richard. *The Color Curtain: A Report on the Bandung Conference.* Cleveland, OH: Dennis Dobson, 1956.

Wu, Judy Tzu-Chun. "An African-Vietnamese American: Robert S. Browne, the Antiwar Movement, and the Personal/Political Dimensions of Black Internationalism." *Journal of African American History* 92, no. 4 (Autumn 2007): 491–515.

Young, Andrew. *An Easy Burden: The Civil Rights Movement and the Transformation of America.* New York: HarperCollins, 1996.

Young, Marilyn. *The Vietnam Wars.* New York: Grafton, 1992.

Yuill, Kevin L. "The 1966 White House Conference on Civil Rights and the End of the American Creed." *Historical Journal* 41, no. 1 (March 1998): 259–82.

Zaroulis, Nancy L., and Gerald Sullivan. *Who Spoke Up? American Protest against the War in Vietnam.* Garden City, NY: Doubleday, 1984.

Zellner, Bob, with Constance Curry. *The Wrong Side of Murder Creek: A White Southerner in the Freedom Movement.* Montgomery, AL: New South Books, 2008.

Ziemann, Benjamin, ed. *Peace Movements in Western Europe, Japan and the USA during the Cold War.* Essen, Germany: Klartext Verlag, 2007.

Zinn, Howard. *SNCC: The New Abolitionists.* Boston: Beacon Press, 1965.

———. *Vietnam: The Logic of Withdrawal.* Boston: Beacon Press, 1967.

———. *You Can't Be Neutral on a Moving Train: A Personal History of Our Time.* Boston: Beacon Press, 1994.

Index

Abernathy, Ralph, 141, 185
Abraham Lincoln Brigade, 15
Acheson, Dean, 20, 27
AFL-CIO, 237, 240
African American press: on the
  abandonment of anticolonialism by
  the newly formed United Nations,
  20–21; on African American soldiers
  in Vietnam, 6, 105, 133–34; on
  Castro's visit to Harlem, 52–53;
  coverage of Ghana's independence,
  43; impact of the Cold War on, 23;
  impact of McCarthyism on, 31; on
  LBJ's 1965 address to Congress
  on voting rights, 144; opposition
  to the Vietnam War under Nixon,
  246; response to the Julian Bond
  controversy, 117; response to
  King's 1965 appeal for an end to
  the Vietnam War, 165; response to
  King's 1967 Riverside address, 196,
  199; response to LBJ's escalation
  of the Vietnam War in 1965, 78–79;
  response to SNCC's 1966 public
  opposition to the Vietnam War, 3–4;
  William Worthy, 41–42, 53–54
African Americans: anticolonialism and,
  23–24, 26, 27; Cold War thaw of the
  mid-1950s and, 38–43; communist
  movement and, 23; dilemma of
  opposition to the Vietnam War in
  1965, 83–84; grassroots activism in
  the 1960s, 44–50; hostility toward
  the Nixon administration, 246; image
  of the good African American soldier
  and, 214; Korean War and, 32–34;
  legacy of the Vietnam War and, 252;
  loyalty to LBJ in supporting the
  Vietnam War, 5; mainstream opinion
  on the events of 1965, 109; members
  of draft boards, 135; military
  service and, 5–6, 32, 97–98, 133;
  National Conference for a New
  Politics, 205–7; 1948 presidential
  election and, 25–27; 1965 March
  on Washington and, 89; 1967 march
  on the Pentagon, 208; opinion
  of King's open antiwar stance,
  203; opinion of the Vietnam War,
  77–79, 114–15, 136; opposition
  to the Nixon administration, 249;
  optimism at the end of World War
  II, 13; response to King's 1967
  Riverside address, 196–98; response
  to LBJ's escalation of the Vietnam
  War in 1965, 77–79; response to
  SNCC's 1966 public opposition
  to the Vietnam War, 3–4; rise of
  anticolonialism in the 1930s and
  1940s, 14–18; Soviet Union and,
  22; Watts uprising and, 94–97
African American soldiers: the African
  American press on, 6, 105, 133–34;
  Simeon Booker's 1965 report on,
  214; disproportionate numbers and
  casualties in Vietnam, 6, 98, 135;
  impact on the civil rights movement
  and its attitude toward the Vietnam
  War, 6, 135, 136–37; military service
  and, 5–6, 32, 97–98, 133; Project
  100,000, 134–35; radicalization
  by the Vietnam War, 136; reasons
  for supporting the Vietnam War, 6;
  response to King's assassination,
  210; Whitney Young's reports on,
  230, 232

CIVIL RIGHTS AND THE STRUGGLE FOR BLACK EQUALITY
IN THE TWENTIETH CENTURY

SERIES EDITORS
Steven F. Lawson, Rutgers University
Cynthia Griggs Fleming, University of Tennessee

Freedom's Main Line: The Journey of Reconciliation and the Freedom Rides
Derek Charles Catsam

*Subversive Southerner: Anne Braden and the Struggle for Racial Justice in the
Cold War South*
Catherine Fosl

*Constructing Affirmative Action: The Struggle for Equal Employment
Opportunity*
David Hamilton Golland

River of Hope: Black Politics and the Memphis Freedom Movement, 1865–1954
Elizabeth Gritter

Sidelined: How American Sports Challenged the Black Freedom Struggle
Simon Henderson

Becoming King: Martin Luther King Jr. and the Making of a National Leader
Troy Jackson

Civil Rights in the Gateway to the South: Louisville, Kentucky, 1945–1980
Tracy E. K'Meyer

In Peace and Freedom: My Journey in Selma
Bernard LaFayette Jr. and Kathryn Lee Johnson

Democracy Rising: South Carolina and the Fight for Black Equality since 1865
Peter F. Lau

Civil Rights Crossroads: Nation, Community, and the Black Freedom Struggle
Steven F. Lawson

Selma to Saigon: The Civil Rights Movement and the Vietnam War
Daniel S. Lucks

In Remembrance of Emmett Till: Regional Stories and Media Responses to the Black Freedom Struggle
Darryl Mace

Freedom Rights: New Perspectives on the Civil Rights Movement
edited by Danielle L. McGuire and John Dittmer

This Little Light of Mine: The Life of Fannie Lou Hamer
Kay Mills

After the Dream: Black and White Southerners since 1965
Timothy J. Minchin and John A. Salmond

Fighting Jim Crow in the County of Kings: The Congress of Racial Equality in Brooklyn
Brian Purnell

Roy Wilkins: The Quiet Revolutionary and the NAACP
Yvonne Ryan

Thunder of Freedom: Black Leadership and the Transformation of 1960s Mississippi
Sue [Lorenzi] Sojourner with Cheryl Reitan

Art for Equality: The NAACP's Cultural Campaign for Civil Rights
JennyWoodley

For Jobs and Freedom: Race and Labor in America since 1865
Robert H. Zieger